Regimes of Inequality

Since the 1990s, mainstream political parties have failed to address the problem of growing inequality, resulting in political backlash and the transformation of European party systems. Most attempts to explain the rise of inequality in political science take a far too narrow approach, considering only economic inequality and failing to recognize how multiple manifestations of inequality combine to reinforce each other and the underlying political features of advanced welfare states. Combining training in public health with a background in political science, Julia Lynch brings a unique perspective to debates about inequality in political science and to public health thinking about the causes of and remedies for health inequalities. Based on case studies of efforts to reduce health inequalities in England, France and Finland, Lynch argues that inequality persists because political leaders chose to frame the issue of inequality in ways that made it harder to solve.

JULIA LYNCH is a professor of Political Science at the University of Pennsylvania, an editor of *Socio-Economic Review*, and serves as an expert advisor to the World Health Organization. She is the author of *Age in the Welfare State: The Origins of Social Spending on Pensioners, Workers, and Children* (2006).

Regimes of Inequality

The Political Economy of Health and Wealth

JULIA LYNCH
University of Pennsylvania

 CAMBRIDGE
UNIVERSITY PRESS

CAMBRIDGE
UNIVERSITY PRESS

University Printing House, Cambridge CB2 8BS, United Kingdom

One Liberty Plaza, 20th Floor, New York, NY 10006, USA

477 Williamstown Road, Port Melbourne, VIC 3207, Australia

314-321, 3rd Floor, Plot 3, Splendor Forum, Jasola District Centre, New Delhi - 110025, India

103 Penang Road, #05-06/07, Visioncrest Commercial, Singapore 238467

Cambridge University Press is part of the University of Cambridge.

It furthers the University's mission by disseminating knowledge in the pursuit of
education, learning and research at the highest international levels of excellence.

www.cambridge.org
Information on this title: www.cambridge.org/9781009087766
DOI:10.1017/9781139051576

© Julia Lynch 2020

First published 2020
First paperback edition 2021

A catalogue record for this publication is available from the British Library

Library of Congress Cataloging in Publication data
NAMES: Lynch, Julia, 1970– author.
TITLE: Regimes of inequality : the political economy of health and wealth / Julia Lynch.
DESCRIPTION: Cambridge, United Kingdom ; New York, NY : Cambridge University Press, 2020 |
  Includes bibliographical references and index.| Summary: "A spectacular thirty-meter high viaduct spans the
  Ouseburn river as it makes its way through Newcastle-upon-Tyne, in the northeast corner of England. Modern,
  bright-yellow and black tram cars ply the viaduct, bringing passengers from working-class Byker to more
  affluent South Gosforth station in a journey that takes roughly ten minutes. But while the Byker viaduct allows
  riders to traverse the physical chasm carved out by the Ouseburn with ease, the social differences that separate
  residents of Byker from their better-off neighbors are much harder to bridge. Twice as many children in Byker
  (two in five) live in poverty as in Gosforth. And while a fifty-five-year-old man from Gosforth can expect to live
  another seventeen years in good health, the average fifty-five-year-old in Byker has only another nine years of
  healthy life expectancy ahead of him (Bambra 2016, 92)"– Provided by publisher.
IDENTIFIERS: LCCN 2019021322 | ISBN 9781107001688 (hardback)
SUBJECTS: LCSH: Medical policy–Europe. | Health services accessibility–Europe. | Welfare state–Europe. |
  Poor–Medical care–Europe.
CLASSIFICATION: LCC RA395.E85 | DDC 362.1094–dc23
LC record available at https://lccn.loc.gov/2019021322

ISBN 978-1-107-00168-8 Hardback
ISBN 978-1-009-08776-6 Paperback

For my children, Kieran Jacob Laskawy and
Eli Bernard Laskawy

Contents

Figures

Tables

Acknowledgments

The public health literature tells us that social support is associated with better health outcomes. If there is a causal link in my case, then I can expect to live a long and healthy life. This book, as is true of all academic endeavors of any scale, is the product of more people's efforts than I can possibly acknowledge. It really does take a village to raise a book, and in this case the village spans several countries, multiple academic disciplines, and more than one generation of Penn undergraduates.

I started thinking about the problems that animated the work on this book as a participant in the Robert Wood Johnson Foundation's human capital programs in the 1990s and 2000s. These programs were the breeding ground in which my thinking about health equity as a problem that political science ought to be paying attention to first took shape. The Health Policy Scholars Program, Investigator Awards Program, and Health and Society Scholars Program brought me into contact with mentors and peers whose support for me and my intellectual growth made it possible to dream about writing this book. Alan Cohen, Mark Schlesinger, Mark Peterson, Kathy Swartz, Craig Pollack, Sarah Gollust, and Elizabeth Rigby all came into my life via the RWJF, and all pushed me to think harder and better about why health equity matters for political life.

At Penn, my colleagues at the Leonard Davis Institute of Health Economics and the Political Science Department have provided me with a secure home base from which to operate, and have supported my disappearances to take classes in demography and public health (thanks to funding from a Mellon New Directions Fellowship) and to do field work without complaint. I am truly grateful. I have also benefited from the help of a number of outstanding Penn students during the process of researching and writing this book. Alexandra Babinchak, Julia Berenson, Chloe Bousquet-Chavanne, Alyssa Kennedy, Capucine LeMeur, Niyati Patel, Saku Rimali, Ilana Wurman, and especially Peter

Manda and Cathy Zhang deserve special mention. My former PhD advisee Isabel Perera has been my right-hand woman from the beginning, navigating French bureaucratic politesse and providing me with continuous substantive feedback on the project with equal aplomb. Isabel, I could not have done it without you; and watching your own star rise as we have worked together on this project has been an unparalleled pleasure.

I have also benefited from the advice of many smart, generous people who have read and commented on portions of the project: Jason Beckfield, Mark Blyth, Melani Cammett, Jane Gingrich, Scott Greer, Peter Hall, Matt Kavanagh Quinton Mayne, Kimberly Morgan, Isabel Perera, Katie Rader, Ted Schrecker, Dawn Teele, and, above all, Kate McNamara. The remaining errors are all mine, but the bulk of the work is so much better because they read it. My profound thanks are also due to the people and institutions who welcomed me during my field work, especially Cornelia Woll at Sciences Po in Paris, Ben Ansell and Desmond King at Nuffield College, Oxford, and Christine Brown at the World Health Organization.

Getting to know the international network of health equity policy experts who served as both my informants and subjects has been a wonderful experience. Without their willingness to answer my questions and point me in new directions, this would have been a different and much worse book. They go unnamed only out of a desire to preserve their anonymity.

Finally, to my long-suffering family, thank you for bearing with me. I'm all yours again ... until the next book.

Abbreviations

General

CVD	Cardiovascular disease
ESS	European Social Survey
GDP	Gross domestic product
HIA	Health impact assessment
HiAP	Health in All Policies
ISSP	International Social Survey Project
MP	Member of parliament
NGO	Non-governmental organization
RII	Relative index of inequality
SBTC	Skill-biased technical change
SDOH	Social determinants of health
SES	Socioeconomic status
VAT	Value-added tax

European-Level

CSDH	Commission on the Social Determinants of Health (WHO)
DG	Directorate general
DG SANCO	Directorate general for health and consumer protection (EU)
DG SANTE	Directorate general for health and food safety (EU)
EMS	European monetary system
EMU	European Monetary Union
ESF	European Science Foundation
EU	European Union
G20	Group of 20
HFA	Health For All strategy (WHO)
IMF	International Monetary Fund
OECD	Organisation for Economic Cooperation and Development

UNICEF   United Nations International Children's Emergency Fund
WHO   World Health Organization
WHO   Regional Office for Europe of the WHO
Europe
WTO   World Trade Organization

England
HEC   Health Education Council
IPPR   Institute for Public Policy Research
NHS   National Health Service

Finland
KASTE   National Development Plan for Social Welfare and Health Care
KTL   National Institute of Public Health
MSAH   Ministry of Health and Social Affairs
NAP   National Action Plan
SDP   Social Democratic Party
STAKES   National Research and Development Centre for Welfare and
                Health
TEROKA   Reducing Socioeconomic Health Inequalities in Finland
THL   National Institute for Health and Welfare
TTL   Institute of Occupational Health

France
ARH   *Agences régionales de l'hospitalisation* (regional hospital
                agencies)
ARS   *Agences régionales de santé* (regional health agencies)
ASV   *Atelier santé ville* (city health workshops)
CGP   *Commissariat général du Plan* (General Planning Commission)
CIV   *Comité interministériel des villes* (Interministerial Committee on
                Cities)
CLS   *Contrats locaux de santé* (local health contracts)
CMU   *Couverture maladie universelle* (Universal Health Coverage)
CNRS   *Centre national de la recherche scientifique* (National Center for
                Scientific Research)
CPOM   *Contrat pluriannuel d'objectifs et de moyen* (multi-year contract
                of objectives and means)
DREES   *Direction de la recherche, des études, de l'évaluation et des
                statistiques* (Directorate of Research, Studies, Evaluation and
                Statistics)
HCSP   *Haute commission/conseil del la santé publique* (High
                Commission/Council for Public Health)
IGAS   *Inspection générale des affaires sociales* (Inspectorate General for
                Social Security)

ISS   *Inégalités sociales en santé* (socioeconomic inequalities in health)
INSERM   *Institut national de la santé et de la recherche médicale* (National
              Institute of Health and Medical Research)
Loi   *Loi "hôpital, patients, santé et territoire"* (Law on hospitals,
HPST   patients, health and territory)
MRS   *Missions regionales de santé* (regional health agencies)
ORS   *Obsérvatoires régionales de santé* (regional health observatories)
PRAPS   *Programmes régional d'accès à la prévention et aux soins des
              personnes les plus démunies* (regional programs for preventive
              and health care services access for the poorest)
PS   *Parti socialiste* (Socialist Party)
RGPP   *Révision générale des politiques publiques* (General Review of
              Public Policies, 2007 public administration reform)
RPR   *Rassemblement pour la République* (Rally for the Republic,
              center-right political party)
SNS   *Stratégie National de Santé* (National Health Strategy)
SROS   *Schéma régional d'organisation sanitaire* (regional health
              organization plan)
UMP   *Union pour un mouvement populaire* (Union for a Popular
              Movement, center-right political party)
URCAM   *Unions régionales de caisses d'assurance maladie* (regional health
              insurance councils)

Explaining Resilient Inequalities in Health and Wealth

INTRODUCTION

A spectacular thirty-meter-high viaduct spans the Ouseburn river as it makes its way through Newcastle-upon-Tyne, in the northeast corner of England. Modern, bright-yellow and black tram cars ply the viaduct, bringing passengers from working-class Byker to more affluent South Gosforth station in a journey that takes roughly ten minutes. But while the Byker viaduct allows riders to traverse the physical chasm carved out by the Ouseburn with ease, the social differences that separate residents of Byker from their better-off neighbors are much harder to bridge. Twice as many children in Byker (two in five) live in poverty as in Gosforth. And while a fifty-five-year-old man from Gosforth can expect to live another seventeen years in good health, the average fifty-five-year-old in Byker has only another nine years of healthy life expectancy ahead of him (Bambra 2016, 92).

Across the rich, industrialized democracies, social inequalities – inequalities of earnings and wealth, of well-being and health – have, beginning in the 1980s, widened dramatically. This is not only the case in liberal welfare states like England,[1] where we might expect governments and the public to accept high levels of market-generated inequality; the growth of inequality has been almost as rapid in the traditionally more solidaristic social democratic welfare states in the Nordic countries. In fact, the phenomenon of rising inequality is so widespread across the rich industrialized democracies that it has come to seem inevitable. But rising inequality is not a straightforward result of abstract economic forces, a universal tendency for the rich to be powerful, or the victory of a neoliberal ideological agenda. I argue in this book that inequality has become a persistent fact of

---

[1] Throughout this book I refer to England as a case study and a country because my analysis of health policy in the United Kingdom is confined to England after the devolution of health policy authority to Scotland, Wales, and Northern Ireland after 1998.

contemporary politics beginning in the 1990s because of the way politicians have redefined what the problem of inequality is.

An important shift occurred in how politicians approached the issue of inequality beginning in the 1990s – a shift that coincided with the rise of a neoliberal policy paradigm in Europe, but that was also decisively shaped by the preexisting welfare regimes of the *trente glorieuses* (the "glorious" thirty-year period of peace and prosperity that followed the end of the Second World War). Politicians' subjective beliefs about which policy tools they could feasibly use to solve the problem of inequality emerged from the interaction of old welfare regimes and the new neoliberal paradigm. These beliefs shaped the way that politicians have defined the problem of inequality in recent decades. The core argument of this book is that a new framing of inequality as a matter of the unequal distribution of human capital, including health, has unwittingly made the problem of inequality much more difficult to solve.

This book examines the political dynamics underlying inequality's remarkable resilience across the rich democracies since 1980 by tracing the largely unsuccessful attempts to reduce socioeconomic inequalities in population health in England, France, and Finland. I approach the larger issue of inequality through the lens of health in part because, if we want to understand why inequality is so resilient, we need to consider inequality in general, and not just the specific instantiation of inequality that is expressed in, say, household income inequality. Health inequalities are related to income inequality and to the latter's underlying causes, but are not the same problem. Since health equity emerges as a distinct public problem during the postwar period at varying times and with varying political valences in different countries, studying the politics of health inequalities encourages us to direct our attention to how the framing of the problem of inequality affects policy responses, and why some policy ideas gain traction while others do not.

Governments have several good reasons for paying attention to health inequalities. The health of a country's population brings economic benefits (Sachs 2001; Lopez-Casasnovas et al. 2005), and the presence of health inequalities brings the average health of a population below where it could be if all members of a society enjoyed the same high level of health. Health inequalities are also an indicator of broader societal well-being. Across countries, the magnitude of health inequalities is correlated with the extent of other social ills like income inequality, poverty, social isolation, and the intergenerational transmission of deprivation (see, e.g., Kawachi et al. 1997; John Lynch et al. 2000; Wilkinson and Pickett 2009; Aizer and Currie 2014). Systematic differences in health across social groups suggest that the political, social, and economic institutions that exert power over health, just as they govern other aspects of social life, may be unjust (Durkheim 1976; P. Hall and Lamont 2009; Foucault 2012). And health is not just any social good: philosophers attach particular importance to health because it is fundamental to our very existence as persons and necessary for full participation in social and economic life (Daniels 1983; Sen 2002).

By studying how political elites grapple with the problem of health inequalities, I have sought to discover whether common logics govern the politics of inequality in income and wealth versus health, or whether instead the different domains of inequality follow systematically different, or even unrelated, political patterns. A key conclusion is that the politics and policy of health inequality and social inequality more broadly are thoroughly intertwined, in ways that suggest that we should think about *regimes of inequality* rather than the politics of economic inequality, or the politics of health inequality, separately. In fact, the interconnectedness of income and health inequalities, and the links between the policies characteristic of postwar welfare regimes and the politics of neoliberalism, give inequality a resilience that would be difficult to understand if we looked at health and wealth, or at politics and policies, in isolation from one another.

Case studies of policy-making efforts to reduce socioeconomic inequalities in health in England, France, and Finland give the empirical basis for these observations about the politics of inequality. In each of the three country case studies, I explain the sources of politicians' beliefs about what policy tools are feasible to use and which are taboo in addressing inequality, show how these beliefs shape their definition of the problem of inequality, and demonstrate how that definition in turn shapes the effectiveness of efforts to limit inequality.

Inequalities in health are every bit as troubling as the more familiar inequalities in income and wealth, even if they have received much less attention from political scientists. Health inequalities are also, as it happens, closely related to economic inequality (Marmot and Wilkinson 2005). Definitions of health inequality vary over time and across national contexts. In the United States, for example, health inequalities are often conceptualized in racial and ethnic terms, while in most European countries today the term "health inequality" refers to "social" inequalities in health, that is, inequalities in health status linked to socioeconomic status or class, as measured by income, wealth, occupation, or education (Docteur and Berenson 2014; Julia Lynch and Perera 2017). Health inequities are usually defined in European policy circles as systematic differences in health status between groups that are avoidable and that are unjust because they result from inequalities generated by the organization of the society and the economy, rather than from biology or individual choices (Whitehead 1991; Kawachi et al. 2002; WHO Regional Office for Europe 2013; see also Chapter 3). To speak of health inequality is thus to make a normative claim about the inequity, undesirability, and socioeconomic origins of differences in health between groups in society.

THE PUZZLE OF RESILIENT INEQUALITY

The last thirty years have witnessed a sustained rise in social inequality in the rich democracies. So problematic are the inequalities that have emerged in western democracies since the 1980s, in fact, that one could say that the failure to tame inequality is a defining political issue of the early twenty-first century.

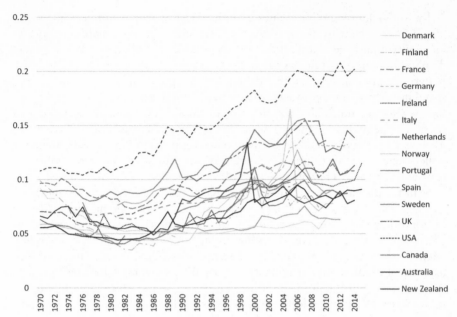

FIGURE 1.1 Share of national income held by households in the 99th–100th percentile of the pre-tax income distribution, 1974–2014.
Data from World Income and Wealth Dataset (http://wid.world/, accessed October 15, 2018)

One frequently used measure of economic inequality is the share of all income (wages, dividends, etc.) in a country that is received by people in the top 1 percent of the income distribution (Figure 1.1). The growth in this top income share measure is most dramatic in the United States and United Kingdom, but shows clear increases from 1980 onward in other rich, industrialized democracies as well. Taxes and social benefits can reduce inequality substantially, but even after taking the redistributive effects of these policies into account, economic inequality has risen dramatically in most of western Europe and North America. Figure 1.2 shows the Gini coefficient for disposable household income, that is, the income a household receives from all sources, including work, investments, and social benefits, minus taxes, adjusted for the size and composition of the household. The Gini coefficient captures the deviation between a perfectly even distribution of income across the population and the actual distribution, with higher values indicating more inequality. As with the top income share measure, the earliest and most dramatic increases in disposable household income inequality came in the United States and the United Kingdom, in the 1980s, with the continental and Nordic countries following suit in the 1990s and 2000s.[2]

---

[2] Income inequality fell in Southern Europe and Ireland in the 1990s, but from a much higher level (Hopkin and Lynch 2016; Matthijs 2016).

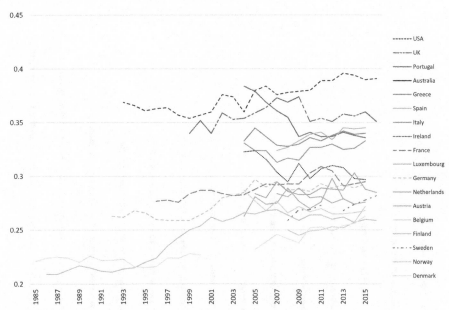

FIGURE 1.2 Inequality (Gini coefficient) of disposable household income, 1974–2009. Data from OECD.stat (https://stats.oecd.org/, accessed October 20, 2018)

It is not only income and wealth that have come to be maldistributed in the rich democracies, however. Inequalities in educational attainment and in social mobility have also increased in many countries over the period since 1980 (Breen 2005; Beller and Hout 2006; Eurofound 2017; OECD 2018). Similarly, inequalities in health grew throughout the 1990s and the first decades of the twenty-first century (Mackenbach et al. 2016, 2017; Gelder et al. 2017). Even in western European countries where the vast majority of citizens have access to affordable medical care, there is a significant gap in life expectancy between the top and bottom income quintiles, educational, or occupational groups, which means that white-collar managerial workers can expect on average to live five to seven years longer than their counterparts who do manual labor.[3] These inequalities extend to health as well as death. For example, in surveys of health status, people with incomes in the lowest quintile of the income distribution are substantially more likely to report being in poor health than those in the top quintile (Figure 1.3). In many

---

[3] Only a small portion of socioeconomic inequalities in health outcomes is attributable to differences in access to health care. The lion's share of mortality gaps even for causes of death that are amenable to medical interventions – 80–90 percent, by some accounts – is attributable instead to underlying inequalities in financial, social, and cognitive resources that shape the conditions of life and behavioral choices that affect people's health (see Chapter 3).

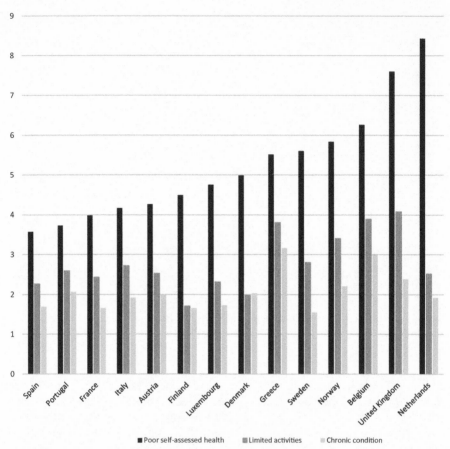

FIGURE 1.3 Relative inequality in self-assessed poor health by country, 2010. Relative risk ratios calculated as prevalence of "bad" or "very bad" self-assessed health; limitations on daily activities; and chronic health problems; among persons with a household income in the bottom quintile for that country, divided by the prevalence among those with a household income in the top quintile for that country.
Data from Beckfield and Morris (2016) based on 2010 EU Survey of Income and Living Conditions

countries, the size of such health inequalities has increased over time, often despite substantial efforts by governments to close the gaps. One commonly used measure of the magnitude of health inequality is the relative index of inequality (RII), which summarizes how strongly related the risk of a particular health outcome is, in a given population, to socioeconomic status (SES). Figure 1.4 shows that the RII for all-cause mortality by educational attainment increased during the period 1970–2009 in all of the European populations for which there are comparable data over time.

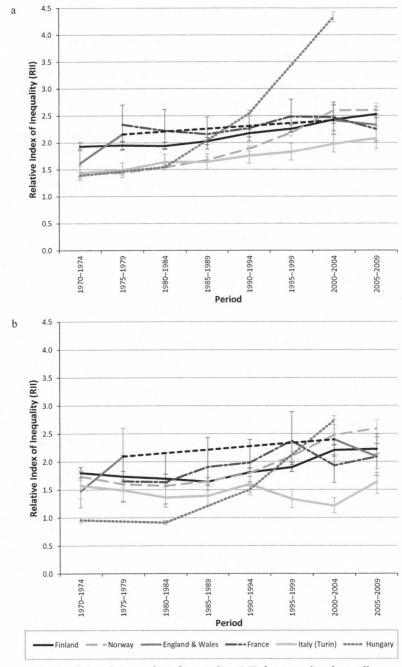

FIGURE 1.4 Trends in relative index of inequality (RII) for mortality from all causes, by education level. (a) RII for men; (b) RII for women. In England and Wales, RIIs for the period 1980–99 could not be calculated because "middle" education was not available. Reproduced with permission from Gelder et al. (2017)

Rising inequality has not gone unnoticed. In 2014, Pope Francis tweeted that "Inequality is the root of social evil."[4] Just weeks later, Christine LaGarde, then managing director of no lesser a "bastion of capitalism," than the International Monetary Fund (Greenhouse 1992), warned of the dangers for democracy and capitalism of "excessive" inequality. "If we want capitalism to do its job," LaGarde remarked, "then it needs to be more inclusive. That means addressing extreme income disparity" (Lagarde 2014). Public intellectuals, too, have taken up the issue. *The Spirit Level: Why Equality Is Better for Everyone*, by two longtime British scholars of inequality, Richard Wilkinson and Kate Pickett (2009), and *Capital in the Twenty-First Century*, written by French economist Thomas Piketty and published in English in 2014, became international bestsellers – the latter becoming the first and, one suspects, likely the last 400-plus-page book containing mathematical equations to ever be a number one bestseller on Amazon. The former linked economic inequality to a variety of other forms of social inequality, including health inequalities, but was by no means the first to do so: both national governments and international bodies have commissioned reports that document growing inequalities in health and lay out policy agendas for reducing them since the 1980s (at the inter-national level, see, e.g., WHO 2008; European Commission 2013; WHO Regional Office for Europe 2013; and Ottersen et al. 2014; at the national level, see Chapters 4–6).

Nor has inequality evoked complacency among electorates. Political scien-tists and politicians alike predicted in the 1980s and 1990s that increasing prosperity and the expansion of the middle class would produce electorates that were unconcerned with inequality and had little appetite for redistributive taxation and spending (see, e.g., Inglehart 1971; Kitschelt 1994). However, these predictions turned out to be at best partially correct. In the United States, opposition to redistributive policies was fueled not so much by prosperity as by a combination of racial resentment and the growing association in the public mind of poverty and welfare with racial minorities (Gilens 2009). And while anti-tax, anti-welfare backlashes did occur in some of Europe's more highly taxed countries in the late 1970s and early 1980s, these were temporary: public support for welfare programs in European countries remained as high in the 1980s as it was in the 1960s (Alber 1988, 195).

In the 1990s and 2000s, data from high-quality cross-nationally comparable surveys such as the International Social Survey Project (ISSP), the European Social Survey (ESS), the Eurobarometer, and the World Values survey revealed that large majorities of the public in European countries continued to support a wide variety of redistributive tax and spending policies, advocated for the government to have an important role in reducing social inequality, and

---

[4] Pope Francis, Twitter post, April 2014, 1:28 a.m., https://twitter.com/pontifex/status/460697074585980928?lang=en.

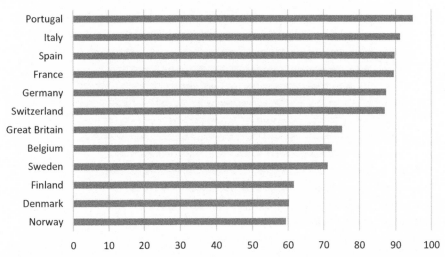

FIGURE 1.5 Percentage agreeing that "income differences in [country] are too large."
Data from ISSP 2009 (www.gesis.org/issp/modules/issp-modules-by-topic/social-inequality/2009/, accessed October 15, 2018)

believed that inequality was too high. Figure 1.5 shows the share of each nation's respondents who agreed in a 2009 ISSP survey with the statement "income differences are too large": at least 60 percent in the most equal, Nordic countries, and over 80 percent in Germany, France, and Southern Europe. Similarly, the ESS survey asked respondents across Europe whether they agreed or disagreed with the statement "The government should take measures to reduce differences in income levels." In no year from 2002 to 2016 (covering the flush period before the onset of the global financial crisis in 2008 as well as the period of austerity that followed) did support for government efforts to reduce income inequality drop below 69.5 percent in Europe as a whole.[5]

There is much less information available about public attitudes toward inequalities in health in Europe, although one small study in England found substantial public aversion to health inequality (Robson et al. 2016). However, an ISSP module in 2011 did ask respondents in several west European countries about inequalities in access to health care: "Is it fair or unfair that people with higher incomes can afford better health care than people with lower incomes?" The share responding that this practice was "unfair" ranged from a low of 45 percent in Great Britain to a high of 80 percent in France (Figure 1.6). Public opposition to tiering of health care by income appears to be lower in countries where access to a wide variety of primary and preventive health care is free at

---

[5] Data from European Social Survey (http://nesstar.ess.nsd.uib.no/webview/), various years.

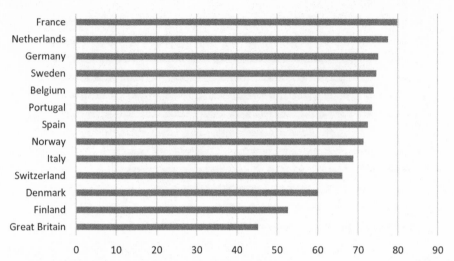

FIGURE 1.6 Share of respondents saying it is "unfair that people with higher incomes can afford better health care than people with lower incomes."
Data from ISSP 2011 (https://dbk.gesis.org/dbksearch/sdesc2.asp?ll=10&notabs=&af=&nf=& search=&search2=&db=d&no=5800, accessed October 15, 2018)

the point of service (the underfunding of the national health service in Sweden, which by the 2000s had resulted in very long wait times and a rapid growth of private voluntary health insurance, may explain higher opposition in that country).

Inequality in both economic conditions and health is rising, then – despite the fact that experts agree that these inequalities are problematic, despite the fact that mass publics in west European countries generally express a desire for considerably more equality than currently exists, and despite, as we shall see, considerable efforts on the part of some governments to try to reverse the growth of inequality. How can we account for the surprising resilience of social inequality?

THE POLITICAL ECONOMY OF RESILIENT INEQUALITY

The standard explanation for rising income inequality in economics is "skill-biased technical change" (SBTC): a shift in production technologies associated with the growth of computerization and other information technologies that rewards higher-skilled individuals with higher wages and greater employment opportunities (see, e.g., Goldin and Katz 2008; Acemoglu and Autor 2011). However, as numerous analyses have shown, SBTC is an inadequate explanation for rising inequality. SBTC cannot account for the rise of non-wage inequalities – in educational attainment or health, for example – that have accompanied the rise of economic inequality but do not obviously result from differences in the productive capacities of workers with different skill sets. Moreover, variation in political arrangements and labor market policies means that economies with similar skill profiles have experienced widely varying growth in inequality (see, e.g., Hacker and Pierson 2010; Hühne and Herzer 2017).

To better account for the growth of economic inequality, economist Thomas Piketty proposed an alternative explanation (Piketty 2014). Piketty shows that under normal circumstances, the rate of return to capital is higher than the rate of growth of the economy as a whole. This leads the share of national income and wealth that is held by individuals at the very top of the distribution to grow over the long term. But while Piketty's theory relies on economic formulas rather than politics to explain trends in inequality, he himself calls for "a political and historical economics" (p. 573) that recognizes the role of politics in generating certain patterns of inequality – including the moderation of inequality during the *trente glorieuses* from 1945 to 1975. Proposals for more progressive income taxation and a global wealth tax made by Piketty and by his longtime collaborator Anthony Atkinson also suggest that political action can moderate the accumulation of capital (Piketty 2014; Atkinson 2015). The sustained growth of economic inequality over the last forty years is a political fact, then, not an economic one, and requires political explanations.

For the past twenty years, though, the dominant lens in political science through which variation across countries and over time in the level of economic inequality has been viewed is a single theory borrowed from a pair of economists: Allan Meltzer and Scott Richard (1981).[6] The Meltzer–Richard model stipulates that policy-makers respond to the political demand for redistribution arising from the median voter, and that the median voter's taste for redistribution is higher when society is more unequal. This is because income and wealth distributions are almost always skewed to the right by the presence of some very high-earning individuals, resulting in the median income being lower than the average income. The more unequal the society, the lower the median voter's income relative to the average, and thus the greater the demand for redistribution. The Meltzer–Richard model leads us to expect that when inequality rises, the median voter will desire more redistribution, and democratically elected governments will compensate by introducing more redistributive policies.

In fact, of course, this is the opposite of what has happened in the rich democracies over the last forty years. Economic models are designed to be parsimonious, to reduce the complexity of human interactions down to a set of rules that can help us understand regularities and predict future outcomes.

[6] Noteworthy examples of applications of the Meltzer-Richard model in political science include Moene and Wallerstein (2001); Boix (2003); Iversen and Soskice (2006); Pontusson and Rueda (2010); Ansell and Samuels (2014); Huber (2017).

We accept a certain amount of imprecision in exchange for ease of application, and if models fail to predict real-world outcomes, we allow that this may be because the unmodeled complexity in the world sometimes generates unexpected outcomes, even if the underlying model is correct. Much of the political science literature on inequality in the last twenty years has operated on this assumption, and instead of rejecting the Meltzer–Richard model outright, has attempted to explain deviations from the expected outcomes by illuminating more of what goes on in the black box between societal inequality and the political demand for redistribution. Aided by the availability of high-quality, cross-nationally comparable sources of public opinion data such as the ESS and Eurobarometer, scholars have produced a large body of empirical research examining whether, how, and under what circumstances inequality affects public preferences regarding redistribution.[7] This work is enlightening, and helps us to see that political and policy institutions, in addition to social and economic structures, shape the level of demand for redistribution in the electorate.

It does not, I would argue, go far enough. In order to explain why there is sometimes more, and sometimes less, redistribution than the Meltzer–Richard model predicts, we need to rethink the model. Redistribution is not simply something that happens in response to demands from the electorate. It is also a result of what politicians are willing to supply in terms of policies to generate social equality.

Research inspired by Marxian class analysis offers a straightforward political explanation for inequality that is more attentive to the supply of (in)equality by governments. In the Marxisant view, inequality persists because it is advantageous to capital holders, who are aided in accumulating surplus value in their own hands by a state apparatus that does their bidding. Even if the state is not simply, as Marx declared in the *Communist Manifesto*, "a committee for managing the common affairs of the whole bourgeoisie" (Marx 1951 [1848], 35), in the Marxisant view capital holders generally get what they want. Ideological hegemony, weak class consciousness on the part of workers, and/or lack of a well-organized and well-resourced labor movement may also contribute to capital holders' grip on power, but at the end of the day, the key to understanding the persistence of inequality, in this view, is that the wealthy prefer to keep most of their wealth, and have the power resources to do so in the face of anything short of revolution or natural disaster. Historian Walter Scheidel's *The Great Leveler: Violence and the History of Inequality from the Stone Age to the Twenty-First Century* (2017) exemplifies this line of reasoning. Echoes of the argument can be found as well in social science scholarship that emphasizes the importance of labor's power resources for

---

[7] See, for example, widely cited articles by Moene and Wallerstein (2001); Linos and West (2003); Iversen and Soskice (2006); Kenworthy and McCall (2008); Lupu and Pontusson (2011); Barnes (2013); Jusko (2015). New research in this genre continues to emerge at a rapid pace.

welfare state development (e.g., Korpi 1985; E. Huber and Stephens 2001), and of the "structural power" of capital in ensuring favorable distributive outcomes (e.g., Gill and Law 1989; Block 1992; Woll 2014).

Closer attention to European political history suggests, though, that governing elites do not always act to safeguard capital accumulation. The threat of expropriation has in fact frequently persuaded economic elites to redistribute preemptively (Piven and Cloward 2012 [1971]; Ansell and Samuels 2014). Indeed, the postwar settlements that ushered in the *trente glorieuses* in western Europe required capital holders to relinquish some of their power to accumulate, in return for workers' acquiescence to employers' control over the capital that they retained (Maier 1981). Welfare regimes built around these settlements codified and managed the acceptable level of socioeconomic inequality within society through policy instruments such as redistributive taxation, social insurance and social assistance programs, regulation of labor markets by law and through neocorporatist bargaining, and public provision of social services such as education and health care. Nowhere in the rich democracies has the capitalist class been given free rein to accumulate.

Moreover, in the postwar period these democracies have generally not been governed solely by elites who represent or work in the interests of capital. In practice, parties and governments, whether of the left or right, are often cross-class coalitions (Przeworski and Sprague 1986; Bartolini 2007). And while the intellectuals who staff academic and government research agencies may not be part of the revolutionary vanguard, neither do they necessarily develop policy proposals simply in order to serve capital-holders. State bureaucrats may have reasons of their own to want the state to carry out redistribution or reduce inequality through other means (Orloff 1993b; Skocpol 1995). In other words, the messy, cross-class reality of democratic government in an era of mass politics means that persistent inequality cannot be attributed solely to the power and interests of capital holders.

Neither economic forces, nor a lack of demand from below, nor a conspiracy of capital holders is enough to explain why, since the 1980s, governments in the rich capitalist democracies have allowed inequality to rise so quickly and so far. Why have center-left governments, in particular, not done more to prioritize policies that would maximize the share of the national income going to lower-income voters? One explanation that has strongly influenced the literature on party systems in Europe, and indeed the behavior of many politicians, connects the lack of interest in reducing inequality to changes in the electorate: specifically, the rise of a "postmaterialist," "left-libertarian" voting bloc beginning in the 1970s. For much of the history of democratic mass politics in these countries, center-left parties (and many Christian democratic parties, too) had strong connections to active labor unions and mass-membership structures. These led to regularized, personal contact between voters and party activists, which helped to recruit people of working- and middle-class backgrounds into party leadership and elected office, and helped ensure that the economic interests of non-elites remained on the agenda. Beginning in the mid-1970s, however, falling unionization rates, the gradual decline of membership-based mass parties, and changing economic and social structures presented a fundamentally changed landscape. The number of party leaders with close connections to the labor movement began to fall, and center-left voters, too, were increasingly drawn from middle-class and service-sector occupations.

Political scientists and sociologists have theorized that during this period, rising prosperity, increased access to higher education, and an occupational structure increasingly dominated by services rather than manufacturing led citizens to prioritize post-materialist values such as personal autonomy, tolerance, and environmentalism over bread-and-butter issues of remuneration and redistribution (Inglehart 1971; Kitschelt 1994; Bell 2008 [1973]). Under these circumstances, left party leaders faced a choice: realign their parties' social and economic priorities to appeal to a left-libertarian coalition of middle-class service-sector and white-collar workers, or remain committed to the materialist issues that appealed to a shrinking blue-collar electorate and cede the new postmaterialist voters to green and liberal parties.

While the timing has varied, many major center-left parties did eventually shift to a programmatic stance consistent with the "left-libertarian" strategy (Kitschelt 1994), which implied deprioritizing efforts to redistribute vertically between higher- and lower-income citizens. This shift has narrowed the distance between the center-left and center-right in Europe when it comes to economic policy, particularly compared to the 1970s (Knutsen 1998; Keman and Pennings 2006). The old postwar consensus based on Keynesianism, which reigned through the 1960s, was replaced, after a period of more polarized politics in the 1970s, with a new economic policy consensus. This policy consensus emerged on the political right in the early 1980s, but by the 1990s had come to include most of the center-left as well. Collectively, the political alliances, ideas, and policies that underlay the new consensus that emerged during this period are often termed "neoliberalism" (P. Hall 1986; McNamara 1998; Blyth 2002).

In Chapter 2, I explain in some detail what I mean by neoliberalism and why I believe the term is a useful one for this analysis. However, it is worth noting right away that neoliberalism is not in itself incompatible with a focus on inequality. The hegemony of neoliberal ideas was never complete, as is vividly illustrated by the conversion of international organizations like the IMF to support efforts to reduce inequality. Moreover, while the neoliberal paradigm rejects many policies that would encourage significant redistribution of income or wealth, it has little to say about the inherent value of other forms of social inequality. Politicians who accept the basic premises of neoliberalism might nevertheless be concerned about inequalities in human capital, and seek to remedy them by means that are unobtrusive with respect to markets or income distribution.

Indeed, that is what many center-left politicians and policy-makers have done: the Third Way policies of Tony Blair, Bill Clinton, and Gerhard Schroeder in the 1990s; the activation turn in the Netherlands, Denmark, and Sweden in the 2000s; and the new interest in health inequalities in the twenty-first century are all examples of efforts by center-left politicians to reframe the issue of inequality, to make it amenable to policy remedies during a period in which the traditional tools of economic management used to mitigate market inequalities are increasingly off-limits.

In the case studies that I consider in this book, I show that center-left politicians believed that that their electorates had changed in ways that made certain forms of inequality less politically pressing, and were strongly influenced by neoliberal ideas about what policy tools were appropriate to use in that context. But they did not entirely abandon either their working-class constituencies or the goal of making their societies more equitable, and in fact took up the issue of health inequalities precisely as a way to rally both working- and middle-class voters around the issue of equity. In order to understand why this political choice did not result in a reduction of inequality, we need to go beyond the structure of the electorate or the threat from capital, and consider what happens when the fundamental structuring institutions of contemporary political economies are brought into question by pressures from neoliberal ideas and practices.

The explanation that I offer in this book for the consistent lack of progress on inequality in European countries is rooted in a broader politics that varies cross-nationally, but in predictable ways. My explanation grounds neoliberalism in praxis in order to understand how it creates inequality; updates welfare regime theory to accommodate the influence of neoliberalism; and helps us understand the conditions under which policy frames do and do not correspond to policy outputs. I argue that the effects of neoliberalism on inequalities in health and wealth manifest differently depending on the distinctive political dynamics that are generated by different welfare regimes' interaction with specific instantiations of neoliberalism in the 1980s and 1990s. These interactions shape how politicians frame the issue of inequality, the tools they use (and avoid using) in order to combat inequality, and ultimately their success or failure in combating rising inequality into the twenty-first century.

THE ANALYTIC STRATEGY

My goal is to understand how inequality functions as a political issue in the neoliberal era, since roughly 1980, by examining the politics of health inequalities. What happens when political actors frame social inequality in terms of health inequalities? What forms of political power do they invoke, reinforce, or undermine by this framing? What ideas are excluded from public debate? The core method that I use in this book to answer the question of why and how inequality has remained so resilient in the face of public and expert opposition, and so resistant to policy efforts to reduce it, is frame analysis. Process tracing and content analysis support the analysis of policy frames that lies at the heart of this work. Process tracing methods (including archival research, interviews, and reviews of secondary literature) are used in case studies of the World Health Organization's Regional Office for Europe (WHO Europe), the European Commission's Directorate General for Health and Consumer Protection (DG SANCO), England, France, and Finland to understand how, at the level of individual polities, health inequality emerges as a political problem, why the problem takes the form it does in different contexts, and what are the consequences for politics and policy. Content analysis – of official government reports on health inequalities and of other relevant materials – is used to assess the content and coherence of policy frames at different times and in different national contexts.

Analysis of Policy Frames

Political science as a field has not adopted a standard definition of a policy frame. Drawing on work in communications studies, sociology, and political science,[8] I define a policy frame as a way of discussing a policy problem that is comprised by five distinctive elements: a definition of the problem, a causal story that explains the sources of the problem, a moral judgment that invokes the necessity for action, attribution of treatment responsibility to particular political or societal actors, and a treatment recommendation laying out how the problem should be solved. By defining who or what is responsible for causing and fixing a problem, policy frames can affect whether an issue gets on the agenda and shape policy responses to a problem. Frames do their work by activating schema in the minds of recipients of messages about social problems, who then use these schema unconsciously to "fill in the blanks" between elements of a problem in order to construct policy responses that seem reasonable (van Gorp 2007). While a policy frame may arise organically, as policy actors come to consensus on a particular set of ideas that just seem to make sense, framing can also be intentional: policy actors hire pollsters, messaging, and marketing experts to develop ways of talking about their priorities that are likely to mobilize supporters and generate the desired results, and allocate resources toward activities that are likely to support their frame.[9]

Frames are distinct from policy paradigms. Peter Hall (1993) defines a policy paradigm as "a framework of ideas and standards that specifies not only the goals of policy and the kind of instruments that can be used to attain them but also the very nature of the problems they are meant to be addressing" (p. 279). In this sense, policy paradigms are similar to policy frames. The distinction

---

[8] See Stone (1989); Entman (1993); Vliegenthart and van Zoonen (2011).

[9] Thomas and Turnbull (2017) distinguish between a frame, which denotes "how I see the world," and the process of framing, which involves actors deciding "how I want you to see the world" in order to legitimate their own preferred policies or impel others to take action.

between the two becomes clear, though, if we consider the difference between Hall's paradigm shifts and lower-order types of policy change. In Hall's framework, paradigm (third-order) shifts involve a change in the fundamental goals behind policy (e.g., refocusing economic policy on creating equity, rather than growth). First- and second-order policy changes involve adjustments to policy *means* – respectively, changing how standard policy instruments are used and introducing new types of policy instruments, but without changing the *ends* to which these policies are deployed. Thus Hall's first- and second-order policy changes, and not only paradigm shifts, could occur in tandem with, or be triggered by, a change in a policy frame. This is because changing any one of the elements of the frame, from problem definition to attribution of treatment responsibility, might imply a need for new or revised policies. In other words, policy frames may be subsumed within policy paradigms, which are marked by fundamental differences in the ends of public policy. The health inequalities problem frame adopted by many center-left governments in the last twenty years is distinct from, and subsidiary to, the neoliberal policy paradigm that has emerged during the same period.

But across time and space, policy actors have framed health inequalities differently. Even before we examine where these different frames come from, whether and how they affect policy-making, and what this tells us about power and politics, simply to recognize that health inequalities are framed differently depending on the political setting has important consequences for our understanding of the politics of inequality. Comparative analysis of framing denaturalizes health inequalities. For public health scholars and advocates, noticing that health inequality is not just "out there" to be measured, but rather actively constructed as a concept, encourages a deeper engagement with dimensions and causes of inequality that might otherwise be missed, and may shed light on new ways to combat inequities.

Political science also benefits from a comparative analysis of framing. Health inequalities are a form of social inequality relatively unfamiliar to most political scientists. This makes it easier for us to see when political actors wittingly or unwittingly frame the issue in ways that highlight or obscure certain facets of the problem, and empower or disempower different actors in the polity. Other, more familiar concepts like income inequality are similarly framed, but because of their familiarity we are often less attentive to the consequences of different framings of the issue. Consider, for example, the implications of discussing income inequality in the United States and elsewhere in terms of top income shares, as occurred after Piketty and Saez's data became available (Piketty and Saez 2001; 2006). Occupy Wall Street picked up this framing, emphasizing the contrast between the "top 1 percent" and the "other 99 percent," phrases that came to dominate news and political speech surrounding inequality in the United States in 2011 and 2012 (Dreier 2011). This frame focused public, policy, and academic attention on wealth, and on the super-rich, contributing to a flowering of policy debates surrounding executive compensation, the appropriate role of the finance sector in modern capitalist economies, the role of money in politics, baby bonds, global wealth taxes, and the like. The "top 1 percent" frame informed a new approach on the part of both academics and policy-makers to inequality in the rich democracies – an approach that has also tended to downplay concerns that were more traditionally at the heart of inequality politics (e.g., wage dispersion, the decline of employment in high-skill manufacturing, the fate of the middle class), and temporarily to suppress the study of rising inequality in the countries of continental Europe, where the gains to top income groups have been more modest than in the United States or United Kingdom.

Why did this frame come about? Who wins and who loses from this frame? Piketty and Saez's data did not cause the "top 1 percent" frame, the frame did not cause these policy issues to emerge, and the emergence of the policy issues did not cause any particular solutions to be adopted. But by analyzing the frame and its constituent parts and trying to understand why it had resonance, we can more clearly see how certain aspects of (income) inequality become more salient and more likely to serve as focal points around which policy-makers may rally. The same is true for frames about health inequalities.

Case Selection

This book is organized around case studies of the framing of health equity in three countries: England, France, and Finland. In each of these countries, center-left politicians and governments have been the most actively involved in promoting action on health inequalities while in government, and so it is to their framing of the problem of inequality that I am most attentive. However, the frames used by center-left actors do not come from nowhere. To understand why the center-left's framing of inequality takes the form that it does in each country, it is necessary to examine ideas about health inequality expressed by the policy elites who constitute the national and international health policy fields in Europe. Policy elites include politicians, spokespersons for national governments and international organizations, as well as the bureaucrats, researchers, and civil society actors who have contributed to forming the knowledge base on which health policy ideas are constructed. Because international organizations and professional networks shape what problem frames are readily available to national-level politicians, I preface the national-level case studies with research on two organizations whose activities have an important effect on domestic health policy actors: WHO Europe and DG SANCO.

WHO Europe and DG SANCO are obvious case studies on which to base a reading of health inequalities frames and framing at the European level. The EU can, if it so chooses, influence member states to undertake policies to address health inequalities via "soft law"; as we shall see in Chapter 3, it has relied on WHO Europe as a critical source of expertise and policy ideas in this area. The WHO's global office in Geneva has had an impact on health policy in

Europe, but on the issue of health equity it has tended to take a back seat to the regional office. Neither the Organisation for Economic Cooperation and Development (OECD), nor the World Bank, nor any other international organization active at the European level has had a similar impact on the health equity agenda.

England, France, and Finland hardly constitute a usual set of cases for comparative analysis, however, so some explanation for their selection is in order. Scholars of comparative politics are often drawn to instances of surprising variation in how states and other political actors behave, and we usually select our cases so that they represent the range of this variation. If we wanted to know, for example, why otherwise similar governments respond to an exogenous shock differently, we would select similar countries that have been subjected to the same exogenous shock, but that vary in their response to it. I began the research for this book with just such a strategy. My goal at the outset was to understand how governments make policies to combat health inequalities, and why these policies might vary across countries in ways that ultimately affect population health. But because there had not been a systematic study of policy responses to health inequalities across European countries, I did not have a strong sense of what the variation in policy responses across countries might be. I did know from my previous work on the politics of health equity, however, that there was some variation in how researchers and policymakers defined and discussed the problem of health inequalities in different contexts (Julia Lynch 2016; Julia Lynch and Perera 2017). I expected that these different policy frames would create different policy outcomes.[10]

As I learned more about the policy responses to the problem of health inequalities in European countries, though, I found a surprising degree of similarity. Despite important differences in the framing of the problem, and despite WHO Europe and DG SANCO's exhortations, as of 2010 many countries lacked a coherent plan at the national level to combat health inequalities. To the extent that action against inequalities was being taken at the local level, it tended to be scattershot and only weakly intersectoral. Even more strikingly, none of the countries had put into place policies that would attack the problem of health inequalities by reducing inequalities in the farthest "upstream" social determinants of health. It was beginning to look like the most puzzling finding of my preliminary research might not be the presence of variation in the

---

[10] As compared to the European literature, American scholarly and policy production around the issue of health inequalities is much more strongly focused on racial and ethnic disparities, and on health care rather than health outcomes (Julia Lynch and Perera 2017). And despite legacies of sharp regional discord in their countries, most Italian and Belgian scholars writing on inequalities in health outcomes in the 1990s and 2000s rarely mentioned regional differences. Meanwhile, French government reports put territorial differences in health front and center, producing reports decorated with scores of beautifully shaded maps (Julia Lynch 2016).

TABLE 1.1 *Case characteristics and policy outputs*

Case Characteristics	England	France	Finland
Welfare regime type	Liberal	Conservative-Corporatist	Social Democratic
Level of socioeconomic inequality	High	Medium	Low
Health care system	National Health Service	Social Insurance	Mixed
Health inequalities	Large	Medium	Medium
Contributions to international consensus health inequality frame	Substantial	Minimal	Substantial
Timing of adoption of international consensus frame	1980s	2010s	2000s
Policy Outputs	**England**	**France**	**Finland**
Intersectoral working	Health centric	Only at local level	Does not include key ministries
National coordination of local efforts	Attempted	Minimal	Minimal
Action on fundamental causes of health inequalities?	No	No	No

framing of health inequalities, but the *lack* of meaningful variation in the policies that emerged out of these different frames.

To make sense of this kind of puzzle, the optimal case selection is a "most different systems" approach (Teune and Przeworski 1970), in which the researcher examines cases that present the greatest possible range of variation in the potential causes of the similar outcome, in order to find the constellation of causes that seems to consistently produce that outcome. The final selection of England, France, and Finland as primary cases came about in order to provide maximum variation on some of the factors that I thought could be plausibly related to the common outcome of interest – governments' failure to enact the policies that would be most likely to help them reduce health inequalities – even after they had put in place national health equity plans (see Table 1.1). They include early (England) and later (France and Finland) adopters of the policy framing of health inequalities that had come to dominate the international agenda by the 2000s; countries in which the problem of health equity has been at the very center of the political agenda (England, Finland) and those where it has been more peripheral (France); Beveridgean (England), Bismarckian (France), and mixed (Finland) health care systems; liberal (England), social democratic (Finland), and conservative-corporatist (France) welfare states; and societies that are quite equal (Finland) as well as those that have moderate income inequality (France) or are very unequal (England). The country cases also differ in the extent to which they were involved in shaping the international health inequalities consensus, which I suspected might affect the speed and thoroughness with which their governments acted on policy recommendations coming out of that consensus. Two of the country cases, England and Finland, shaped the approach of the international organizations, as well as being shaped by it. France, which rejected the international framing in favor of its own problem definition until quite recently, has more of a one-way relationship with the international organizations, as a "taker" rather than a "maker" of ideas about health inequalities.

A combination of least- and most-likely cases for the full adoption of policies compliant with the international consensus health inequality policy frame made it possible for me to begin to work through the potential causes of the puzzling similarity in policy outputs. Considering how strongly British scholars contributed to the development of the international consensus approach to health inequalities and the sustained attention to health inequalities under Labour governments from 1997 to 2010, England would seem to be a most likely case for the implementation of the international health inequalities consensus policy recommendations. However, very high levels of income inequality and a strong liberal intellectual tradition made England a potential outlier when it comes to dealing with inequality.

France is an obvious contrasting case, considerably less likely to implement the recommendations of the international consensus. French health policy-makers are weakly integrated into international networks, and until quite recently were neither fully aware of nor particularly concerned to follow WHO Europe and DG SANCO's recommendations. Furthermore, France's social insurance health care system and transfer-heavy conservative-corporatist welfare state made its institutions a poor fit with the mental model held by many of the British and Scandinavian policy entrepreneurs working to establish a consensus policy frame at the international level.

Finally, Finland, like England, was likely case for the straightforward transposition of WHO-inspired health policy into national law. Finnish epidemiologists had been involved with developing the WHO's expertise in population health at least since the 1970s, and Finland had independently undertaken a world-renowned project to reduce regional disparities in cardiovascular health already in the 1980s. Finland also volunteered to be the pilot case for the WHO's Health For All program in Europe in the 1980s, and Finnish expertise, particularly in the area of cross-sectoral policy-making, has continued to feed into the international consensus right up to most recent period. Moreover, Finland was led by governing coalitions that included social democrats in the 1950s through 1970s and again in the mid- to late-1990s. This meant that unlike the United Kingdom or France, Finland landed squarely in the social democratic world of welfare and should be expected to pursue higher levels of social equality.

The fact that none of these three countries succeeded either in fully implementing the international consensus set of policy recommendations or in meaningfully reducing health inequalities suggests that even under the most favorable circumstances, something was getting in the way.

Data Collection and Analysis

In researching this puzzlingly similar outcome, I drew on a variety of sources and methods to understand how ideas about health inequalities spread, and how policies did or did not respond to these ideas, in each case. My starting point was to survey the academic research literature on health inequalities for each country. I conducted systematic searches of online databases and individual journal websites to identify relevant English- and French-language publications by scholars of social medicine and public health, epidemiologists, demographers, geographers, economists, and political scientists, dating back in some cases to the 1940s. Reading these materials gave me a sense of what kinds of questions researchers in each country were asking about health inequalities, which academic disciplines tended to dominate, what kinds of data were available to them, and who their funding sources and policy audiences were. Beginning in the 1990s, a secondary literature discussing health inequalities as a research and policy field had begun to develop. In some settings, like England, a great deal has already been written by other observers about the politics of and policy responses to health inequalities, so I rely on secondary sources to provide a wealth of useful information. This volume and detail was not available for the other countries or at the European level, however, so I turned to a variety of primary materials to piece together the story of how health inequalities emerged as a political problem, and why it has elicited the set of policy responses that it has.

I began the work of process tracing the emergence of health inequalities as a political issue by reading official reports about health inequalities that had been produced by the WHO, the EU, and national governments, at the request of these entities, or by outside groups in an effort to influence these entities, beginning with the Black Report in the United Kingdom in 1980. These reports gave me a sense of the main terms of the debate about health inequalities in each setting: What kinds of inequalities, concerning what kinds of outcomes, were discussed in the reports? Who did their intended audience seem to be? What bodies of research did they draw on, and what other reports were they citing? What kinds of solutions were they suggesting, if any?

Each of these reports has a history and a backstory, so I read as much as I could find in online archives about the genesis of the reports, the tenor of the drafting process, and what might have been included in earlier versions and then dropped. Because tracing the process of how these reports came about was not the main object of my research, however, I did not conduct a comprehensive review of all of the archival material related to these reports, particularly when it was not readily accessible electronically. Instead, I relied on the experts who produced these reports to fill in details about the process.

In fact, the most important initial source of information about influences on policy-making in the area of health inequalities came from my in-depth interviews. In each country, I interviewed three broad types of people involved with health inequalities: researchers, policy-makers, and politicians or their staff. In the countries I studied there is a great deal of movement between academic and government research positions, and even between research and policy roles. While the more senior policy positions in France and Britain are reserved for career civil servants, many of my interviewees held both academic and government roles, and often quite senior ones. And while in general few party leaders, prime ministers, or even health ministers had backgrounds as health inequalities researchers, I did interview several senior academics who had run for or been elected to public office. The lines dividing academia from government, research from policy, and policy from politics are thus not bright ones in this sample of respondents. Nevertheless, the distinction was useful in guiding my sampling and interview protocols.

To begin with, in each case I contacted the most prolific researchers in the health inequalities field in each country, whom I identified through a thorough review of the academic literature. I next drew on government reports to identify and contact any other academics and policy experts who had contributed to major reports on health inequalities commissioned or produced by the government. These experts helped me identify an initial set of contacts in the agencies responsible for formulating and implementing policies aimed at reducing health inequalities, and for communicating with the WHO and DG SANCO. Finally, I interviewed actors in the political sphere, including elected officials and the health specialists and other staff members working as advisors to political parties, prime ministers, and health ministers. The vast majority of the individuals I contacted agreed to be interviewed, and many suggested further contacts. A complete list of interviews is included in the References section.

Interviewing participants in the health inequalities research and policy field of course meant that I risked immersing myself in the world of people who care about the issue and have something at stake in portraying it as important, when in fact the issue has very little salience beyond that community. Speaking with journalists, academics, and policy-makers who were not specialists in the topic of health inequalities but who knew about politics and policy-making in their countries more broadly was an important corrective. However, the interviews with "insiders" served a number of very important functions in my research.[11]

---

[11] Interviews were semi-structured and generally lasted between one and two hours. For the most part I met with participants in their places of work, although a few interviews took place in public locations or via Skype. Interviews concerning England, Finland, and the WHO were conducted entirely in English, while those concerning France and the EU took place in English, French, or a combination of the two. Interviews were audio recorded, and participants were granted anonymity in accordance with guidelines for the protection of human subjects participating in research studies. The research and policy communities devoted to health inequalities in

The academic researchers, policy experts, and politicians I spoke with all provided important background information and helped me to construct complete inventories of government statements on and policy responses to health inequality. Interviewing a broad sample of academic researchers on health inequalities from a variety of disciplines allowed me to learn about how the "raw materials" that government reports drew on came into existence. I was particularly interested in whether there was a relationship between what data sources were available and how scholars defined the problem of health inequalities, to what extent the supply of research funding and demand for information from policy-makers influenced their research agendas, and the types of connections that existed between research and policy communities both at the domestic level and internationally. The researchers and other experts who participated in producing major reports on health inequalities provided me in addition with detailed information about how and why these reports came into being, and why they took the form that they eventually took.

Members of the policy bureaucracy were often able to provide additional insights into the motivations behind the reports, and of course were also a source of information about policies that were made in response to these reports. My conversations with politicians – elected officials and their staffers – focused on their rationales and motivations for taking up the issue of health inequalities, and for pursuing a particular set of policy responses to the problem. I interviewed fewer politicians than other types of participants, though, because I believed that politicians would be less likely to speak candidly about their motivations for framing the issue of inequality in one way or another.

Interviews provided me with valuable information about how health inequalities were framed as a public problem, and how responses to that problem were crafted. However, even the most knowledgeable participants in the health inequality research and policy fields in Europe could speak only to their own experiences. Neither did extensive reading of the research literature on health inequalities or secondary analyses of health policy-making allow me to gain a full overview of the scope of activity in this policy domain. To understand how ideas about health inequalities flowed through networks of scholars and policy, and to measure concretely the similarities and differences between health inequalities discourses and policy responses in different contexts, I turned to content analysis of other sources of primary data.

Policy frames are mental constructs, made of ideas, but they become visible in the communications among policy elites and between elites and the public. Records of these communications – the contents of newspaper articles, campaign press releases, party manifestos, parliamentary questions, scholarly journal articles, minutes of ministerial meetings, and many other sources of

these countries are small, and to maintain confidentiality I report only the most general professional roles of individual respondents when discussing the results of the interviews.

text – thus provide data for the reconstruction of frames that political and policy actors refer to when advocating for, making, and justifying public policies. In Chapter 3, I use quantitative content analysis of official reports to demonstrate that there is in fact a comprehensive policy frame that is widely shared among a defined set of international policy actors – health equity experts and bureaucrats writing on behalf of WHO Europe and the EU – and I describe the contents of that frame. In subsequent chapters I examine government reports and other bodies of text to assess the salience of the health inequality frame, the degree to which policy frames at the domestic level match the international health inequality consensus, and to what extent policies enacted in the name of reducing health inequalities match the treatment recommendations in either the domestic or international frames. The methods used to analyze these texts are described in greater detail in the chapters in which they are used, and in the Appendix.

PLAN OF THE BOOK

The common inability of governments in so many countries to make policies that could meaningfully reduce inequalities in either health or the underlying social determinants of health is a puzzling regularity that demands explanation. In the public health literature devoted to health inequalities, this phenomenon is generally attributed either to difficulties in carrying out the complex policy coordination across multiple sectors required to work effectively on the social determinants of health inequalities, or to opposition from forces committed to a neoliberal economic agenda.[12] Neither of these explanations is wrong – indeed, both are important parts of the puzzle. But even taken together, they cannot fully explain why efforts to reduce health inequalities have foundered in the way that they have. In the chapters that follow, I argue that efforts to reduce health inequalities have been largely unsuccessful because, despite differences in underlying political-economic arrangements, policy-making in each country follows a common trajectory: First, the interaction between postwar welfare regimes and a rising neoliberal policy paradigm generates political taboos that center-left politicians then seek to avoid by reframing the problem of inequality as an issue of health. Medicalizing inequality results, however, in shifting the range of appropriate policy options for dealing with inequality away from the traditional tools of economic management and toward a battery of policies that are unfamiliar, difficult to wield, and ultimately incapable of reducing health inequalities.

Chapter 2 lays out in greater detail the central argument of the book, situating it in an examination of the relationship between welfare regimes,

---

[12] Wismar et al. (2013) and Greer and Lillvis (2014) review research evidence on the difficulties of cross-sectoral policy-making for reducing health inequalities; Shrecker and Bambra (2015) provide an excellent overview of the literature linking health inequalities to aspects of neoliberalism.

neoliberalism, and health inequalities. I take care to define each of these three concepts and explain how they have been used in political science and public health, in the hope of promoting a better-informed dialogue between the two scholarly disciplines.

Chapter 3 explores the development and transmission, through an international epistemic community fostered by WHO Europe and DG SANCO, of ideas linking health inequalities to underlying socioeconomic inequality. For readers unfamiliar with basic concepts in social epidemiology, this chapter will be particularly helpful. The international consensus framing of health inequalities whose development I describe in this chapter was influenced strongly by policy actors in the United Kingdom and Finland, among other countries, but also serves as a resource for national-level policy-makers across western Europe. The international framing is thus an important backdrop for the political and policy-making processes outlined in the next three chapters.

Chapters 4–6 show how, at different times and in slightly different ways, politicians in England (Chapter 4), France (Chapter 5), and Finland (Chapter 6) embraced health inequalities as a political problem in order to claim the mantle of protectors of equity, while avoiding the sticking points generated in their countries by the collision between postwar welfare regimes and transnational neoliberalism. Each of these chapters is divided into two main sections. In the first, I demonstrate that center-left politicians reacted to the collision of their postwar welfare regime with a rising neoliberal policy paradigm by creating self-imposed taboos against using certain kinds of policy levers to deal with inequality. In each country the taboos were different, unique products of their historic welfare regimes and the specific instantiations of neoliberalism that were most challenging to the regime's central methods for containing inequality. The second halves of Chapters 4–6 show how politicians responded to the new taboos by reframing the issue of inequality. In the English case, New Labour redefined the problem of social inequality writ large, introducing health inequality as a substitute for discussions of income inequality that would invoke the taboo topic of redistribution. In Finland and France, the reframing occurred within the field of health, as political and policy actors redefined the problem of health inequality in terms of upstream social determinants of health in an effort to avoid taboos against increased public spending (France) and market regulation (Finland).

In Chapter 7 I show how, in all three countries, reframing inequality redirected attention toward policy tools that were inadequate to the challenge of reducing inequality, with results that were, at least in hindsight, predictably disappointing. Chapter 7 thus presents the meat of the argument about why it is so difficult for governments to reduce health inequalities, which may be of particular interest to a public health audience. Chapter 8 concludes with a synthesis of the cross-case findings and implications for political science theorizing about inequality, for public health, and for the future of the center-left.

2

Theorizing Regimes of Inequality

Welfare, Neoliberalism, and the Reframing of a Social Problem

INTRODUCTION AND KEY CONCEPTS

Solving the puzzle of resilient inequality requires coming to grips with how higher-than-desirable levels of inequality have come to be reproduced in so many of the rich democracies simultaneously. In Chapter 1, I showed that the normal explanations for this phenomenon offered by political science and economic theories fall short, and took the first steps toward laying out an alternative argument. In this chapter, I make a more comprehensive case for my claim that political solutions to the problem of inequality are shaped both by legacies of the past and by the way politicians talk about the problem of inequality in the present. As the central institutions for containing the growth of inequality in the welfare regimes of the postwar period collided, beginning in the 1980s, with a rising neoliberal economic policy paradigm, politicians on the center-left responded by changing how they framed the issue of inequality. This shift in framing had unanticipated consequences, however: instead of making the problem of inequality more politically tractable, as politicians hoped, the new framing of inequality as a matter of health made it more technically intractable by prompting policy-makers to eschew the simplest, most effective policy remedies. Before laying out my argument in full, I must clarify how I understand three core concepts – health inequalities, welfare regimes, and neoliberalism – that are necessary background for the argument, but that may have different resonances for different audiences.

Health Inequalities and Their Causes

For the purposes of this volume, I define health inequalities as preventable inequalities in health status between groups that are characterized by different positions in the social, economic, and political structure. Inequalities in health related to differences in income, occupation, and social class have been documented in Europe for hundreds of years (Villermé 1826; Engels 1987 [1845]; Virchow 2006 [1848]), though epidemiologists still debate the precise pathways linking socioeconomic status (SES) to health. On the one hand, poverty itself is surely a cause of poor health: People with very low incomes are often unable to gain access to the goods and services that are necessary to ensure good health and, as a result, tend to live shorter, less healthy lives and die at higher rates, even from preventable causes. This relationship between poverty and poor health is observable at the level of nation-states, at the level of neighborhoods, and at the level of individuals, and is so widely observed that it has achieved the status of a social fact. But poverty alone is not the sole cause of health inequalities. In most of the rich democracies today, a small percentage of the population lives below the income threshold that is needed to allow for adequate nutrition and shelter; in west European countries, moreover, access to medical care is guaranteed to all but the most marginalized groups. Moreover, differences in health have been observed across the entire social spectrum not only between the poor and the rich. If poverty and access to medical care cannot account for the full social gradient in health, can economic inequality?

There is some disagreement among specialists on this point. Cross-sectional studies of countries in Europe at a single point in time have found larger health inequalities in countries with lower income inequality (e.g., Mackenbach et al. 2008) – the opposite of the pattern we would expect if socioeconomic inequality was driving health inequalities. However, longitudinal studies that measure changes over time in health inequality in the same country have found increasing health inequalities as income inequality has grown (Truesdale and Jencks 2016), and a recent study found that income inequality, as distinct from poverty, is associated robustly with inequality in life expectancy in a group of twenty-eight countries observed from 1974 to 2011 (Neumayer and Plümper 2016). These disagreements should not be papered over: if the jury is still out on whether socioeconomic inequality causes health inequalities, then policymakers taking an evidence-based approach would be well advised to steer clear of trying to address the problem of health inequalities by reducing economic inequality. Of course, much policy-making – including policy-making in the area of health inequalities – is not strictly evidence-based (see, e.g., Smith 2013a). But regardless of the truth value of the claim that there is a causal relationship between socioeconomic inequalities and health inequalities, health policy actors at the international and national level often act as if were true, and recommend reducing income inequality as a way to reduce health inequalities.

If we accept that economic inequality and health inequality are causally related, we need an explanation for why this is so. Public health scholars offer a number of different types of complementary explanations. Most obviously, one way that greater social inequality occurs is when there are larger numbers of people living in poverty, which is correlated with a larger number of people who lack the material resources necessary to live a healthy life, and who are as a result more exposed to and/or more vulnerable to a variety of risk factors for poor health and early death. But differences in the level of economic inequality can result from differences in the distribution of income at the top end, as well as at the bottom end. Moreover, this "materialist" explanation for the link between economic and health inequalities cannot account for the full social gradient in health.

"Psychosocial" explanations for health inequalities focus on the effects on individuals of living at any rung of the ladder below the top in stratified societies, and are hence better suited to explaining the gradient. The chronic stress associated with social subordination and lack of control sets off biological processes in the body that result in inflammation, weathering, and microcellular degradation that can lead to excess mortality. The steeper the inequality, the more acute the stress, and the sharper the health inequalities.

Explanations that focus on individuals and their exposure to epidemiological risk factors – be they material or social in origin – help to establish potential mechanisms, but they do not explain why people at lower rungs on the ladder face greater exposure. Moving "upstream" to consider the "causes of the causes" of health inequalities offers more leverage for understanding how and why social inequality is linked to health inequalities. For example, dietary choices are individual behaviors, but they are also correlated with socioeconomic status and shaped by food availability, cost, palatability, and dietary mores within a given cultural milieu that may also be correlated with SES. To understand inequalities in the incidence and prevalence of diseases that are associated with dietary choices, for example, cardiovascular disease, diabetes, or certain cancers, we need to move upstream to understand the forces that shape dietary choices.

Upstream causes of health inequalities include the living, working, educational, family, and community environments that shape individuals' exposure to risks that ultimately contribute to health status – collectively referred to as the "social determinants of health" (SDOH). Socioeconomic inequality has been described as "the mother of underlying causes" (Dorling 2015) because the financial resources over which individuals have command have such a large impact on the environmental conditions that they experience. People with more resources have greater choice over things like where and with whom to live, or what kind of work and how much of it to do, which can have profound health impacts.

In fact, there seems to be something special about money that results in its status as a "fundamental cause" of health inequalities (Link and Phelan 1995). The health risks to which we are exposed, and the factors that protect us from these risks, are always changing. For example, in wealthy countries, smallpox, cholera, and tuberculosis have given way as leading causes of death to cardiovascular disease and cancers. As new causes of illness (e.g., sedentary lifestyles) and new health technologies (e.g., screenings that can detect cancers at an early stage) emerge, those who possess resources associated with high SES – particularly money, but also knowledge, political power, prestige, and beneficial social connections – can deploy these flexible resources in new ways to meet emerging risks to health, even as access to protection against older health risks diffuses to lower-SES groups. In this sense, inequalities in the flexible resources associated with higher SES, including money and education, are the "causes of the causes" of socioeconomic inequalities in health.

Apart from the direct effect of individuals' command over resources on their health, income and wealth inequalities may also have indirect effects on health inequalities that operate by way of the political process (see, e.g., Daniels et al. 2000). Where income inequality is high, there tends to be less investment in public education, which leads to gaps in cognitive resources and knowledge, which in turn leads to larger inequalities in health. Economic inequality can also erode social cohesion, leading to inequalities in political participation and to governments that are more responsiveness to the wealthier than to the worse-off. High levels of income inequality can also result in spatial segregation by socioeconomic status, with less-well-resourced communities experiencing more crime and violence, a lower quality of public services, and less social cohesion – all of which are associated with worse health (Kawachi et al. 1997; Miller and Chen 2013).

The living and working environments that are the "causes of the causes" of health inequalities are also heavily influenced by public policies, which are in turn influenced by political processes. So how politics is organized, and in particular how responsive politicians are to lower- versus higher-SES constituencies, can also affect health inequalities. If income inequality is the mother of underlying causes of health inequalities, then politics is the grandmother; to understand why health inequalities occur, we need to understand the politics behind the distribution of economic resources. Political institutions as broad as democracy, and as specific as proportional representation systems, have been found to be associated with better health outcome and less health inequity (Houweling et al. 2007; Patterson 2017). In the context of the rich, industrialized democracies, however, the political institutions most consistently invoked to explain inequalities in both wealth and health are welfare regimes and the influence of neoliberalism.

Welfare Regimes

Among the rich, industrialized democracies, it is possible to delineate a small number of recurring ideal-typical responses to the central problem of how to combine economic growth with enough equity to guarantee social peace (while recognizing that in any given country the precise combination of policies, institutions, and political patterns may deviate somewhat from the ideal type). In his seminal 1990 book *Three Worlds of Welfare Capitalism*, Gøsta Esping-Andersen constructs a typology of "welfare regimes" that, despite subsequent debate that has resulted in refinements and extensions of the typology (Esping-Andersen 1990; see, e.g., Orloff 1993a; Ferrera 1996; Wood and Gough 2006; Bambra 2007), nevertheless remains the basis for much analysis of the comparative political economic of advanced industrialized democracies (Arts and Gelissen 2002). Esping-Andersen's typology is a particularly useful starting point for thinking about the politics of inequality, since the outcomes on which he sorts countries into types – stratification and decommodification – are both centrally concerned with inequality.[1]

Welfare regimes are interconnected bundles of public policies, norms, and laws governing relationships between employers and employees and producers and consumers; patterns of political mobilization and competition; and ideas about the proper organization of the economy.[2] In Esping-Andersen's scheme, each of the three welfare regime ideal-types (liberal, social democratic, and conservative-corporatist) is built on a distinctive political foundation composed of ideologies and patterns of political competition and alliance. Each of these political foundations implies a particular set of demands for stratification and decommodification, which in turn generates a distinctive set of interconnected policy features – e.g. patterns of taxation, rules governing social insurance eligibility and replacement rates, regulation of the labor market, collective bargaining arrangements – that produce these outcomes.

Historically, in the liberal world of welfare, working-class parties were unable to govern alone, and instead entered into an alliance with free-market liberals. This arrangement left room for only limited public intervention to correct inequalities generated by the market. In the ideal-typical social democratic welfare regime, on the other hand, generous and relatively uniform social transfers and near full employment were enabled by social democratic party dominance. The ideal-typical conservative-corporatist welfare regime of continental Europe aimed to avert social conflict by redistributing enough to prevent penury but at the same time to preserve church- and society-sanctioned social hierarchies. This was achieved through graduated social benefits tied to occupational status.

In each of the welfare regimes of the postwar period in western Europe, a core political task was to maintain the level of socioeconomic inequality within acceptable bounds – narrower in the social democratic regime, where regulation of internal markets for labor, goods and services, redistributive taxation,

---

[1] Stratification refers to differentiation between social groups in terms of life chances and socio-economic endowments. Decommodification is "the degree to which individual, or families, can uphold a socially acceptable standard of living independently of [labor] market participation" (Esping-Andersen 1990, 37). The extent of stratification and decommodification in society is determined by the arrangement of policies in a welfare regime, which in turn is determined in part by the underlying values about inequality held by the members of the political coalition involved in the construction of the welfare regime.

[2] Other compelling categorizations of political economies emerging from the postwar settlements are also available (e.g., Shonfield 1965; P. Hall and Soskice 2001). Esping-Andersen's (1990) typology of welfare regimes is the most useful starting point for analyzing the politics of inequality, in my view, because it is designed to account for variation in the amount and kind of permissible inequality.

and extensive state provision of social services ensured an inclusive society despite exposure to international markets; wider in the conservative-corporatist regime, where state spending provided a backstop for political economies that had the potential to create strong insider/outsider divides in the labor market; and wider still in the liberal regime, where an ideological tolerance for market-generated inequalities and minimalist social protection institutions on the part of the right required the periodic presence in office of left-labor parties to enact redistribution (Esping-Andersen 1990).

The notion of how much and what kind of inequality was acceptable varied across the different postwar welfare regimes, but so too did the policy levers that were most important for containing inequality within acceptable bounds in each of the regimes. The liberal welfare regime, which lacked corporatist institutions or social insurance systems through which to carry out redistribution, relied on having a left party that could periodically enter government and enact a redistributive tax and spending agenda in order to contain inequality. The conservative-corporatist regime used public spending to backstop social insurance systems, especially during times of economic transformation when the latter were least reliable as social shock absorbers. The social democratic welfare regime developed in small, open economies, and so the key mechanisms for containing inequality – regulation of internal markets combined with high levels of taxation to fund generous social services – were designed to buffer citizens from exposure to markets while also protecting their ability to participate in them.

These regime types were not static constructions, however, and by the late twentieth century had developed beyond the initial outlines suggested by the political coalitions in place at the time of their formation. Comparative political economy scholars in the 1990s and 2000s thoroughly evaluated how welfare regimes responded to changes brought about by the internationalization of trade and increasing competition from low-wage economies (this literature is reviewed by Pierson 2001; Swank 2005; and Levy 2010). Esping-Andersen identified the potential "Achilles heel" of each welfare regime as it confronted the shift to a post-industrial economy: the characteristic structures that pushed each regime to change in particular directions when confronted with new environment (Esping-Andersen 1990, chapter 9; 1996; Iversen and Wren 1998). But we know less about how different welfare regimes have weathered the shift to neoliberalism that took place across the rich democracies beginning in the 1980s. I argue that we can learn a great deal about the politics of inequality by locating the aspects of the underlying welfare regime likely to be most challenged by specific instantiations of neoliberalism, and tracing the political responses to inequality that follow from those challenges.

Neoliberalism

In the Keynesian paradigm on which the welfare regimes of postwar western Europe were built, expansionary fiscal policies and redistributive social spending ensured economic growth by sustaining a robust demand for goods and services on the part of working- and middle-class families. Excessive inequality was deemed dysfunctional in the Keynesian paradigm because when too-large shares of the national product are concentrated in the hands of a few, consumption by the majority, and so demand and economic growth, will necessarily be low. In the neoliberal paradigm that began its rise to dominance in the 1980s, on the other hand, inequality is regarded as functional to economic growth: only when capital accumulation is permitted can sufficient reinvestment to ensure a robust economy occur. Policies consistent with the neoliberal paradigm include reducing social transfer spending, cutting taxes on wealth and profits, and deregulating labor markets to allow for more flexibility in setting wages at both the high and low end of the market. All of these policies tend to result in increasing inequalities in income and wealth.

Like many political scientists, I understand neoliberalism not only as an economic philosophy but as an economic policy paradigm. Such paradigms consist of the overarching goals of policy, as well as the policy instruments and settings of those instruments used to achieve those goals (P. Hall 1993). The overarching economic goal that animates neoliberal policy-makers is to safeguard economic growth in an open international trade and financial order by ensuring that domestic economic policies are credible with financial markets and that national industries are internationally competitive (Ban 2016). The policies and settings associated with these economic policy goals include targeting low inflation, controlling deficits, and reducing the regulation of markets for finance, labor, goods, and services in order to make them externally open and competitive.

Neoliberalism became a widely used analytic concept in the social sciences during the late 1990s, reflecting scholarly efforts to characterize and understand the sweeping changes that had taken place in the political economies of both developing and rich, industrialized countries in the 1980s and 1990s. In the 1990s and 2000s, overuse of the concept, conceptual stretching of neoliberalism to include aspects that went far beyond the core concept (Sartori 1970), and the fact that the term often was used pejoratively, together led some scholars to characterize neoliberalism as a useless catch-all used to describe an unspecified and meaningless set of subsidiary ideas and practices (see, e.g., Boas and Gans-Morse 2009). In my own graduate training, I was urged to avoid using the term "neoliberalism" and instead to identify the causal effects of its component parts.

However, a ban on using the word "neoliberalism" is as damaging as its overuse. As it has been employed in several recent accounts, the term is able to accommodate both the insight that something important changed about the way economies were managed beginning in the 1980s and the fact that these changes occurred in different ways, producing different packages of policies and outputs, in different places (Prasad 2006; Ban 2016; Vail 2018). This book adopts a similar stance. I argue that neoliberalism has common effects, in that it led politicians in all three of the countries that I studied to impose upon themselves taboos against discussing certain policies and goals; that this in turn prompted a reframing of the problem of inequality; and that this reframing consistently makes it more difficult to reduce inequality. But the specific effects of neoliberalism on frames, policies, and outputs is different in each of the country cases, due to the way that different neoliberal ideas, practices, and power configurations interacted with preexisting institutions and orientations in each case.

I rely on Cornel Ban's definition of neoliberalism as a collection of "historically contingent and intellectually hybrid economic and policy regimes" (Ban 2016, 10) that nevertheless share a common goal: promoting economic growth in a context of open international markets for goods and finance by ensuring that domestic economic policies promote competitiveness and credibility with international financial market actors. "Intellectually hybrid" means that neoliberalism on the ground is never a pure expression of economic theory, not even of the monetarist and supply-side models that were the hallmark of global neoliberalism in the 1970s and early 1980s. Still, on-the-ground instantiations of neoliberalism share a common core: "No matter how many Keynesian, structuralist, or 'populist' impurities are absorbed into these historical hybrids, the end result can still be characterized as neoliberalism if its advocates espouse the need for institutionalized trade/financial openness, public finances benchmarked by financial market credibility, and growth strategies based on the relative competitiveness of the national economy" (Ban 2016, 10).

Neoliberalism is "historically contingent" for Ban in the sense that it takes different forms in different places. Ban describes two main variants of neoliberalism, which reflect how governments typically resolve the conflicts or trade-offs between social demand for equality or the demand of firms for protection, on the one hand, and the perceived need to pursue efficiency and market credibility, on the other. In "embedded" neoliberal regimes, these trade-offs "are generally resolved using ideas that maximize the policy space for *downward* redistribution of income and opportunities to compensate society against market dislocations" (Ban 2016, 14, emphasis in the original). Downward redistribution of income and opportunities can occur in the fields of public health, education, or income, through instruments and settings such as progressive taxation, labor laws that protect the employment rights and benefits of workers, macroeconomic policies that support employment, and social benefits. Examples of embedded neoliberal regimes include the Nordic countries, who embedded neoliberalism via "strong universal safety nets" and "democratic neocorporatist systems" (p. 15), and southern Europe before the financial crisis, where less generous but still universal social policies combined with "state-led corporatism and regulated markets that privileges insiders" (p. 15). On the other hand, in "disembedded" neoliberal regimes, policy trade-offs "are generally resolved in favor of *upward* redistribution of income and opportunities (i.e. toward high-income groups and corporations)" (p. 15, emphasis in the original). This can be carried out through policies such as tax cuts that benefit high earners, regulations that disempower labor unions, or privatization of public services.

This distinction helps us see how the three country cases in this study, which are quite different in terms of their historic and current levels of social inequality, may all nevertheless be characterized as having adopted neoliberal policy regimes by the 1990s. Finland until about 1995, and France throughout the entire period I study, are well described by Ban's notion of embedded neoliberal regimes. England under New Labour and Finland after 1995 are hybrids, in which downward and upward redistribution of income and opportunities coexist. In all three countries, though, the consensus on the core goals of neoliberalism – assuring credibility with financial markets, ensuring openness to external trade, and safeguarding international competitiveness – was shared by actors on the center-left and center-right throughout the period of study (the mid-1990s until 2008 in England, the early 1980s to 2016 in France, and the mid-1980s to 2016 in Finland).

The global turn to neoliberalism beginning in the 1980s constrained policy-makers in ways that make reducing inequality difficult. It is not inaccurate to claim broadly, as some have, that neoliberalism is responsible for the rise in income inequality in the rich democracies, or even that "neoliberalism kills" by creating health inequalities (e.g., Mooney 2012). But neoliberalism, as an umbrella concept, affects different types of political economies in different ways (Kus 2006; Prasad 2006). Rather than attributing the rise and resilience of inequality to a disembodied force that operates uniformly across national contexts, I highlight how the work that neoliberalism does in shaping inequality is carried out in the interaction between specific instantiations of neoliberalism – for example, the policy ideas carried by particular actors, or pressure for specific forms of marketization from specific sources – and particular features of domestic welfare regimes put into place in the post–World War II period.

PUBLIC HEALTH APPROACHES TO WELFARE REGIMES AND NEOLIBERALISM

Research in public health has been very attuned to the effects of both welfare regimes and neoliberalism on health inequalities. While the few cross-nationally comparative studies of health inequalities carried out prior to the 1990s had Scandinavian countries at the top of the league table for health equity, in the late 1990s new research showing larger health inequalities in the social democratic welfare states than in the less egalitarian continental and Anglophone countries captured the attention of policy-makers and researchers alike (Mackenbach and Kunst 1997; Bambra 2013). Overall health was generally found to better in the social democratic welfare states; absolute inequalities in health between social groups (e.g., the number of years' difference in life expectancy between high- and low-SES groups) were small; and relatively small numbers of people were in the lowest-SES groups compared to, for example, the share of the population living in poverty in the United Kingdom (Bambra 2013; Popham et al. 2013). But relative inequalities in health – the percentage difference in health status between the higher and lower group – tended to be larger in the social democratic welfare states than they were elsewhere in Europe (Mackenbach and Kunst 1997; Dahl et al. 2006; Huijts and Eikemo 2009; Lahelma and Lundberg 2009).

Driven at first by an implicit assumption that social outcomes ought to reflect the egalitarian underpinnings of social democratic welfare states, scholars of public health began to look more closely at the nature of the relationship between welfare regimes and health inequalities. A body of literature emerged claiming that social democratic party control of government is salutary in its own right (see, e.g., Navarro et al. 2003; 2006; Coburn 2004; Mackenbach et al. 2016), but welfare regimes are composed of multiple, sometimes contradictory elements, whose independent and joint effects need to be evaluated. Recent research has done just this (see, e.g., Hurrelmann et al. 2011; Beckfield et al. 2015; Jutz 2015; Rathmann et al. 2016). Welfare policies are also now understood to affect different groups in society (e.g., by age, gender, ethnicity) differently, resulting in aggregate health effects that are patterned in complex ways (see, e.g., Pongiglione and Sabater 2014; Niedzwiedz 2016; Kim and Kim 2017).

A core, albeit not universal, finding of the literature on welfare regimes and public health is that welfare regimes do have a significant impact on socio-economic inequalities in a number of specific health measures, and among several segments of the population. Welfare regimes frequently mediate or moderate the effects of individual-level predictors of poor health (e.g., financial distress, low education) in ways that produce distinctive forms of aggregate health inequalities in different settings. The most recent findings suggest that social democratic welfare states do not always generate the most egalitarian results in health terms, but they often do; and that liberal welfare states generally do the least to moderate the effects of social and economic inequality on health (Niedzwiedz 2016; Muntaner et al. 2017; Leão et al. 2018).

While welfare regimes remain distinctive in terms of their effects on at least some forms of health inequality, the adoption of neoliberal macroeconomic and social policy paradigms by policy-makers across different welfare regimes may dampen this distinctiveness. In the literature on public and population health, neoliberalism is usually conceptualized in one of three ways: as a body of ideas and disciplinary procedures reinforcing individual responsibility for health (e.g., Brown and Baker 2012); as a harbinger of corporate influence, especially via trade and investment policies that enhance the power of multinational corporations peddling unhealthy products (e.g., Stead et al. 2013); and as the source of policy changes that have led to a progressive diminution of social rights and increasing income and wealth inequality, leading to large inequalities in the social determinants of health (e.g., Farrants and Bambra 2018). These different aspects of neoliberalism are not "unconnected phenomena, products of happenstance," but should instead be understood as "elements of a complicated but coherent political project" that have health effects which may push in the same direction: toward greater socioeconomic inequalities in health (Schrecker 2016b, 477–78).

Some analysts in public health, just as in political science, complain that neoliberalism has often been used to explain public health outcomes in ways that are too simplistic: reducing neoliberalism to "the 'it' which does the explaining, rather than the political phenomenon that needs to be explained" (S. Phelan 2007, 328), or failing to specify "how, where and in what forms do the various processes of neoliberalism impact public health'" (K. Bell and Green 2016, 241). This critique may be somewhat overdrawn: the literature on trade policy and health, for example, is very clear about the mechanisms – the World Trade Organization agreement on Sanitary and Phytosanitary Standards, investor-state dispute resolution mechanisms embedded in trade and investment treaties – that lead or are expected to lead to adverse health outcomes (see, e.g., Koivusalo 2014). But even in the most sophisticated research connecting neoliberalism to the social determinants of health, it is not always clear what is ultimately responsible for increasing health inequalities. For example, Farrants and Bambra (2018) demonstrate clearly and carefully how specific policy changes in Sweden contribute to increasing health inequalities. However, in labeling multiple policy changes as instantiations of "neoliberalism," their analysis bypasses systematic assessment of the political processes that led Swedish policy-makers to make the changes they did.

Despite the contributions of public health analysts using welfare regime theory and neoliberalism, then, there are continuing calls to develop a more sophisticated political economy of public health that can help explain why health inequalities take the forms that they do, and why they have been so resistant to efforts to reduce them. One of my goals in writing this book was to fill that gap, drawing on my training as a political scientist who has spent much of the last twenty years studying the politics of inequality. The next section of this chapter lays out how welfare regimes and neoliberalism have shaped the politics of inequality over the last several decades, and have contributed to the persistence of both health inequalities and the broader socioeconomic inequalities that underlie them.

THE ARGUMENT OF THE BOOK

I will show that across the rich democracies, a common, three-step process links the shape of postwar welfare regimes to current regimes of inequality, via politicians' failure to enact policies that could successfully counteract the growth of inequality prompted by the rise of neoliberalism. The first step in this process is the collision between postwar welfare regimes and the rising neoliberal policy paradigm in the 1980s, which led politicians to generate taboos against advocating particular types of policy remedies for growing inequality. Second, to avoid these taboos, politicians, particularly on the center-left, reframed the problem of inequality in ways that seemed less likely to generate political opposition. Third, the reframing of inequality refocused policy attention on a set of technocratic policy solutions that proved difficult to enact and ineffective at reducing inequalities.

The Genesis of Neoliberal Policy Taboos: Welfare Regimes and Neoliberal Sticking Points

By the 1980s, the mechanisms for managing inequality that had developed in the welfare regimes of the postwar *trente glorieuses* began to operate in a new context that was increasingly dominated by neoliberal ideas and practices, and in which certain market actors (e.g., capital holders, international financial market actors, and multinational corporations) had become newly powerful. Where mechanisms for managing inequality that were central to the identity and operation of postwar welfare regimes were challenged by aspects of neo-liberalism, political "sticking points" (Locke and Thelen 1995) – sites of potential political conflict – developed.

The sticking points were different in the different welfare regimes, as summarized in Table 2.1. The center-left's convergence on neoliberal ideas in the liberal welfare states resulted in a rejection of redistribution, which denatured partisan alternation in government as a means for controlling inequality. In the conservative-corporatist welfare states on the European continent, the importance of the European project, including the construction of the Eurozone, put public spending off-limits. And as the social democratic welfare states in Scandinavia joined the European market, public provision of services, broad-based taxation, and direct controls over product markets became potential political flashpoints. What was common across regimes, however, was that in order to avoid provoking destructive political conflict around these sticking points, center-left politicians began to impose upon themselves taboos against proposing activating old mechanisms for containing inequality.

These taboos arose out of politicians' desires to avoid the potential for political conflict that surrounds such discussion, and adopting them was, in each case, a partially strategic decision. However, labeling this behavior a "taboo" also highlights that it is partially internalized. A taboo is a social custom that prohibits or restricts certain kinds of behaviors, but that requires little enforcement above and beyond social actors' own desire to avoid breaking the taboo. Taboos are thus ultimately self-imposed, and in our cases, politicians could have discussed the policy mechanisms that were most strongly challenged by the neoliberal policy paradigm openly, but choose not to. This is important because it reminds us that politicians, even when they are fearful of the electoral or reputational consequences of their actions, have agency. And this, in turn,

TABLE 2.1 *Welfare regimes, neoliberal sticking points, and taboos*

	England	France	Finland
Welfare Regime	Liberal	Conservative-Corporatist	Social Democratic
Key Attributes	High inequality, market-driven social protection, thin institutional apparatus for redistribution	Moderate inequality, robust social insurance, tendency to dualization between labor market insiders and outsiders	Low inequality, robust public provision of social services, openness to trade
Central Mechanism for Controlling Inequality	Alternation of center-right and center-left in government produces periods of high taxation and redistribution	Public spending to mitigate effects of labor market dualization	Redistribution, public service provision, and regulation of internal markets to protect citizens from effects of external trade exposure
Most Challenging Aspects of Neoliberalism	Ideological convergence of center-left and center-right; pressure from international financial markets	Pressure from international financial markets; liberal EU financial architecture	Pressure from international financial markets; liberal EU product and service markets
Taboo	Redistribution	Public spending	Market regulation

reminds us that neoliberalism is not a force of nature; it is, rather, a social and political force. Another important reason why I have chosen to use the word "taboo" to label the practice of avoiding discussion of redistributive mechanisms challenged by neoliberalism is that interviewees themselves used the word. The English term taboo and the French *tabu* are direct cognates, of course. Finnish interviewees more frequently used the term "ethos" to describe the limits on what was and was not politically feasible. This term emphasizes the beliefs themselves, rather than the fear of punishment.

Having imposed upon themselves taboos against discussing certain types of egalitarian policies, politicians who were still committed to the idea of equity and/or to serving an established electoral base that demanded it needed to find new ways to discuss inequality. Reframing the problem of inequality in a way that would invoke a different set of policy tools for solving it allowed politicians on the center-left to stake out a position in favor of social equity without running afoul of the new taboos. Social investment, activation, and flexicurity – all buzzwords of the 1990s–2000s center-left – offered new ways to think about what the problem of inequality was, and how welfare states might counteract it without engaging directly in taboo issues like redistribution, fiscal expansion, or market re-regulation (Abrahamson 2010; Jenson 2010; Smyth and Deeming 2016). In many cases, politicians expanded their vocabulary in the area of inequality to include several of these buzzwords simultaneously. Reframing inequality as a problem of socioeconomic inequalities in health linked to upstream social determinants, as politicians did in the United Kingdom, France, and Finland beginning in the 1980s, was another strategy from the same play-book.[3] As one English interviewee put it, members of the Labour Party "are keen to talk about health inequalities providing they don't have to talk about income and wealth inequalities.... They are terrified of being labeled as a tax-raising party" (interview UK5).

My aim in this book is not to demonstrate why politicians take up the issue of health inequalities in particular, nor to explain why they choose to reframe inequality in terms of health rather than, for example, education. Instead, I am keen to show that some reframing of the issue occurs, to understand why that is, and to explore what happens as a result. And in order to understand this process, we need to understand why health inequalities was even on the list of available reframings of inequality when neoliberalism hit.

The Reframing of Inequality

Health inequality was a non-issue in politics in most countries until the early 2000s. After all, for the last half-century, give or take a decade or two depending on the country, citizens of even modest means in most west European countries have been able to see a doctor, fill a prescription, or have life-saving surgery without mortgaging their homes or their futures. Beginning in the late 1970s, it became increasingly evident in many European countries that near-universal access to health *care* did not erase inequalities in *health*; but in most countries it took several more decades for health inequalities to be transformed from an academic problem into a public problem. In sociologist Joseph R. Gusfield's memorable phrase, it took time for health inequality to become "Something about which 'someone ought to do something'" (Gusfield 1984, 5).

The first sign that health inequalities had potential as a politically useful issue came with the Black Report in the United Kingdom (Townsend et al. 1992). Commissioned by a Labour government, published in 1980 and promptly buried by Margaret Thatcher's newly elected government, resurrected publicly

---

[3] In Finland, where equity is a core value for parties across the political spectrum, the center-right has also adopted the issue of health equity (see Chapter 6).

by Labour activists, and widely read by public health advocates outside the United Kingdom, politicians and policy-makers learned from the Black Report episode that health equity could be a potent political and partisan issue, especially in a neoliberal policy climate. With the development of the WHO's Health For All (HFA) strategy and its diffusion to some national governments from the mid-1980s through the 1990s, an international consensus on key elements of a health inequalities policy frame began to emerge. Intensified collaboration between the WHO's Regional Office for Europe and the European Commission beginning in the 2000s allowed the WHO's approach to health inequalities, which was by this time firmly anchored in the social determinants of health theoretical framework, to emerge as a standard for health equity policy approaches in European countries.

The policy frame that emerged at the international level defines health inequalities primarily as avoidable, unjust differences in health status across groups defined by their SES. To the extent that most lay people (including politicians who are not experts in public health policy) think about health inequalities, they generally attribute them to difficulties in accessing health care or to individuals' choices about lifestyle. As we have seen, these explanations are not wrong, but they are insufficient in the eyes of most social epidemiologists and public health specialists because they overestimate the impact of medical care on health and underestimate the extent to which individual choices about diet, exercise, or tobacco consumption, for example, are influenced by broader socioeconomic structures including class. Most specialists instead use the concept of social determinants of health to explain the sources of socioeconomic inequalities in health.

Social determinants of health encompass the material and social conditions in our communities and workplaces that affect our health, as well as more distal factors like income, wealth, education, and political power that in turn determine those conditions. The idea of social determinants as a cause of health inequalities came into widespread usage among epidemiologists in the late 1990s, and has been deployed differently by different policy actors, even within the WHO. Some usages focus on relatively proximate, "downstream" determinants of health, such as the availability in a neighborhood of spaces for recreation, or the level of particulate matter in the air. Others, like the final report of the WHO's Commission on the Social Determinants of Health (CSDH) (WHO 2008), assign primary causal power to upstream structural determinants of these material and social resources, such as income, occupation, and education. Still others, like the British Black Report (Townsend et al. 1992) or the Norwegian Plan of Action to Reduce Social Inequalities in Health (Norwegian Directorate for Health and Social Affairs 2005), assign ultimate causality to the political and power context that produces structural inequalities in socioeconomic status.

These differences are significant: where in the full SDOH chain of causation one locates the causes of health inequalities affects what precise policies would be needed to reduce them. However, these stories all share an emphasis on socioeconomic inequality, rather than faults in the health care system or individuals' lifestyle choices, as the most important vector for health inequalities. This shared vision implies at the very least that governments, as the architects of the policy systems that regulate inequality, are responsible for solving the problem of health inequalities.

As we shall see in the next chapter, a uniform set of policy recommendations followed from the SDOH causal interpretation, was promoted by international bodies, and was ultimately adopted by national governments. Chief among these recommendations was that governments should look beyond the health sector and reduce or eliminate inequalities in the underlying social (as well as medical and behavioral) determinants of health – including income inequality. As compared to older policies for dealing with social inequality directly, however, political and policy discussion about socioeconomic inequalities in health was alluringly discreet. Talk about health inequality helpfully shifted attention away from the traditional tools of economic management that had come to seem "too hot to touch" in a neoliberal environment, while still allowing politicians to be "for" greater equality. This is one important reason why some politicians chose to medicalize inequality, discussing it in terms of health rather than income and wealth. Medicalizing inequality did not, however, make it any easier to solve. On the contrary, framing inequality as a problem of health, rather than income and wealth, has actually made it more resilient.

Shifting the Overton Window: Why Reframing Inequality Makes It More Resilient

To understand why reframing the issue of inequality around health did not result in policies that could help reduce both health inequalities and the underlying socioeconomic inequalities that produce them, it is helpful to imagine a spectrum on which policy ideas might range, from completely unthinkable to popular, to actual policy. This analogy is the basis of the Overton window, named for Joseph Overton, founder of the Mackinac Center for Public Policy (Lehman n.d.). Overton's key insight was that policy advocates can shift the window to include or exclude particular policy solutions to public problems by changing the way they talk about both the problems and the solutions. One way policy advocates can do this is by initially proposing policy ideas that are completely unthinkable (e.g., ending public funding of primary and secondary education altogether) in order to make a preferred policy that is currently outside the window of acceptability (such as public financing of for-profit private educational providers) appear more acceptable by comparison.[4]

---

[4] See, e.g., "Morning Feature: Crazy like a Fox?," *Daily Kos*, 2009. www.dailykos.com/stories/2009/11/5/800804/-Morning-Feature:-Crazy-Like-a-Fox%202009.

Another way policy advocates can shift the window in their favor is by redefining the problem such that a particular policy solution that they would rather not use lies outside the Overton window, and more politically appealing tools lie within it. This is what happened with health inequality.

Under the neoliberal policy paradigm, the most effective tools for reducing economic inequality – redistributive tax and transfer policies, expansionary fiscal policy, and public provision of a wide range of social services at low or no cost – were outside the window of acceptability. As one interviewee remarked, the British Labour Party of the 1990s "would *never* have framed what they were doing in terms of reducing the gap between the rich and the poor. That would be political suicide" (interview UK3). Reframing inequality from mainly a problem of the unequal distribution of financial resources in society to a problem of unequal health did not bring these old tools back within the window of acceptability, but it did bring a new set of tools into the range of "reasonable" responses to inequality: To reduce inequalities in health, policy advocates recommended taking coordinated action across a range of sectors including health care, housing, social services, poverty alleviation, transport, environment, agriculture, and urban policy. Since community empowerment was seen by many advocates as an essential mechanism for producing better health, and since many of the appropriate policies were in the hands of local or regional, rather than national, governments, national-level leadership would be required to stimulate and coordinate subnational efforts without stepping on the toes of local actors.

Taken as a group, the policies that fell within the Overton window around the problem of health inequalities tended to be more complex, to demand more multilevel and multiagency coordination, and to take longer to produce effects on inequality than the old tools of economic management that had come to seem unthinkable under neoliberalism. In practice, these new policies were extremely difficult to implement, and ultimately did little to reduce health inequalities even where there were good-faith efforts over an extended period of time, as in England under the Labour governments of 1997–2010. While there were small improvements in some measures among the population groups most intensely targeted by policy innovations designed to reduce health inequalities (e.g., infant mortality among lone mothers), the overall results were disappointing (Bauld et al. 2005; Mackenbach 2011; Bambra 2012).

But the unexpected complexity of cross-sectoral "Health in All Policies" work was not the only way in which the health inequalities frame, which was appealing in theory, turned out in practice to be disappointing. Health inequality appeared to be a way to talk about inequality without discussing sticky issues of taxation and redistribution. The latter implied a zero-sum relationship between capital and labor, or between haves and have-nots, while reducing health inequalities appeared to be an issue where everyone would win, and nobody would lose. In the words of an influential WHO publication, health inequalities were to be reduced by "levelling up," bringing the health of lower-status groups up to the level enjoyed by those at the top – and certainly not by taking away the health of the wealthy (WHO Regional Office for Europe 1991, 16).

The health framing of inequality was also appealing because it fit well with the new, neoliberally inflected social investment paradigm developing in Europe during this period. Unlike Keynesian demand-management policies, spending on health (like spending on job training or education) could be cast as a form of investment, a way to prepare citizens to be more active participants in the labor market. The health inequalities frame, which emphasized the importance of prevention and reducing the overall burden of disease, also allowed policymakers to talk about improving the performance of health care systems without promising to increase spending. As one French analyst put it, "The politicians needed to affirm that they have some big plan for reforming health without spending any money. The social inequalities in health framing allows them to show political will without actually spending any money" (interview FR34). The health framing of inequality unexpectedly led politicians back to policy levers rendered taboo under neoliberalism, however. While health status tends to improve among the better-off without much effort, it requires much greater investments in improving the conditions of the worse-off in order to narrow the gap. This means that while "levelling up" might be non-zero-sum in health terms, in economic terms it could well require significant redistribution. Social investment, just like any other kind of investment, requires money, which in turn often requires redistribution of the benefits from growth and/or the burdens of taxation. But if these facts about what would be needed to really reduce health inequality were foreseeable by experts, the politicians who "discovered" the health inequalities frame and put it to use were for the most part not experts. A Finnish expert explained that health inequalities seems like an "easy issue" for politicians, because everyone agrees about the importance of health equity. But once politicians come to understand that "this may require redistribution of resources, then we are in a hot political area. And this link remains somehow untouched if possible because it is too difficult" (interview FI5).

A lack of clarity about the nature of the causal links between health inequalities and socioeconomic inequalities also made it easier for politicians to elide the two issues in ways that were politically convenient, but that ultimately meant that neither would be solved. By the late 1990s, experts were advising that it would be necessary to tackle social inequality, and not only poverty, in order to reduce health inequalities. Many policy advocates who embraced the new public problem of health inequalities recognized that economic inequalities were the fundamental cause of inequalities in health. As the CSDH report baldly asserted, if "social inequality is killing people on a grand scale," the appropriate response was for governments to "tackle the inequitable distribution of power, money, and resources" (WHO 2008). But while some advocates proposed redistribution as a solution to health inequalities, they remained largely "silent on the topic of whose resources, and how and through what instruments" they ought to be redistributed (Navarro 2009). Politicians were for the most part eager to follow suit. European governments have undertaken poverty reduction, but not income redistribution, as a way to reduce health inequalities.[5] Reframing inequality as a problem of health left redistribution on the table in principle, but in practice, as I show in the case studies of England, France, and Finland, the Overton window around health inequality did not include tools that would reduce the underlying inequality. The net result of reframing the problem of inequality was not to reduce inequality using new tools, but rather a retreat into a technocratic politics of inequality that sought to avoid the central moral conflict surrounding equity in contemporary society.

EMPIRICAL AND THEORETICAL CONTRIBUTIONS OF THE ARGUMENT

Some might argue that politicians who engineered this frame shift did so in order to avoid confronting inequality, not in order to confront it more effectively. I admit that when I began this project, this was my suspicion. After interviewing scores of politicians and policy-makers and reading reams of policy documents and parliamentary proceedings in multiple countries, however, I came away convinced that this was not the case. Most politicians who engaged with the problem of health inequalities truly did want to improve the lives of the worse-off in order to make society more equal, and hoped that reframing inequality as a problem of health would help them do that. Why, then, did reframing the issue of inequality not produce the desired results?

The case studies of English, French, and Finnish policy-making in Chapters 3–6 show that reframing inequality shifted the Overton window around inequality in a way that was compatible with neoliberal ideas and policy pressures in each country, but that hampered efforts to reduce inequality. The policy tools that the new approach to inequality implied were complex, unfamiliar, and ultimately ineffective. This is the proximate cause of the failure of the frame shift to reduce inequality.

Behind that proximate cause, though, lies what I argue is a fundamental interpretive error on the part of center-left politicians about their room for maneuver in confronting inequality. Guided by their own presumptions about what changes in their electorate might mean for public opinion, by fear of

---

[5] Only in Norway did the national government pass a health inequalities plan that was centered on reducing income inequality overall as the most efficient way to reduce inequality (Norwegian Directorate of Health and Care Services 2007). Even in Norway, however, devolution of responsibility for reducing health inequalities to underfunded subnational governments and difficulties in cross-sectoral coordination have stymied efforts to reduce health inequalities (Strand and Fosse 2011; Wel et al. 2016; Synnevåg et al. 2018).

exclusion from the developing European markets for capital and goods, and by their belief in the technocratic promise of neoliberalism, center-left politicians imposed upon themselves taboos against the very policy solutions that could have helped them contain the growth of inequality. That these taboos were a response to fears that had some basis in truth does not change the fact that adopting them was an act of interpretation that constrained future policy responses to the problem of inequality. In other words, center-left politicians chose a destiny in which they could not credibly claim to be acting to protect society from inequality.

Their failed efforts to create more equitable societies in a neoliberal era are also related to deeper, structural constraints, and help to demonstrate how tightly connected current inequality is to the postwar welfare regimes that were constructed to contain inequality. The central tools for containing inequality in the welfare regimes of the *trente glorieuses* shaped, beginning in the 1980s, a politics of inequality that turned out to be counterproductive. The political practices and policy institutions that gave form to the old welfare regimes shaped the reframing of inequality that occurred once political taboos had developed against discussing the sticking points between old welfare regimes and neoliberalism. In their quest to avoid political conflict around the core tools of income redistribution and social solidarity that neoliberalism called into question, politicians blocked themselves from addressing the underlying causes of inequality. In aiming to keep inequality within manageable bounds, the institutions of postwar welfare regimes also, paradoxically, established a perimeter around the possibilities for reducing inequality in a neoliberal era.

The literature on framing in public policy tends to assume as a starting point that successfully reframing an issue – defining a problem in a new way that gains widespread, even if not unanimous, political agreement – will result in a reorientation of policy outputs to match that frame (see Bergeron et al. 2014). But deeper institutional analysis allows us to understand why, in some instances, reframing a policy problem does not make it easier to solve. The political taboos arising from the clash between postwar welfare regimes and neoliberalism are our guideposts to the institutionally rooted "logic of appropriateness" (March and Olsen 1998, chapter 3) that structures policy-making in the arena of inequality. This logic constrains policy efforts to reduce health inequalities, just as it constrains efforts to reduce the underlying social inequalities that cause them – and shifting the frame from income and wealth to health inequalities is not sufficient to subvert that logic.

This implies that if we want to understand why inequality is so resilient, we need to consider *regimes* of inequality, and not only income inequality or health inequality in isolation. "Regimeness" has two attributes: interdependence and institutionalization. Interdependence refers to the tight coupling between multiple instantiations of inequality and between those instantiations and the underlying drivers of various forms of inequality. Institutionalization refers to the constraints on policy innovation and regime change that arise from the tendency of new forms of social organization to replicate key aspects of the older forms that they are intended to replace.

Both interdependence and institutionalization imply that even when political or policy actors want to reduce a specific instantiation of inequality, their efforts are likely to reinforce the basic underlying logic of inequality in the system as a whole. The interaction of old welfare regimes with the new market orthodoxy of neoliberalism generated points of tension that shape the new regimes of inequality. Addressing the problem of inequality in the current, neoliberal era is thus constrained and shaped by the tight coupling of health and income inequalities with each other and with the political and policy institutions built up during the postwar period.

CONCLUSION

My focus on the structural forces shaping regimes of inequality may give the impression that there is little room for agency or judgment in pursuit of great equality. But politicians and policy-makers make choices about how to inter-pret the will of the electorate or whether to attribute veto power to other actors, whether and how to reframe the problem of inequality, and ultimately what policies to pursue, with what degree of alacrity. The fact that they make analogous choices in different settings merely signals that both welfare regimes and neoliberal pressures exert a strong influence over those choices.

Chapters 4–6 examine the choices made by politicians in England, France, and Finland that led to the ultimately unsuccessful approaches to containing inequality in the 1990s–2010s. However, there is an additional factor, beyond welfare regimes and neoliberalism, that shapes politicians' choices about reframing inequality as a matter of health: the development, since 1980, of a consensus among internationally active researchers and policy activists and at the level of the WHO and the EU about the nature of health inequalities as a policy problem. Chapter 3 explores the content and development of the inter-national health inequalities consensus, which was itself strongly influenced by earlier policy approaches in the United Kingdom and, to a lesser extent, Finland.

3

Health Inequalities

The Emergence of an International
Consensus Policy Frame

INTRODUCTION

Intellectual histories of health inequalities and of social epidemiology generally trace the modern "discovery" of health inequalities to the middle of the nineteenth century, when states began collecting sufficiently detailed data on mortality to allow for comparisons of death rates across small geographic areas or groups of individuals with particular occupations (see, e.g., Berkman and Kawachi 2000; Adler and Stewart 2010). In the 1820s and 1830s, Louis-René Villermé studied the link between poverty and mortality at various geographic scales from the street to the *département*[1] in France, and in the 1840s he documented differences in life expectancy among workers in different industries, linking them to differences in lifestyles and working conditions (Julia and Valleron 2011). Rudolph Virchow, a pathologist and representative of the German Progress Party (*Deutche Fortschrittspartei*) in the Prussian parliament, was working around the same time on the spread of typhus; his 1848 research convinced him that "medicine is a social science and politics is nothing more than medicine on a large scale" (Mackenbach 2009). In 1845, Friedrich Engels, comparing working-class residents of Manchester, England, to their better-off neighbors, identified mechanisms linking socioeconomic status (SES) and health (Engels 1987). These authors and others laid the groundwork for the disciplines of social medicine and social epidemiology, whose central task is understanding how social conditions affect health in the population at large.

Advances in medical science meant that biomedical, rather than social, approaches dominated the study of population health for much of the twentieth

---

[1] The French *départements* constitute the level of government immediately below the regional level and above the municipal level in France. As of 2018, there are 101 *départements*; 96 are part of mainland France, and the other five are overseas.

century; but by the turn of the twenty-first century, a near-consensus about the social and economic nature of health inequalities had reemerged among researchers, policy advocates, and policy-makers active at the international level in Europe. High-level reports geared toward a global audience, such as the final report of the World Health Organization (WHO) Commission on the Social Determinants of Health (CSDH) (2008) and the report of the Lancet-University of Oslo Commission on Global Governance for Health (Ottersen et al. 2014), presented a coherent framing of the problem of health inequality that I refer to in this chapter as the "international health inequalities consensus." This frame offers a definition of the nature of the policy problem that the term "health inequalities" invokes, which in turn entails a series of other claims about who and what is to blame for causing health inequalities, who is responsible for fixing them, and how best to do that.

This chapter is divided into three parts, which trace the historic emergence of an international consensus on health inequality that, once it was available, facilitated domestic redefinitions of the problem of social inequality more broadly. In the first section, I lay out some key stylized facts about health inequalities that most specialists in the field accept as conventional wisdom, but that are non-intuitive to many in the lay public, including most social scientists and non-specialist policy-makers. These stylized facts are important because they are the premises on which both the international consensus and subsequent domestic policy responses rest. The second part of the chapter presents a selective history of the institutional and intellectual developments that laid the groundwork for the international health inequalities consensus as it exists today, focusing on the period following the release of the Black Report in Britain in 1980. This part of the chapter draws on existing secondary literature on public health policy in Europe, and on my own archival research. In the final section of the chapter, I present results of qualitative and quantitative analysis of documents produced by or for WHO Europe and the European Union since the 1990s, details of which are available in the Appendix. This analysis establishes that by the early 2000s, a consensus health inequalities problem frame had in fact emerged at the international level. While not every document agrees with or even addresses every idea in the frame, taken together, they offer evidence for a shared view on what the problem of health inequality is and what governments ought to do about it, from which domestic health policy-makers in Europe could draw in the course of their own efforts to frame and address the problem of inequality.

A HEALTH INEQUALITIES PRIMER

Before embarking on a history of the international consensus problem frame, it will be helpful to lay out the key components of the frame, as well as the premises that policy "elites" – the researchers, academic experts, policy advocates, and elected officials and civil servants who make policy – working in this area would likely take for granted when thinking about health inequalities.

The five components of the international health inequality consensus frame define health inequalities as differences in health status between socioeconomic groups in society that are avoidable, rest on a causal interpretation that prioritizes social inequality as the key driver of health inequalities, place the blame for social inequality on economic and societal forces as well as government (in)action to mitigate inequality, hold governments at least partially responsible for solving the problem of health inequality, and offer a policy solution to health inequality.

The international consensus health inequality frame defines health inequalities as differences in health status between socioeconomic groups in society that are avoidable, because they can be affected by human agency, and that are unfair, because they arise from inequalities in society (Whitehead 1991). This means that the focus is on health, rather than health care; and on groups defined by socioeconomic status, since distinctions of class, education, occupation, or income result from political choices about how to organize the economy. Unlike in the United States, where the problem of "health disparities" has been defined primarily in terms of access to medical care and groups defined by race or ethnicity, other group differences (e.g., by race, ethnicity, gender, or geography) are of secondary importance (Docteur and Berenson 2014; Julia Lynch and Perera 2017).

Second, in contrast to earlier problem definitions prevalent in the health policy field, the frame rests on a causal interpretation that prioritizes social inequality, rather than access to health care or individual behaviors like smoking or diet, as the key driver of health inequalities. In the international consensus frame, health inequalities are caused by inequalities in the "social determinants of health" (SDOH) (Raphael 2011a, 223).[2] SDOH are "social," as distinct from biological, causes of health or illness, because they have their origins in human agency, and in particular in the social, political, and economic organization of society. They are "determinants" of health in the sense that they are known (or at least believed) to have a causal relationship with the health status of individuals and populations. Social determinants of health include both proximate or "downstream" determinants – for example, access to health care, nutritious foods, safe housing, or clean air and water – and more distal, or "upstream" determinants including social status, wealth, income, and education (Braveman et al. 2011). I use the upstream/midstream/downstream metaphor throughout this book to distinguish between proximate and distal social determinants of health.[3]

[2] Raphael credits Tarlov (1996) with "the modern introduction of the term" (Raphael 2011a, 223).
[3] Braveman et al. (2011) illustrate the upstream/downstream metaphor in the following way: "[C]onsider people living near a river who become ill from drinking water contaminated by toxic chemicals originating from a factory located upstream. Although drinking the contaminated

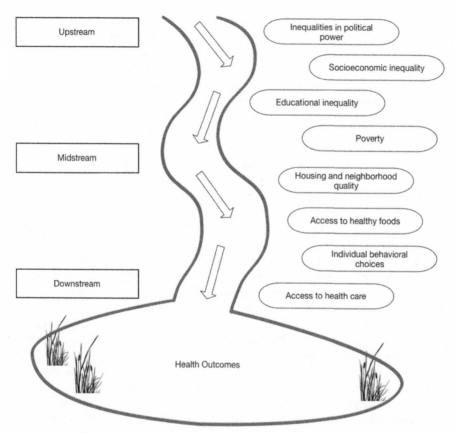

FIGURE 3.1 Upstream and downstream social determinants of health

Figure 3.1 shows the relationship between upstream and downstream determinants and health outcomes. Upstream social determinants of health can also be considered "causes of the causes" of health (see, e.g., WHO 2008), because they act on health in part by affecting downstream determinants. For example,

water is the most proximate or downstream cause of illness, the more fundamental (yet potentially less evident, given its temporal and physical distance from those affected) cause is the upstream dumping of chemicals. A downstream remedy might recommend that individuals buy filters to treat the contaminated water before drinking; because more affluent individuals could better afford the filters or bottled water, socioeconomic disparities in illness would be expected. The upstream solution, focused on the source of contamination, would end the factory's dumping. Although these concepts may make intuitive sense, the causal pathways linking upstream determinants with downstream determinants, and ultimately with health, are typically long and complex, often involving multiple intervening and potentially interacting factors along the way. This complexity generally makes it easier to study – and address – downstream determinants, at the risk of failing to address fundamental causes" (p. 383).

a lack of income (upstream) may be causally related to inability to purchase nutritious foods (downstream). Inequalities in upstream determinants of health often have a larger impact on health inequalities than inequalities in downstream determinants do, because upstream inequalities affect multiple downstream determinants (e.g., not only nutrition but also housing quality, occupational and environmental safety, access to health care) and may act through multiple pathways (e.g., not only through individuals' ability to purchase health-promoting goods but also through the exercise of political power to regulate markets or provide social benefits.)

Third, the combination of the definition of health inequalities as avoidable and unfair and the social determinants of health causal interpretation leads to a moral evaluation that places the blame for health inequalities on the economic and societal forces – including less-regulated capitalism – that generate social inequality, and on government action (or inaction) to mitigate this inequality. This element of the frame implies that many things, such as individual choices about lifestyle and consumption, the behavior of medical professionals, or the actions of community organizations, may contribute to widening or narrowing differences in health, but that health inequalities are nevertheless a moral wrong that cannot be righted solely through action by individuals or civil society. For this reason, the fourth key element of the frame is that it makes government – and particularly national governments – at least partially responsible for solving the problem of health inequalities.

Finally, the international consensus frame offers a policy solution that is in line with the previous four elements. National governments must commit to coordinated actions across "the whole of government" to reduce inequalities in the major social determinants of health. This means multisectoral action that reaches beyond the health sector to reduce or eliminate the inequalities in downstream determinants like health care, nutrition, and occupational safety, as well as tackling "the inequitable distribution of power, money, and resources" that are the "causes of the causes" of health inequalities (WHO 2008). This approach is often referred to as the "Health in All Policies" (HiAP) approach.

The international consensus frame that I have just outlined rests in turn on five basic premises about the nature and causes of health inequalities. Most social epidemiologists would accept these premises as given, but they are unfamiliar to most political scientists and even most health policy-makers. We can think of these five premises as stylized facts about health inequalities: First, health inequalities refer to differences in health status between population groups, and not only to differences in individual access to or use of health care. Second, this is because health care accounts for only a relatively small share of inequalities in health status. Third, some of the remaining share is due to individual lifestyles and behaviors, but larger social structures condition individuals' choices so powerfully that it does not make sense to think of lifestyles as freely chosen. Fourth, some of the remaining gaps in health between social groups can be explained by resource deprivation and absolute poverty, which make it particularly difficult to maintain healthy lifestyles. Fifth, health inequalities are not simply a result of absolute deprivation, but are caused as well by relative inequality. By examining each of these premises in a bit more detail, we will be in a better position to explore where they came from and how they are used in politics.

Defining and Measuring Health Inequalities: A Priority on Outcomes

The international consensus frame defines health inequalities as preventable, unfair differences in health or in the distribution of SDOH between different population groups. This apparently straightforward definition hides a great deal of complexity, even if we leave aside for a moment the obviously thorny questions of what makes an inequality "preventable" or "unjust," and what is or is not a "determinant" of health. Part of this complexity comes from the many different ways that both health and inequality can be measured.

When epidemiologists speak of health inequalities, they normally refer to differences in the average health status of a population group, which can be measured using a wide variety of indicators, and aggregated to the group level in a number of different ways. Indicators of health can include a general feeling of well-being, the absence of long-standing limitations on the activities of daily living or chronic disease, or simply being alive. Indicators of poor health, or the absence of health, can include self-reported illness, evidence of morbidity gleaned from medical and insurance records or from disease registries, and deaths.

While health varies in practically infinite ways across members of the human species, the term "health inequality" is reserved for variations in health across groups that are defined by social categories that are arranged hierarchically, and over which the discovery of health inequalities might constitute a problem of injustice. In northwestern Europe, much research and policy discussion follows the international frame's convention of focusing on comparisons across groups defined by SES (measured as income, wealth, employment status or occupation, and/or educational attainment) or class.[4] However, the social groups most frequently used to discuss health inequalities vary from country to country. They may include (in addition to or instead of SES) race, ethnicity,

---

[4] Each of these SES indicators can in turn be measured in a wide variety of ways – for example, occupation can be measured as one's own current occupation (which might be retired or unemployed), one's former occupation, the occupation of one's parent or spouse – and grouped according to the International Standard Classification of Occupations (ISCO), a national classification scheme, or a rubric specific to a particular survey or researcher. These different groupings might be designed to capture different attributes of occupation – the degree of prestige of an occupation, its average earnings, the level of control a worker has over her actions, the extent of physical exertion required for the job, the likely degree of exposure to harm – each of which could have a slightly different effect on health.

or national origin; sex; age; sexual orientation; or geographic designations representing differences in health within or between countries (Julia Lynch 2016; Julia Lynch and Perera 2017).

Health is measured at the individual level, but to make meaningful statements about health inequalities, health status must be aggregated to the group. Aggregating from the health of individuals to the health of groups could involve, for example, estimating the average self-reported health status in a group from a survey sample, estimating the rate of morbidity in a population from administrative records, or constructing standardized mortality rates or life expectancy at different ages as compared to a reference population. Alternatively, the effect of being in a particular social group (e.g., of having a household income below 50 percent of the median, of living in a rural area, or of belonging to a minority ethnic group) on some indicator of health may be estimated using a variety of forms of statistical regression analysis. The proliferation of indicators of health status and group and the multiple sources of data and methods for aggregating those data complicate efforts to compare the size of health inequalities over time, across countries, or among different groups, let alone to determine with certainty what causes health inequalities to grow or shrink.

Another set of methodological choices that can affect how researchers and policy-makers understand the problem of health inequalities is the choice of absolute versus relative measures. Absolute measures take the form of difference in the mean health or rate of morbidity or mortality of population groups. For example, in 2017 the life expectancy at birth for French men in the top 5 percent of the earnings distribution was 84.4 years, while for those in the bottom 5 percent it was 71.7 years (Blanpain 2018). The absolute rich/poor inequality in life expectancy for men in France is thus 12.7 years (84.4 − 71.7). Relative measures express the difference between groups as a ratio (in this example, 84.4–71.7, or 1.18). This ratio tells us that French men in the highest income group can expect to live on average 18 percent longer than their poor compatriots.

Absolute and relative measures capture the same underlying relationship, but on different scales. Whether absolute or relative inequalities appear large or small also depends on whether the health outcome is rare or frequent in the population as a whole. Generally speaking, the lower the incidence of a particular health outcome, the smaller the size of absolute differences, since there is a lower bound of zero. This implies that countries with population that are generally in very good health will tend to report smaller absolute inequalities than those where mortality or morbidity is higher, but relative inequalities may still be large. This can help explain, for example, why (relative) health inequalities appear to be quite stark in the Nordic countries, despite high levels of social protection and good health for most. Despite competing recommendations on best practices, most contributors to this debate agree that both absolute and relative measures capture distinct aspects of the relationship between groups that are advantaged and disadvantaged in terms of health, but should be interpreted in light of the overall prevalence of a health outcome in the population.

Let us put measurement complexity aside for a moment, though. The most important part of the WHO's definition of health inequalities is that it refers above all to inequalities in health, and only secondarily to inequalities in health *care*. Indicators of health determinants, including health care utilization or accessibility, are sometimes reported as measure of health inequality. This feeds the impression among many policy-makers and members of the public that health inequality is mainly a problem related to health care. This brings us to our second key stylized fact about health inequalities.

Distinguishing between Health Inequalities and Health Care Inequalities

Within both public policy and political science, it is commonplace to elide health inequalities and health *care* inequalities. This is natural: most of us think of our health mainly when we lose it, which is when we come into contact with the medical care system. Furthermore, curative medical care consumes the vast majority of resources within the health policy sector, with public health and primary prevention like cancer screenings, immunizations, and well visits making up only a small slice of health budgets. However, medical care is not the most important determinant of health in most rich, industrialized countries, and as a result, inequalities in health care access or utilization are not the most important determinants of inequalities in health. Estimating the precise size of the share of health inequalities due to health care is difficult. However, researchers have found only limited associations between measures of health care supply and avoidable mortality (Mackenbach et al. 1988; Kunst et al. 1998), and recent estimates suggest that no more than one-fifth of the variation in population health is due to medical prevention and treatment (McGinnis et al. 2002, 83; House 2016, 607).

The limited impact of health care on health inequalities is so counterintuitive to most non-specialists that it is worth exploring the logic behind this stylized fact in some detail. The presence of illness is a result of a combination of exposure to risks, vulnerability to those risks, and treatment. For example, whether a child contracts chicken pox will depend on whether others in her environment have the disease (exposure) and whether she has been vaccinated (vulnerability). Or, to take another example, workplace harassment (exposure) may lead to depression in one who has few other social supports (vulnerability), but the depression could be alleviated with appropriate health care (treatment). Some causes of ill health are more amenable to medical treatment than others, which is why epidemiologists who study the effects of health care on health and mortality are particularly interested in "amenable causes" of morbidity and mortality – that is, those causes of illness and death that can actually be prevented or ameliorated by timely and appropriate medical care. Medical care such as vaccination can affect whether an illness is contracted after exposure to a risk. Medical care can also determine whether and when an illness is detected, how it is treated (if it is treatable), and, within limits, a patient's prognosis. However, medical care does not often determine whether a person is exposed to a particular risk factor to begin with, nor (with the exception of vaccination) does it affect their vulnerability or resilience in the face of that risk.

Health inequalities are determined by a combination of differences in the exposure and vulnerability to health risks across population groups, and the extent to which the conditions caused by these risks are amenable to medical intervention. As an example, consider mortality from traffic accidents. Anyone might die from a car accident if he or she does not have access to good treatment (trauma care), but some people are far more likely than others to be exposed to the risk of a car accident to begin with. The rate of automobile accidents has many non-medical determinants, such as the quality of roads, access to public transport, isolation of pedestrians from automobile traffic, safety features in automobiles, alcohol consumption, and driving while tired or distracted. Access to trauma care may vary by geographic region – for example, the average distance to the nearest trauma center is generally greater in rural than in urban areas – but is unlikely to be as strongly correlated with factors such as SES, ethnicity, age, or gender, since car accident victims are generally routed to the nearest available trauma center for treatment.[5] However, the other, non-medical determinants of traffic accident fatalities may vary considerably not only geographically, but also across other social groups. Hence, we observe not only geographic inequalities in traffic-related mortality in many European countries, but also socioeconomic inequalities that are not fully accounted for by the correlation between SES and geography.

Most health problems in the rich, industrialized world today are in fact more similar to car crashes than to chicken pox. The major killers of people living in western Europe and North America are accidents and non-communicable illnesses like cardiovascular disease and cancers. While timely medical treatment can help slow the progression of some of these conditions, their onset is strongly linked to the environments in which we live and work, and to health behaviors that are in part structured by those environments. These environments and behaviors, in turn, are strongly associated with socioeconomic factors. This brings us to our third stylized fact.

Health Behaviors Are Socially Structured

In most of the rich democracies today (except the United States, of course), a person of even limited means can go to see a medical provider and receive

---

[5] An important caveat to this generalization is that even within areas characterized by a given level of rurality or urbanness, socioeconomically or ethnically marginalized populations may reside further from trauma care facilities (see, e.g., Hsia and Shen 2011).

antibiotics that will prevent serious health consequences from a bacterial infection. However, people with lower incomes are more likely to work with hazardous chemicals or dangerous machines, more likely to live near major pollution sources like highways or smokestacks, less likely to be able to afford to eat fresh fruits and vegetables daily, and more likely to begin smoking and less likely to quit once they begin. Exposure to health risks that are related to the major causes of illness and death in the rich democracies are socially patterned well before medical treatment even enters the picture. This is one reason why access to health care does not account for all, or even most, of health inequalities in rich, industrialized societies.

While McGinnis et al. (2002) estimate the contribution of medical care to early deaths in the United States to be less than 10 percent, they attribute a much larger share – 40 percent – to behavioral patterns: "the daily choices we make with respect to diet, physical activity, and sex; the substance abuse and addictions to which we fall prey; our approach to safety; and our coping strategies in confronting stress" (McGinnis et al. 2002, 82–83). Interventions to induce behavioral change have been a major component of public health policy in many countries for decades. However, many social epidemiologists and public health advocates argue that health behaviors are structured by social and economic determinants over which individuals may have little conscious choice. Inadequate resources to consume more healthful products, targeting of advertising to disadvantaged groups, class-specific social norms that encourage risky behaviors, and prolonged exposure to psychosocial stressors from which risky health behaviors offer some relief all help to explain why poor health behaviors tend to concentrate in disadvantaged groups, even when people are aware of the health risks posed by these behaviors (see, e.g., John Lynch et al. 1997; Gatrell et al. 2004; T. Smith et al. 2004; Krueger and Chang 2008).

This means that even health-promotion strategies that are successful at the level of an entire population often fail to generate improvements among the most disadvantaged groups, leading to increases in health inequalities (F. Baum and Fisher 2014, 215). This phenomenon occurs because "peoples' abilities both to respond to health promotion messages and improve their health and risk factor status as a result of the messages vary significantly, and the overall impact is likely to be greater in economically advantaged groups" (F. Baum and Fisher 2014, 216). By the time anti-smoking, pro-exercise, or pro–safe sex messages reach us, each of us has already accumulated a set of experiences and resources that condition how we are likely to respond to these messages. For example, John Lynch et al. (1997) found striking associations between obesity, smoking, and alcohol consumption among adults and markers of their family's socioeconomic status when those adults were infants. Inequalities in health behaviors are, thus, at least partly due to structural causes, and not only to freely made individual choices about lifestyle.

Social Hierarchy and the Social Gradient

So far, we have been speaking of health inequality as a societal phenomenon that exists because of the worse health of low-income, disadvantaged, or excluded groups. This is not a full description of the problem, however. At every step up on the ladder of income, education, or occupational status – not only on the first step above the bottom – health tends to improve. This is what epidemiologists mean by the *social gradient*.

The existence of a relatively smooth social gradient in health, and not only a gap between the best- and worst-off, was demonstrated forcefully by the Whitehall studies of civil servants in the United Kingdom, carried out in the late 1960s to early 1970s and the mid-1980s by Marmot and his collaborators (Marmot et al. 1984; 1991). These studies showed that among British civil servants, none of whom was poor (and all of whom had access to health care free at the point of service from the British National Health Service), age-adjusted morbidity and mortality from a wide range of diseases decreased with every increment in status and salary across six job categories ranging from clerical assistant to senior executive officer. "It is not simply that those in the lowest status jobs had the worst health and the greatest clustering of potential risk factors," they concluded (Marmot et al. 1991, 1392). Rather, "It should be emphasized that the usual pattern of association between job status and health measures is a gradient" (p. 1392). Similar findings have since been reported in scores of studies.

Why does this gradient exist? It is easy to understand how severe material deprivation could lead to illness and even early death. Being able to afford decent food, shelter, and clothing would seem to be a prerequisite for decent health, even if medical care is available free or at low cost, as it is in much of western Europe. And if the lowest items on Maslow's hierarchy of needs (Maslow 1943) are secure, we might nevertheless intuit that the daily slings and arrows of living in a low-income neighborhood deprived of amenities, or working in a dull or dangerous job with little autonomy, might do damage to one's health. How are we to make sense, though, of the fact that the top executives in the British civil service had less cardiovascular disease than their immediate subordinates (Marmot et al. 1991), or that Academy Award and Nobel Prize winners on average live several years longer than nominees who do not take home an Oscar or receive the call from Stockholm (Redelmeier and Singh 2001; Rablen and Oswald 2008)?

Chronic stress is one mechanism that could account for inequalities in health not only between the rich and the poor, but also between the rich and the slightly less-rich. For primates, including humans, being in a subordinate position in a social hierarchy causes ongoing stress (Sapolsky 2005). This provokes cellular-level changes that can result in illness and premature aging (Juster et al. 2010). Chronic stress associated with poverty, but also with a lack of autonomy at work and with experiencing discrimination, has been linked to poor health outcomes at the population level in scores of studies (useful reviews are offered by A. Baum et al. 1999; Brunner and Marmot 2005; and Thoits 2010). The systematic association between one's social status and the level of chronic stress helps explain the social gradient in health. Explanations that focus on status and control as the key mechanisms producing health inequalities that follow a social gradient are known as psychosocial explanations.

Psychosocial explanations for the social gradient need not substitute for, but may complement, materialist explanations that attribute the relative health of social groups to graduated access to resources that promote health. Psychosocial explanations focus on the effects of social domination and subordination on health via chronic stress, and lead to the conclusion that where hierarchies in social status are steeper and more strongly associated with levels of autonomy and control in one's life, health inequalities will also be larger. Materialist explanations make a similar case for the distribution of resources: greater inequality in resources, particularly in the flexible resources of money and education, will lead to greater differences across the gradient in access to health-promoting environments and goods, and ultimately to greater differences in health. Even above a threshold of absolute deprivation characterized by insufficient food, shelter, or clothing, people occupying different positions in the social hierarchy are unlikely to have equal access to all the things that we know contribute to health. With social status comes not only relief from the chronic stress of subordination, but also a wide variety of financial, educational, and social resources. These resources permit the individuals who possess them, if they choose, to access the things that tend to improve health (e.g., water filters, fresh foods, passenger side airbags, fitness club memberships, the most up-to-date medical technologies), and to avoid the things that harm health (e.g., living in an apartment with lead paint, working night shifts, consuming mainly processed foods). Greater social status also tends to change the environment and the community around an individual in ways that indirectly support her health. For example, attending a secondary school where few of one's peers smoke, or living in a community where residents band together to oppose the entry of new liquor stores or demand streets that are safer for pedestrians, will almost certainly lead to better health. These circumstances are more common for people with more income, education, and power.

The resources that increase with higher social status, particularly money, power, and education, are so strongly associated with health that they are sometimes referred to as *fundamental causes* of health (Link and Phelan 1995). These resources are fundamental not only in the sense that they are necessary for accessing many of the further downstream social determinants of health like safe housing, good food, good jobs, and health care, but also because they can be deployed flexibly, in ways that allow the people who possess them to take advantage of new opportunities for enhancing their health as these opportunities arise through advancements in knowledge about the causes of health and disease. Fundamental resources are distributed unequally across society, in the form of a social gradient. The health consequences of this distribution thus also take the form of a gradient, and not merely a gap between the most and least privileged.

Social Inequality Itself Is a Cause of Health Inequalities

Our final stylized fact about health inequalities derives from the presence of the social gradient: economic and social inequality causes health inequalities. Socioeconomic inequalities are clearly responsible for inequalities in many of the downstream determinants of health: for example, people with higher incomes are better able to afford housing that is warm in winter, cool in summer, and free of lead paint, mold, and other health hazards. But inequalities in money, power, and education also seem to cause health inequalities through other pathways, including the psychosocial pathway outlined above. Some researchers are skeptical that socioeconomic inequality is the primary cause of health inequalities, citing the potential for reverse causation (less healthy individuals tend to earn less and have lower educational attainment) and a lack of direct causal identification in most statistical analyses (see, e.g., Montgomery et al. 1996; Mellor and Milyo 2001; Deaton 2002; Beckfield 2004). Nevertheless, the epidemiological literature is replete with macro-level evidence supporting such an association (see Pearce et al. 2006; Leyland et al. 2007; Singh and Kogan 2007; J. Phelan et al. 2010; B. Thomas et al. 2010), and the international consensus regarding health inequalities has largely embraced it.

Both the psychosocial and materialist explanations for the health gradient highlight the importance of social inequality itself in generating health inequalities, but they suggest quite different conclusions about the possibilities for reducing health inequalities in hierarchical societies. If the main reason for health inequalities is psychosocial, then reducing the stigma and loss of control associated with lower social status could reduce inequalities, even without changes in the underlying distribution of resources. The materialist framework, however, sees socioeconomic resources as themselves inherently generative of health inequalities. Because wealth and education are flexible resources that can be redeployed to meet new health challenges as existing causes of poor health become easier and less costly to deal with, attempting to eliminate health inequalities by reducing inequalities in downstream social determinants will simply result in a game of "whack-a-mole."[6]

Imagine, for example, a world in which lead poisoning from chipping lead paint is the main cause of health inequalities related to housing quality, and that

---

[6] Whack-a-mole is a carnival game in which the player, armed with a mallet, faces a playing surface pocked with holes out of which figures of small rodents pop up at random. As the player whacks a mole back down into its hole with a mallet, another mole inevitably emerges from a different hole. The goal is not to eradicate the moles, but to whack as many of them as possible back into their holes in the allotted time.

medical science has discovered an effective and widely available remedy for lead poisoning (in fact, there is currently no safe level of lead ingestion for children). People with more money and knowledge might still be better able to avoid living in housing contaminated by chipping lead paint in this brave new world, but inequalities in mental health due to lead poisoning would be minimized by the widespread availability of treatment. In this imagined world, the pathway between income inequality and health inequality via housing (a downstream determinant) would be disrupted – but many other sources of health inequalities would remain in place, and some new ones might be on the horizon. For example, imagine that scientists in this world discovered that exposure to radiation emitted by ubiquitous wireless devices like cell phones and wi-fi routers caused harmful brain tumors (in reality, there is no conclusive evidence that this is the case). People with greater awareness of the problem of deadly wireless radiation and greater financial resources to update their equipment with new wired versions would be the first to see declines in brain tumors, creating a new inequality in exposure to replace the old chipping lead paint. In fact, as Phelan et al. (2010) show, there are many examples in the real world of this phenomenon. As old forms of health inequality are lessened, new ones arise, as long as the underlying distribution of flexible resources is unequal.

Socioeconomic inequality can additionally cause health inequalities because financial and cognitive resources are associated with enhanced political voice for those at the top of the social hierarchy (Bartels 2016; Elsässer et al. 2017), and because inequality tends to reduce social cohesion (Wilkinson and Pickett 2009). The concentration of financial and cognitive resources at the top of the social hierarchy leads to hoarding behavior, as those at the top of the hierarchy seek to protect their status (Reeves 2017). If the rich and powerful lose interest in paying for health-promoting collective goods like public schools, public housing, or public health services that are likely to be consumed by others, social inequality can lead to health inequalities (see, e.g., Kawachi 2000; John Lynch et al. 2000; Bergh et al. 2016). Both psychosocial and materialist theories of health would thus lead us to expect a causal link between social inequality and health inequalities.

THE EMERGENCE OF THE INTERNATIONAL HEALTH INEQUALITY CONSENSUS FRAME

The stylized facts enumerated in the previous section form core of the knowledge base of social epidemiology, and have come to be taken-for-granted premises that underlie the international consensus framing of health inequalities as a public problem. This section develops a narrative that culminates with the publication in 2014 of the WHO's *Review of Social Determinants and the Health Divide in the European Region*, representing the apotheosis of the international consensus health inequality frame. Highlights of this narrative are summarized in Table 3.1. But the emergence of anything like a consensus

TABLE 3.1 *Key events in the development of the international health inequalities consensus frame*

Year	Event
1948	WHO founded; constitution recognizes impact of social conditions on health.
1978	Alma Ata joint declaration with UNICEF states that inequality in the health status of people within and between countries is "politically, socially and economically unacceptable"; launches Health For All agenda.
1979	WHO sponsors meeting of experts in Mexico City to discuss "the socioeconomic determinants and consequences of differential mortality."
1980	UK Black Report documents social inequalities in health status in Britain despite universal health care; attributes health inequalities to class inequalities in British society.
1980	WHO Europe launches regional Health For All strategy.
1984	Results of first Whitehall Study show a social gradient in health among British civil servants.
1984	WHO Europe announces reducing social inequalities in health status by 25 percent as top priority for Health For All.
1991, 1992	WHO Europe publishes Dahlgren and Whitehead's discussion papers. The papers define health inequities as inequalities in health status between groups that are preventable and unjust, and introduce the rainbow model of social causation.
1997	EU Treaty of Amsterdam requires the EU to promote and protect the health of EU citizens, and to foster cooperation between member states in the area of public health.
1998	EU DG SANCO created; first European Public Health Programme launched.
1998	WHO Europe commissions Wilkinson and Marmot to write *Social Determinants of Health: The Solid Facts* to inform update of HFA strategy.
1999	WHO Europe publishes *Health21: The Health For All Policy Framework for the European Region*; introduces Health Impact Assessment as a core strategy.
2005	WHO Europe releases second update of HFA program; EU commences work on second Health Programme.
2005	WHO global office convenes Commission on Social Determinants of Health (CSDH) under the direction of Marmot.
2005, 2006	EU rotating presidency held by the United Kingdom and Finland. Both highlight health inequalities and commission major reports on health inequalities and potential policy responses in the European region.

Year	Event
2006	EU convenes Expert Group on Social Determinants and Health Inequalities within the High Level Committee on Public Health in DG SANCO.
2007	EU adopts third comprehensive Health Strategy, *Together for Health*; initiates joint action with WHO Europe to map health inequalities and determinants at the regional level in Europe and to assist policy-makers in taking action to reduce health inequalities.
2008	WHO CSDH releases final report, blaming health inequalities on a "toxic combination" of "poor social policies and programmes, unfair economic arrangements, and bad politics," and arguing, "Inequities are killing people on grand scale."
2009	Communication by DG SANCO "Solidarity in Health: Reducing Health Inequalities in the EU" sets out Commission's plans to address health inequalities.
2011	European Parliament resolution "Reducing Health Inequalities in the EU"
2012	WHO Europe releases *Health 2020: The European Policy for Health and Well-Being*; commissions a "European Marmot Review" to make concrete policy recommendations.
2013	WHO Europe publishes Marmot's *Review of Social Determinants and the Health Divide in the WHO European Region*.

approach to the problem of health inequalities in Europe was not a foregone conclusion, particularly given important differences in the nature, understanding, and political valence of the problem at the national level in different countries in an earlier period. Some of the individual elements that characterize current international thinking are probably quite contingently linked to the very strong influence of single experts. For example, Michael Marmot played a central role in promoting the concept of the social gradient in health and the accompanying psychosocial explanation for the link between socioeconomic inequality and health inequalities. The British epidemiologist contributed to or led both the inquiries that served as the basis for the British government's approach to health inequalities in the 1990s and 2000s (Acheson 1998; Marmot et al. 2010), and the health equity strategies guiding the WHO's global and European regional levels (WHO Regional Office for Europe 1998; 2013).

However, even some of the most widely shared and most fundamental parts of the policy frame, including the very definition of what health inequalities are, were far from inevitable. If French or Finnish experts had led the meetings convened by European international organizations to discuss health inequalities in the 1980s, for example, the international consensus might have turned out to be that health inequalities are really an issue of regional variations in health care supply. Instead, British, Dutch, and Scandinavian experts did, and as a result Europeans now define health inequalities mainly as class-based differences in health status.

As contingent as the development of the current international health inequality consensus may have been, though, its past nevertheless shaped its present in discernible ways. In this section I trace that past, focusing on three key periods that helped to define how the frame would come to operate in political life. The first of these key periods followed the publication of the Black Report in the United Kingdom in 1980, at the very beginning of Margaret Thatcher's term in office. The Black Report was widely disseminated outside the United Kingdom, and its framing of the problem of health inequalities as an issue of unequal health outcomes linked to social class inequalities profoundly influenced the international field of scholars and policy advocates interested in health equity. In the aftermath of the Black Report, policy-makers also learned that health equity could be a potent political and partisan issue.

A second important stage in the construction of the international health inequality consensus was the development of the European Health For All (HFA) strategy within the WHO European region and its diffusion to some national governments. During the Health For All period, which began in the mid-1980s, action across multiple policy domains became a central component of the treatment recommendation for dealing with health inequalities. Equally importantly, the HFA strategy stimulated the growth of an international network of epidemiologists working on health inequalities in Europe and so laid the groundwork for faster flow of core ideas in the health equity frame across national borders.

The third key stage in the development of the international health inequality consensus was the WHO's adoption of the social determinants of health framework as a core principle for its global work. When the WHO global office in Geneva formed a Commission on the Social Determinants of Health, the organization decisively supported a framing of the issue of health inequalities that had been taking shape for years in the European regional office of the organization. The Commission's report did not succeed in overturning the WHO's health-system centric vision at a global level, but it lent legitimacy to the European Regional Office's efforts in this area and in so doing paved the way for intensified collaboration between the Regional Office and the European Commission. As a result of this collaboration, the WHO's approach came to be the standard against which health equity policy approaches in European countries would be judged, often quite explicitly.

From Social Medicine to the Black Report: World War II to 1980

From World War II until the publication in 1980 of the Black Report, biomedical approaches to health, which take patterns of human health and illness to arise from the natural dynamics of contagion or from the more-or-less random allocation of biological endowments or environmental exposures, generally dominated the health policy field. But the social approach has nevertheless enjoyed moments of influence. In 1948, the newly founded World Health Organization adopted a constitution that "clearly acknowledge[d] the impact of social conditions on health" (Irwin et al. 2008, 64). In the 1960s, after a period in which the biomedical approach dominated, a social approach to health resurfaced within the organization, bringing with it an emphasis on reducing socially determined inequalities in health within and between countries. Community-based health programs adopted in many developing countries in the 1960s and 1970s had "a holistic model of health attentive to social and environmental determinants" and focused on intersectoral action to address non-medical determinants of health like agriculture and clean water (Solar and Irwin 2006, 181). During the 1970s, delegates to the WHO from China, the Soviet Union, and several African states began advocating for the organization to adopt an approach to health rooted in primary health care and attention to the social and economic causes of illness (F. Baum 2007, 34). In 1977, delegates to the WHO's World Health Assembly declared the attainment of "health for all" by the year 2000 as a central goal. As the editors of a 2000 WHO publication note, "The term *all* referred to the promotion of equity in health" (WHO Regional Office for Europe 2000, 1).

In 1978, the WHO and UNICEF, meeting in the city of Alma Ata in Soviet Kyrgyzstan, issued a joint declaration on primary health care stating that health is a fundamental human right and that the "existing gross inequality in the health status of the people" both within and between countries is "politically, socially, and economically unacceptable" (WHO 1978, 1). The next year, the WHO sponsored a meeting of experts in Mexico City to discuss "the socio-economic determinants and consequences of differential mortality" (Fox and Carr-Hill 1989, 7). This meeting inspired attention to the issue internationally and led to the convening of a series of workshops on the same topic funded by the European Science Foundation (ESF) (Fox and Carr-Hill 1989, 9).

One of the participants in both the WHO and ESF workshops was John Fox, a statistician who was at the same time providing expert assistance to the working group preparing the British Black Report. This report was commissioned by a Labour government in 1977, and issued in 1980. The key finding of the Black Report, which is described in greater detail in Chapter 4, was that the social inequalities in mortality in Britain that persisted despite universal access to free medical care were due to class and income inequalities. The notion of social causation had, as we have seen, been in circulation for well over a century, and researchers had been producing evidence to this effect in Britain for some years before the Black Report was released. But the Black commission's report would go on to be a central reference point for future research and policy on health inequalities throughout Europe.

The release of the Black Report was a critical step in the development of the current international health inequality consensus because, in considering and refuting the main alternative causal claims circulating in research circles at the time, it helped to define health inequalities as a problem related to social class. Conventional wisdom at the time was that worse health outcomes in lower social strata were due to "artifact," which had mainly to do with difficulties in measuring social class position; "selection," that is, the tendency of people in worse health to go on to lesser occupational attainment and lower earnings; or individual behaviors and preferences. The Black Report argued against each of these alternatives, accumulating enough evidence to cast doubt on them and to introduce a "materialist" causal story that linked poor health to unequal access to resources.

The new problem definition and causal story that the Black Report introduced went on to form the basis of the international consensus framing of health inequality as a policy problem. This "seminal" work influenced subsequent reports not only in the United Kingdom, but also in the Netherlands, Chile, China, and at the WHO (Freeman 2006). In fact, "Most academic writing on health inequalities has subsequently tended to adopt its agenda, questions, concepts, and definitions, and to debate its conclusions. It has been influential not only in the way it responds to the problems but more importantly in the way it poses the questions" (Vågerö and Illsley 1995, 219).

A less widely recognized contribution of the Black Report to the international health inequality consensus, however, was political rather than intellectual or evidentiary, and it was entirely unintended. The report was commissioned by a Labour government, but, as described in Chapter 4, the final version of the report was delivered to Margaret Thatcher's newly elected Conservative government, which attempted to bury the findings. Left-leaning policy advocates capitalized on the whiff of scandal and adopted health inequalities as a political cause, using it as a "propaganda weapon" (Whitehead 1998, 481). The Thatcher government's reception of the Black Report, and the response of policy experts and activists to that reception, demonstrated that the issue of socioeconomic inequalities in health could be used as a way to advocate for equity even when the politics of economic policy had taken a sharp neoliberal turn.

The Health For All Period: 1980–2005

Despite the influence of the Black Report, health inequality did not become salient as a public issue in most countries of western Europe until considerably later than 1980. But developments that began in the early 1980s, in both the WHO Regional Office for Europe and the European Union, laid the groundwork for pushing the issue onto many domestic national policy agendas in Europe by the 2000s.

Under the leadership of Halfdan Mahler, the WHO announced its global Health For All strategy at Alma Ata in 1978. The Health For All agenda aimed to put health – defined as a state of well-being that would allow a person to lead an economically and socially productive life – within reach of everyone.

This was to be achieved through continued progress in making medical care and public health services widely available, largely through an emphasis on expanding primary health care, as well as through interventions in areas such as literacy, housing, communications, agriculture, and industrial policy (WHO 1981). Progress on the HFA movement soon stalled at the global level, when attention in developing countries to what would later come to be called the social determinants of health was diverted to a more biomedically oriented "selective primary health care" model (Lee 2008, 75). In Europe, however, the regional office of the WHO launched its own European Health For All program in 1980. The Regional Health Development Advisory Committee – chaired by British health economist Brian Abel-Smith, who had helped to set up the British Black Report and was a key social policy advisor to Labour governments in the United Kingdom – was charged with producing a written program document, which it released in 1982 (WHO Regional Office for Europe 2000, 5).

In western Europe, the Health For All targets and strategies were developed in the context of well-developed health care systems, economic stagnation, and a perceived crisis of already well-established welfare states (Mishra 1984).[7] As a result, the emphasis on expanding access to primary health care in the global HFA agenda was translated, in the European region, into a push for appropriate, community-based care as an alternative to the existing, costly, hospital-focused health policy paradigm. Similarly, "healthy public policy" – which in developing countries of the global south mainly meant increasing literacy, infrastructure development, and agricultural outreach – was reinterpreted in Europe to mean developing cross-sectoral action in support of health equity, predominantly through developing and, in some cases, combatting the retrenchment of non-health social policies (Tervonen-Gonçalves and Lehto 2004, 3–4).

Targets in support of the European Health For All program were published in 1984, with reducing social inequalities in health status by 25 percent as the top priority among thirty-eight targets.[8] These targets were not legally binding, but member countries agreed to use them to set similar national targets and priorities, and to participate in regular data collection and monitoring.[9] The inequality target, while rather vague and lacking teeth, nevertheless "helped in putting inequalities in health on the policy agenda in many European countries" (Mackenbach and Bakker 2003, 29). According to the WHO, this was

[7] In some west European countries, including Finland, a lack of primary health care services was still perceived in rural areas.

[8] These targets were the result of a consultation process convened by WHO Europe in which more than 250 experts from across the region developed a list of 82 targets for consideration by the Regional Committee. These were eventually reduced by the committee to the set of 38 targets adopted unanimously in 1984 (Ritsatakis 2000, 7).

[9] Initially the plan was to monitor implementation every two years (beginning in 1983), and effectiveness every six years (beginning in 1985). The Regional Committee assessed progress toward the regional targets every three years, in 1985, 1988, 1991, 1994, and 1997.

the first time that all members of the European region had agreed to a common health policy as the basis for further developments (WHO 1985 Targets for HFA, cited in WHO Regional Office for Europe 2000, 5). Moreover, as Ritsatakis et al. (WHO Regional Office for Europe 2000) noted, "Whether or not they were fully aware of the wider implications at the time, in 1984 the WHO European Member States adopted a policy based on clear ethical principles of promoting equity in health" (p. 11).

Developing the European Health For All strategy was not a purely bureaucratic exercise. It relied on international expert networks to provide data and analysis. At the start of the global Health For All agenda, in 1979, the UN had convened a global meeting of experts and the WHO encouraged regional meetings to facilitate the exchange of information and more systematic study of the causes of socioeconomic inequalities in health (Fox 1989, 7–8). The European Science Foundation provided funding for a series of interdisciplinary workshops in 1984, 1985, and 1986 on inequalities in health in European countries, which were attended by thirty-five researchers from thirteen European countries (Fox 1989, 9). The collaboration resulted in a volume edited by British statistician John Fox, who had authored the 1971 decennial occupational mortality supplement on which the Black Report drew heavily. *Health Inequalities in European Countries* was the first systematically comparative work on health inequalities in Europe, with contributors from the United Kingdom, France, Sweden, Denmark, Finland, West Germany, Spain, Greece, Hungary, and Israel documenting and attempting to explain differences in socioeconomic inequalities in mortality and morbidity across European countries (Fox 1989).

At the same time, and partly in response to the recession in the late 1970s, WHO Europe had formed an equity program within the regional office. The program was originally focused on issues of unemployment and poverty, later expanded to include other vulnerable groups, and finally, by the second half of the 1980s, turned its focus to examining the causes of health inequalities. During this period the regional office also built up a network of experts in academia and research institutions (Ritsatakis 1994, 204–5).

The Health For All strategy was significant in the development of the international health inequality consensus frame because it committed member countries in the European region to reducing health inequalities as a primary objective of health policy. However, during the 1980s and 1990s, WHO Europe also promoted the health equity agenda in other ways. WHO Europe had underwritten the production and dissemination of three discussion papers written for non-specialists. The first, released in 1985, was written by Dutch epidemiologists Anton Kunst and Johan Mackenbach, and offered a guide to measuring and monitoring health inequalities. Two further papers, by British public health scholar Margaret Whitehead and Swedish economist and civil servant Göran Dahlgren, were made available in 1990, with the aim of raising awareness and stimulating debate about the issue of health inequalities among a wider audience (Ziglio 2006, viii).

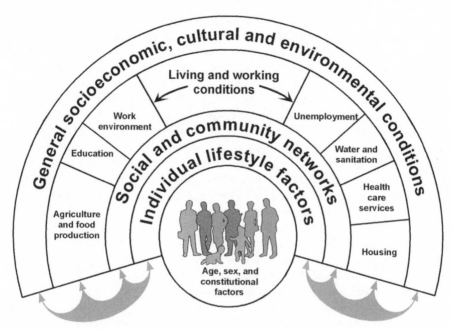

FIGURE 3.2 The Dahlgren–Whitehead rainbow model of health causation.
Reproduced with permission from Dahlgren and Whitehead (1993).

This aim was clearly achieved. The definition of equity put forth in *Concepts and Principles of Equality in Health* (Whitehead 1991) is still widely cited in WHO, EU, and country-level policy documents. The second paper, *Policies and Strategies to Promote Equality in Health* (WHO Regional Office for Europe 1991), introduced the concept of social causation and the term "determinants of health" to a wide audience, depicting these concepts in a "rainbow model" (see Figure 3.3). The rainbow model shows health as a product of proximate causes nested within more distal ones: individual lifestyle choices within community and social networks, within the range of public policies that affect the conditions in which people live and work, and within general socioeconomic and environmental conditions. The rainbow model has been widely reproduced in health inequalities reports throughout the world. The image and the conceptual model underlying it have been so influential, in fact, that the British Economic and Social Research Council highlighted it in 2015 as one of fifty landmark social science research achievements of the last fifty years (ESRC [Economic and Social Research Council] n.d.).

According to Whitehead, the decision to produce the second of the discussion papers reflected the WHO regional office's desire take a more active role in promoting policy solutions to achieve the HFA inequality reduction target

(Whitehead 1998, 477). The paper discussed interventions ranging from the very local to the transnational, and aimed at affecting the production of health inequalities on each of the levels of the rainbow, from individual health behaviors to the broader socioeconomic and environmental conditions. The emphasis, however, was on the highest two levels. Because multiple factors negatively affecting health are often present for disadvantaged groups, the authors argued that structural interventions that reduce the level of disadvantage are likely to be more effective entry points than more proximate determinants. Similarly, while policies in a number of areas are discussed in the paper (e.g., housing quality, workplace safety, food pricing, the quality of educational, social, and health services to which people at different income levels and in different geographic areas have access), Dahlgren and Whitehead (WHO Regional Office for Europe 1991) are attuned particularly to government policies affecting the distribution of income and the level of employment. Providing a rationale for this focus, they cite British scholar Richard Wilkinson's estimate, published earlier that year in the *Guardian*, that three-quarters of observed inequalities in health status were due to underlying socioeconomic inequalities (WHO Regional Office for Europe 1991, 15).

Dahlgren and Whitehead's two papers were extraordinarily influential, and laid out clearly many of the premises that would become incorporated into the international health inequality consensus: the idea that socioeconomic inequalities in health were unfair because they were linked to political choices about how to organize social and economic life, the notion of broader and narrower determinants of health, the necessity for policy changes across multiple sectors and levels of government, and the priority accorded to reducing underlying economic inequality as a "master key" for reducing health inequalities.

In laying out a political strategy for achieving a policy environment more conducive to health equity, Dahlgren and Whitehead were particularly emphatic on two points. First, they argued that appropriate organizational and bureaucratic structures to support the development of equity-enhancing policies across multiple sectors were not in place in most countries, and would be needed if health inequalities were to be reduced. Second, they pointed out that citizen involvement is critical, but that unless and until political leaders offer policies that are likely to reduce health inequalities, the people whose lives would be most improved by reducing health inequalities are unlikely to become engaged. To that end, Dahlgren and Whitehead offered a set of sample policies that political parties and politicians might offer to voters as part of a plan to reduce health inequalities. First on the list was reducing existing income inequalities.

Dahlgren and Whitehead did not limit their attention to what national-level policy-makers could do to reduce health inequalities. In their 1991 paper, they also leveled scrutiny at economic policies being undertaken or proposed as part of European integration, emphasizing both the beneficial and harmful roles that the European Community could play in regulating pollution, the staffing of health services, and the price and availability of food, tobacco, and alcohol

(WHO Regional Office for Europe 1991). Dahlgren and Whitehead noted that regulations that had already been floated under the Single European Act (the 1987 agreement that aimed to introduce a single internal market by 1992) would worsen health inequalities in many countries by reducing tobacco and alcohol taxes, and making it easier for wealthier countries in the region to poach qualified health care professionals from poorer ones. It was important, they argued, that European integration policies be evaluated for their impact on health equity.

This eagerness to consider what could be done at the European level likely reflected growing interest in health matters within the European Commission. The Maastricht Treaty of 1992 stated that European Community policies in all areas should be consistent with assuring a high level of health protection in member states, and throughout the 1990s the EU "gradually developed a set of activities such as health promotion, education, information, and training" and began to develop EU-level sources for health data (Seychell et al. 2013, 2). The EU "identified research on inequalities in health as a priority for its public health program" during this period (Whitehead 1998, 472), and funding commenced for a number of international research initiatives on health inequalities, including a group based at Erasmus University in Rotterdam that would go on to be a central node in the EU's network of expertise in this area.

In 1994, the European Commission and the Council of Europe sponsored a ministerial-level European Health Policy Conference organized by WHO Europe. Meanwhile, the European Commissioner for Social Affairs tasked Brian Abel-Smith (the British health economist who authored the initial European Health For All report and was a key advisor to WHO chief Halfdan Mahler) with producing a report to jump-start European health policy collaboration. The result was *Choices in Health Policy: An Agenda for the European Union* (Abel-Smith 1995), which combined recommendations for both health services and public health sector reforms.

The EU itself began to take on a more significant role in public health in the late 1990s, largely in response to the "mad cow disease" (bovine spongiform encephalopathy) crisis (Guignier 2006, 233). The 1997 Treaty of Amsterdam introduced a public health title, Article 152, that required the European Union to promote and protect the health of EU citizens and to foster cooperation between member states in the area of public health. In 1999, main responsibility for health was moved from the European Commission's Directorate General dealing with employment and social affairs to a separate Directorate General for Health and Consumer Protection (*Direction Générale Santé et Consommateurs*, abbreviated DG SANCO).

When the Commission first began work in the area of public health, its staff had limited technical expertise, and so relied heavily on the WHO for programmatic ideas and expert guidance to legitimate its own activities in the health field (Guignier 2006, 229 and 234; Kurzer and Cooper 2011). Even now, the EU's own capacities in public health remain limited. The work of carrying out treaty obligations under Article 152 occurs not through legal instruments, which would run afoul of the principle of subsidiarity as applied to health policy, but through guidelines, communications, and encouragement of cooperation among member states (Randall 2001). Furthermore, work relevant to public health and health equity remains fragmented across various directorates general (DGs) and agencies, including the DGs for research, agriculture, and the environment, and the European statistical agency (McKee et al. 2010, 234–35).

However, despite these limitations, and despite the fact that EU public health capacities may have been initially expanded in order to deal with an infectious disease crisis rather than health inequalities or the social determinants of health, the work of DG SANCO quickly became closely intertwined with WHO Europe's Health For All program and with other efforts in the area of health equity. As compared to the WHO (though not by any means in absolute terms), the Commission had far greater budgetary resources and leverage over member state governments. This allowed it to assert itself as a public health actor in its own right and, through funding of data collection, research, and NGOs, to develop its own networks and sources of expertise (Guignier 2006, 236–37; Greer et al. 2013, 7–8). Furthermore, the EU's structure allows (with some effort) for activity across multiple sectors of government and society, a fact that dovetailed with the WHO's growing emphasis on multisectoral action on social determinants in the late 1990s (Guignier 2006, 237–38).

In 1998, WHO Europe began a publicity campaign to encourage action on social determinants of health, and commissioned British scholars Marmot and Wilkinson to write *Social Determinants of Health: The Solid Facts* (WHO Regional Office for Europe 1998).[10] This report recommended action across ten key areas of public policy affecting the social determinants of health. Another opportunity to reinforce the message of the need for cross-sectoral action on the SDOH also occurred in 1998, as that year also marked the first scheduled update to WHO Europe's Health For All program. The Regional Committee had approved revised Health For All targets in 1991, which continued to hold equity in health as a primary objective. But when the Health For All strategy was re-renewed at the global level in 1998, the European regional office revised the entire strategy, resulting in *Health21: The Health For All Policy Framework for the European Region* (WHO 1999). There was considerable continuity in the strategy – "equity in health" was the second of its twenty-one targets – although a new emphasis on casting health as a human right implied a somewhat increased focus on gender equity. Like the original HFA policy, *Health21* called for "multisectoral strategies to tackle the determinants of health" (target 14). What was new was the introduction of Health Impact Assessment (HIA) as one of four core strategies put forth in the document,

[10] An expanded edition of the report including the scientific evidence behind the recommendations was published in book form in 1999 (WHO Regional Office for Europe 1999).

to ensure the accountability of all sectors for the effects of their policies and actions on health. With funding from the EU, the government of Finland was tasked with carrying out a project to map the state of the art in HIA and provide guidance for further action.

Meanwhile, in April 1998, the European Commission launched its own process to develop a new public health policy for the EU. The resulting first EU Public Health Programme (2003–8) was announced in 2002. The new public health strategy had three strands: improving information for health, rapid reaction to health threats, and tackling the determinants of health through health promotion and disease prevention. These were to be accomplished by "conducting research, building networks, coordinating health activities, sharing experiences, and educating and disseminating relevant information and knowledge to improve health by preventing diseases and disorders and protecting health" (Oortwijn et al. 2007, 3). According to Greer and Kurzer (2013), WHO Europe "was instrumental in convincing the EU council (representing the political leaders of the member states) to endorse a new public health program for Europe" (p. 157), and indeed, the year 2000 marks the beginning of closer cooperation between the WHO and the EU (Guignier 2006; Burci 2015).

In 2003, the regional office released an updated second edition of Marmot and Wilkinson's *Social Determinants of Health: The Solid Facts*, and work began on the second update to the European Health For All program, which was released in 2005 (WHO Regional Office for Europe 2003; Marmot and Wilkinson 2005). This update reaffirmed *Health21* and its focus on solidarity and equity as the basis for health policy throughout the region. While the previous iterations of the HFA program had established targets (quantitative in 1984 and 1991, notional in 1998) for the reduction of health inequalities, the third did not. Instead, the Regional Director, Marc Danzon, offered the HFA "process" as a "forum for exchanging information and experiences, generated at the national and subnational levels" (WHO Regional Committee for Europe 2005, vii).

Coinciding with the 2005 release of the updated Health For All strategy by WHO Europe, the EU commenced work on a second Public Health Programme (the word "public" eventually dropped out of the title). In accordance with the new emphasis on social determinants of health and health impact assessment, one of the three core objectives at the beginning of the work on the program was mainstreaming health across all EU policies. This approach did not survive in the final version of the program, but at the European Parliament's insistence, the goal of tackling health inequality was strengthened – including, in the second reading, adding explicit language regarding the reduction of inequalities to the Commission's rather vague objective of "promoting health for prosperity and solidarity" (McKee et al. 2010, 242–45).

The EU's second health program made almost 114 million euros available for research and interventions related to health promotion, including action on the social determinants of health. My own accounting, which relies on information in the publicly available database of projects funded under the second health program, suggests that DG SANCO allocated at least 7.2 million euros to projects related to health inequalities generally, with an additional 2.1 million euros dedicated to particular mechanisms for reducing health inequalities (e.g., reduced tobacco and alcohol consumption) or to health inequalities affecting specific populations (e.g., Roma, immigrants, children, and teens).[11] These projects (and others funded by the DG for research during the same period) contributed to further developing the expert consensus around a definition of health inequalities as a policy problem related to social inequity, produced and potentially remedied by policies that went well beyond the health sector.

National governments were responsible for developing and implementing their own policies in pursuit of the goals of the HFA strategy, and to the extent that they undertook actions consistent with the goals of the HFA process, it was not even always as a result of the activities of these international organizations. Of the national health policy documents analyzed in the WHO HFA 2005 Update, thirty-two of the forty explicitly reference HFA as a "framework or source of inspiration" (WHO Regional Committee for Europe 2005, 27). However, some of the most important national-level developments either occurred independently (as with the founding of the French High Commission for Public Health in 1991 and the eventual passage of a major new public health law in 1994) or used the HFA framework as a way to legitimate policies desired by domestic constituencies (as with the Finnish HFA-inspired Health 2015 program) (WHO Regional Committee for Europe 2005, 29–30).

But European institutions played an important role in setting a focal strategy and in funding data collection, research, and dissemination. WHO Europe and EU activities from the 1980s through 2005 centered on developing and refining the Health For All strategy, and affected national policy (and health inequalities) mainly through classic soft law mechanisms. In the process the WHO and the EU contributed to building a robust international network of scholars who influenced not only each other but also policy development at the European and national levels.

THE CSDH ERA: 2006 ONWARD

In March 2005, the Director General of the WHO convened a Commission on the Social Determinants of Health (CSDH). The CSDH was deeply influenced by the reframing of the Alma Ata primary health care agenda that came out of the European region during the Health For All period. In the developing world

---

[11] Data from DG Research (http://cordis.europa.eu/home_en.html), DG SANCO (http://ec.europa .eu/health/social_determinants/projects-o_en), and the European Commission (https://webgate .ec.europa.eu/chafea_pdb/health/).

in the 1980s and 1990s, the primary health care agenda had been reinterpreted as (or supplanted with) a drive to improve medical care and advance disease-specific programs often involving medical interventions (Youde 2012). The appointment of Marmot to head the CSDH signaled a "swing back toward social medicine" on the part of the WHO global office, and an emphasis on social, rather than biomedical, factors as causes of health and illness (Lee 2008, 96). As we have seen, this emphasis was already present in Europe: Marmot and Wilkinson's *Social Determinants of Health: The Solid Facts* (WHO Regional Office for Europe 1998), which had informed the WHO Europe's second Health For All update in 1998 and had already been revised and re-released once, in 2003.

Marmot's intellectual calling card was the idea, which he first documented in his Whitehall studies beginning in the late 1960s, that health inequalities existed across the entire social gradient, and did not only affect the very poor. The key policy implication of this finding did not become clear in WHO documents, however, until the "social determinants era," starting around 2006. Even the 2005 Health For All update stated, "One of the most effective ways to deal with a widening gap in health status within a population is to target the social determinants of health, *notably poverty*" (WHO Regional Committee for Europe 2005, 65, emphasis added). The final report of the CSDH, however, took a stronger stand against inequality, and not only poverty. *Closing the Gap in a Generation* came with an attention-grabbing sound bite: "Inequities are killing people on grand scale." It went on to describe the commission's findings that inequalities in health are caused by a "toxic combination" of "poor social policies and programmes, unfair economic arrangements, and bad politics" (WHO 2008, 26).

Some critics have argued that the CSDH report failed to live up to its progressive promise. Navarro, for example, notes that while the report "does emphasize, in generic terms, the need to redistribute resources," it is "silent on the topic of whose resources" ought to be distributed, "and how and through what instruments" (Navarro 2009, 440). Even so, the health equity frame advanced by the CSDH report was bolder than most earlier incarnations at the European level. Some earlier domestic reports, including the Black Report, had contained equally scathing critiques of current socioeconomic arrangements; and the Norwegian government had announced in 2007 its intention to try to reduce health inequalities by flattening the income distribution. But such a policy idea had, until the CSDH report, not been promoted by the WHO or the EU.

At the same time the CSDH was taking up the torch of social determinants from the WHO regional office, the EU was also becoming more active in this issue area. The British and Finnish governments had their turns in the rotating presidency of the EU in 2005 and 2006, and both presidencies chose to focus on health inequalities – areas in which their own governments had already innovated. The UK presidency, in the second semester of 2005, held a summit on "Tackling Health Inequalities," and commissioned two major reports on health inequalities in the European region. The first was led by Johan Mackenbach of Erasmus University, the second by a collaboration between Scottish researchers and the Brussels-based NGO EuroHealthNet (Mackenbach 2006; UK Presidency of the EU 2006). The Finnish presidency, in the second semester of 2006, held a high-level conference on Health in All Policies (the successor concept to Health Impact Assessment), and issued a companion report (Finnish Ministry of Social Affairs and Health 2006).

In 2006, the EU formalized its network of researchers and policy experts, convening an Expert Group on Social Determinants and Health Inequalities within the High Level Committee on Public Health in DG SANCO. The group met roughly twice a year to share information and best practices and to advise the DG on policy. In 2007, the EU adopted its third comprehensive health strategy, Together for Health, which took up the new language of Health in All Policies and provided funding via the EU Health Programme (2008–13) to projects aimed at promoting health and reducing health inequalities. One of the key initiatives funded under the program was a "joint action" with WHO Europe focused on health inequalities and social determinants. The joint action had two main objectives: to map health inequalities and determinants at the regional level in the EU and neighboring countries and to build on the global CSDH's work to develop resources to assist policy-makers in taking action to reduce health inequalities (WHO Europe n.d.).

The first major policy statement on health inequalities to come out of the European Commission itself was a 2009 joint Communication by DG SANCO and the Directorate General for employment titled "Solidarity in Health: Reducing Health Inequalities in the EU" (European Commission 2009). The Communication set out the Commission's plans to address health inequalities, which included doing more to assess the impact of existing EU policies on health inequalities and collecting and disseminating more data on the extent of inequalities and the effects of interventions to reduce them. The Spanish presidency (first semester of 2010) took up these themes, producing a report on "Monitoring Social Determinants of Health and the Reduction of Health Inequalities" (Hernandez et al. 2010), followed closely by the Belgian presidency's (second semester of 2010) high-level conference on "Reducing Health Inequalities from a Regional Perspective: What Works, What Doesn't?" In 2011, the European Parliament adopted a resolution, "Reducing Health Inequalities in the EU," drafted by Portuguese MEP Edite Estrela.[12] The resolution's strong emphasis on gender equity in health proved to be something of a liability, attracting the ire of members of the European Parliament concerned over increasing access to abortion,[13] but it nevertheless passed.

---

[12] European Parliament, P7_TA (2011) 0081, "Reducing Health Inequalities in the EU," March 8, 2011.

[13] European Parliament, "Debates – Monday, 7 March 2011: Reducing Health Inequalities (Short Presentation)."

The growing interest in health inequalities within the EU was supported by a renewed interest in public health in the WHO's regional office, following a decade during which much of the office's attention had been focused on reforms to health care systems (Hunter 2012, 871). The new regional health policy framework, *Health 2020: The European Policy for Health and Well-Being*, was adopted in September 2012 after two years of work, and rested on a conceptual foundation of social determinants causation and cross-sectoral, "whole-of-government" responsibility for reducing health inequalities (WHO Regional Office for Europe 2012). The policy had two "strategic objectives": improving health for all and reducing health inequalities and improving leadership and participatory governance for health (p. 13), and six "headline targets," of which the third was to reduce inequalities in health in the European region (p. 16). At the same time, the policy declared the intention of the regional office to work even more closely with the EU on health matters "as the European Region's repository of advice and evidence on what works," and noted that cooperating with the EU brought benefits in terms of "legal and financial mechanisms" for implementing cooperation and common policies (p. 21). The policy itself recommended few concrete actions, but argued that "[i]nequities in health cannot be reduced without addressing inequities in … the distribution of power, money and resources" (p. 63) and pointed out that "[t]he gradient approach implies a combination of broad universal measures with strategies targeted at high-risk groups. An approach targeting only disadvantaged groups would not alter the distribution of the determinants of health across the whole socioeconomic spectrum" (p. 64).

More specific policy recommendations to flesh out *Health 2020*'s call to take "actions on the social determinants of health" were included in a report led by Michael Marmot, A *Review of Social Determinants and the Health Divide in the WHO European Region* (WHO Regional Office for Europe 2013), as part of the preparations for *Health 2020*. The report describes the main actions the European Commission took to implement its Communication on health inequalities since 2009, and develops recommendations and "specific actions" for achieving the objectives and targets in *Health 2020*. Interventions to increase equity in the social determinants of health are to take place in multiple settings (schools, workplaces, communities) and across the life course. However, Marmot also devotes chapters to the "wider society" and "macro-level context," in which recommendations concerning social protection and redistribution are found. While the "specific actions" highlighted under Recommendation 2(a) concern "the level and distribution of social protection," the report also recognizes income inequality as a related but distinct problem requiring government action.

The report connects the level of social spending and income inequality, arguing that "[i]f those at the higher end of the socioeconomic distribution take a larger share of the rewards from production than is generated by their activities, less is available for others. This type of income inequality can, in particular, affect the amount of money available to pay a minimum standard for healthy living" (WHO Regional Office for Europe 2013, 90). To overcome this problem, "[g]overnments can influence income inequality in a number of ways. They can alter their taxation regimes in isolation, or adjust the overall package of charges and social protection benefits to ensure minimum incomes are sufficiently high.... They could enforce maximum wage differentials within companies to increase the money available to pay workers, or limit bonuses. Similarly, government contracts could be awarded only to companies meeting a minimum wage and wage ratio. Legislation is not always needed, of course, and responsibility deals could be struck if found to be effective" (WHO Regional Office for Europe 2013, 90).

The European Marmot Review (WHO Regional Office for Europe 2013) presented all of the elements of the current international health inequalities consensus: the definition of the problem of health inequalities as a problem of socioeconomic inequalities in health status; the causal attribution of health inequalities to inequalities in the underlying social determinants of health, including income as a fundamental driver; the designation of health inequalities as unfair; the assignment of treatment responsibility to government, rather than solely to individuals, market actors, or civil society; and the prescription of core policy mechanisms (cross-sectoral action with national-level leadership) and actions (reduction of inequalities in the social determinants of health). Content analysis of European health equity documents demonstrates in greater detail how these themes are presented in European-level health policy documents in the period from 2003 to 2013.

THE INTERNATIONAL HEALTH INEQUALITY
CONSENSUS IN PRINT

The dominant policy frame used by officials of WHO Europe, the European Commission's DG for Health and Consumer Protection, and many internationally oriented policy experts when discussing the issue of health inequality has strongly influenced national-level policy-makers in many member countries. This frame is not universally accepted; as we shall see in the following chapters, the consensus as a whole is more widely shared in England, for example, than in France. Competition with the consensus frame comes from domestic definitions of equality and equity as applied to the health field, from continued medical dominance of many health policy levers, from behavioral approaches within public health, and from a neoliberal policy paradigm that posits the market as a solution to most social problems. Nor is the international health inequality consensus entirely stable even over the very near term. The financial and debt crises that plunged Europe into economic depression after 2008 left their mark on the international health inequality consensus, whose roots were in the less austere earlier part of the decade, and the current influx of refugees and migrants into Europe will surely shape it further.

Nevertheless, the international health inequality consensus frame is by now the backdrop against which most high-level domestic policy-makers and politicians in Europe operate when they talk about health inequalities. Particularly since the WHO released the final report of the Commission on Social Determinants of Health in 2008, the outlines of the international health inequality consensus are repeated frequently in both international and national policy documents in Europe. Even in the United States, where since the mid-1980s health inequalities have been predominantly discussed in ways that are quite different from the dominant paradigm in Europe, major foundations and government agencies have now adopted a similar language of social determinants and health equity (Julia Lynch and Perera 2017).[14] This makes the international health inequality consensus a useful measuring rod against which to compare national-level politics and policies in the area of health inequalities. National-level policy-makers are also being judged against that standard by the EU (through its open method of coordination) and by domestic policy experts who have been influenced by the international consensus.

If we are to use the international health inequality consensus as a standard against which to measure national approaches, though, we need first to know exactly what that standard is. Moreover, we need to understand which parts of the "consensus" are really consensual, which are central to the frame, and which are more peripheral. The systematic analysis of the contents of a corpus of policy documents produced by WHO Europe and the EU, presented in the Appendix, will fill in some of these details.

The present work is the first to examine systematically a broad sample of health inequality documents produced at the European level. However, the reports of governments and intergovernmental organizations have been used frequently as a source of information about how health policy elites understand health inequalities (see, e.g., Graham 2004a; Vallgårda 2007; 2008; Blakely 2008; Raphael 2011a; 2011b; Docteur and Berenson 2014; Julia Lynch 2016; Julia Lynch and Perera 2017). As Freeman (2006) explains, "Government is a text-based medium, no less in public health than in other areas of public policy, and a feature of the politics of health equity across countries is that it turns on the production of a key text" (p. 52). Reports are important not only because they express the sentiments of key actors about a policy problem, but also because the process of producing government reports helps build constituencies for particular ideas and policies within the policy elite. As contributors negotiate over common language, the documents themselves become "a source of authority, a means by which influence is established and exerted, such that the

---

[14] Health equity reports by the US government and health NGOs have emphasized racial and ethnic inequalities much more strongly than is the case in most European documents, and, for reasons related to the lack of universal health care provision, have focused much more strongly on the health care system as a driver of and solution to the problem of health inequality.

production of the document may be thought of as a process of underwriting as much as writing" (see also Freeman 2006, 54; Raphael 2011a; 2011b).

The corpus of WHO and EU reports that I examine is not authoritative in the sense that governments of member states are required to act on the reports (they are not), but they do carry weight because they represent the views of those experts and policy-makers who have chosen, or been chosen, to participate in constructing an international consensus around this issue. Both the WHO and the EU issue a large volume of statements about health and health policy in the countries that make up their membership. (Further details about the selection criteria used in sampling these reports are presented in the Appendix.) These statements allow us to construct a portrait – not quite a snapshot, since the documents come from a period of roughly a decade – of a policy frame at a particular period of time.

Many attributes of the documents could fruitfully be examined. For example, Freeman (2006) analyzes how health inequalities documents in the United Kingdom, the Netherlands, the United States, Chile, and China establish authority, in addition to how they define and propose acting on the problem of health inequalities; and Vallgårda (2008) finds that British and Scandinavian health inequalities policy documents differ in whether they discuss SES inequalities in health by singling out the problems of distinctive groups or looking across the entire income gradient. I focused on the five key elements of the international health inequality consensus that are the most generalizable elements of any policy frame: the definition of the problem (how health inequalities are referenced in the report); the moral language used to describe the problem (inequity or injustice versus the more neutral term "inequality"); the causal story or stories about where the problem comes from; which actors, at which levels of government or society, were cast as responsible for solving the problem; and the recommendations for how the problem could be solved (how health inequalities could be reduced).

The problem of health inequalities is defined in this corpus primarily in terms of health status outcomes across socioeconomic groups, and the words used to discuss health inequalities convey a distinct moral judgment that health inequalities are unjust. The dominant causal story in the corpus is that health inequalities arise from inequalities in the social determinants of health, rather than primarily from health care services or from individual behaviors that are not shaped by other inequalities. Unlike in much popular discussion of health inequalities, where causal explanations relating to individual-level and downstream causes of health inequalities are common, the documents in our corpus emphasized structural causes. While not mentioned at all in the earliest EU or WHO documents, economic inequality and systemic political economy causes became more prevalent explanations for health inequality beginning in 2006.

Finally, I consider how the WHO and EU documents in this corpus propose that the problem of health inequalities ought to be solved. The documents attribute responsibility for correcting the problem of health inequalities to a wide variety of agents, including supranational, national, or subnational organs of government; health system actors; private-sector actors; schools; communities; and individuals. Most of these documents make it clear that solving the problem of health inequalities should not be a task for the people adversely affected or for the health care system alone. Governments bear primary responsibility for solving the problem in all reports in the corpus. The policies most frequently recommended were actions to reduce inequalities in the social determinants of health outside the health sector. Remarkably, given the radical implications, 14 percent of treatment recommendations in the corpus involved a call for fundamentally changing the political and/or economic system to reduce inequalities in power and resources, and so create better conditions for health equity.

CONCLUSION

If the international consensus frame is coherent, it is not entirely consensual. At no level of governance, either domestic or international, has there ever been complete consensus on the right way to define or deal with health inequalities, and as we saw in Chapter 2, even relatively disinterested researchers may disagree over some fundamental aspects of the frame, such as how exactly socioeconomic inequality causes health inequalities. Furthermore, the "international" consensus is not divorced from domestic politics. Domestic problem definitions affected the work of policy entrepreneurs who went on to contribute to the international consensus, and many of the policy recommendations tied to the international consensus frame can be enacted only at the domestic level. Even so, the frame is international in the sense that it has been propagated through a network of internationally oriented academic researchers and policy experts that spans national borders and given its fullest expression as an aspiration for policy in the work of two intergovernmental organizations: the World Health Organization's Regional Office for Europe and the European Union.

Tracing the emergence of health inequalities as a political problem in European countries thus requires examining both the national and international contexts. In this chapter, the attention has been on how a specific definition of the problem of health inequalities emerged at the transnational level in Europe, such that it could subsequently influence national policy-making communities. In Chapters 4 and 5, I take up the domestic forces shaping how health inequality functions as a political issue in England, France, and Finland. But as we have seen, the international consensus was itself strongly influenced by British experiences, scholars, and activists, along with Dutch, Scandinavian, and Finnish contributions. This means that the international consensus frame is likely to interact differently with policy formulation in England and Finland as compared to France.

The international consensus frame treats inequalities in health status as an outcome of upstream inequalities in power and resources, which have consequences for how more proximate determinants of health are distributed in society. The main policy remedy is thus cross-sectoral action on multiple social determinants of health, coordinated by national governments, and including efforts to reduce inequalities' upstream determinants, such as income, wealth, and political influence. This is, on the face of it, a radical position, particularly in the context of the neoliberal times (though surely no more radical than IMF managing director Christine LaGarde's calls to reduce economic inequality). Yet by the mid-2000s, many governments in Europe had taken up the issue of health inequalities and issued plans and programs to combat them.

Under what circumstances might we expect cautious politicians to bring the international framing of health inequalities into political discourse? The detailed analysis of the premises behind the international consensus undertaken in this chapter gives us some clues. If politicians do not fully grasp those premises, and so fail to understand that reducing socioeconomic inequality is essential for reducing health inequality, the international consensus frame might not seem particularly threatening. Alternatively, politicians may hope to engage in cheap talk, adopting the international frame without intending to follow through on the more challenging parts of it. Either of these circumstances could lead to the result that we observe in the following chapters: that governments did take up the international framing of health inequalities when it suited their purposes, but generally did not try to enact the most difficult element of the policy recommendation, reducing socioeconomic inequalities, in order to reduce health inequalities. While the data that I have collected on national experiences do not allow me to distinguish decisively or with any quantitative precision between the two possible causes of this outcome, in each country there appears to be some cheap talk as well as a great deal of honest befuddlement on the part of politicians about what it would actually entail to reduce health inequalities in a meaningful and permanent way.

4

New Labour, the Redistributive Taboo, and Reframing Inequality in England after the Black Report

INTRODUCTION

In 2002, speaking at a school in east London, Prime Minister Tony Blair promised to "redistribute power, wealth, and opportunity." This uncharacteristic – and perhaps unguarded, given the venue – remark was "one of the first times the prime minister has used the word 'redistribute' unprompted," according to the *Guardian* reporter who covered the speech (*The Guardian* 2002). The surprised reporter went on to declare that redistribution was "previously a taboo expression in New Labour."

Indeed, throughout the period in which Tony Blair and his centrist allies led the Labour Party and the government of the United Kingdom, redistribution was rarely discussed, but health inequality, a problem whose very solution would require redistribution, moved to the center of the Labour's rhetoric and policy agenda. This chapter explores how and why Labour came to view redistribution as "taboo" (Cook 2004; Irvin 2008) and reframed the problem of social inequality as a matter of health rather than of redistributive policy – a decision that would ultimately hamper their ability to reduce either health inequalities or socioeconomic inequality in England.

As we saw in Chapter 3, British policy-makers and public health experts have been at the center of the international health inequalities field since the 1970s. British politicians also led the international shift away from the Keynesian, redistributive postwar consensus and toward a neoliberal ideational and policy consensus in the 1980s and 1990s, with elites on both the right (Conservatives) and the left (Labour) developing neoliberalism as an intellectual and policy agenda that would later be adopted elsewhere. Fear of a changing electorate and of punishment by economic elites and the media for being economically irresponsible led Labour leaders in the late 1990s to view redistributive rhetoric as a taboo, not to be discussed in public.

That said, Labour did not abandon equity as a goal. Even the most centrist of Labour's leadership in this period were committed to advancing a policy agenda that would improve the lives of lower-income citizens, and to a certain extent they succeeded. But Labour had acceded to a neoliberal policy paradigm as the basic foundation on which all other policies must be built, and ceased to attempt to woo voters through talk about redistribution or income inequality. Reducing inequality by limiting or taxing top incomes had also become taboo. This circumstance – a party whose candidates and voters cared about equity, but could not bear to utter the word "redistribution" – paved the way for health inequality to become an important electoral issue for "New Labour," as the party temporarily rebranded itself under Tony Blair's leadership.

Because both European neoliberalism and the international consensus framing of health inequality were so strongly influenced by developments in Britain, the British experience with the transformation of inequality from a problem of socioeconomics to a problem of health is something of an ideal type, and central to understanding the politics of inequality more broadly. Health policy autonomy was devolved to the United Kingdom's constituent nations in 1999, and the Scottish approach to health inequality, in particular, has diverged from the English (Greer 2004). Because most policy that affects the structural and "upstream" social determinants of health in England is still made by the Westminster parliament – not the case for the devolved governments of Wales and Scotland – the political choices of Westminster politicians are reflected most strongly in English health policy. That is where this chapter focuses. It is in the English context, and particularly during the period of New Labour under Blair, that we can see most clearly how economic inequality became a taboo topic and was reframed as a health issue.

THE ENGLISH HEALTH INEQUALITY FRAME IN BRIEF

The issue of socioeconomic inequalities in health has been driving policy in Britain as far back as the 1832 Poor Law, but began to receive renewed attention in expert circles in the late 1970s. This was due partly to emerging intellectual currents in the international public health field, to which British scholars and experts were well connected, and partly to the fact that British life expectancy had begun to fall behind that in other European countries. Two major reports on health inequalities in the United Kingdom, both commissioned by Labour governments and delivered into Conservative hands – the 1980 Black Report, which concerned all of the United Kingdom, and the 2010 Marmot Review for England – bookend the English case study. From 1980 to 2010, the Labour Party embraced health inequality as a political issue whose value derived from its connection to Labour's long-standing identity as the party of the National Health Service (NHS). After 1994, with the party's rebranding as New Labour, health inequality had even greater utility as a signal of commitment to social equality that nevertheless did not require overt discussion of redistribution. The major events in English politics and policy-making in the area of health inequality during this period are summarized in Table 4.1.

English health equity reports commissioned by Labour during the period 1980–2010 were, like the international consensus on health inequality, dominated by language about social inequality as a cause of health inequality. High-level recommendations for how to solve the problem of health inequalities have been closely aligned with this interpretation. However, there is slippage between this causal framing and the actual policies proposed in English documents as a solution to the problem (and still greater slippage when it comes to implementation). General treatment recommendations espoused in English health policy documents have proposed to fight the battle against health inequalities on two main fronts: by reducing income inequality and by reducing inequalities in the midstream social and environmental determinants of health. Policy recommendations, on the other hand, have focused further downstream, on attempts to reduce poverty and to coordinate actions on housing, transportation, education, community development, and the like in order to produce healthier physical and social environments. Interventions to reduce wage dispersion or limit the accumulation of wealth – both of which would be clearly supported by the British literature linking class inequality to health inequality – have been conspicuous in their absence.

This combination of a rhetorical linking of health inequalities to socioeconomic inequality and a practical focus on cross-sectoral policy-making rendered health inequality an irresistible political issue for a Labour Party that was struggling, by the mid-1990s, to shed the "loony left" moniker with which it had been branded by the media, and redefine itself as a party committed to equity but accepting of neoliberal policy orthodoxy (on the origins and content of the "loony left" label, see Petley 2005; J. Thomas 2005). The connection to class inequality made health inequalities seem like a natural issue for Labour, as the party of social equality, while the call for joined-up government and evidence-based interventions across a wide variety of policy areas shifted attention away from fundamental economic reforms and toward technocratic forms of governance.

Labour politicians avoided discussing inequality as a matter of class contestation over the fruits of the national economy, and instead adopted a technocratic discourse focused on social investment into which the health inequalities frame that had been developing at the international level fit neatly. Unlike in France and Finland – where, as we shall see, neoliberal challenges to the welfare state prompted policy-makers to reframe the problem of health inequality in a way that more closely matched the international consensus – in England health inequality since the Black Report (UK Department of Health and Social Security 1980) had all along been largely consistent with the international consensus

TABLE 4.1 *Timeline of major events in English health inequality politics*

Prime Minister	Years	Events
James Callaghan (Labour)	1977	Working Group on Inequalities in Health commissioned by government to produce Black Report .
Margaret Thatcher (Conservative)	1980	Black Report delivered; Labour Party conference resolution calls on next Labour government to implement Black Report's recommendations.
	1983	Labour Party campaigns on farthest-left platform in decades, loses decisively.
	1985	Labour Party leader Neil Kinnock delivers speech marking turning point between "old" and "New" Labour.
	1986	Health Education Council (HEC) commissions Margaret Whitehead to update Black Report's analysis.
	1987	Whitehead's *The Health Divide*, released in March, identifies growing homelessness, unemployment, and child poverty as threats to public health. In April, the HEC is disbanded by the government and replaced with the less powerful Health Education Authority.
John Major (Conservative)	1992	The Conservative health strategy, *Health of the Nation*, discusses health "variations" in passing.
	1995	*Variations in Health: What Can the Department of Health and the NHS Do?* (Metters Report) recommends substantial funding for research into health inequalities.
Tony Blair (Labour)	1997	Newly elected Labour government commissions Acheson Report to guide strategy to reduce health inequalities, appoints first-ever Minister for Public Health, and establishes cabinet committee to coordinate efforts of various government departments whose work affects public health.
	1998	Health Action Zones established with the goal of reducing health inequalities and improving population health through coordination of local activities.

Prime Minister	Years	Events
	1999	*Saving Lives: Our Healthier Nation* public health strategy emphasizes the goal of reducing health inequalities. Beginning of Sure Start program, a multisectoral initiative aimed at reducing health inequalities by addressing the conditions of children living in poverty.
	2001	Government sets targets for reducing inequalities in infant mortality and life expectancy to be achieved by 2010.
	2002	Treasury Department carries out Cross-Cutting Review to evaluate and better coordinate action on multiple social determinants of health. NHS reorganization replaces local authorities with smaller primary care trusts, fragmenting expertise and capacity.
	2003	Health Action Zones curtailed after failing to meet expectations for quick gains.
	2004	White Paper *Choosing Health: Making Healthy Choices Easier* emphasizes individual responsibility for health, government role offering information, advice, and support.
	2005	Public health standards included in assessment of performance of NHS bodies.
Gordon Brown (Labour)	2007	Department of Health releases *Tackling Health Inequalities: 10 Years On*, which reviews limited progress toward reducing health inequalities and highlights failures of cross-sectoral coordination and lack of progress in reducing inequalities in SDOH.
	2009	House of Commons Health Committee report highlights failure of cross-departmental coordination to reduce health inequalities. Brown government commissions external review of health inequalities in England from Sir Michael Marmot.
David Cameron (Conservative-Liberal Democratic coalition)	2010	Marmot Review for England delivered to Coalition government. Coalition public health strategy *Healthy Lives, Healthy People* prioritizes "personal responsibility" for health.

frame described in Chapter 3. Of course, this is in no small part because the Black Report and British policy advocates have had an exceptionally strong influence on the international consensus.

In English policy documents, health equity is defined primarily in terms of class or socioeconomic differences, rather than differences across populations defined by race, ethnicity, national origin, gender, or region of residence. These other group designations are not absent from research or from the policy debate, but socioeconomic status is the dominant lens through which health inequalities are reported and analyzed. Area-based analyses of social inequality, in which health outcomes are compared across postal codes, neighborhoods, local health authority boundaries, or other small areas, have become a prominent feature of academic research, and are also found in government reports and media coverage. To a very large extent, though, these area-based analyses are meant as a proxy for socioeconomic deprivation at the level of resident individuals or households, and/or at the level of the community as a whole.

English analysis of health inequalities as a policy problem has also focused mainly on health status outcomes such as mortality, morbidity, and self-assessed health, rather than on access to health care as an outcome of interest in its own right. There has also been periodic attention to problems of resource allocation across regions and localities within the NHS. However, the policy debate around health inequalities has long been premised on the notion that class-based inequalities in health status are surprising and unfair precisely because they exist *despite* the equalizing influence of universal access to health care free at the point of service.

In the English health inequality policy frame, then, the main causes of health inequalities are generally taken to lie outside the health care system. Many politicians and health policy-makers in England, attribute poorer health on the part of people with lower socioeconomic status (SES) may be attributed to "downstream" factors such as smoking, diet, and exercise, over which individuals are assumed to have control. Among experts, though, this behaviorist interpretation of health inequalities is generally recognized to be incomplete. Instead, the dominant causal stories explaining the existence of socioeconomic inequalities in health status are based in further-upstream social determinants that influence individual choices: class habitus and psychosocial pressures springing from economic deprivation shape individual choices about diet, alcohol, and tobacco consumption, for example. This causal story also acknowledges that these upstream social determinants have direct effects on health through the material conditions of living and working that are linked to the level of income – for example, housing quality, safe outdoor space, workplace safety, food availability, and the like.

A prominent and distinguishing feature of the English policy discourse around health inequalities has been the focus on class inequality, rather than simply economic deprivation, as a cause of health inequalities. Psychosocial dimensions of class position – the stress of unemployment, insecurity, or living in an area with multiple, concentrated forms of deprivation – as well as the class system itself play important roles in generating health inequalities. Some of the most influential contributors to British health inequalities policy debates, including Richard Wilkinson and Michael Marmot, have shown that health inequalities exist across the entire social gradient, and not only between the very deprived and the rest of society. Material and psychosocial dimensions of inequality have been consistently presented, from the Black Report to the Marmot Review (UK Secretary of State for Health 2010), as the primary underlying causes of health inequalities.

Epidemiological theory is one thing; governing is another. Labour's policy approach to health inequalities once in government recognized that poverty and social exclusion were harmful for health, but generally declined to make a strong link to income inequality. While still in opposition in 1996, Labour's spokesperson on health matters promised that "Labour will attack unjustifiable health inequalities," criticizing the Conservative government for "refus[ing] to address the problem with fairer economic, education, and employment policies." He promised that Labour "will use all the avenues open to us" but limited his recommendations to "developing a long-term strategy to lift people out of poverty and to secure opportunities for employment for all," "interdepartmental action to tackle health inequalities," and setting targets for health inequality reduction (Bayley et al. 1996, 6). Labour's 1997 manifesto similarly promised to "attack the root causes of ill health," enumerating "poverty, poor housing, unemployment, and a polluted environment" as key determinants (Labour Party Manifesto 1997). Reducing income inequality through redistributive taxation or regulating wages was not on Labour's official agenda, although in fact their policies once in office did direct more resources to lower-income people than had the Conservatives' policies. How and why did this reframing inequality from a matter of unequal income and wealth to one of unequal health come about?

SETTING THE STAGE: FROM THE BLACK REPORT TO
NEW LABOUR

Labour's framing of inequality as an issue of health in the 1980–2000s has its roots in a tradition dating back to the mid-1800s, when British social reformers became closely attuned to the link between social class and health. However, a hiatus in political attention to social inequalities in health occurred after the introduction of the National Health Service in 1947, because policy-makers presumed that universal access to medical care free at the point of service would eliminate these inequalities. In the 1970s, however, public health researchers and policy experts began to discover that this was not the case, and in 1977 the Labour government established a commission to report on health inequalities, to be chaired by Sir Douglas Black, chief scientist at the Department of Health and Social Security and President of the Royal College of Physicians (UK Department of Health and Social Security 1980). The commission's Black Report, as it came to be known, reintroduced the issue of health inequality into British politics, making it available for New Labour to mobilize it in the 1990s and 2000s as an alternate frame for equity that downplayed contentious issues of redistribution.

The key finding of the Black Report was that inequalities in mortality in Britain, which persisted despite universal access to free medical care, were due to class and income inequalities. The notion of social causation had been in circulation for well over a century, and researchers had been producing evidence to this effect in Britain for some years before the Black Report was released. But the Black commission's report would go on to be a central reference point for future research and policy on health inequalities not only in the United Kingdom, but throughout Europe. As described in Chapter 3, the international consensus framing of health inequalities was based in large part on the Black Report. The report was the first comprehensive, government-commissioned report devoted to the problem of health inequalities in any of the rich democracies, and its nine chapters plus appendices systematically reviewed all of the available research findings related to health inequalities in Britain.

The Black Report's main intellectual task was to evaluate alternative claims about the causes of health inequalities circulating in research circles at the time. The Working Group on Inequalities in Health had been commissioned in 1977 by Labour Secretary of State for Social Services David Ennals. Researchers and policy advocates who were involved with the Black Report have reported a number of possible motivations for its commissioning, including Britain's declining position in the world league-tables for mortality (Aiach and Carr-Hill 1989, 46; Townsend et al. 1992, 4–5); lingering concern over high mortality among coal miners (Berridge 2002, 134); the personal influence of poverty activist Brian Abel-Smith on Ennals (Berridge 2002, 133); epidemiologist Richard Wilkinson's open letter to Ennals, published in *New Society* in 1976 (Berridge 2002, 121); and hope that the report, whose release was initially planned to coincide with the thirtieth anniversary of the NHS, would show that there had been improvement in health inequalities (Berridge 2002, 132–33).

Whatever the precise motivations, Ennals expected that the report would be done in time for the Labour government to receive its recommendations. However, after drafting an initial version of the report in 1978, the members of the working group disagreed over whether hospital resources should be cut in order to free up resources for broader social interventions (Berridge 2002, 139), and the final version of the report was not completed until late 1979. In the meantime, early elections had been called, resulting in the election of a Conservative government led by Margaret Thatcher. Patrick Jenkin, Thatcher's Secretary of State for Social Services, received the working group's report and released it over the August bank holiday, declining to endorse its recommendations and producing only 260 copies. The Thatcher government's decision to minimize the impact of the report backfired spectacularly.

British medical journals remarked pointedly on the government's attempted "cover-up." Contemporary articles in the *Lancet* and the *British Medical Journal* bemoaned Jenkin's "frosty reception," "flat rejection," and "sustained campaign of demolition" of the report and its recommendations (quoted in Gray 1982, 373). Health-related trade union groups quickly published summaries of the report, and "quite exceptional efforts were made by bodies connected with the health and welfare services to bring the evidence and arguments in the report to a wide audience" (Townsend et al. 1992, 4–5). One correspondent for the *Lancet* wrote that the report had "acquired the novelty of an underground *samizdat* publication from Eastern Europe" (quoted in Gray 1982, 350). An interviewee who attended a pre-release presentation of the report's results in London admitted that at the time he was not appropriately impressed; he realized the importance of the report only later, when "efforts to suppress it made it more interesting" (interview INT4). Participants in the working group that produced the report recalled that the Labour Party and unions showed a great interest in the report after its suppression by the Thatcher government, and carried the issue forth throughout the period of the Conservative rule (Berridge 2002).

A resolution passed at the Labour Party conference in October 1980 called on the next Labour government to implement recommendations of the report when it came into office (Townsend et al. 1992, 5). Margaret Whitehead, who participated in the working group, noted that Labour and other political parties "'adopted' the report (and health inequalities in general) as a cause" (Whitehead 1998, 482) and used "health inequalities as a propaganda weapon" against the Thatcher government (p. 481). This did not go unnoticed by those on the receiving end. Writing for the Economic Intelligence Unit, a neoliberal think tank with strong ties to Thatcher, Rudolf Klein accused the Black Report's authors and supporters of using health inequalities "as a way of generating more political support in the battle against poverty: a campaign which was otherwise flagging" (Klein 1988, 9). "A new industry has developed," he said, "designed to demonstrate the link between deprivation and poor health, with a not so hidden agenda of trying to prove that Conservative policies are widening inequalities in health" (p. 10). He concluded that "[health] inequalities have, in effect, become political property" (p. 12).

The Thatcher government's reception of the Black Report and the response of policy experts and activists to that reception showed that the issue of health inequality could be a potent political weapon, even when the neoliberal climate made attention to other forms of inequality politically treacherous. Ongoing work by researchers and civil servants made it possible for Labour to take up the issue of health inequality in its campaigns against the Conservative government, which it did with increasing fervor at every passing election.

Thatcher's government downplayed the issue of health inequalities; for example, Secretary of State Jenkin attempted to dismiss the Black Report's findings, arguing that it did not adequately explain the causes of health inequalities and that therefore its expensive recommendations could not be implemented (Aiach and Carr-Hill 1989, 47). More generally, the Thatcher government "denied that health inequalities were caused by material factors and attributed them to statistical artifact, social mobility, or, more often than not, individual behavior" (Baggott 2010, 383). When it could not avoid addressing the issue, the government used the less inflammatory term "health variations" rather than inequalities.

However, ignoring the issue entirely proved difficult. The furor around the Thatcher government's handling of the report led, according to one member of the working group, to "an enormous growth of research interest in this area, the growth of networks of researchers, a kind of underground culture of inequalities research and debate which continued throughout the 80s and early 90s" ("History of the Black Report" 1999). In each year following the report there were at least forty publications on health inequalities in Britain (Macintyre 2002, 204). The Economic and Social Research Council, the Medical Research Council, the Health Education Authority, the British Medical Association, and the King's Fund all financed major research initiatives in the field in the 1980s and early 1990s (Macintyre 2002, 205). Data from Britain's first longitudinal study of mortality differentials, which had begun with the 1971 census, became available during this period and confirmed that inequalities in health were growing.

Alongside the boom in research on health inequalities, and despite an inhospitable environment in Parliament, policy-makers at the local level and within the civil service remained engaged with the issue of health inequalities. Local and regional initiatives to document and reduce health inequalities were given impetus by the growing international interest in health promotion, by WHO initiatives such as the Healthy Cities program and the Health For All strategy (to which the United Kingdom had signed on in 1985), and by personal contacts between public health researchers and professionals in the United Kingdom and abroad (see, e.g., Berridge et al. 2006, 29–36; interview INT4).

The civil service also helped to keep the issue of health inequality alive (Macintyre 2002, 209). One civil service body – the Health Education Council (HEC), an agency under the Secretary of State for Social Services – was a particular thorn in the side of the Thatcher government. A front-line public health practitioner at the time recalled that "a Tory government found the existence of [the HEC] and, indeed, health promotion, to be uncomfortable. As a new secretary of state appointee to the Council in 1981, I recall frequent challenges to policies and programmes from the [Department of Health and Social Security] 'minder'" (quoted in Berridge et al. 2006, 32). In 1986, the HEC commissioned Margaret Whitehead to update the Black Report's analysis. Her report, *The Health Divide*, which was released in March 1987, identified growing homelessness, unemployment, and child poverty as threats to public health, and criticized the government for failing to deal with these problems. Just after the report was released, in April 1987, the HEC was disbanded and replaced with the similarly named Health Education Authority, which, however, had significantly less autonomy (K. E. Smith and Bambra 2012, 104).

In 1992, John Major's Conservative government issued a new health strategy, *Health of the Nation*, which mentioned health "variations" only in passing (UK Secretary of State for Health 1992). But by the early 1990s, the growing impact of Conservative government policies on social inequality was becoming impossible to ignore. Poor health among lower-SES citizens was making it difficult for the government to achieve its overall targets for health improvement, and medical professionals, who could see the effects of growing poverty, unemployment, and homelessness in their practices, were growing critical of the government (Baggott 2010, 383–84). In 1994, the government responded to this pressure by establishing a committee to examine "what steps the Department of Health and the NHS should be taking to tackle variations" (Benzeval and Meth 2002, 205). Of course, as Marmot remarked, "That made life a little difficult for many of us on the committee as it concluded, in line with Black, that variations in health services were not the prime cause of variations in health" (Marmot 2001, 1166). The result was the 1996 report, *Variations in Health: What Can the Department of Health and the NHS Do?*, also known as the Metters Report, which recommended substantial funding for research into health inequalities, but otherwise could go little farther (Great Britain Department of Health 1996).

Despite the Thatcher and Major governments' attempts to downplay health inequalities, researchers and civil servants kept the issue alive throughout the Conservative period. Labour did not pass up the opportunity to use the issue of health inequalities to their political advantage. As one health inequalities researcher who was also a Labour Party activist at the time remarked, "The way we kicked the Tories was to say that they were literally killing people. Labour absolutely loved the early health inequalities [research] because it said you are child killers, your trickle-down isn't working" (interview UK4).

Labour's 1983 manifesto promised to "reduce inequalities in standards of health care for all those who need it," and announced plans to give greater emphasis to prevention and primary care within the NHS. It also promised to reestablish school meal and milk programs cut by the Tories, in order to "offset the inequalities, for example in nutrition, highlighted by the Black Report" (Labour Party Manifesto 1983). In 1987, Labour once again highlighted health inequality, noting that Tory rule had brought about "[e]ight years of growing division – in health, in opportunity, in housing conditions, in work, and in income – between regions, communities, classes, families, white and black, rich and poor." In 1992, Labour's manifesto made only a single reference to inequality, despite the fact that income inequality had risen quite dramatically under Thatcher – and it was to inequality in health. "We will set new targets to cut the inequalities in health between social classes and ethnic groups," promised Labour. The manifesto contained no mention of redistribution, proposing only "fair taxation" along with benefits changes that could be "self-financing" (Labour Party Manifesto 1992).

With the *British Medical Journal* publishing research showing that voters in Labour districts tended to have higher mortality (G. D. Smith and Dorling 1996; 1997), the 1997 Labour campaign manifesto outlined the party's vision "to tackle the division and inequality in our society." They promised to create a new minister for public health who "will attack the root causes of ill health, and so improve lives and save the NHS money." The party also vowed to "set new goals for improving the overall health of the nation which recognize the impact that poverty, poor housing, unemployment and a polluted environment have on health" (Labour Party Manifesto 1997). During the campaign, Labour emphasized the conservative government's failure to act on the Black Report, and their excessive focus on lifestyle choices as explanations for health inequalities. They also promised to launch their own follow-up to Black Report (K. E. Smith and Bambra 2012, 96), which they did almost immediately following the installation of the new government.

THE TABOO: HOW NEW LABOUR ADOPTED NEOLIBERALISM AND ABANDONED REDISTRIBUTION

Labour's adoption of health inequality as a key political issue during its campaigns of the 1990s occurred against the backdrop and as a result of another key decision: the decision by Labour's leadership to abandon redistribution as a political issue. Britain's encounter with neoliberalism, in the form of Thatcherism and Labour's eventual acquiescence to the idea that "there [was] no alternative" to it, generated the potential for political conflict that would threaten the very core of the liberal welfare regime. New Labour's decision to make redistribution politically taboo was in this sense both constitutive of and a response to the clash between a liberal welfare regime's core mechanism for ensuring redistribution – partisan alternation in government – and the most threatening aspect of neoliberalism in that context: partisan convergence on a neoliberal economic policy paradigm. This section describes how redistribution became a taboo topic for New Labour in this context.

Labour Made Redistribution Taboo

After the Second World War, both Labour and Conservative governments contributed to expanding the welfare state in Britain. But despite the construction of entitlements to universal, tax-financed public education, old-age and unemployment insurance schemes, and the National Health Service, Britain's remained a fundamentally liberal welfare regime. Residualist, means-tested income support measures implied that relatively little income redistribution would be carried out automatically through social insurance, and uncoordinated management of the liberal market economy meant that wage setting was either absent or the result of sporadic government intervention, rather than of institutionalized, solidaristic wage bargaining. To maintain inequality within acceptable bounds, then, the British welfare state relied not on the thick institutional apparatus characteristic of social democratic and conservative-corporatist welfare regimes and coordinated market economies, but instead on partisan politics: on periodic adjustments carried out by incumbent governments of tax, benefit, and wage policies that suited, in rough alternation, the working-class base of the center-left Labour Party and the economically better-off, who were represented by the Conservative Party.

Like most other rich countries, Britain in the late 1970s experienced a combination of inflation and societal unrest. Both of these were linked to the growing strength of organized labor at the end of the 1960s: wage gains made by workers contributed to high inflation (whose main cause was the rapid increase in oil prices), and labor unions' responses to the government's efforts to combat inflation by capping wages fed fears of social disorder and ungovernability. In the United Kingdom, this culminated in the 1978–79 "Winter of Discontent," during which public sector workers staged labor actions to protest wage caps. Against this backdrop, Margaret Thatcher's Conservative party successfully wrested control of government away from the Labour Party, and embarked on an ideologically motivated effort to transform the British society and economy, rather than simply managing it for the duration of her time in office.

Conservative policies, from Thatcher's immediate drive to dismantle the labor unions to the deliberate construction of a "stakeholder society" through privatization of state assets to eventual moves to expand the role of international financial markets in the British economy, not only led to a massive increase in socioeconomic inequalities in Britain, but also fundamentally reshaped the political landscape around inequality (Hopkin and Shaw 2016). The radical changes to British economic policy and the ideas underlying it that accompanied Thatcher's accession to power have been widely documented. Not all of Thatcher's attempts to restructure the economy and the welfare state were successful, but the policy ideas that Thatcher brought to government transformed the postwar Keynesian economic policy consensus (P. Hall 1986). Under the emergent neoliberal paradigm, economic growth and social stability would be secured not by ensuring that the mass of workers had adequate incomes to consume and spur new investment, but by releasing the productive forces of capital from the constraints of government regulation and the necessity to cooperate with labor.

The basic tenets of Thatcherism – freer markets, less regulation, prioritizing control of inflation over growth of employment and wages – justified policies that created a surge in inequality in Britain. The Thatcher government passed laws that cut income tax rates across the board, leading to greater gains for high earners; severely restricted the mobilization capacities of private and public sector trade unions, often buttressing the restrictions with the use of police force; privatized national industries; and encouraged the City of London's emergence as a lightly regulated trading center for international financial capital. Predictably, income inequality rose dramatically under the Conservatives.

The first years of the Thatcher government were economically rocky, marked by high unemployment and a recession. Hoping the working class's economic woes would carry them to victory, Labour ran its farthest-left campaign in decades in 1983. By that time, however, the economy in general had improved, and the war in the Falklands had bolstered the government's popularity. Some centrist Labour MPs defected to form the Social Democratic Party (SDP), which resulted in Labour losing a number of marginal constituencies, and the Conservatives gaining a large majority in parliament.

After its crushing loss in 1983, the Labour Party began the process of transforming itself from a labor-based party into one that could win the votes of "Middle England." Labour's defeat in 1983 was probably a result of several factors: the party's self-positioning played a role, but so too did Thatcher's skillful mobilization of nationalist sentiment around the war in the Falklands, increasingly hostile press coverage of the "loony left," and the defection of Labour's right wing to form a new party. Nevertheless, subsequent analyses and self-analyses of the Labour defeat in 1983 focused on Labour's sharp rhetorical and programmatic turn to the left during the campaign. In a corrective move, centrist currents within the Labour Party assumed control, and began to shift Labour's approach to achieving social equality rightward. During this period, Labour engaged in a deep but also quite public introspection about its goals, policies, and language, particularly with respect to inequality, redistribution, and class. The end result was the birth of a "New" Labour, a party whose leadership would no longer speak about or advocate redistribution as the route to a more equitable society.

Labour nevertheless remained a center-left party. That meant retaining a commitment to economic equality and social justice, two hallmark principles that had, in various guises, defined the British left since the Victorian era (Jackson 2007). What changed was not the commitment to an equitable society but the Labour leadership's beliefs about what types of solutions would bring about equality and the language that party leaders used to discuss the problem of inequality. Under New Labour, any discussion of income redistribution became quite explicitly taboo (Cook 2004; Irvin 2008). Of the forty-nine Labour Party leader speeches in the online British Political Speech Archive for 1984–2010, only three contain the word redistribution ("British Political Speech" n.d.). The first of these speeches, Kinnock's 1985 Parliamentary Report, was subsequently regarded as the speech that marked the turning point between "old" and "New" Labour. In this speech, Kinnock promises to do what is needed to shed Labour's "reputation of being a party that is solely concerned with redistribution, of being a party much more concerned about the allocation of wealth than the creation of wealth" (Kinnock 1985).

Labour Party manifestos of the period are similarly reticent on the issue of redistribution. During the 1983 electoral campaign, Labour had announced plans "for the redistribution of wealth and power in our society," promising to "reform taxation so that the rich pay their full share" and to "reduce the huge inequalities in inherited wealth" (Labour Party Manifesto 1983). But by 1987, even while noting that Tory rule had brought growing class divisions, systematic redistribution was not offered as a solution (Labour Party Manifesto 1987). Instead, there was a more limited promise to reverse Thatcher's tax cuts on the richest 5 percent of Britons and to "allocate that money instead to the most needy" (Labour Party Manifesto 1987). By 1992, Labour's manifesto contained no mention of redistribution, despite the fact that income inequality had risen dramatically since 1979. In 1992, Labour replaced their plans for a wealth tax with a slightly more progressive income tax under the mild banner of "fair taxation," promised to make tax and benefits changes that were "self-financing," and made only a single reference to inequality, which concerned not income or wealth, but health: "We will set new targets to cut the inequalities in health between social classes and ethnic groups" (Labour Party Manifesto 1992).

While Labour did promise in its 1997 manifesto to introduce a "reasonable" national minimum wage (set "not on the basis of a rigid formula but according to the economic circumstances of the time"), its program made it clear that Labour was not planning to return to its socialist roots when it came to running the economy. The party pledged not to increase income tax on average or high earners for at least its first five years in office (though it planned to reduce high marginal tax rates on low incomes), not to exceed the public spending levels planned by the Tories for two years after the election, and to maintain a target inflation rate of 2.5 percent (Labour Party Manifesto 1997).

The Labour Party's taboo on discussing redistribution was not merely a matter of rhetoric. Labour remained committed, as it always had been, to a vision of a more equitable society, but the type of equality that New Labour espoused was truly new (for Labour). It presumed that outcomes produced by the market were fair, as long as there was equal opportunity for participation in paid work (Hickson 2004, 130; Levitas 2005). The policies that Labour pursued while in office conformed to this new vision of inequality: there was substantial redistribution toward the very bottom of the income distribution, but the growth of high incomes went unchecked, and wealth accumulation was relatively lightly taxed. The policy approach could be summed up in New Labour architect Peter Mandelson's now famous off-the-cuff remark to a group of computer executives in California in 1989: "We are intensely relaxed about people getting filthy rich as long as they pay their taxes." While Labour maintained its belief in the possibility of public action for the collective good, it had accepted "the gospel of market fundamentalism" (S. Hall 2003, 19, 13–14).

Why Labour Made Redistribution Taboo

Why did Britain's main center-left party change its basic orientation toward the problem of inequality so dramatically from the early 1980s to the late 1990s? At one level, of course, changes in party organization that ensured the victory of Labour's "modernizing" wing over the old left factions were essential preconditions for the philosophical and policy changes of New Labour to have any effect. But these organizational changes were largely endogenous to changes in the balance of power already under way in the party. Labour adopted its new attitude toward inequality and redistribution partly out of fear: fear that the rhetoric of redistribution would not appeal to a rising middle class, which made up the bulk of their potential electorate by 1997, and fear of being labeled by the newspapers and the business elite as economically incompetent and unfriendly to capital. However, while fear may have been responsible for Labour's initial decision to try to court a different kind of voter using different language around inequality, there was also, as we shall see, an element of true belief.

Chief among the Labour leadership's worries when the taboo against redistribution emerged was a fear that their core working-class electorate was shrinking (Heath et al. 2001, chapters 2 and 5). According to two of the most comprehensive studies of the Labour electorate during this period, the Labour leadership was largely correct in their assessment of the sociological shifts under way (Heath et al. 2001; Evans and Tilley 2017). By the mid-1980s, Labour's traditional base among unionized working-class voters had shrunk considerably as a share of the electorate from its postwar peak. This process was related in part to broader technological changes taking part throughout the advanced economies, but was also accelerated by Thatcher's policies that weakened unions and reduced employment in highly unionized sectors. Working-class voters by and large retained a sense of class distinctiveness, a distaste for inequality, and an appetite for redistribution – but they had become too few in number to dominate Labour's electorate (Evans and Tilley 2017, chapters 2–4). Blair was correct, then, in remarking in 1992 that Labour had lost the last four elections because "society had changed and we did not change sufficiently with it" (quoted in Sopel 1995, 138).

Labour leaders further diagnosed the desires of the aspiring middle-class electorate to which they would need to appeal as fundamentally antithetical to taxation and redistribution: "When the majority were have-nots, and the vested interests that held them back were those of wealth and capital, the idea of people acting together, through the state, to reform social conditions and redistribute power became a strong political force," Blair said in June 1992. However, he went on to say that "the majority of people, as they prospered, earned more and began to pay the tax to fund the state, became more skeptical of its benefits" (quoted in Cronin 2004, 336). Indeed, another key modernizer, Mo Mowlam, went so far as to say that "we exist as a party to make people as affluent and free as possible.... People want more money, a decent house, a good car – and so do all of us in the Labour Party" (quoted in Cronin 2004, 336). To a large extent, then, Labour leaders rejected the rhetoric of redistribution because they feared that it did not fit with the preferences of the electorate that they needed to reach.

Evidence from long-running social surveys might have put their mind at rest. Throughout the 1990s, between 65 and 95 percent of people in all occupation and education groups told the British Social Attitudes Survey that "the gap between those with high and low incomes is too large," numbers that had in fact increased since the mid-1980s. At the time Labour decided to stop mentioning "the R word" (redistribution), between 40 and 70 percent of respondents, depending on their income or education, agreed that "the government should redistribute income from the better-off to those who are less well-off" (McKnight and Tsang 2013, 100–103). Nevertheless, Labour's public diagnosis of its electoral failures rested on mistaken beliefs about voter preferences. In an earlier era, Labour leaders had expected to mobilize the party's electorate around a vision of the good society, shaping voter preferences rather than simply responding to them (Heath et al. 2001, 5). Labour's rejection of redistribution thus suggests that more had to change in Britain than just the makeup of the electorate, to so fundamentally reshape the party's approach to economic and social policy.

Labour feared not only the voters, but how Britain's increasingly antagonistic newspapers would portray their policies to voters. As one interviewee described it, Labour politicians "are totally driven by the reaction of the newspapers .... They've been scarred" (interview UK5). As recently as 2003 more than half of Britons were still regular newspaper readers (Evans and Tilley 2017, 92), so what the national papers said mattered. The press's particularly virulent coverage of Labour's campaign in 1992 loomed large in the party's thinking. Thomas's (2005) study of partisan press coverage supports this view, as did the *Sun*'s famously self-congratulatory, all-caps headline the morning after the election, "IT'S THE SUN WOT WON IT."

In order to prevent a repeat of what happened in 1992, Labour worked hard to engineer a less contentious relationship with the media. Their ultimate success in this endeavor was enabled by media-hostile policies undertaken by the Conservatives, by John Major's lesser charisma, and by the Labour Party's own discipline and savvy in relation to the media. In fact, so successful were they in courting the approval of the press, particularly Murdoch-owned papers, that Labour leaders were later accused of betraying their voters in order to attract the papers' endorsement (J. Thomas 2005, chapter 6).

While in opposition, Labour sought to convince not only the public and the media, but also business leaders, that a Labour government would be both competent and friendly to capital. In the delightfully monikered "prawn cocktail offensive," Shadow Chancellor John Smith and close Blair associate MP Mo Mowlam met key members of the financial services industry in a series of private lunches to reassure them of Labour's friendly intentions. Labour politicians operated in the shadow of the finance industry's considerable structural power. This was perhaps less evident during the campaigns of the 1990s than it was once Labour assumed office. Labour's spending plans relied heavily on continued growth of the finance sector, which was so large that, despite being rather lightly taxed, it supplied almost 14 percent of total tax revenues in 2007 (Hopkin and Shaw 2016, 358). Stamp duties on the residential real estate market, whose value was also inflated by a permissive financial regulatory environment, were another important source of revenue for the government. With the potential veto power of the finance sector, it is not surprising that Labour would rather appear to be "intensely relaxed" about high income growth occurring in the finance sector than to advertise any redistributive intentions.

If Labour's taboo against discussing redistribution was linked to social changes in the electorate and the potential veto power of the press and capital holders, at the end of the day it was also about ideas. Labour modernizers' disdain for a heavy-handed state and appreciation for freer markets as the engine of growth seems to have sprung from genuine conviction. This was likely due to both changes in the social class background of Labour leadership and a shift in the intellectual *zeitgeist*.

Much as Labour's electorate transformed during the 1980s and 1990s from a working-class one into a middle-class one, changes in party recruitment and selection during this period also generated a sociological shift within the party leadership. The new slate of Labour MPs who entered parliament in 1997 were overwhelmingly middle class and university educated, in contrast to those in older cohorts who were more likely to have backgrounds in organized labor. Labour MPs are now no less likely to have attended university than are Conservative ones, and the gap between the parties in the share of MPs having attended Oxford or Cambridge has nearly closed (Evans and Tilley 2017, chapter 7). These changes accelerated dramatically in the period between 1985 and 1997, precisely when Labour's language and policy efforts were pivoting away from working-class concerns. As Labour's leadership has become less likely to have been recruited through the trade unions, and more likely to have come out a background of higher education and political internships (Cairney 2007), they may have also become more likely to believe that an economy geared around the needs of capital is a good idea.

However, this central tenet of neoliberalism is in fact so widely accepted in British politics that it may not be necessary to attach its rise within the party to Labour MPs' changing occupational or educational background. Thatcher had succeeded in constructing a hegemonic neoliberal belief structure (Gamble 1996). From the mid-1980s, key elements of Thatcherism had produced "a transformed discourse which continues to be drawn on in official texts by the Labour Party .... By the beginning of the 1990s, it had become the dominant discourse of political debate in Britain" (Phillips 1998, 853). At the level of ideology, elements of liberalism and neoliberalism had become prominent in Labour's approach, particularly as concerned questions of social justice and equality (see, e.g., Hay 1999; Driver and Martell 2002, chapter 4; S. Hall 2003; Hickson 2004; Shaw 2007). New Labour did not echo Thatcherism in every detail of its discourse and policies, but Labour leaders came to share the core goal of neoliberalism as described by Ban (2016): to make economic policy that would avoid antagonizing finance or impairing international competitiveness, in order to ensure that Britain could grow while remaining open to international markets.

In sum, then, despite evidence from public opinion surveys in the 1990s that showed that a majority of Britons thought inequality was too high, the British Labour Party dropped redistribution from its vocabulary. The reasons for this include the decline of working-class voters as a share of Labour's electorate and a subsequent desire to appeal to middle-class voters, concerns not to antagonize the "capitalist press," the growing importance of the finance sector as a source of tax revenue with which to undertake social programs, and the diffuse but pervasive ideological hegemony of neoliberalism in a post-Thatcher era.

The taboo against advocating redistribution of income and wealth between classes as the means to a more equitable society rendered the main mechanism for containing inequality in the liberal welfare regime, partisan alternation in office, inert. Nevertheless, the Labour Party and many of its leaders and policy-makers remained committed to the end goal of equity. As one interviewee in a high-level policy position said, "Generally politicians don't like to talk too much about inequality, but nobody wants to be *for* inequality, either" (interview UK2). This tension provided an opening for health inequality policy advocates to push the issue of reducing health inequality to the fore of Labour's discourse: if Labour took up the issue of health inequality, it could remain committed to equity but avoid talking about redistribution.

INEQUALITY REFRAMED: FROM CLASS INEQUALITY TO SOCIAL INVESTMENT AND HEALTH

That British political discourse about inequality changed between the 1970s and the 2000s is undeniable. Figure 4.1 shows the relative prevalence of discussion about economic redistribution versus health inequalities in the parliamentary record. There is a decline from 1970 to 2004 in the number of distinct interventions by MPs and Ministers discussing redistributive policy, while interventions regarding health inequalities increased substantially after 1985.[1] In 1997, the

---

[1] I searched the historic Hansard database of parliamentary records (http://hansard.millbanksystems.com/search, accessed May 24, 2017) using two search strings: "'health inequality'" (quotation marks included in the search string) and "tax income redistribution" (quotation marks not included). These search strings were developed iteratively to balance sensitivity and specificity. I retrieved all entries in the Hansard database for the 1970–2004 parliamentary seatings in which variants on the search terms appeared. Entries containing the words "Scotland" or "Scottish" were omitted in order to restrict discussions to England, which is the focus of health inequalities

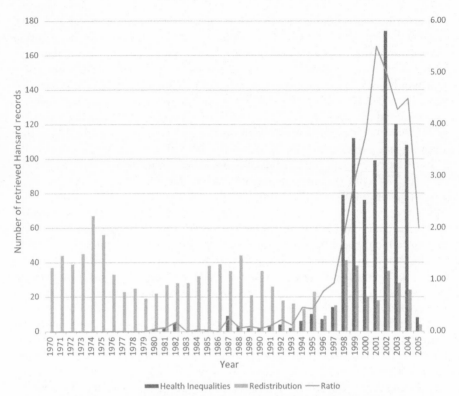

FIGURE 4.1 Change over time in parliamentary speech about redistribution versus health inequalities. Left axis: number of records retrieved; right axis: ratio of health inequalities to redistribution mentions. Records retrieved from database of parliamentary records, 1970–2004. Search strings were "'health inequality'" (quotation marks included in the search string) and "tax income redistribution" (quotation marks not included); variants on those words and phrases were also retrieved. Records containing "Scotland" or "Scottish" were excluded.

Source: Historic Hansard database (https://api.parliament.uk/historic-hansard/index.html, accessed May 24, 2017)

first year of Labour's government, there were more than five times as many parliamentary interventions related to health inequalities than to income taxation or redistribution.

Some of this change was due to Labour's changing approach to the politics of inequality. We have already seen that Labour's party manifestos in the 1980s

policy made in Westminster after devolution in 1998. Since many entries contained interventions by multiple speakers, I was unable to cleanly distinguish between speech by Labour and non-Labour MPs.

and 1990s took up the issue of health inequalities while gradually abandoning discussion of class inequality and redistribution. Manifestos are of course a very partial selection of political discourse, and are read by less than one-third of voters (Dathan 2015). But British parties are often held accountable for failing to meet key pledges, and manifestos are useful for analysis of framing because parties do play close attention to their construction (Bogdanor 2015). The fact that health inequality appears in Labour manifestos just as redistribution disappears lends some textual confirmation to the claims of secondary sources (from both the left and the right of the political spectrum) that Labour sought to politicize the issue of health inequalities, and to do so in a way that allowed them to bolster their claim to be a champion of social equality more broadly.

It also supports a contention of several policy advisors and activists whom I interviewed: that the party leadership was interested in the issue of health inequality in part because it allowed them to avoid the taboo topic of redistribution. According to a Labour MP centrally involved with health policy, health inequalities was taken up as an issue in the 1980s mainly because it was a way of discussing inequality that did not create further division between the left and right wings of the party: "It was an issue that the left and right of the party would have agreed on. The right of the party was probably closer to being socialist on this issue than in any other part of their world view" (interview UK1). A former policy advisor to the Blair government explained that "[t]he Labour government didn't define their agenda in terms of addressing income or wealth inequalities. But they were committed to a focus on equity more generally." As a result, they were keen to work on health inequalities – but they "didn't want to explicitly address income inequality. They would *never* have framed what they were doing in terms of reducing the gap between the rich and the poor. That would be political suicide" (interview UK3). "They are keen to talk about health inequalities," an external observer noted, "providing they don't have to talk about income and wealth inequalities" (interview UK5).

This unwillingness to advocate redistribution as a solution for health inequalities is not surprising in light of what we already know about Labour's taboo against discussing redistribution, but it is at odds with the advice that the party was receiving from experts about how to reduce health inequalities. At the behest of former NHS Chief Medical Officer Donald Acheson, who hoped that the incoming Labour government would establish a standing royal commission on health inequality, the King's Fund had published a report on the issue of health inequality in 1995 (Benzeval et al. 1995).[2] The report contained numerous specific recommendations for policies that a future government could pursue in order to reduce health inequalities, organized

---

[2] Fearing that the report's conclusion was too radical and would "rock the boat" with Labour, Acheson distanced himself from the report's conclusions, declining to participate in any publicity surrounding its release (K. Judge, personal communication, 2018).

according to Dahlgren and Whitehead's rainbow model of causation (WHO Regional Office for Europe 1991). The report included, in addition to recommendations for reducing inequalities in downstream and midstream health determinants, a series of interventions designed to affect upstream economic inequalities: abolish the ceiling on taxable income for national insurance contributions, reduce tax deductions for higher-income earners, increase the top income tax rate, and shift the balance of taxation from regressive consumption taxes to more progressive income taxes. The authors of the report recognized that "taking money from large numbers of people" would be politically difficult, and so further recommended that "in pressing for such measures there should also be nurtured a political consensus for the purposes for which the money is spent" (Benzeval et al. 1995, 80). In other words, a Labour government setting out to reduce health inequalities must persuade the public of the need to tax and redistribute.

Ken Judge, one of the report's authors, met regularly with the Labour shadow secretaries for health and their chief advisors before Blair's government was installed, and communicated the report's policy recommendations directly (K. Judge, personal communication, 2018). A 1996 policy brief from the Labour think tank Institute for Public Policy Research (IPPR) (Coote and Hunter 1996), which outlined a general approach to health inequalities for the party, also referred its readers to the King's Fund report for policy specifics. The contents of the report, then, would have been known to party leaders. However, the incoming Labour government did not take up the report's recommendations regarding income inequality. Indeed, it did not accept the King's Fund report as a policy blueprint at all, instead charging a new commission, led by Donald Acheson, with developing a health inequalities policy agenda for the government.

During the campaign Labour had said "that we would have a new Black Report" (Labour MP, quoted in Smith 2013a, 76), and the Acheson Report (1998) was their answer to that promise. But rather than taking the Black Report's recommendations as a starting point, the government asked the inquiry team to "conduct – *within the broad framework of the Government's overall financial strategy* – an independent review to identify priority areas for future policy development" that would be "likely to offer opportunities for Government to develop beneficial, cost effective, and affordable interventions to reduce health inequalities" (UK Secretary of State for Health 1998, 156, emphasis added). The government promised that evidence-based conclusions of the Acheson Report would be the basis for its health policy (K. E. Smith and Bambra 2012, 96).

The Acheson Report made thirty-nine main recommendations, encompassing seventy-four subsidiary recommendations. Three of the recommendations were singled out as "crucial": health impact assessment for all policies likely to affect health, prioritizing the health of families with children, and taking steps to "reduce income inequalities and improve the living standards of poor households" (UK Secretary of State for Health 1998, xi). At a conceptual level, then, the Acheson Report was clearly concerned with the relationship between health and both inequality and poverty. The authors noted that "available evidence is insufficient to confirm or deny a causal relationship between changes in income distribution and the parallel deterioration in inequalities in some areas of ill health," but asserted that "[n]evertheless, we take the view that these changes are likely to be related." They also asserted that "[t]he penalties of inequalities in health affect the whole social hierarchy and usually increase from the top to the bottom," and accordingly promised to "[address] the socioeconomic determinants of health as they affect the whole social spectrum" (UK Secretary of State for Health 1998, xi).

As the Acheson Report moved from causal theories to policy recommendations, however, concrete plans to reduce socioeconomic inequality as a way of reducing health inequalities fell by the wayside. The three concrete policy recommendations related to "reducing income inequalities and improving living standards" did not include any of the redistributive tax measures recommended by the King's Fund report, nor those cited in the Acheson review's own analysis, which had established that a "fairer tax system" could boost the incomes of lower-wage earners and that "shifting the tax burden from regressive to more progressive forms of taxation and fiscal policies ... would help mitigate the effects of income inequalities." The Acheson Report instead limited itself to interventions on the benefits side: increasing benefits in cash or in kind to reduce poverty among women of childbearing age, expectant mothers, young children, and older people (recommendation 3.1); increasing welfare benefits and pensions to "narrow the gap between their standard of living and average living standards" (recommendation 3.2); and unspecified measures designed to increase the take-up rate of means-tested benefits.

The report justified this approach by noting that "[f]or the least well-off members of society ... it is the benefit system which is the principal determinant of living standards" and that the difference between the incomes of those who relied on means-tested benefits – which included almost a quarter of all households – and those with other income was a "major determinant of income inequality." But focusing on upgrading social benefits rather than addressing the income distribution as a whole made even more political than economic sense. The mandate to the Acheson review committee was clear: come up with policy proposals "within the broad framework of the Government's overall financial strategy" – a framework that included a Labour Party campaign promise not to increase spending above the level projected by the outgoing Conservative government for three years. The report accordingly noted approvingly where the government had already made commitments to act to reduce poverty and applauded its initiatives for a minimum wage and reforms to the tax system that would incentivize working-age people receiving means-tested benefits to move into employment.

Michael Marmot, who served on the Acheson review commission, remarked, "We took the view that as a scientific group we were charged, as stated in our terms of reference, with 'identifying priority areas for future policy development,' not with telling the finance minister at what level to set the rate of taxation and benefits" (quoted in Exworthy 2002, 181). However, given that the report did make several other very specific policy recommendations, it seems likely that the members of the commission demurred because they did not believe that pressure to reduce inequality further would be welcome by the government. Benefits reform, on the other hand, was already on the government's agenda, and that is where the report focused its recommendations with regard to income.

The Acheson Report, in declining to advocate income distribution, set the tone for subsequent government policy (Pickett and Dorling 2010). Since the Acheson Report, "[o]bjectives have always been defined very vaguely, referring at best to the general concept of 'reducing' or 'tackling' health inequalities. Similarly, the targets selected appear either limited in scope or not entirely consistent with the emphasis placed on the socioeconomic dimension of health inequalities" (Sassi 2005, 89). The problem of income inequality, both as it related to health inequalities and elsewhere in New Labour's policy agenda, was overwhelmingly conceptualized as a problem of poverty, not inequality.

Labour sought to alleviate poverty through several types of policy approaches. Cash transfers and tax expenditures directed at families with children and pensioners were upgraded, resulting in a significant reduction of poverty among both groups. As unemployment was known to be a chief cause of poverty, the Blair government changed the tax code to remove disincentives to part-time and low-wage work, and introduced a series of New Deals aimed at, inter alia, young people, the long-term unemployed, single parents, and people with disabilities. The New Deals combined individualized counseling, training in basic skills designed to enhance employability, and, in the case of youth and long-term unemployed, mandatory transitions from welfare to work. Finally, the Blair government introduced a National Minimum Wage, which had been a key pledge of Labour campaigns for years. The low level at which the minimum wage was set, as well as the fact that most minimum-wage workers were not primary breadwinners and not living in poor households, meant that the minimum wage policy did not have a significant effect on overall poverty rates (Gregg 2010). Nevertheless, taken as a whole the Blair government's initiatives to reduce poverty did have an effect on low incomes, especially among pensioners and lone-parent families with children.

But poverty and inequality are distinct phenomena with quite different relationships to health, and poverty and inequality do not always move together; thus, attempting to reduce health inequalities only by reducing poverty is unlikely to be successful. As we saw in Chapter 3, some materialist explanations for health inequalities draw on strong associations between absolute material deprivation, such as would be experienced by those in a state of poverty, and ill health. Psychosocial and political explanations, on the other hand, point to equally robust associations between experiencing *relatively* low income (or, more often, relatively low social status associated with lower income) and poor health, and argue that socioeconomic inequality itself, above and beyond poverty, creates health inequalities. If reducing poverty necessarily resulted in reducing inequality, one could hope to kill the materialist, psychosocial, and political birds with one stone. However, there was no logically necessary link between poverty and inequality, even with the relative poverty measure (60 percent of median size-adjusted disposable household income) preferred by Labour.

On the one hand (and despite Conservatives' assertions to the contrary [Lansley 2011]), it was theoretically entirely possible to eliminate relative poverty by bringing households in poverty above the 60 percent of median income threshold and without moving anyone who was below the median to above it. This could be achieved in practice by upgrading social benefits and introducing a modest minimum wage, without making major changes that would benefit earners in the 40–50th percentiles of the income distribution. The result would be a dramatic reduction in poverty without affecting the position of the lower middle class relative to higher earners. Inequality could also rise without increasing poverty if (some) incomes above the median were to rise rapidly, but incomes below the median grew at a slower rate. A combination of these two scenarios – impressive improvements for poor households, modest growth in the middle of the distribution, and very large increases in net top incomes despite some taxation – was exactly what occurred under Labour (see Gregg 2010 for a comprehensive discussion), leading Acheson eventually to complain before the House of Commons in 2000, "I should like to see some more redistribution of wealth" (Sir Donald Acheson, House of Commons, 2000, question 116, quoted in Sassi 2005, 78).

In addition to anti-poverty initiatives, efforts to reduce inequalities in the distribution of other social determinants of health took place across a wide variety of policy areas during the Labour governments of 1997–2010. In 2001, the Joseph Rowntree Foundation commissioned a review, published in 2003, of progress in implementing the recommendations of the Acheson Report (Exworthy et al. 2003). The review team mapped policy actions taken in each of the seventy-four areas identified by the Acheson Report and found that a number of government departments and agencies had taken steps toward implementing the recommended policies. The most active, according the review, were the Departments of Health; Education and Skills; Work and Pensions; Environment, Food and Rural Affairs; and Transport, Local Government, and the Regions (later the Office of the Deputy Prime Minister and Department for Transport) (Exworthy et al. 2003, 9). After 2002, the treasury took on a larger role, joining the Department of Health in coordinating policy activity across multiple sectors – though it still declined to put its own, powerful policy levers of taxation and macroeconomic policy to work reducing health inequalities (Exworthy et al. 2003; Sassi 2005).

In line with a government-wide emphasis on "Joined-Up Government," the Blair government also initiated a number of cross-sectoral efforts to reduce health inequalities. Even before the Acheson Report was formally released, the government introduced its Health Action Zone program, which targeted health inequalities in twenty-six deprived areas of England through multiagency partnership actions coordinated at the local level. Health Action Zones focused on health behaviors, employment, housing, education, and substance abuse, among other issues. The Health Action Zones were small enough to allow for significant local autonomy in priority setting and methods of actions, and were conceived essentially as pilot programs, receiving only "relatively modest resources accompanied by guidance – more evangelical than practical – from central government" (House of Commons Health Committee 2009). The Health Action Zone program ended in 2003.

The Sure Start program, loosely modeled on the Head Start program in the United States, was introduced in 1999 as a multisectoral initiative aimed at reducing health inequalities by addressing the conditions of children living in poverty (the Labour government had promised to halve child poverty by 2010 and eradicate it by 2020). The main elements of the initiative, which was targeted initially at the most deprived areas, were increasing the availability of child care, improving health and development among children, and supporting parental employment.

At the national level, the government put into place a number of working groups, task forces, and reviews in order to facilitate joined-up working. A specialized Cross-Government Group on Public Health and Inequalities was formed, and supplemented the work of several other cross-departmental units, such as the Social Exclusion Unit and the Sure Start Unit, whose work bore directly on health inequalities. And in 2002, the treasury was asked to carry out a Cross-Cutting Review to evaluate and better coordinate action across government departments.

Despite Labour's causal analysis that health inequalities were rooted in social determinants, the health sector also played an important, even dominant, role in health inequalities policy. The Cross-Government Group on Public Health and Inequalities was led by the Department of Health, and NHS bodies played a critical role in the Health Action Zones. It was the Department of Health that advised setting health inequalities targets (reducing income difference in infant mortality and geographic inequalities in mortality), which the government did in 2001. The NHS itself was charged with reducing health inequalities by reducing inequalities in access to care; meeting disease-specific targets for reducing inequalities in, for example, cardiovascular disease and cancer; and appointing Directors of Public Health to coordinate health inequality reduction efforts by local and regional bodies of the NHS. Starting in 2002, NHS funding to local areas was also tied to the size of health inequalities.

Labour continued to highlight health inequality as a political issue even after the first few years of its strategy had failed to produce meaningful reductions.

Labour's manifesto for the 2002 general election included a pledge "to improve the nation's health" by "tackl[ing] the longstanding causes of ill-health and health inequality." Their strategy included fighting against cancer, heart disease, and stroke; reducing deaths in poorer communities and among poor children; improving prevention and screening; offering smoking cessation services; and (in a pledge reminiscent of Herbert Hoover's 1928 promise to put a "chicken in every pot") giving "a piece of free fruit every day" to schoolchildren aged four to six years (Labour Party Manifesto 2001).

Perhaps reflecting growing concern about the slow progress of the government's initiatives to reduce health inequalities, in 2005 Labour began to back away from its materialist, structural framing of the problem and instead reverted to the classic behavioralist tropes of promoting personal responsibility for health lifestyles. Labour's plan was to reduce health inequalities between the rich and poor by introducing "health trainers" to "help people maintain their healthy choices" (Labour Party Manifesto 2005). Nevertheless, health inequalities continued to play an important political role for the party until the financial crisis overshadowed the issue beginning in 2008.

Internal policy documents issued during Gordon Brown's government continued to prioritize government action on the social and economic determinants of health, and in 2009, Brown's government commissioned an external review of health inequalities in England in anticipation of the expiry in 2010 of the health inequalities targets set after the Acheson Report (UK Secretary of State for Health 2010). To lead the report, they chose Michael Marmot, who had participated in the Acheson review committee and who had just completed a high-profile stint as chair of the WHO's Global Commission on the Social Determinants of Health. Marmot was publicly committed to the social determinants model of causation and to the impact of inequality above and beyond material deprivation in driving health inequalities. Not surprisingly, given Marmot's intellectual pedigree, the review emphasized the social gradient in health and the need for society to act to counter the "organization of misery"[3] created by underlying socioeconomic inequality. However, recognizing the limitations imposed by the outgoing Labour government's commitment to austerity policies in the wake of the financial crisis of 2008, as well as the fact that the report would be delivered into the hands of a Conservative government, the Marmot Review made few concrete recommendations about how a reduction in underlying inequality might be achieved, instead focusing on upgrading minimum income benefits and acting on midstream social determinants.

By 2010, Labour's manifesto for the general elections made no mention of inequality, not even health inequalities. Labour's platform with regard to health

---

[3] The epigraph to the report is a quote from Chilean socialist and poet Pablo Neruda: "Rise up with me against the organisation of misery."

mainly concerned the NHS, with population health reduced to a private affair: "We all have a responsibility to look after our own health, supported by our family and our employer." Labour promised that "[t]he ambitious Change 4 Life programme will support a more active, health-conscious country" (Labour Party Manifesto 2010). However, this program was essentially limited to exhorting Britons to eat better and exercise more. By the end of Labour's time in government, then, health inequality had been disconnected from the problem of income or class inequality, and had lost the potential to reduce inequality in either health or its upstream causes.

CONCLUSION

Neoliberal ideas and policies reshaped Britain in the years following Margaret Thatcher's election in 1979 in a way that probably even she would not have dreamed possible: the opposition Labour Party came first to believe, and then to embody, Thatcher's famous slogan, "There is no alternative." Ideological and policy convergence between the Conservative and Labour parties had an unintended consequence, however. Convergence meant that partisan alternation in government, a core mechanism for maintaining inequality at manageable levels in a liberal welfare regime, came under threat. To avoid engaging in the political conflict that would have emerged by confronting this fact openly, Labour instead imposed upon itself a taboo against discussing redistribution.

Labour politicians were keen to find a new way of discussing inequality once redistribution had become politically taboo, and the way that the Black Report framed health inequality as a policy problem facilitated Labour's embrace of health inequalities as a core equity issue. Health was a perfect issue for New Labour: well-informed politicians and policy-makers understood that health inequalities were linked to underlying inequalities in income and health, but not so closely linked as to signal to the public or to business interests that Labour was interested in redistribution.

In office, Labour's implementation of its promises to reduce inequality excluded use of policy levers like taxation and macroeconomic policy, and initially instead focused on cross-sectoral collaboration and area-based initiatives. But by the end of its term in office, Labour's health inequality strategy had devolved into little more than exhorting individuals to take more responsibility for their own health – a far cry from the socioeconomic framing of health inequalities that had characterized Labour's stance in the 1980s and 1990s, and one that was entirely unsuited to create any real reduction in the problem of either health inequality or the social inequality that was its root cause.

This chapter has described how a political taboo against discussing redistribution emerged on the center-left in England in the 1980s through 2000. This taboo was generated when the ideological convergence of Labour and Conservative leaders on a neoliberal economic program highlighted the potential for the liberal welfare regime's core mechanism for containing inequality – partisan alternation in government to enact relatively short-lived redistributive tax spending programs – to cease functioning. Hoping to avoid the political fallout that would come about if they either angered a middle-class electorate that they thought was opposed to redistribution or openly acknowledged having abandoned reducing inequality as a central goal, Labour politicians reframed the issue of social inequality. No longer was Labour's central concern disparities in income or class; moving forward, equality of opportunity – including the opportunity to live a healthy life – would be the main issue. The consequences of this reframing of inequality for Labour's efforts to create a more equitable society are discussed in detail in Chapter 7, which will show how medicalizing inequality unwittingly made both the problem of health inequality and the ultimate goal of reducing the underlying societal inequalities more difficult to achieve.

Readers who wish mainly to understand the English case may skip directly to Chapter 7. Those with an interest in seeing how the three-step process of reframing inequality plays out in quite different settings, France and Finland, are advised to proceed to Chapters 5 and 6.

Territory, Austerity

Hea... quity in France since the U-Turn

INTRODUCTION

In Chapter 4 we saw that, when the postwar welfare order in Britain came into contact with a rising neoliberal current, center-left politicians reframed the problem of social inequality in terms of health. In order to avoid violating a self-imposed taboo against discussing redistribution, Labour leaders took up the issue of health inequality, which appeared to allow the party to maintain its long-standing commitment to a more equitable society without raising the specter of taxing high incomes. Health inequality has played an analogous discursive role in French politics, allowing French center-left leaders to avoid discussing a sensitive topic made salient by the collision between France's conservative-corporatist postwar welfare order and the neoliberal paradigm that came to dominate Europe in the 1980s.

In the 1960s and 1970s, France's political elite steered the economy via regulation, credit allocation, state ownership, and currency devaluation in order to deliver desired levels of growth and equality (Shonfield 1965; Zysman 1984; P. Hall 1986). Beginning in the early 1980s, however, under pressure from international financial markets to cease devaluation and reduce the state's control over the economy, French *dirigisme* (interventionism) gave way to the "social anesthesia state" (Levy 2005). Public spending was used to paper over the growing social divide between highly protected "insiders" (workers and pensioners in the formal, unionized, often public, sectors) and "outsiders" (the long-term unemployed, irregularly employed, and those in unprotected sectors), which had been revealed by slower overall growth. This pattern of public spending became one of the central methods for controlling inequality in conservative-corporatist welfare states beginning in the 1980s (Esping-Andersen 1996; Palier 2010). However, the "social anesthesia" strategy directly challenged another *bête noire* of international financial markets: deficit spending. In order to ensure France's place at the center of the euro area and the European Union, goals that governments of both the right and left in France have shared, French politicians have acceded, at least rhetorically, to fiscal restraint.

But because embracing fiscal restraint undermines the core mechanisms for containing inequality in the conservative-corporatist welfare regime, it creates an ongoing potential for existential political conflict that is damaging for the center-left. While in Britain center-left politicians were keen to avoid discussing redistribution, in France, the political taboo that politicians sought to avoid by discussing social equality in terms of health was public spending that would enlarge the deficit. Redistribution itself has not been off-limits for politicians and policy-makers on the left in France; on the contrary, politicians associated with the Socialist Party (*Parti Socialiste*), as well as those further to the left, continued to invoke class inequality as a political issue well after President François Mitterrand abandoned the left's interventionist economic approach after 1982. But even as the rhetoric of class conflict persists on the center-left in France, a taboo has developed around the use of public spending to contain inequality, particularly if that spending would threaten France's standing in Europe by signaling fiscal irresponsibility.

As the taboo against public spending has strengthened, the problem of inequality itself has been reframed in areas such as health where reducing inequality might require substantial state spending. I focus in this chapter on how French discussions of health inequality changed beginning in the 1980s. Traditionally, discussion of health inequalities in France had a strong spatial dimension, with depictions of inequality across geographic designations within France appearing more frequently than the class-based language of inequality that was so central in England.[1] This territorialized conceptualization of inequality was rooted in the French Republican vision of equality before the state that required French citizens living anywhere in the "hexagon" of metropolitan France to have access to the same services.[2]

By the mid-2000s, however, French policy-makers and politicians had adopted the international consensus definition of health inequalities as unfair differences in health status between groups defined by income, education, or occupation, as opposed to the more territorial, health care–centric definition that had dominated French health policy-making previously. I argue that a new framing of health inequalities as *inégalités sociales en santé* (socioeconomic inequalities in health, or ISS) came to prominence in France around

---

[1] Spatial designations such as "deprived areas" are common in English discussions of health inequalities, but these designations are generally proxies for socioeconomic status. In France, until the most recent period, such spatial designations tend to reflect larger geopolitical designations such as regions.

[2] In practice, a much lower standard of services was acceptable in the twelve territories of France's *outre-mer*.

2010 because the ISS frame allowed politicians to advertise a concern for equity and continuing support for the French social model while at the same time recommitting France to the even greater fiscal austerity required by the neoliberal financial architecture of the euro area at that time. In other words, the ISS frame allowed French politicians to be for health, and for equality, without being against the fiscal constraints that were part and parcel of France's membership in Europe.

THE EMERGENCE OF THE FRENCH TABOO AGAINST SOCIAL SPENDING

In France, as in other conservative-corporatist welfare states, the economic changes of the post-oil shock period and the transition to a neoliberal order in Europe both led to new forms of social inequality and made it more difficult to deal with them. As growth slowed, dualized labor markets and semi-permanent forms of social exclusion emerged in France. The new, market-conforming adjustment strategies that had replaced the old *dirigiste* growth model after Socialist President François Mitterrand's "U-turn" in 1982 generated some winners and many losers among the French population. Successive governments attempted to contain growing inequality by targeting social spending at those who had lost out from the transition to neoliberal policies (Vail 2018, chapter 3). This strategy of "social anesthesia" (Levy 2005) was common to the conservative-corporatist welfare states throughout Europe beginning in the 1980s, and was tenable as long as international finance markets and European agreements were willing to permit the public spending levels necessary to sustain it.

By the 1990s, however, social anesthesia spending and public investments in services like education and health care that supported social equality ran up against limits, as first currency and then sovereign debt markets challenged France's budgetary position, and as the European fiscal and monetary architecture coalesced ever more firmly on German preferences for tightly controlled inflation and fiscal probity. The social anesthesia state gave way to "managed austerity" (Vail 2009). In order to maintain France's credibility with financial markets and thus its position at the center of Europe, both the center-left and the center-right ceased advocating publicly for levels of spending that were needed to maintain social equality within acceptable bounds. Politicians wishing to promote policies aimed at containing inequality would need to find a new way to present them that did not imply greater spending. Later in the chapter we will see how French politicians and policy-makers changed discourse about health inequalities in order to advance the dual goals of fiscal responsibility and societal equity. But to understand why this occurred, we must first understand the origins and nature of the French taboo against public spending.

Dirigiste Keynesianism Confronts the Global Economic Order

The French social model during the postwar *trente glorieuses* was premised on two fundamental principles agreed to by leaders from both the left and right: social peace via vigorous economic growth, and engagement with the European community to protect the sovereignty of the French state. The first principle was to be assured through state-directed industrial modernization, which involved high levels of public investment and extensive intervention in credit and product markets (Shonfield 1965; Zysman 1984; P. Hall 1989). The second principle was European engagement.

At the dawn of the Fifth Republic, there was no apparent conflict between the expansionary French social model and French leadership in Europe. The fragmentation of the left into multiple parties and labor unions meant that there was little pressure for redistribution, and governments, which were led by the right, emphasized a state-led industrial policy as a way to generate high levels of growth. Meanwhile, President Charles de Gaulle saw French membership in and leadership of the EU as a means to assert the nation's power, not as a constraint on French leaders' policy autonomy. Center-right leaders, beginning with de Gaulle in 1958, had cast French leadership of the European project as a *"multiplicateur de puissance"* (multiplier of power), a source of strength and sovereignty that would allow France to exercise power in Europe, and in the world through Europe (Schmidt 2007, 998).

But major social upheavals in 1968 demonstrated that growth was not a rising tide that would lift all boats. In the wake of 1968, the government began a rapid expansion of social welfare spending in an effort to secure social peace. With the right still in power, the emphasis was on social insurance, which resulted in substantial redistribution across the life course and between family types but relatively little vertical redistribution. Throughout the 1970s, the French model of social and economic organization comfortably accommodated expansionary statist management of the economy along with compensatory social policy, all in a polity with a strong orientation toward Europe.

Some Communists and left-wing Socialists feared Europeanization would lead French workers to be exposed to dangerous market liberalism, but Mitterrand had prevailed on the *Parti Socialiste* in 1973 to include a plank in its platform calling for developing French socialism and European integration in tandem, in the hope of appealing to both center-right pro-European voters and potential coalition partners and left-wing skeptics of Europe (Schmidt 2007, 999; see also Parsons 2003, 159). This strategy proved successful, and in 1981 Mitterrand, the first Socialist President of France's Fifth Republic, came to power on a platform promising nationalization of key industries and services, employment generation, wage increases, expansion of social security, and cooperation with Europe.

By late 1982, however, it had become clear that this was not a tenable combination. The French system of *dirigiste* Keynesianism was at odds with the global economic order. France developed a serious balance of payments crisis, and successive runs on the franc threatened France with expulsion from the European Monetary System (EMS). In response, Mitterrand (after much consultation and under pressure from domestic policy advisors as well as European partners and the United States) opted in early 1983 for an economic policy "U-turn" that committed France to a set of policies – including denationalization, deregulation, and spending cuts – that joined the nation's future to that of the European project's now unambiguously neoliberal economic agenda.

France's European Aspirations Reinforce the Taboo on Public Spending

In the wake of Mitterrand's economic policy reversal, participating in the European project became a critical justification for French socialists' domestic economic policy choices. The strategy was to use membership in the EMS as an external monetary anchor whose rules would encourage domestic economic reforms, rather than relying on devaluation to produce competitiveness (Gourevitch 2015). By the end of the 1980s, European integration was regularly used by domestic political actors "to impose or accompany measures of liberalization," in sectors from financial services to transportation (Grossman 2007, 986), and questioning either the economic policies necessary to maintain a *franc fort* or France's place in Europe came to be off-limits for mainstream politicians. Until 1997 there was "a virtual taboo among mainstream parties against criticism of EMU [European Monetary Union]" (Schmidt 2007, 1002).

Politicians of the mainstream French right, even though they tended to be more statist and nationalist in orientation than many conservatives in Europe, by and large took the positions on economic policy and on Europe that one would expect given their placement on the political spectrum. More remarkable is the transformation of the dominant factions in the *Parti Socialiste* to fiscal orthodoxy in the context of a commitment to Europe. Mitterrand's allies and successors believed that fiscal restraint and a stable currency were necessary for France's economic well-being. Socialist Prime Minister Lionel Jospin's finance minister, Dominique Strauss-Kahn, declared in 1999 that the era in which the French left was "identified with the continuous expansion of the public sphere was long gone" (Strauss-Kahn and Sautter 1998). In 2001, Jospin's government adopted new budget procedures that set strict limits on spending increases. Socialist party platforms from the 1980s, 1990s, and 2000s routinely called for fiscal restraint and deficit reduction.

Pierre Bourdieu, a leading public intellectual of the period, remarked in an interview with the newspaper *Le Monde* in 1992, "Ten years of Socialist government have completed the demolition of belief in the state and the demolition of the welfare state that was started in the 1970s in the name of liberalism" (Bourdieu 1998, 6). But while Bourdieu was correct that the new international economic orthodoxy was fundamentally at odds with French *dirigisme*, politicians did continue to use social spending to smooth over some of the tensions generated by the seemingly incompatible necessities of retaining France's social model and maintaining France's place in Europe. After the U-turn, governments expanded some parts of the welfare state in order to compensate for market liberalization, austerity, privatization, deregulation, and flexibilization of the labor market, all of which had made French workers more vulnerable (Levy 2000). This expansion of social spending was possible even in the face of external pressure for fiscal orthodoxy because economic elites in France conceptualized the crisis in the early 1980s as being centrally concerned not with welfare spending, but instead with the declining competitiveness associated with *dirigiste* policies (Kus 2006).

Politicians were also, paradoxically, able to use the idea of Europe itself as a way to demonstrate their commitment to the French social model. On the one hand, *Parti Socialiste* programs from the 1980s to 2000s consistently advocated for a more "social" Europe, with greater protections for workers. On the other, and despite Europe's clear association with the neoliberal economic restructuring of the period that rolled back the state's role in the economy, increased individual responsibility, and prompted growing unemployment and poverty, the *Parti Socialiste* presented Europe as a shield against globalization and encroaching neoliberalism (see also Schmidt 2002, 275–77). The *Parti Socialiste*'s 1988 program, for example, decried unregulated international trade, and warned that relying on the invisible hand of the market would not protect France from recession. Instead, it invoked membership in the European Union as a means of protecting the French economy from broader forces of neoliberal globalization: *"L'Europe du progrès sera solide et solidaire, une puissance qui affirme ses valeurs et défend ses intérêts dans une mondialisation régulée"* ("The Europe of progress will be strong and united, a power that affirms its values and defends its interests within the framework of a regulated globalization"). The 1998 program similarly linked economic success with Europe: *"Cette politique en faveur de l'emploi s'inscrit dans une double exigence: la construction de l'Europe et la poursuite du redressement de notre économie"* ("these policies in favor of employment meet a double demand: for the construction of Europe, and for the pursuit of the recovery of our economy") (Parti Socialiste 1988).

Despite everyday political discourse that rejected globalization, neoliberalism, and attacks on social entitlements, French governments of the left oversaw a slate of reforms consistent with economic liberalization in the 1980–2000s: privatization of publicly owned companies, liberalization of the finance sector, deregulation of the labor market, and establishment of an independent central bank. Socialist governments committed themselves to meeting the convergence criteria laid out in the European Union's Maastricht Treaty, and European engagement was used as a policy anchor that could enforce reforms at the domestic level.

Paradoxically, though, linking membership in Europe to defense of the French social model added to the strength of the taboo against any discussion of withdrawing from the European economic order. Even when parties of the far left and far right began in the 2000s to mobilize a public fearful that the EU could be a Trojan horse for unwanted neoliberal reforms rather than a shield against them, the center-left and center-right increasingly came to present European integration as simultaneously a cause of necessary economic policy changes and a safeguard against further disruption to the French social model.

In the mid-2000s, some mainstream politicians in France did begin to reconsider their anodyne position toward European integration (Grossman 2007, 986; Schmidt 2007, 1004). During the 2005 referendum on the European Union constitution (a referendum called by President Chirac in which he argued that an EU constitution would act as a barrier against neoliberal economic policies), a contentious debate emerged within the *Parti Socialiste*. Party leader François Hollande was contested by a "no" faction led by the party's deputy leader that described the EU as a threat to the European social model and the source of unwelcome neoliberal reforms. However, "[g]overnmental, economic and bureaucratic elites continue[d] to support European integration" (Grossman 2007, 988–89). In the 2007 presidential campaign, despite its coincidence with the fiftieth anniversary of the Treaty of Rome, discussion of Europe was largely absent (Grossman 2007, 989; Schmidt 2007), and Bernier (2014) argues that even the radical left in France, which "advocates a different, more socially solidaristic Europe," had stopped short of calling for a break with the European monetary and legal order. The taboo among mainstream politicians against questioning France's engagement with Europe's neoliberal market-making project remained powerful in France right up to the eve of the 2008 crisis, despite increasing public awareness and occasional expressions of discontent.

With the onset of the global financial crisis in 2008, the international economic policy community briefly endorsed Keynesian stimulus. By the June 2010 G20 meeting in Toronto, however, the priority internationally had once again returned to "growth-friendly fiscal consolidation" (Blyth 2013), that is, cuts in public spending. France's AAA bond rating was under threat, and the country entered into the European Union's Stability and Growth Pact's excessive deficit procedure in 2009. Fearful of the response from finance markets and constrained by EU demands for deficit reduction, the center-right prime minister oversaw major cuts to government spending. When the *Parti Socialiste* regained the presidency in 2012, President Hollande inherited his predecessors' promises to the EU to cut the deficit to 3 percent by 2012, and had the additional burden of seeking to placate financial markets, which Socialists believed were particularly mistrustful of center-left governments (Clift 2014, 2). Hollande's austerity budgets were a key part of his "strategy to demonstrate French economic credibility with financial markets and European partners" (Clift 2014, 8).

From Mitterrand to Hollande, and despite ongoing disagreements over economic policy and membership in the European Union among different factions of the *Parti Socialiste*, the French center-left in government has made it clear that it would prioritize fiscal consolidation in order to remain at the center of Europe. Unable to induce German leaders to abandon their own ordoliberal aspirations for strict monetary and fiscal policy and to apply the French social model to Europe, French leaders eventually acquiesced to a European financial architecture largely on German terms, with low inflation targets and tight control over deficits. In light of the cross-party agreement on the desirability of remaining in Europe, this imposed on French domestic politics a strong taboo against advocating expansionary public spending or even the type of social anesthesia spending that had characterized much of the 1990s and 2000s.

Internal Pressures for Austerity and the Self-Imposition of Taboo

International finance markets and France's European partners have considerable coercive power as long as French leaders remain committed to remaining in the euro area, but pressure to adopt neoliberal constraints on spending has never been entirely exogenous in France. While neoliberal ideas were not connected to influential think tanks, journalists, and lobbyists as they were in the United Kingdom, neoliberal thinking pervaded technocratic circles and was an important component of the French intellectual and policy scene from the 1970s onward (Fourcade-Gourinchas and Babb 2002; Prasad 2005; 2006; Gentile 2010). A broad spectrum of policy elites in France "came to see in the internationalization of the French economy (via integration with Europe in particular) the means to pursue its historic mission of modernization" (Fourcade-Gourinchas and Babb 2002, 567).

Another endogenous source of strength for the taboo against social spending in France came from the electoral arena. By the 2000s, French Socialist politicians had come to believe, as Labour politicians had in the United Kingdom, that middle class support was contingent on lower taxes, which they could offer only if public spending was contained. In 1999, Jospin had called for a "new alliance" between the socially excluded, the "popular classes" (i.e., "people who work hard, in a constrained environment, and do not earn much"), and the middle class, a group that was playing "an increasing role in French society," but to whose "legitimate aspirations" Socialists had not been paying sufficient attention (Jospin 1999). After revelations in August of that year that tax revenues were higher than expected, which sparked media attention to the level of taxation and fear that the *Parti Socialiste* could lose the next election on the issue of taxes, the prime minister declared his support for a tax cut. According to Touzet (2017, 15), from that point "belief that taxation needed to be cut to cater to middle-class voters pervaded the direction of the socialist party" through the early 2000s. At the same time, Touzet notes, French Socialists took care to remain attractive to their base in the "popular classes," and turned to tax credits as a means of supporting low incomes while at the same time upholding an "ideational ban on public spending" (Touzet 2017, 16).

As in the United Kingdom, then, French politicians decided not to discuss openly the full range of policy tools available to them for dealing with inequality in part because external forces constrained them, but in equal measure because politicians chose to believe that those constraints were material and worth abiding by. In this sense, the post-1982 French Socialist taboo against advocating public spending to reduce inequality was self-imposed, just as the post-1985 British Labour taboo against discussing redistribution was. At the same time, French politicians on the center-left continued to see themselves as champions of the core French Republican values of *égalité* and *fraternité*, just as Labour politicians saw themselves as the historic defenders of Britain's working class.

Touzet (2017) shows that in both Britain and France in the 1990s, supporting low incomes via tax credits versus direct spending provided a way for policy-makers to express commitment to an equitable society while at the same time reshaping the welfare state to accommodate an emerging neoliberal orthodoxy (Touzet 2017). Proposals to reduce health inequalities in the 2000s and 2010s served the same purpose: they allowed politicians to reframe inequality in a way that removed attention from off-limits tools for containing inequality.

INEQUALITY REFRAMED: FROM TERRITORIAL TO SOCIOECONOMIC INEQUALITIES IN HEALTH

In France, political and policy attention to socioeconomic inequalities in health status shifted the conversation in health policy away from the extra spending that would be required to ensure territorial equality in health service provision and toward the potential cost savings associated with a greater emphasis on primary health care and prevention. In this way, the reframing of health inequality in France both obscured and reflected the need to limit public spending, which had been the French welfare model's main tool for containing inequality within acceptable bounds, but which had been rendered taboo by French political elites' acceptance of the neoliberal economic orthodoxy necessary at the core of the European project.

Beginning in the 2000s, talking about "social" inequalities in health (i.e., inequalities in health status associated with socioeconomic status [SES]) provided French political elites with an opportunity to characterize policy measures that they believed would be cost-cutting – shifting of resources within the health system from medical treatment "upstream" to prevention – as a means to promote equity.

But the *inégalités sociales en santé* framing was relatively new in France: unlike in Britain, until quite recently most French policy-makers, politicians, and members of the public have understood the problem of health inequalities to be primarily concerned with the distribution of health care services over the French territory, rather than the distribution of health outcomes over social groups. Underlying this framing of the problem was the Republican view that *egalité* is a matter of citizens' equality before the state rather than with one another, and is linked to the equal availability of state services wherever in the hexagon they might reside.[3]

The shift in the 2000s to the ISS framing of health inequality reflected an intensification of budgetary pressures after the financial and eurozone crises. The new, international framing of health inequalities as a problem that was related to socioeconomic inequalities in health outcomes offered the hope of replacing costly medical care spending with a slate of much less expensive local initiatives aimed at improving health status through upstream prevention and targeted social services. A combination of more effective public health messaging, health visitors, and greater access to green space, for example, not only would reduce health inequalities and improve population health; it would obviate the need for more hospitals, outpatient facilities, and expensive specialist visits.

Of course, there have long been significant segments of the French health policy elite, including but not limited to the small number of social epidemiologists, economists, and geographers with strong ties to international research collaborations, who viewed the problem of health inequalities in a way that was congruent with the international emphasis on socioeconomic disparities in health, morbidity, and mortality. Until quite recently, though, this view has not been dominant in French policy circles. By contrast, beginning around 2010, politicians and policy-makers have come to discuss the problem in a way that looks more similar to patterns in northern Europe and at the international level. Analyzing official reports about the problem of health inequalities since 1980 in France reveals this transition, which has itself allowed for at least temporary and partial reframing of the broader underlying issues of social inequality that had come to seem, by the mid-1980s, impossible to address using the old mechanisms of compensatory social spending.

Health Inequalities: Discourse in French Government Reports

As noted in Chapter 3, government reports are a standard source of information about how health policy elites understand health inequalities (see also, e.g., Graham 2004b; Vallgårda 2007; Docteur and Berenson 2014). The universe of relevant reports is smaller for France than for England: since 1980 there have been just five major reports commissioned or produced by the national-

---

[3] French overseas territories have not generally enjoyed the same intensity of social citizenship as residents of metropolitan France and are little discussed in general health equity documents.

level executive or legislature bodies and primarily concerned with health inequalities (see Table 5.1, which presents a timeline of the major reports in their political and economic context). The first major report dedicated exclusively to health inequalities in France in the modern era was *Les inégalités devant la santé* (Inequalities in Health), produced at the request of the newly appointed Communist health minister and released in 1985 (Ministère des Affaires Sociales et de la Solidarité nationale 1985). The issue of health inequalities surfaced again in preparations for the General Planning Commission (CGP)'s eleventh national plan, for which a working group was charged with preparing a brief on health inequalities to be included in the health system planning document *Santé 2010* (Commissariat Général du Plan 1993). However, the next major freestanding report on health inequalities in France did not emerge until 1998. The High Commission for Public Health (HCSP) issued *Allocation régionale des ressources et réduction des inégalités de santé* (Regional Allocation of Resources and Reduction of Health Inequalities) in response to changes in the health care financing system that were prompted by *Santé 2010* (1999). It is the first report from the country's main public health body that uses the term "health inequality" in the title. A second HCSP report on health inequalities, *Les inégalités sociales de santé: sortir de la fatalité* (Social Inequalities in Health: Escaping Fatalism), came more than a decade later (2009), followed in 2011 by a health inequalities document prepared by the Inspectorate General for Social Security (IGAS 2011). Finally, a relatively minor report, *Inégalités territoriales, environnementales et sociales de santé. Regards croisés en régions: de l'observation à l'action* (Territorial, Environmental, and Social Health Inequalities: Regional Perspectives, from Observation to Action), was released by an interministerial committee for sustainable development in 2014 (Besse et al. 2014).

Evidence of the French government's approach to health inequality can also be gleaned from chapters or sections devoted to health inequalities found in serial documents on the nation's health. Beginning in the 1990s, two serial publications reported regularly on population health in France, and contained sections dedicated health inequalities. The HCSP, which was charged with contributing to public health planning by advising the government on prevention, health risks, and health care system performance, published a series of reports on *La santé en France* (Health in France) in 1994, 1996, 1998, and 2002 (HCSP 1994; Ministère du Travail et des Affaires Sociales and Haut Comité de la Santé Publique 1996; HCSP 1998; Ministère del'Emploi et de la Solidarité and Haut Comité de la Santé Publique 2002). The public health law of 2004 specified one hundred public health objectives, two of which included reducing health inequalities, to be achieved by 2008. These objectives necessitated systematic monitoring and data collection, which was undertaken by the *Direction de la recherche, des études, de l'évaluation et des statistiques* (DREES, the Directorate of Research, Studies, Evaluation and Statistics), a research organ attached to the Ministry of Health and Social Affairs, and published

TABLE 5.1 *Timeline of major events in French health inequality politics*

President	Prime Minister	Year	Event
François Mitterrand (Socialist)	Pierre Mauroy (Socialist)	1982	Mitterrand makes economic policy "U-turn" in response to intense pressure from currency markets.
	Laurent Fabius (Socialist)	1985	Publication of *Les inégalités devant la santé* (the LeRoux report), the first major report dedicated to health inequalities in France in the modern era.
	Édith Cresson (Socialist)	1991	Regional health planning bodies created under hospital reform law.
	Pierre Bérégovoy (Socialist)/Édouard Balladur (RPR[a])	1993	The report *Santé 2010* is released as part of the *Commisariat du Plan*'s 11th Plan.
Jacques Chirac (RPR[a])	Alain Juppé (Republican)	1996	Regional hospital agencies created to allow for increased central government oversight of health insurance expenditures.
	Lionel Jospin (Socialist)	1998	High Commission for Public Health (HCSP) releases report *Allocation régionale des ressources et réduction des inégalités de santé* in response to changes in health care financing.
		1999	*Atelier santé ville* (ASV) or "city health workshops" established by inter-ministerial committee on cities to help cities prioritize the reduction of socioeconomic and territorial health inequities.
		2000	*Couverture malaise universelle* (CMU), providing health insurance for low-income residents who have no other form of coverage, introduced by Socialist government. *Les inégalités sociales de santé*, an edited volume produced by INSERM researchers, is widely read by health policy specialists and sparks further discussion of SES inequalities in health.

(*continued*)

TABLE 5.1 *(continued)*

President	Prime Minister	Year	Event
		2001	New budget procedures adopted by Socialist government set strict limits on increases in spending.
	Jean-Pierre Raffarin (UMP[b])	2004	Public health law specifies 100 public health objectives to be achieved by 2008, including reducing territorial and socioeconomic inequalities in health.
	Jean Pierre Raffarin (UMP[b])/Dominique de Villepin (UMP[b])	2005	Referendum on the European Union constitution
Nicolas Sarkozy (UMP[b])	François Fillon (Republican)	2008	Global financial crisis; international economic policy community briefly endorses neo-Keynesian stimulus.
		2009	France enters the EU Stability and Growth Pact's excessive deficit procedure. *Loi HPST* devolves responsibility for reducing health inequalities to newly created Agences régionales de santé (Regional Health Agencies, or ARS). *Les inégalités sociales de santé: sortir de la fatalité* published by the HSCP. Report adopts international consensus framing of health inequalities.
		2011	*Les inégalités sociales de santé: déterminants sociaux et modèles d'action* is published by the Inspectorate General for Social Security (IGAS).
		2011	ARS directors sign first *Contrats pluriannuels d'objectifs et de moyens* (CPOMs) with the state to outline the goals of their ARSs, including how they plan to reduce health inequalities.

President	Prime Minister	Year	Event
François Hollande (Socialist)	François Fillon (Republican)/Jean-Marc Ayrault (Socialist)	2013	EU Fiscal compact enters into force, requiring France to adhere to strict budgetary conditions. *Stratégie National de Santé* announced by Hollande's health minister Marisol Touraine.
	Jean-Marc Ayrault (Socialist)/Manuel Valls (Socialist)	2014	Short report *Inégalitiés territoriales, environnementales et sociales de santé* released by inter-ministerial committee for sustainable development.
	Manuel Valls (Socialist)/ Bernard Cazeneuve (Socialist)	2016	*Loi Santé* passed, aims to facilitate universal access to health care across the French territory and to promote health equity. Interministerial committee for health convened.

a RPR = Rally for the Republic (*Rassemblement pour la République*), center-right.
b UMP = Union for a Popular Movement (*Union pour un mouvement populaire*), center-right.

beginning in 2006 in a series of reports on *L'etat de santé de la population en France* (The State of the Health of the Population) (DREES 2006; 2007; 2008; 2010; 2011; 2015).

Quantitative analysis of the ideas and elements appearing in the French reports as compared to the international health inequality consensus frame is presented in the Appendix. The results of this analysis suggest a health inequalities discourse that is distinct from the international frame in many regards, but similar in others. All of the French reports, even recent ones, emphasize territorial inequalities and inequalities in health care to a much greater extent than in the international consensus, where socioeconomic inequalities in health status are core elements of the definition of health inequalities. Like the international documents, French reports are attentive to the role of social and environmental factors in producing health inequalities, but are less inclined to use the specific language of "social determinants." In two of the reports (HCSP and Ministère de l'emploi et de la solidarité 1999; IGAS 2011) there is a strong emphasis on health care as a cause of inequalities. Where the French reports differ most strongly from the international reports, however, is in their recommendations for solving the problem of health inequality, and their attribution of responsibility for doing so. The French reports are far more reluctant than the international ones to recommend action on the part of national or supranational bodies, instead attributing most of the treatment responsibility to subnational government, to the health care system, or to the private sector, community groups, and individuals. In none of the French reports are structural solutions – those aimed at reducing inequalities in the social, economic, or political determinants of health – the dominant recommendations; instead, these reports highlight the need to make changes to the health system and to collect more data on health inequalities.

In fact, most French health inequality reports make very few concrete policy recommendations beyond data collection and actions in the health care system. The exception is the early LeRoux report, whose origins in the office of a Communist health minister may have encouraged policy recommendations focused on workplace-related interventions, including worker participation in oversight of health conditions. The 2009 HCSP report and 2011 IGAS reports, both of which drew extensively on UK and WHO expertise, call for generating political will to tackle the problem and cooperation across government departments and levels to resolve health inequalities, but even these reports do not recommend specific policy interventions outside the health care sector. Finally, none of the French reports – not even those explicitly recognizing the role of income inequality in shaping health inequalities – makes a policy recommendation that would entail significant redistribution of economic resources or power.

Qualitative examination of the French corpus confirms that French government reports on health inequalities have been quite attentive to territorial aspects of health inequality. The LeRoux report details the health consequences of hard, lightly regulated labor in France's countryside, factories, fisheries, and office buildings, but the report is nevertheless deeply territorialized in its structure, such that each chapter devotes some or all of its time to describing geographic inequalities. *Santé 2010* (also known as the Soubie Report, after its lead author) was not itself a report on health inequalities. However, the report of the working group dedicated to the subject of *Les inégalités sociales de santé* notes that despite a generally equitable health care system, certain gaps in health persist – first among which is "territorial situations [characterized by] contrasts in mortality, in the density of health care supply, and in the level of health expenditure" (Atelier no. 1 1993, 103). The report mentions disparities between socio-professional groups, but the text's main concern is with regional variation in health care spending, which is argued to be unjust because it did not match the regional variation in health status and health care needs.

The HCSP's 1998 report *Allocation régionale des ressources et réduction des inégalités de santé* (Regional Allocation of Resources and Reduction of Health Inequality) was written in response to changes in the health care financing system that were prompted by the Soubie Report. As such, the report is really about health care financing and not about inequalities in health per se. The report begins by noting that there are large differences in both health and health care supply between the regions, with the north of France generally disfavored on both counts. The report concludes that the best way to reduce inequalities in health status between regions would not be through health care spending, but by way of a regional policy that devoted supplemental resources to disfavored regions (HCSP and Ministère de l'emploi et de la solidarité 1999, 23). Annex II of the report is dedicated to indicators of health and health care needs. These are conveyed via a series of maps and tables showing the best- and worst-off regions. This report shows more clearly than any other the importance of territorial (in this case, regional) inequalities in French policy discourse about health inequalities.

Serial health publications of the era paint much the same picture, albeit with slightly more information on health inequalities across socioeconomic categories. The first of the HCSP's *La santé en France* reports, in 1994, outlines four main objectives for health policy in the medium term, the last of which is reducing health inequalities (HCSP 1994, 209). Both "inequality between the most and least favored social categories" and "inequality between regions" are to be targeted (HCSP 1994, 209). The remaining reports are similar in their joint emphasis on ISS and territorial inequalities, but are visibly weighted toward a territorial analysis: all of the *Santé en France* reports feature maps: two in 1994, twelve in 1996, four in the 1994–98 report, and eleven in 2002.

Given the salience of ethnicity in French discussions of social exclusion, it is noteworthy that race and ethnicity are largely absent from the reports, with only two mentions of racial or ethnic group differences in the entire sample, both in the earliest document. This is almost certainly partially a result of the fact that the French government is prohibited by law from collecting data on individuals' race or ethnicity. Analysis of small-area variations in health, which is prominent in more recent French reports, could provide insight into racial and ethnic disparities, given the spatial concentration of ethnic minorities in France. However, government reports do not explicitly link small-area variations in health to the racial/ethnic makeup of these areas, instead leaving it to the audience to draw their own conclusions about whether racial and ethnic inequalities are problematic or, indeed, even exist.

The Territorial Frame in French Health Inequalities Policy Discourse

Why did policy elites in France in the 1980s and 1990s discuss the problem of inequalities in health in a way that differs so markedly from the international consensus, with the French embedding social inequalities in the territory and the international consensus viewing health inequalities as rooted in socioeconomic inequalities? The modernization theory implicitly espoused by the WHO (Whitehead et al. 2014) and the EU (e.g., UK Presidency of the EU 2006) argues that France was simply a laggard on the "health equity action spectrum." Internally, France is also sometimes self-described as a "bad pupil" (interviews FR28; FR31) when it comes to adopting WHO or EU policy models. The fact that French discourse about health inequalities is, in its territorial focus, less consonant with the dominant discourse at the international level likely contributes to the impression that French policy elites were late to fully recognize that health inequalities are an important policy problem. But the volume of documentation relating to health inequalities demonstrates that there is no lack of interest in health equity on the part of the French. French concern with health inequalities was, until the late 1990s, different from, but not necessarily less abundant than, the concerns expressed in the United Kingdom or as part of the international consensus.

The greater emphasis on health care, as opposed to health per se, has several likely causes. First, France's social health insurance system, with its generous reimbursement of fee-for-service medical care, had by the 1980s generated larger numbers of providers and health care facilities per capita and higher health care consumption than in any other country in Europe (Dutton 2007). The high cost to the state of this massive health care apparatus had become a source of political tension by the late 1970s, and the attention of policy elites was drawn to health care, rather than health outcomes, as the central issue of concern for the health policy domain. Second, the French public health establishment is weak relative to the social insurance and medical providers, and also heavily biomedical in its orientation (Briatte 2010; Bergeron and Nathanson 2012). Public health policy elites were thus not powerful enough to serve as a counterweight to the medical care apparatus and, with the little power they did possess, were disinclined to advocate for an approach to population health grounded in social causation.

A final reason that French health inequalities discourse focused on health care more than on health outcomes in the 1980s and 1990s is that health care was directly related to the territorialized view of health inequality that dominated in France until the mid-2010s. For example, when restrictions on the number of new medical graduates (the so-called *numerus clausus* introduced in the 1980s) took effect, medical demography – the unequal distribution of doctors over the territory – emerged as a prominent theme in media coverage of health policy. As the overall numbers of doctors declined, the idea of the medical "deserts" (*déserts médicaux*) came into common parlance. The territorial differentiation of *dépassement* – the practice of doctors charging fees above those reimbursed by the national insurance – became a newsworthy topic somewhat later, with frequent stories of patients being unable to find a single doctor in their area willing to accept the regular fees (interview FR3). Such geographic differences in health care supply fed a sense that the important inequalities in health in France are linked to health care, and to territory – and hence, in the words of a senior health advisor, violate a "strong principle," "shared by all people," that "health has to be the same everywhere in the country" (interview FR3).

The importance of this "strong principle" is undoubtedly aided by the importance of rural areas in French politics. The French *cumul de mandats* allows the same office-holder to be elected to serve simultaneously as a mayor or departmental or regional councilor, and in the national legislature in France. Mayors of towns with fewer than 3,500 inhabitants can additionally serve in the regional/departmental legislature *and* in the national assembly or senate, resulting in an over-representation of rural areas at the national level. Several interviewees noted that an important cause of the territorial framing of health inequalities in France is their apparent link to issues of concern to rural areas. As one remarked, "the problem of *déserts medicaux* is linked to a larger discourse about the withdrawal of services from rural areas" (interview FR20) – a discourse that has been taken up most recently by the *gilets jaunes* protesters.

Territoire is a concept that goes beyond rurality, though, and is weighted with multiple meanings in France. As a French expert on regional politics put it, territory has "a political, social, historical thickness about it. It has a state dimension; it's also about institutions, political systems, political networks, political exchange. It's also about history. So, it's a very thick notion" (interview FR4). One of the primary valences of territory in France is equality. The equation of equality with territorial uniformity is deeply rooted in France. A key threat to inequality and national cohesion in French political discourse, dating back to the realm of Louis XIV and gaining full expression during World War II, is the lack of access in France's "deserts" to the amenities and privileges of the Parisian way of life. The juxtaposition between Paris and less well-served parts of the country entered mainstream policy thinking with J. F. Gravier's 1947 book *Paris et le désert français*, which argued that since the Napoleonic period, more and more power had been concentrated in Paris, to the detriment of the rest of France. Gravier's ideas were influential in the post–World War II period and led to his appointment as head of the *Commissariat général au Plan* (Baudoui 1999). The determination to remove the disparities implied in the concept of *déserts* became a cornerstone of postwar French planning. A consequence of this idea is that for French policy-makers, territory becomes "a metaphor to focus on the issue of policy implementation" (interview FR12).

The *département* has, since Napoleon, been the most important unit of the French state for policy implementation. However, starting in the 1960s, the French state made periodic attempts first to create and then to enhance the power of regions, in part as a way to counteract the power wielded by local notables who dominated departmental politics. After the first oil shock in 1973 created pressure to contain public sector costs, policy-makers in France also turned increasingly to the regions as loci for state control of expenditure in health, which was growing rapidly.[4] When pressure mounted to reduce government spending, "the central government tried to subject the health system to state planning, and to create a link [between health spending and] health needs" (interview FR19). French planning was by its nature a territorial exercise, and "[t]here was already a known problem with territorial inequities in health

---

[4] A boom in hospital construction after the war fueled direct government expenditure, while the health insurance system, which was regulated by the social partners and received very little oversight from the central government, grew unchecked (Dutton 2007).

spending. For a long time, there had been a higher level of expenses in Paris and in the south than in the north, independent of the health status of population" (interview FR19). In order to have the necessary information to better match health spending with health status, and so reduce expenditure overall, an official report commissioned by the prime minister in 1980 recommended that Regional Health Observatories (*Obsérvatoires régionales de santé*, or ORS) be created in each region (interview FR19). The creation of the ORS in turn made it possible for French public officials and researchers to report on health inequalities in regional terms.

All of these factors help to explain the territorialized framing of the problem of health inequalities in French policy discourse, which was further reinforced by policy developments aimed at rationalizing medical expenditure through regionalization in the 1980s and 1990s. Regionalization of the French health care system began in the early 1990s, as a "direct consequence" of the fiscal pressures generated by the financial crisis of the late 1970s (interview FR34). The hospital reform law of 1991 organized hospitals and affiliated care establishments into regional health planning bodies, *Schéma régional d'organisation sanitaire* (SROS, the Regional Health Organization Plan), in order to better rationalize and balance health care spending. In 1996, decrees creating regional hospital agencies (*Agences régionales de l'hospitalisation* [ARH]) and increasing central government oversight of health insurance expenditures were passed as part of center-right Prime Minister Alain Juppé's planned reform of the social security system (even as other parts of his initiative were abandoned after general strikes). A 2004 law reforming the health insurance system introduced partial coverage of voluntary health insurance costs for low-income people, but also reorganized the governance of the health insurance system along regional lines. The law created *Missions regionales de santé* (MRS, Regional Health Agencies) that grouped together the ARH and newly formed regional health insurance councils (*Unions régionales de caisses d'assurance maladie*, URCAM). The implementation decree specified that the first directors of each MRS would be appointed by the Health and Social Affairs ministers, subject to approval by the Director General of the national body representing the health insurance funds. Further reforms to the governance of the French hospital system took place during the 2000s, culminating in 2009 with the *Loi "Hôpital, Patients, Santé et Territoire"* (the Law on Hospitals, Patients, Health and Territory, commonly abbreviated as *Loi HPST*).

The *Loi HPST* was an administrative revision of the 2004 Public Health Law, but was an important piece of legislation in its own right, extending regionalization beyond hospital care and health insurance to include the entire French health system. Its centerpiece was the merger of several department- and regional-level health care agencies into regional health agencies (*Agences régionales de santé*, ARS) that would be responsible for the planning, coordination, and delivery of medical care in the regions, and also for public health. The law also marked an important inflection point in French health inequalities discourse: it was the high-water mark of the territorial approach to health inequalities, and at the same time the beginning of a turn in French public discourse toward a view of health inequalities that was more consonant with the international health inequalities consensus, and promised even deeper cost containment.

Toward Adoption of the International Health Inequalities Consensus in France

Title 1, Chapter 1, Article 1 of the 2009 *Loi HPST* defines "*la lutte contre l'exclusion sociale*" (the fight against social exclusion) as an essential function of the health system, and the law set out provisions (discussed below) for tackling inequalities in health. However, many experts and policy-makers doubted that the ARS, still relatively new at the time I conducted my interviews in 2012–14, would be able to deliver significant reductions in either socio-economic or territorial health inequalities. A large number of my interviewees concluded that the framing of the law in terms of health equity was, as one put it, "primarily rhetorical" (interview FR22; see also FR4; FR10; FR20). The Health Minister's presentation of successive drafts of the proposed legislation and the eventual text of the law all equated reducing health inequalities with reducing territorial variation in health care supply and access, not reducing socioeconomic inequalities in health status.

While the *Loi HPST* was billed rhetorically as an effort to reduce territorial inequalities in access to health care, its true aim seems to have been to provide policy-makers with new sources of leverage to control health care expenditure. The regional health agencies were charged with coordinating policies affecting hospitals, insurance, public health, the elderly, and people with disabilities, all formerly competencies of the departments and, to a lesser extent, regions. The reorganization of competencies facilitated the underlying goal of controlling health care costs in three ways: First, for historical reasons the social insurance funds did not have an organizational presence at the regional level (regional bodies representing the health insurance funds were created only in 2004) and could thus be more effectively sidelined by the ARS than at the national or departmental level, where their power was better institutionalized (interviews FR1; FR3; FR20; FR34). Second, the law would accelerate the process of hospital consolidation and reform by reinforcing the power of centrally appointed administrators at the regional level over local and departmental political elites and doctors (interview FR34). Finally, as with other contemporary regionalization initiatives, the law promised to generate savings by reducing duplication of bureaucracies and personnel. In short, the law, which one technocrat described as "a child of the RGPP" (the center-right government's 2007 public administration reform), and had "primarily budgetary objectives" (interview FR34).

While the *Loi HPST* had a familiar focus on territorial inequalities in health care and on controlling health care costs, the rhetorical framing of the law as a response to social inequalities in health reflected a transition in wider French health policy circles, already under way since the early 1990s, toward a new, more socioeconomic understanding of health inequalities. Several circumstances combined during that period to draw more attention to socioeconomic inequalities in health.

First was a changing understanding of the link between poverty and health that had its roots in the French Left's "rediscovery" of poverty, in the form of *la nouvelle pauvreté* (the new poverty) and social exclusion, upon their return to power in the late 1980s. This rediscovery involved a new consciousness that the structure of French social and economic life prevented many people – and not only the very most marginalized members of society – from enjoying social goods that were previously (and erroneously) assumed to be widely shared. One of these social goods was access to health care, and one expert interviewee argues that health inequalities "arrived on the political agenda via the question of social exclusion" (interview FR37).

Preparations for the introduction of the *Couverture maladie universelle*, (CMU), a new program of publicly funded health insurance for low-income citizens designed to reduce inequalities in access to health care and enacted by Jospin in 1999, prompted a flurry of publicly funded research on health status inequalities at the National Institute for Demographic Research (INED), the National Center for Scientific Research (CNRS), and the National Institute of Health and Medical Research (INSERM) (interview FR37). A related 2000 publication by INSERM researchers, *Les inégalités sociales de santé* (INSERM 2000), was widely read by health policy specialists, its publication "a key turning point" after which the subject of SES inequalities became a "legitimate" topic for research (interview FR29). The issue of SES inequalities in health status first appeared in law in France in 2004, with a new public health law whose provisions regarding health inequalities were "mainly driven by a concern for improving health outcomes for the poor by improving access to care" (interviews FR21; FR22).

Developments in public health in the 1990s also contributed to a rising consciousness about socioeconomic inequalities in health status. The spread of HIV/AIDS and a scandal over France's tainted blood supply had led to the formation of the HCSP in 1992. The HCSP's main concerns were population health surveillance and health safety, and its orientation was largely biomedical. However, key policy entrepreneurs within the HCSP were eventually able to promote a more social-epidemiological reading of health inequalities. The landmark HCSP report on health inequalities in 2009 was widely referenced in parliamentary and ministerial work on health policy during the period, even if many of its lessons went unheeded (interviews FR27; FR30; FR32).

Finally, the problem of socioeconomic health inequalities was linked in the 1990s and 2000s to pension reform politics. As the state sought to gain control over public pension spending by, among other things, raising the retirement age and lengthening the required number of years of contribution for enjoyment of a full pension, policy-makers who were not health policy experts became aware of disparities in life expectancy between manual workers and those in less strenuous occupations (interviews FR21; FR27; FR29; FR38).

Within the health policy community, several interviewees noted a "paradigm shift" (interviews FR5; FR23) in the mid- to late 2000s, after which both researchers and policy professionals increasingly came to understand the problem of health inequalities as disparities in health status linked to the social gradient. According to two key players, 2009 was the decisive turning point (interviews FR21; FR29). In that year, two signal events in addition to the release of the HCSP report on health inequalities took place: the second French Cancer Plan, led by a nephrologist with no background in health inequalities research, surprised the health policy world by establishing reducing inequalities in cancer as a major objective,[5] and the *Loi HPST*, which (albeit rhetorically) prioritized reducing health inequalities, was enacted. After those events, "if you went to the [health directorate] in the Ministry of Health, people understood what social inequalities in health were, and they were being written about everywhere" (interview FR29). After 2009, awareness of socioeconomic inequalities filtered even into public discourse: media attention to the issue spiked, and some parts of the medical profession began to take the issue of social causation seriously (interviews FR13; FR21; FR23).

The emergence in France in the late 2000s of a policy discourse about health inequalities that is more attentive to socioeconomic inequalities in health is clearly visible in French government reports on health inequalities as well. Territorial inequalities still figure prominently: the 2007 DREES report[6] on *L'etat de santé de la population en France* notes in the introduction that there are important *"disparités géographiques"* as well as *"disparités sociales"* in France (DREES 2007, 14), and the 2008, 2009–10, and 2011 reports combine territorial and SES inequalities in a single subsection. The DREES reports are also liberally sprinkled with multishaded maps showing the diversity of health outcomes, health behaviors, and health care utilization across French regions. Nevertheless, socioeconomic inequalities in health status are addressed both in a stand-alone section of the later reports and as an issue cutting across other indicators, a novelty in French health policy discourse.

Similarly, *Les inégalités sociales de santé: sortir de la fatalité*, the report released by the HCSP in 2009, was explicitly addressed to "social" (i.e., socioeconomic) inequalities in health. The report characterizes SES health inequalities as connected to territorial inequalities in health, arguing, "The geographic

---

[5] In France, medical doctors, with the exception of some primary care doctors, have generally not been the main advocates of greater attention to ISS.

[6] The 2004 public health law had stipulated that each edition of DREES's *L'etat de santé de la population en France* document socioeconomic differences in health indicators.

environment constitutes one of the determinants of health. Social inequalities in the occupation of territory can be clearly identified in France, so it is natural to reflect on [these inequalities] jointly" (HCSP 2009, 22). It goes on to state, "The territorial, local, or regional dimension is extremely important for the question of social health inequalities.... As we have emphasized, territorial and social inequalities are intricately tied to one another" (HCSP 2009, 75). But the territorial analysis carried out in part in the report is at a finer-grained level than much previous government analysis in France. Data are presented at the level of the community or neighborhood rather than *départements* or regions, allowing for closer mapping to the sociodemographic characteristics of place. And unlike earlier reports, this one casts territorial inequalities primarily as containers for SES inequalities: SES inequalities are "anchored" in *les territoires* (HCSP 2009, 76).

If the 2009 HCSP report shifted the connotation of territorial health inequalities closer to SES health inequalities by focusing on the socioeconomic composition and context of geographic designations, and by recommending solutions like "improving the conditions of daily life" and "redistributing power and income" that are squarely in the ISS playbook, it did not abandon the French discursive tradition of treating territorial inequalities in health and health care as important in their own right. The report culminates with recommendations that the new public health law call for indicators on health inequalities to be collected by socioeconomic category, but broken down by geographic area (HCSP 2009, 13), and for developing a geographic indicator of deprivation to "track the link between territorial development and health" (p. 14). These recommendations are in line with the then-state-of-the-art epidemiological focus on small-area variation as a proxy for SES. Nevertheless, the specific language that the HCSP proposes for the primary and secondary objectives regarding health inequality in the new law seems designed to leverage the ambiguity in the language of "territory" to link long-standing political concern in France with inequalities across larger-scale territorial aggregations.[7]

The 2011 report by the Inspectorate General for Social Security (IGAS) follows a similar pattern. *Les inégalités sociales de santé: déterminants sociaux et modèles d'action* (Social Inequalities in Health: Social Determinants and Models of Action) is once again nominally directed at social inequalities in health, and it adopts the international consensus language on health inequalities. For example, social inequalities are defined as avoidable differences in health; they concern social justice, follow a gradient, require multisectoral action, and are best addressed with proportionate universalism. France is placed on Whitehead's (1998) equity action spectrum, and the WHO

---

7 "**Objectif général:** réduire les inégalités sociales et territoriales de santé. **Objectifs spécifiques:** réduire le gradient social et territorial des états de santé en agissant sur l'ensemble des déterminants de la santé; réduire les obstacles financiers à l'accès aux soins" (p. 13).

Commission on the Social Determinants of Health's report is referenced as providing the most up-to-date model of causation (table 2 [p. 14] in fact reproduces the WHO causal model diagram). At the same time, the imprint of the older territorialized analysis remains. The introduction to the report states, "Classically, three types of health inequalities can be distinguished: those between women and men, between socio-professional categories, or between territories" (IGAS 2011, 7), and the report goes on to argue that "public policies need to take into account the relationships that link social inequalities in health with other forms of inequality, above all territorial inequalities" (IGAS 2011, 22). The authors of this report understand and articulate the political consequences of choices about how they frame the causes of health inequalities – "to act on the determinants of health implies in effect choices about economic and social regulation" (IGAS 2011, 12) – and have chosen a framing that resonates with long-standing concerns about regional inequalities in France, while at the same time shifting policy discourse in the direction of the international health inequalities consensus.

Explaining the Growing Salience of the ISS Frame

Why, given the presence of a thread of research on socioeconomic inequalities in health outcomes in France dating back centuries, did the ISS framing only become layered on top of the territorial framing in the late 2000s? The fact that the turn toward a more socioeconomic approach to health inequalities discourse became fully actualized in 2013, the year in which the EU Fiscal Compact requiring France to adhere to strict budgetary conditions entered into force, offers some clues. The new ISS framing of health inequality allowed politicians to advertise a concern for equity and continuing support for the French social model while recommitting France to fiscal austerity and the neoliberal financial architecture of the eurozone. In other words, the new frame allowed French politicians to be for health, and for equality, without being against the constraints on spending that were part and parcel of France's membership in Europe. Let us examine how.

The *Stratégie National de Santé* (SNS) announced by the Hollande government in 2013 remained recognizably French in its territorial orientation and its emphasis on access to care, but it also adopted all elements of the international consensus framing of health inequalities. The introduction to the document characterizes social and territorial inequalities, and inequalities in health status and access to health care, as "injustices" (Ministère des Affaires Sociales et de la Santé 2013, 3). But, in line with the international consensus, it explained health inequalities as a result of "determinants of health" – "social and environmental problems," including financial difficulties, unemployment, working conditions, overcrowding, and unsafe housing – that "account for 80 percent of health inequalities, be it directly or indirectly as a result of their influence on behavioral factors" (p. 6). And the SNS documentation argued that "[h]ealth status generally, over the long term, results ... from environmental, economic and social conditions that go well beyond the health care domain" (p. 9).

The strategy's main treatment recommendation when it came to equalizing health status was cross-sectoral policy action on the social determinants of health. The text references a publication in the *British Medical Journal* demonstrating that "increasing social spending has a larger impact on health than increasing health care spending" and argues that previous reforms to the health system have "too often forgotten" the need "to act on the totality of these determinants of health" (p. 6). The strategy notes that while policy attention is usually directed to health care, "good health flows also from political choices in the realms of economics, education, environment, and labor, but also transportation, urban policy, sport, and social cohesion" (p. 9). Just as prescribed by the international consensus framing of health inequality, to facilitate coordinated attention to policy domains outside health care that affect health status, a major new policy innovation was proposed as part of the SNS: an interministerial committee for health, working under the prime minister. In March 2014, as if to demonstrate the SNS's credentials as a plan compliant with the international health inequality consensus, the Minister of Social Affairs and Health published a summary of the Strategy in the British medical journal *The Lancet*, which had in 2008 also debuted the main findings of the WHO Commission on the Social Determinants of Health (CSDH) (Marmot 2005; Touraine 2014).

The SNS was developed as part of the preparations for a new health law that the government had promised for 2016. The *Loi Santé*, which passed on April 14, 2015, was framed in the typical double-barreled French way: as a measure to facilitate universal access to health care across the French territory and SES groups, and to promote health equity. It targeted persistent inequalities in health outcomes across socioeconomic groups by increasing coverage of eyeglasses and dental care, and introducing a third-party payment system (*tiers payant*) to cover the up-front costs for medical visits for those with low incomes. It also mandated actions in the arena of public health, addressing food, hygiene, sexuality, health behaviors (e.g., smoking, alcohol consumption), and health education, and established plans to create a national health data system to bring together major medical administrative databases, which would allow for analysis of risk factors leading to illness and premature death.

The *Loi Santé* was passed six months after I completed my field work for this book, and its impact on how health inequalities policy will actually be implemented remains uncertain. What is clear, though, is that by the time the law was being crafted, health policy discussions in France were qualitatively different from the discussions of a decade earlier. "I don't know if it's really changing the way decisions are made," remarked one informant, "but *inégalités sociales en santé* are now in the debate. We do think about it now. And that's quite new" (interview FR33).

Indeed, socioeconomic inequalities in health have recently entered political debate as well as expert conversation, appearing for the first time since at least

1980 in campaign materials of the French center-left. No *Parti Socialiste* manifesto from 1980 to 2017 made specific mention of any inequality in health outcomes by socioeconomic group, but there were references to territorial inequalities in health care provision and health outcomes in the 2002, 2007, 2012, and 2017 presidential campaigns, and one reference to SES inequalities in access to health care in the 1988 and 2017 campaigns. But the 2017 presidential candidate Emanuel Macron's *En Marche!* website (*En Marche!* 2017) highlighted inequalities in life expectancy between blue-collar workers and executives and differences in oral health between the children of farmers and executives as examples of socioeconomic disparities that must be addressed.

French discourse about health inequalities has, then, undergone an incomplete transformation. In contrast to the dominant international health inequalities consensus frame, the problem of health inequalities in France continues to have a strong territorial inflection and to be centered on issues of health care rather than on health outcomes. However, in the last decade, French government reports and legislation have paid more attention to socioeconomic inequalities in health outcomes and to the social determinants of health as key entry points for policy. This change is likely due to a number of factors ranging from data availability to the participation of French researchers in international networks. However, a key motivation for politicians and policy-makers to adopt both the territorial frame and, more recently, to shift to the international consensus frame was the perception that advancing equity would have to be done without increasing fiscal imbalances. This rationale is on full view in the 2013 SNS, which repeatedly notes the need to limit spending and to be mindful of fiscal sustainability, even as it proposes an ambitious agenda to reduce inequalities in health.

Other forces, too, may have pushed policy-makers to frame health inequalities in the way that they did. One potential influence on how researchers and policy-makers frame the issue of health inequalities is the availability of data. Indeed, in a US context, the relative dominance of attention to racial disparities in health over attention to socioeconomic inequalities has been attributed to the fact that the United States has long collected data on the race of citizens, but not on their economic situation (Krieger 1992; Reed and Chowkwanyun 2012). We have already noted that the rise of the regional health observatories in the 1980s promised to make readily available data on mortality and health status at the regional level, facilitating territorial analysis. It is also possible that the ban on collecting government data on ethnicity in France could help explain the more recent rise of small-area analyses of health inequalities, which can serve as a proxy for the spatial concentration of ethnic minorities. However, data on socioeconomic inequalities in both health care and health status have been available in France since 1965, and revealed "irrefutable evidence of social differentials" – without, however, any "discernable political debate or policy impact" (Aiach and Carr-Hill 1989). So, the relative inattention to these data prior to 2009 requires further explanation.

One possible reason is the presence of a disconnect between researchers and government officials and between data gatherers and data users within the French bureaucracy (Aiach and Carr-Hill 1989; interviews FR21; FR33; FR35). Among researchers, participation in international research collaborations (some of them funded by the European Commission and the European Research Council) has undoubtedly increased exposure to the international health inequalities consensus, but it is possible that this has not filtered into the policy-making sphere. Many of the health inequalities researchers in France whose work is most closely aligned with the international consensus have participated in international collaborations headed by researchers such as John Fox, Michael Marmot, and Johan Mackenbach, who are closely identified with the international consensus. Some researchers who participate in international research collaborations have attempted to shift the perspective of some policy-makers. For example, one interviewee described how a senior researcher affiliated with the HCSP "has been trying to get [policy-makers] in a position where they can't ignore the data – forcing them to look at the results of the French participation in international initiatives, to meet with UK officials interested in this theme, assembling a report of EU policies in this area so that they can't claim they don't know about the problem or how to address it" (interview FR10). Another interviewee recounted that "[i]n 2000, a bunch of people from France went to a big conference on health inequalities in the UK [organized by the UK presidency]. The researchers who went were shocked that there were no French government officials there. They wrote a little piece in the newspaper to try to shame the government into paying more attention" (interview FR35). Yet French participation in international research collaborations predates by decades the changing political discourse around health inequalities in France, and a disconnect between research and policy has blunted the influence of the international consensus in France. One very senior researcher opined, "Policy-makers don't read anything. They only read what they themselves have written, and only in French" (interview FR2). Another explained that the participation of French researchers in the EU Joint Action on health equity "didn't have any impact on policy-makers" because "nobody from the French government came" (interview FR29).

International policy trends may have had a more significant influence on French policy regarding health inequalities than did international research collaborations. According to one high-level government researcher, "My intuition is that the question of social health inequalities came from the outside, from the EU or Great Britain" (interview FR22), and a senior academic researcher speculated that the WHO's CSDH report "probably had big impact" on French policy-makers (interview FR22). Policy ideas generated at the international level can exert an influence, albeit sometimes difficult to quantify, on domestic political discourse. "When an idea is constantly on the table at the WHO it has an impact. People start to think differently.... [T]hose kinds of ideas are coming to France through this international pressure" (interview FR31). The emergence of EU requirements for national governments to produce European Core Health Indicators has also likely raised the profile of the issue in France. "For a long time in France, there was an interest in looking at the US to say it isn't good, and looking at Canada because in Quebec they speak French. Looking at Europe wasn't interesting. But now we have to do it.... [C]learly there are some indicators on which we are not good. And then you have to think about what policies, maybe in other sectors, are responsible," recounts one respondent (interview FR31).

However, attention on the part of policy-makers to international trends can be a double-edged sword. Interviewees pointed out that highly favorable rankings of the French health care system by the OECD and WHO have led some politicians to be uncritically defensive of the system, and have undermined efforts by other policy-makers within the national government to push for reforms that would make the system more equitable (interviews FR29; FR31). In the words of one policy advocate, "If you look at mortality statistics comparing France to Europe, France is the worst. But perceived health inequalities are among the smallest in France. French people think the health care system is the real explanation for health, and they think the health care system is very good. The WHO told us so" (interview FR29).

On the other hand, when WHO recommendations reflect poorly on France's performance, they may be ignored. One researcher stated that France snubbed WHO recommendations to reduce SES differences in outcomes: "We just don't do it!" (interview FR21). A health ministry official explained that politicians in France rarely take WHO or EU initiatives into account: "Politicians say 'No, France is France! It's self-governed.' I recently met with the *chef du cabinet* of the health minister. I brought [the health ministry's liaison to the EU] with me, to say, 'Hey, you know Europe exists, there are some directives we could look at more attentively, maybe we could be more proactive....' But there was not a positive response. Europe is very far from French politics" (interview FR28). Another researcher echoed this sentiment, saying, "France is very far from the European level" (interview FR18): closed off from international-level policy discussions, impermeable to international pressures and influence, defensive of its sovereignty, and desirous of remaining self-governed.

While international trends in research and health policy may have had limited impact on France's take-up of the international health inequalities consensus, specific policy entrepreneurs within the French state have been important in advancing the health inequalities as a matter linked to underlying social inequality, rather than simply as a result of insufficient access to medical care. Interviewees cited INSERM, DREES, and above all the HCSP as particularly important sites of innovation and entrepreneurship in this regard (interviews FR2; FR5; FR6; FR20; FR29; FR35; FR38). According to one researcher, the HCSP is "the main source cited in recent parliamentary reports on health inequalities," and its highly publicized reports have been "instrumental in disseminating information about health and health care inequalities" (interview FR5). Insiders report that the HCSP's 2009 report and the transversal health equity working group set up within the organization were bottom-up initiatives led by individuals with a particular interest in the topic, and were not directed from above or undertaken because of any perceived pressure from or desire for such a focus on the part of the health ministry or other government officials (interviews FR29; FR35; FR38).

In this sense the health equity advocates within the HCSP acted as true policy entrepreneurs. Their influence at the level of discourse was unequivocal; however, the HCSP itself has little formal leverage, and its directors do not participate in the key health policy decision-making bodies (interview FR5). Moreover, it is a mistake to regard the HCSP as operating totally autonomously. One high-level Ministry official explained that key figures in the HCSP and the Ministry had been working on the issue of ISS in parallel for many years before finally joining forces to promote the issue:

That's something we, and the public health community, had been putting forward for quite a while. The *exposé des motifs* for the public health law [in 2004] included a statement about [ISS], and then we kept talking about it again and again and again. The way we have tried to promote the idea is, for example, we asked the group at HCSP to write a report on health inequalities. That's one way to try get these ideas out. Just after that, when we almost had a new public health law in 2010, we had a conference here on health inequalities where Marmot came and did his number. [*Laughs.*] [A representative from the HCSP] also presented, and so on.... So there are different ways. We [at the Ministry] were very interested to see [the theme of ISS] emerge and happy that it came. Now it seems that it's a commonly accepted thing. (interview FR30)

The rise of a health inequalities agenda that is attentive to socioeconomic as well as territorial disparities, and to the role of social determinants as well as health care access in producing health inequalities, is thus not fully explained by data availability, international influences, or domestic policy entrepreneurship. The more consistent through-line relates health inequalities discourses in France since the early 1980s to perceived fiscal constraints.

High costs in the health care system were an obvious target for cuts in the 1980s and 1990s, and regionalization of the health care system was a key tool of both center-right and center-left governments for gaining control over health spending. Territorial health inequalities became a central part of the national conversation about health policy in the 1990s and 2000s as a way to motivate the need for these regionalizing reforms. By the 2010s, however, EU- and self-imposed austerity measures following the onset of the eurozone crisis meant that France's fiscal room for maneuver became even more straitened. Some redistributive policy aimed at improving economic conditions for the lowest earners and the marginalized was still possible in France, because the left was willing to tax high incomes, but the usual strategy of "social anesthesia" spending to reduce the impact of inequitable growth more broadly had been set off-limits in the new era of austerity. As one official put it, "The crisis changed everything. After that there was no money to do anything" (interview FR36). At that point, the socioeconomic framing of health inequalities, which had become established as an international policy consensus and had gained a significant number of adherents among the French public health research and policy elites, broke through. Shifting attention to the socioeconomic causes of health inequalities justified rationalizing health care spending, and held out the promise of future reductions in spending, all while maintaining a commitment to equity.

CONCLUSION

This chapter has discussed how the French framing of health inequalities changed from the 1980s to the mid-2010s, in response to a political taboo against discussing substantially increased public spending. The core mechanism for controlling inequality in France's conservative-corporatist welfare state beginning in the 1980s was public spending, but as the financial and monetary architecture of the European currency area became increasingly neoliberal, this mechanism came into conflict with a cross-party consensus on the need for France to be a central player in the EU. In response, center-left politicians in France who might once have spoken openly in favor of increased public spending as a way to manage inequality adopted a self-imposed taboo. This taboo was nurtured by the growing convictions of center-left politicians that the electorate would not tolerate high taxes, that financial markets would not tolerate deficit spending, and that the route to economic growth lay in protecting France's competitiveness in open markets within a European framework.

Throughout the 1980s and 1990s, pressures for reduced public spending were refracted into French health policy through the lens of health care spending, which successive governments sought to rationalize by aligning regional spending more closely with health care needs. This resulted in a French framing of the issue of health inequalities that focused on territorial differences in access to health care. But by the 2010s, as fiscal room for maneuver became even tighter, French politicians and policy-makers increasingly adopted the international consensus framing of health inequality as socioeconomic inequalities in health status. This framing allowed politicians to express their concern for equity without having to promise any new spending, since the problem of ISS would be solved through integrating cost-effective prevention and primary care better with already-existing social services, rather than spending on medical treatments. As one interviewee succinctly put it, "The politicians needed to affirm that they had some big plan for reforming health without spending any money. The *inegalités sociales en santé* framing allows them to show political will without actually spending any money" (interview FR34).

The *Loi HPST*, France's central health policy reform of the 2000s, was justified rhetorically as means to promote health equity by reducing territorial inequalities in access to care and health status, but was in reality closely connected to the broader agenda of public sector cost-cutting. Spending on health care service provision was largely in the hands of the medical profession and the social insurance funds, neither of which was motivated to control spending. But the French government was ultimately responsible for financing health care spending overruns, and as one senior health policy bureaucrat remarked, "[T]he main issue [motivating the *Loi HPST*] is cost-control because the system of *médecine libérale* can't do that" (interview FR3). "We are counting every euro now," said one health ministry official (interview FR20).

In the 2010s, health inequality discourse at the political level in France caught up with international conventions, shifting to incorporate a stronger emphasis on upstream social determinants of health and primary prevention. This subtle change in the way politicians talked about health inequalities masked an underlying continuity of purpose: to generate fiscal space by controlling health sector spending. As one high-level health bureaucrat put it, "Prevention is always supported by people who want to say they are reforming the system without cutting – like those on the left of the [*Parti Socialiste*].... The idea is to take money from hospitals without saying it" (interview FR27). A *Parti Socialiste* operative confirmed that the political strategy behind the health messaging in Hollande's campaign for the presidency in 2012 was above all about reducing spending. One aide reported, "Hollande's strategy all along was, 'We have to balance the budget.' He would say, 'I'm warning you, we have to balance the budget.' And then you can ask about any policy, and he will say, 'We have to balance the budget. It's good to have X policy, but my priority is to balance the budget. That is what I will be elected on'" (interview FR36). Once Hollande had been elected, "both the president and the prime minister had decided that the priority was to balance the budget, period – even if it will have a cost for people who are sick, or can't afford to see a doctor" (interview FR36).

The *Stratégie National de Santé* process paved the way for further health system reform culminating in the 2016 *Loi Santé*. As with the *Loi HPST*, the health reforms in this period were justified as a way to reduce territorial and socioeconomic inequalities in health. The attention in the SNS to reducing inequalities in socioeconomic health inequalities was, in the opinion of one health policy researcher I interviewed, merely "window dressing" (interview FR34). Indeed, alongside the equity motivation, in the SNS ran an explicit goal of reducing overall health sector spending: "The SNS aims to reduce social and geographical inequalities in health, reduce premature mortality and improve healthy life expectancy. It must both set the course and the path to achieve this, by setting up an appropriate organization of the health system, while respecting the overall framework of public spending" (Ministère des Affaires Sociales et de la Santé 2013, 8). The broader context within which the SNS was articulated was "a strong contraction of the budget, including within health insurance. This is not a politically popular agenda!" (interview FR34).

The effects of the reframing of health inequality as a political and policy issue in France, which did not occur fully until 2013, are still unclear. Even when more time has elapsed and more data are available, it will be difficult to disentangle the effects of the financial crisis and austerity from the effects of shifting the framing of health inequality to focus on a broader set of upstream interventions beyond the health care system. Chapter 7 explores the limited data currently available on changes in health inequality in France from the beginning of the frame shift, circa 2009, until the present, and finds little impact on trends in socioeconomic health inequalities of new tools designed to solve the problem. Chapter 7 also shows that the new approach to health inequalities beginning in the 2010s shifted the focus from tools for containing inequality that were off-limits but at least partially effective, to a new set of tools that were less politically problematic, but also less likely to stem the growth of inequality.

6

From Risk Factors to Social Determinants

How the Changing Social Democratic Welfare Regime in Finland Reframed Health Inequality

INTRODUCTION

In 1964, a nationwide survey of health and health care utilization in the Finnish population revealed striking inequalities. Finnish citizens living in rural areas, where access to medical services was limited, had higher mortality, and poorer people in Finland were more frequently ill than their higher-socioeconomic status (SES) neighbors, yet less likely to see a doctor. In response, an innovative program, organized at the municipal level, was rolled out in 1972. It provided integrated public health, prevention, and primary health care and services free of charge, and focused on the poorest areas first. A review of health policy by the tripartite Economic Council that same year articulated the joint goals of improving population health and ensuring a more equal distribution of health, a dual formulation that would later be repeated in the WHO's Health For All agenda (interview FI5). The North Karelia project, Finland's internationally renowned, multisectoral effort to reduce regional inequalities in cardiovascular mortality, was also launched in 1972.

Health inequalities have been on the policy agenda in Finland for a long time, then. For most of the postwar period, however, proposed solutions to the issue of health inequalities were located well "downstream" of the socioeconomic interventions that would later be embraced by the international consensus (see Chapter 3). Until the 2000s, health inequalities in Finland were linked in public debate and in the minds of most politicians to inadequacies in the health insurance system and in access to health care. Meanwhile, the public health field in Finland focused on reducing health inequalities by seeking to modify downstream risk factors such as diet and smoking. These attributes of Finnish health policy persist in contemporary political and policy discourse, just as in France territorial inequalities in access to health care remain at the top of the agenda even as the idea of *inégalités sociales en santé* has become more prominent. Since the early 2000s, however, Finnish health policy regarding inequalities has come into much closer alignment with the international health inequalities consensus frame. Finnish politicians of both the left and right now refer to socioeconomic inequality in health as an issue of social inequity, rather than as a problem of insurance or access to care, and government policy is oriented toward cross-sectoral action to reduce health inequalities by reducing inequalities in upstream and downstream social determinants of health.

How can we explain the reframing of public health discourses in Finland in recent years? As in the British and French cases, the political taboos generated by the collision between the postwar welfare regime and a liberalizing European order help to explain the nature and timing of the reframing of health inequalities in Finland. In the 1990s in Finland, neoliberalism took the form of an ideological convergence between the center-left and center-right and increasing exposure to liberalized international markets for finance, goods, and services. Against this backdrop, the social democratic welfare regime's traditional tools for managing inequality – provision of extensive public services funded by broad-based taxation and regulation of internal markets – became politically impossible. But the very rapid growth of inequality in Finland in the late 1990s put pressure on politicians who were, for electoral and ideological reasons, still concerned with maintaining equality within acceptable bounds. One response was to prioritize the issue of health inequalities in political debate, but in a new way, focusing on "upstream" drivers of health inequalities such as income and educational inequality, rather than on downstream risk factors related to health behaviors and health care access.

Given the strongly egalitarian political culture in Finland, both center-left and center-right politicians were concerned to demonstrate their interest in controlling inequality. This meant that the reframing of inequality was a more consensual political project in Finland than it was in either Britain or France. The long history of public concern with health inequalities in Finland also meant that inequality and health were already closely linked in political discourse. But as integration with liberalized European markets made the traditional policy tools associated with the social democratic welfare regime more problematic for Finnish policy-makers to wield, and as social inequality skyrocketed started in the mid-1990s as a result, health inequalities were reframed as a problem of broader social inequalities that required coordinated policy action across a variety of domains outside the health sector. What changed in the early 2000s was not so much the salience of health inequalities relative to other forms of inequality (as was the case in Britain in the 1990s), but, as in France, the way that politicians and policy-makers conceptualized and mobilized health inequality itself as a public problem. In Finland this involved elevating elements of the international health inequality consensus frame that had previously been less prominent, most importantly the emphasis on reducing health inequalities by reducing inequalities in the upstream social determinants of health.

This chapter follows the pattern of the previous two. The first section examines the consequences for the politics of inequality when Finland's post-war welfare regime came into contact with the intellectual and market forces associated with neoliberalism in the 1980s and 1990s. I then show how, in the 2000s, reframing inequality – in this case, a shift in the way that policy actors conceived of the problem of inequality in health – was a response to the political taboos generated by the clash between the old and new socioeconomic models. Compared to the English and French case studies, this chapter relies less on primary analysis of government documents and mainstream media, which I did not have the language skills to access, and more on English-language interviews and secondary sources. I forgo comprehensive content analysis of Finnish government reports on health inequalities, instead focusing in depth on the documents that have official English translations available. In an effort to make up for the paucity of Finnish-language resources, I conducted extensive interviews with a wide range of academic experts and health policy elites, including authors of the most significant government reports dating back to the 1970s, and made a thorough study of the secondary literatures in English on political economy, social policy, and public health in Finland. Table 6.1 presents a timeline of the major government actions related to health inequalities and contextualizing events that are discussed in the chapter.

THE TABOO: FROM SOCIAL DEMOCRATIC INTERVENTION TO RESPECTING MARKETS

In Chapters 4 and 5 we saw that the specific characteristics of the liberal and conservative-corporatist welfare regimes generated distinctive taboos when they confronted the rise of neoliberalism in England and France in the 1980s and 1990s. Center-left politicians responded by reframing the issue of inequality in terms of health (in England) and reframing the issue of health equity in terms of social determinants (in France). In Finland, the same process was at work, but different taboos and responses were generated because the characteristics of a social democratic welfare regime rendered policy and politics vulnerable to different aspects of neoliberalism than in England or France.

In the social democratic welfare regime's postwar order, social equality was maintained at levels lower than anywhere else in the industrialized world, through a commitment to redistributive taxation and social spending on a broad array of high-quality services. The small countries that make up the social democratic world relied on liberal external trade regimes in the postwar period to produce levels of economic growth that could maintain full employment, which was essential to finance an encompassing welfare state. Internally, however, these countries favored rather heavy intervention in markets for labor, goods, and services in order to buffer society from the market and ensure the desired high level of social equality.

TABLE 6.1 *Timeline of major events in Finnish health inequality politics*

Prime Minister (party)	Year	Event
Urho Kekkonen (Agrarian)	1955	Finnish government embarks on program to improve access to curative medical care.
Reino Ragnar Lehto (Independent)	1964	Nationwide survey reveals inequalities in health status and health care utilization by region and SES.
		Universal, public sickness insurance program introduced to complement existing occupationally based insurance.
Rafael Paasio (Social Democratic)	1972	Primary Health Care Act establishes a system of public health centers run by municipalities, providing preventative, primary, and social care services free at the point of service.
		Report of the Finland Economic Council establishes dual aim of health policy as improving population health and reducing inequalities in health status.
		Launch of the North Karelia project, a multisectoral effort to reduce regional inequalities in cardiovascular mortality.
Kalevi Sorsa (Social Democratic)	1986	Finland volunteers as pilot country for WHO's Health for All program.
Harri Holkeri (National Coalition)/Esko Ahno (Centre)	1991	Deep recession, caused by collapse of Soviet Union and liberalization of banking sector, results in mass unemployment.
Esko Ahno (Centre)	1993	Finland revises Health for All strategy to place a greater emphasis on health equity.
		Reform of system of central government financing of municipalities provides greater discretion and initiates gradual reduction of spending on health promotion and preventive services.
	1994	Start of rapid growth in socioeconomic inequality in Finland due to reductions in social benefits and revisions to tax code.
Esko Ahno (Centre)/Paavo Lipponen (Social Democratic)	1995	Finland joins the EU.
Paavo Lipponen (Social Democratic)	2001	Health 2015 National Public Health Program launched.
Matti Vanhanen (Centre)	2004	Estonia joins the EU, resulting in easier importation of alcohol into Finland.

(*continued*)

TABLE 6.1 *(continued)*

Prime Minister (party)	Year	Event
		Finland reduces alcohol taxes in response. Launch of TEROKA (acronym for Reducing Socioeconomic Health Inequalities), a pilot program with the goal of reducing health inequalities.
	2005	TEROKA and Ministry of Social Affairs and Health begin work on a multisectoral action for reducing health inequalities.
	2007	TEROKA releases *Socioeconomic Health Inequalities: An Essential Societal Challenge in Finland. A Memorandum for Socio-Political Ministerial Group* as background for a national action plan.
	2008	The government begins its multisectoral Health Promotion Program.

Among the Nordic countries, Finland is perhaps the furthest from the ideal-typical social democratic welfare regime. Finland retained more occupational social insurance features for longer than was the case in Sweden, Denmark, or Norway, achieving fully universal coverage in some areas only in the 1980s (Fellman 2008). Finland's economic policy has also tended to be more pro-cyclical than its Scandinavian neighbors, with less appetite for public spending during periods of recession and state spending generally subject to budget constraints set to current tax revenues (Pekkarinen 2005). But as a small, open, egalitarian economy, Finland nevertheless exhibited many of the characteristics of the social democratic welfare regime that created potential for political friction with the internationalization and liberalization of the European economy beginning in the 1980s.

The market-liberalizing trends of the 1980s that affected liberal and conservative-corporatist welfare states were no less consequential for the countries in the social democratic world of welfare. In the social democratic welfare states, the 1980s-era integration into increasingly internationalized markets for capital and goods challenged the postwar political economy regime. In Finland during the 1980s, policy-makers on both the center-left and center-right began to conceive of market liberalization as essential for the country's economic survival (interview FI4). Appetite for high levels of taxation waned as compared to the earlier postwar period, and there was a new emphasis on incentivizing investment and eliminating market distortions (D. Ornston, personal communication, 2018). Banking and credit markets were liberalized, and economic policy-making shifted to prioritize maintaining a strong *markka* rather than promoting exports via devaluation. At the same time, preparations began for transforming the public sector in line with neoliberal New Public Management principles, which aimed to make the public sector more efficient by importing private-sector management techniques and focusing on customer (client) service (Temmes 1998; Timonen 2003).

Partly as a result of financial market deregulation, a deep recession hit Finland in 1991 that opened a window of opportunity for policy changes that had already been under discussion in the 1980s. This would alter the postwar welfare regime in important ways. Entry into the European Union in 1995, to which there was agreement across most of the political spectrum in Finland, offered additional justification for changes in the regulatory, tax, and public sectors, which in turn led to increasing economic and social inequality, as well as health inequalities. Beginning in 1995, Social Democratic Party leader Paavo Lipponen's coalition government introduced reforms to the tax structure and liberalization of the welfare state and product markets that were closely aligned with what policy-makers believed to be the expectations of international financial markets and the EU.

By the mid-1990s, liberalizing pressures from international finance markets and the EU combined with domestic political and intellectual ideas favoring greater liberalization to generate significant friction with the Finnish postwar model of political management. The resulting sticking points generated, for mainstream politicians, political taboos against using the mechanisms for political economic management and public health intervention that had most informed the old Finnish model of economic management: income redistribution and regulation of markets. As in England and France, external actors made more powerful by liberalization (e.g., international financial market actors, multinational corporations) and international constraints (in the form of EU market rules) limited Finnish politicians' room for maneuver, but my use of the term "taboo" signifies that the new restrictions on what policy levers were permissible or politically tenable were also partly self-imposed. And while new styles of policy-making under neoliberalism had some elements of continuity with the past – the language of "economic necessity" and budgetary constraint has long motivated Finnish policy in the socioeconomic realm (Pekkarinen 2005; Kettunen 2006) – the fundamentally neoliberal form that the doctrine of economic necessity took by the mid-1990s was new. While the Finnish political economic model of the postwar period had emphasized providing, to the extent possible given budgetary conditions, solidaristically financed, publicly provided services and intensive regulation of product markets in the name of public welfare, politicians operating under the neoliberal paradigm believed these tools to be off-limits.

Politicians of both the center-left and center-right in Finland continued to express support for the goal of social equality. But with these taboos in place, they needed to find new ways of proposing to promote social equality without resorting to taxing high incomes, asserting a public role in service provision, or re-regulating markets. As I argue in the next section, reframing the problem of health inequality offered politicians and policy-makers a way to appear to be doing something about inequality despite these taboos. First, though, let us examine in greater detail the origins and nature of the taboos.

Creating Taboo: A Social Democratic Welfare Regime Collides with Neoliberalism

The contours of the social democratic political economic regime and its status as a model, ideal type, heuristic, or empirical cluster have received a great deal of attention in literature on comparative social policy and comparative political economy (see, e.g., Korpi 1983; Esping-Andersen 1990; Kautto et al. 2001; Ryner 2007). Despite variations in the emphasis placed on particular definitional attributes, though, most scholars recognize the social democratic (or Nordic) postwar political economic model as comprising a set of interlinked institutions that worked together to make social citizenship "compatible with economic stability and international economic competitiveness" in small, trade-exposed countries at the fringes of Europe (Katzenstein 1985; Ryner 2007, 62–63).

Relying on a liberal external trade regime led to a perception of vulnerability to the external environment that in turn "generated an ideology of social partnership that ... acted like a glue for the corporatist politics of the small European states" (Katzenstein 2003, 11). International liberalization was thus linked to domestic compensation (see also Cameron 1978; Garrett 1998). The social democratic welfare states taxed at a high rate to support high-quality, publicly provided, universal child care; education; health care; and social services designed to prevent social exclusion before it started. The Nordic states also provided generous cash transfers to support citizens who were unemployed or unable to work, and were committed to fiscal, monetary, and trade policies that promoted the full employment needed to sustain such an expansive set of social rights.

The Finnish social model of the postwar period was a variant – albeit somewhat later-developing and more reliant on benefits linked to occupation – of the social democratic welfare regime. The Finnish state (often in cooperation with social partners) acted forcefully to curb market-generated inequality and created the conditions for a society that was markedly less stratified along socioeconomic lines than elsewhere in the rich, democratic world. Despite getting a late start, Finland had by the 1980s become a fully developed social democratic welfare state in terms of its employment protection and level of social benefits (Fellman 2008), and enjoyed the lowest level of income inequality in western Europe. As in other small states in western Europe, domestic compensation via the welfare state was always tied to Finland's openness to trade, which also generated an ongoing sense of vulnerability to market forces. Finnish policy-makers and politicians have long justified social and economic policy with reference to what is needed to ensure Finnish competitiveness (Kettunen 2006). During the "golden age" of the social democratic welfare regime, social equality in Nordic states, including Finland, was seen as compatible with and even necessary to the functioning of the economy (interview FI4; D. Ornston, personal communication, June 19, 2018).

But the 1980s marked a "paradigm shift in economic policy thinking where neoliberal ideas became much more prominent" (interview FI7) and a "turning point in Finnish politics, a shift toward a neoliberal belief structure, and a change in what 'economic necessity' meant" (interview FI4). Since then, "[t]he imperatives of global competition have become an integral part of the rhetoric of national community and are widely adopted as determinants of the political agenda" in Finland (Kettunen 2004, 305). Several Finnish interviewees used the word "ethos" to describe a new belief structure that emerged in Finland in the 1980s and intensified in the 1990s: a belief structure that involved a growing faith in the positive effects of unfettered market forces and a concomitant lessening of the priority placed on social solidarity and equity (interviews FI6; FI7; FI8).

Paavo Lipponen, who would become the Social Democratic Party leader in 1993 and held high-profile positions in the party beginning in 1979, led the transformation of the SDP from a social democratic to a neoliberal center-left party (the last references in Social Democratic Party platforms to socialism as an economic model occurred in the early 1980s [interview FI7]). But Lipponen himself had always been "fairly far to the right" (interview FI12), and so his ideology alone is not enough to explain the shift in the SDP's policy positions. The composition of the SDP's electorate was also changing: electorally, the SDP had "started to see its vote share decline as a result of secular changes in the Finnish economy, like the decline of traditional manufacturing and paper exports and the rise of professionals" (interview FI14), and had become by the 1980s "fundamentally a party of those who are in employment – a middle-class party" (interview FI12) in which "most of these new middle class actually work for the welfare state" (interview FI14). According to one interviewee, the interaction between the changing electorate and the orientation of the social democratic welfare regime made "the SPD's shift to a more neoliberal approach" (interview FI14) eminently logical: "If you want to make economic policy that will favor export competitiveness without devaluing, and at the same time not be seen as being against the welfare state, an ideological shift that frames policies in terms of an economic necessity, and saving the welfare state by enhancing growth, is the way to go" (interview FI4).

Neoliberal Taboos against Devaluation, Taxing Capital, Public Spending

Finland's exposure to international markets, including both capital markets and the European single market, came together with a central ideational element of the social democratic model – the need to combine social equality with economic competitiveness – to render key elements of the postwar social democratic political economic bargain off-limits in a liberalizing Europe. The social democratic welfare regime has seen important changes since the 1980s in the political regulation of the labor market, in how social services are provided, in the degree of conditionality attached to social transfers, and in the resulting level of income inequality. While social equality remains a core value that is shared across the political spectrum (Kuisma 2017), certain tools for achieving equality have become politically taboo because politicians see them as unwise to discuss openly, for fear of antagonizing financial markets, firms, or voters.

In Finland, the steep economic downturn that began in 1991 – the deepest recorded recession in any OECD country to that point – was partly a result of policy-makers' decision to take currency devaluation, which had been used extensively in the 1970s, off the table as a tool for economic management. The "strong *markka*" policy that dominated during the 1980s, combined with significant liberalization of banking and finance regulations in Finland, resulted in an influx of foreign capital. But the collapse of the Soviet Union, a major trading partner, along with other conjunctional reasons, left Finland unable to defend to value of the *markka* in the early 1990s, resulting in a major outflow of capital. This experience resulted in the introduction to Finnish politics of two additional taboos.

First, taxing capital incomes at high rates was taken off the table in order to minimize threats of future exit by domestic and foreign capital. Legislation introduced in 1993 by the center-right Aho government (1991–95) reduced taxes on capital income relative to the rate on labor income, resulting in a widening gap between high-income earners, who were also more likely to have income from capital, and low earners. But even in the face of very rapidly increasing income inequality after 1995, the Social Democratic–led Lipponen governments (1995–2003) maintained low tax rates on capital income, raising them only a small amount in 1996 and again in 2000 (Ganghof 2006, chapter 6). Regarding the tax law change, one interviewee summarized: "The Social Democrats have not resisted this at all, the idea that capital has to accumulate so we can invest" (interview FI5).

A second result of the transition in Finland to prioritizing a strong currency was that public expenditure as a share of GDP – one of the prime indicators for financial market actors of whether a government is financially "responsible" (Mosley 2000) – became an even more important target for reformers than it had been previously. In the immediate wake of the financial crisis in 1991, the center-right government sought spending freezes and fiscal discipline in order to halt speculative attacks on the currency and "prove their credibility to currency markets" (Timonen 2003, 46). Proposals for New Public Management–inspired reforms of the public sector had been floated in Finland in the 1980s, mainly aimed at increasing the responsiveness of municipal governments (the main service providers in Finland) and the quality of services by introducing quasi-markets. By the time these reform proposals were passed into law in the early 1990s, however, the main goal had become restraining expenditure. The 1993 reform of the system for financing social services, which replaced direct payments from the central government with block grants to municipalities, was "a way of gaining firm control of the totals of municipal spending at a time of great budgetary pressure, and of delegating painful decisions about spending priorities down to municipal leaders" (Pollitt and Bouckaert 2017, 278).

Cutbacks to the social sector under Lipponen's first, Social Democratic–led "rainbow coalition" government were relatively minor, and even in the face of shrinking budgets municipalities continued to prioritize health and social spending (interviews FI8; FI10). But to assuage financial markets, politicians and policy-makers avoided proposing new spending. In fact, "[a]ll left-wing, centre, and right-wing parties that participated in the Finnish ... governments between 1991 and 1998 considered low inflation and reduction of the budget deficit the most important goals of economic policy. There were some differences in emphasis ... but a broad consensus prevailed nonetheless over what was feasible" (Timonen 2003, 45). A consensus on what was not feasible emerged during this period as well: Finnish welfare state restructuring in the 1990s was a result of "the inability and unwillingness of decision-makers to use 'old' policy tools" like devaluation, taxing capital incomes, and deficit spending (Timonen 2003, 60).

European Taboos against Public Service Provision, Product Market Regulation

Finland joined the European Union on January 1, 1995. There was never any serious question that Finland would join (and then remain) a member of the EU. The major political parties, interest associations, key players in the private sector, and the media all favored Finnish entry.[1] Debate on Finnish entry into the EU began only in 1990, after the Maastricht Treaty had established that the EU market would be a liberal one, so one might have expected substantial opposition to integration from left-of-center political elites. However, such opposition was considerably more muted in Finland than it was in Sweden or Denmark (let alone Norway, which joined the European Economic Area but not the EU) (Ingebritsen 2000). The center-left in France staked its credibility after 1981 on remaining in Europe despite the disruption that European market integration caused for the French model, but it did so against internal opposition. The Finnish SDP, by contrast, more enthusiastically embraced market integration, with little heed to the consequences for its social model,

---

[1] In fact, until the recent emergence of the Euroskeptic Finns party, there was remarkable cross-party support for EU membership in Finland, fostered in part by media consolidation, self-censorship, and courses for elite indoctrination (Ornston 2018, 63).

and in particular for its reliance on social services as a mechanism for keeping inequality in check.

To be sure, the Finnish SDP's membership and voters were by no means uniformly in favor of EU entry. But support from Lipponen and other party leaders drove the party's decision to come out strongly in favor of entry in 1991, of Finnish participation in the third stage of EMU starting in 1999, and of deeper European integration on social issues (Raunio and Tiilikainen 2003). Apart from the deepest years of the recession in 1992–94, Finland had a generally favorable deficit and debt-to-GDP ratio, which meant that meeting the fiscal preconditions for participating in the European project was in some ways less challenging than was the case for France. Nevertheless, reported one social policy expert, "The Lipponen government took a pretty tough line [on public spending], because of a fear that ... we had to compete in the EU" (interview FI5). This interviewee noted that "heading into joining the EU, the economic criteria were quite tough. I don't think the Germans ever met the deficit criteria, but Finland did, even when we were in the deepest depression of that century.... Subsidies were cut, and there were cuts in social security benefits. Even though the economy turned up again by 1995, and we had seven fat years after that, we didn't return the social security benefit level to what it was before" (interview FI5).

Since joining the EU, the Finnish government under both center-right and center-left leadership has generally supported further integration, rather than working to undermine or change the direction of the single market. Indeed, compliance with the EU's market-making and market-enforcing endeavors has received widespread support across all mainstream parties. This in turn has generated taboos on devaluation and increasing public spending linked to Finnish politicians' desires to meet the conditions for membership in the EU and in the eurozone, thus limiting the resources available to fund the array of social welfare benefits and services that Finland had previously relied on to promote social equality.

Finland's entry into the EU made the old social democratic strategy of promoting social equality through extensive public service provision complicated for another reason, too. The specific form that the European single market took made exclusive state provision of welfare services to reduce social inequality legally problematic. European Union jurisprudence in the 1990s established that health services were to be treated as services subject to international market law rather than as social insurance, over which the member states retained more control (Greer 2014, 16). As a result, health services delivery in Europe must comply with administrative law on competition and state aids (Hatzopoulos 2010; Hancher and Sauter 2012). For the Finnish health system, this has implied an ongoing opening of previously public municipal health service provision, including the vaunted multidisciplinary primary health centers, to competition from private, often non-Finnish providers, with potentially negative consequences for the quality, quantity, and equity of services. As one respondent summarized, "It's been very difficult for Finland to maintain its health care services within the EU frame" (interview FI5).[2]

The EU cross-border services directive was still in the process of being implemented at the time of my interviews, but interviewees expressed concern that it would likely impose considerable additional costs on the Finnish government and disrupt the system of publicly provided services. The cross-border services directive would require Finland to reimburse the costs of all treatment received overseas, even if the Finnish government would not have covered the treatment under its own national health service, and even if the service costs more when provided in a fee-for-service context. Furthermore, not only does the cross-border services directive threaten to increase costs in the Finnish system, it also would likely reduce equity, since "[p]oor people can't go abroad for services because they have to pay up front [there]. If you're rich you can just pay up front," and get more health care by seeking treatment abroad (interview FI6). The key difficulty, according to one respondent, was that EU law was written "from the point of view of social insurance-based systems," which are based on reimbursing private providers, making it especially disruptive to public health service models such as Finland's (interview FI6).

Forces other than the European market also pushed in the direction of increasing choice in service providers in Finland, of course. New Public Management–inspired goals of increasing competition among publicly financed services, and the desire to curb employment growth in public services after a ten-year period in which 90 percent of new jobs created were in the public sector (Timonen 2003, 118–19; interview FI8), certainly played a role. However, European regulations imposed limits on what kinds of strategies Finnish policy-makers could advocate to reduce social inequality through the provision of health and social services.

European integration also coincided with, but was not solely responsible for, the rise of a second major taboo, this one against product market regulation. This affected Finnish governments' ability to regulate the level of inequality in society. Finnish policy-makers' long-standing concern with inequalities in health status had led them to develop not only integrated community health centers, but also extensive intervention in markets in the form of taxes and state subsidies for products ranging from alcohol and tobacco to fruits and vegetables. Many of these interventions were disallowed under EU competition law,

---

[2] The same interviewee described the process that complying with EU competition law engenders for municipal health care provision in a rural area in Finland: "When we organize health care in the countryside, municipalities outsource health centers, and there is a tender. The municipalities may not have even one lawyer, but the multinational service provider organizations who come in to make their bids know very well how to make these contracts favorable to them. We are doing this outsourcing also in elder care, and with children taken into custody. In health care and elder care especially, you really need continuity of care. And when you are putting things up for bid every five years, there are always cuts" (interview FI5).

and Finland's entry into the EU forced a major revision in the Finnish government's public health strategy that had developed in the wake of the successful North Karelia project.

The North Karelia project was a twenty-five-year public health intervention, running from 1971 to 1997, that aimed to reduce Finland's very high mortality from cardiovascular disease and other chronic illnesses. In the late 1960s, prevalence of cardiovascular disease was found to be unusually high in Finland as a whole, compared to other rich countries, but especially so in the largely rural region of North Karelia. After the results of a major epidemiological survey were released in 1970, the governor of North Karelia successfully petitioned the central government for state aid to combat the high rates of cardiovascular disease in the region, and a large-scale intervention was launched in 1972. For the first five years of the project, interventions were confined to North Karelia, but very encouraging results led the government to expand the project's reach to the whole of Finland in 1979.

The project's interventions included health education campaigns, training of preventive health service providers, work with local volunteer organizations, and a series of measures designed to alter the environment to encourage healthier dietary choices. A 2009 English-language monograph describing and celebrating the project describes "collaboration" with food manufacturers and food service providers on "legislation, labelling, mass communication, and advertising using health arguments, food processing, new product development, pricing policy, information exchange campaigns, and financing of the project's programs" (Finnish National Institute for Health and Welfare 2009, 61). This rather bloodless description of "collaboration" conceals the fact that the North Karelia project involved extensive market intervention – regulation of product composition and prices, revocation of existing subsidies, limits and requirements on advertising, mandated spending by firms, and so on – all with the "underlying purpose" of making it possible for people "to buy healthy products at competitive prices" (Finnish National Institute for Health and Welfare 2009, 61).

Entry into the EU complicated this strategy, and rendered some policy levers unavailable. For example, at the time Finland joined the EU, a series of taxes and subsidies were in place in Finland to encourage the production and consumption of margarine and low-fat milk, and to discourage butter, full-fat milk, and cheese. Entry into the EU facilitated equalization of the tax rates on animal fat and vegetable oil production, which aligned with the North Karelia project's objective of replacing a significant portion of butter and lard intake with margarine and canola oil (Puska et al. 2002, 248). But EU law also provided subsidies for inclusion of full-fat milk and cheese in school lunches. An interviewee who was closely involved in the project reported that, having just "convinced [Finnish] schools to switch to skimmed milk," Finnish members of the European Parliament were "furious" that the EU regulations were undermining public health achievements in Finland (interview FI3).

Product market regulation also came under pressure from processes linked to, but not always directly caused by, European integration. For example, the Finnish and Swedish governments had long relied on a state monopoly on alcohol production and sales to contain problem drinking, which was responsible for considerable excess mortality among low-SES groups. The EU granted some exceptions to alcohol market liberalization when Sweden and Finland joined, but the bans on alcohol advertising and on drinking in public had to be lifted to comply with EU law, and borders opened to allow alcohol purchased elsewhere in the EU to be brought into Finland without duty. These changes resulted in an increase in alcohol consumption, which further increased after neighboring Estonia joined the EU. With Tallinn just a ferry ride away from Finland, Estonia's much lower tax rates on alcohol cut into Finnish alcohol sales and revenues, which in turn stimulated a downward revision of Finnish taxes, in spite of epidemiologists' warnings about the effects on population health and health equity (interviews FI3; FI12).

For some products, like tobacco, EU regulations were more stringent than in Finland. But because the social democratic welfare states relied more heavily on product market regulation to protect their citizens than did most others in Europe, this dynamic is more the exception than the rule. Overall, respondents reported that the impact of joining the EU on the ability of the Finnish government to regulate product markets to promote population health and health equity has been significant and largely negative (interviews FI3; FI6; FI9).

As was the case for fiscal and monetary policy and public service provision, Finland is subject to pressures to liberalize not only from the EU but also from international market actors. "Increasingly, the main issues [getting in the way of health promotion] are with market interests," stated one respondent (interview FI9). In the case of product market regulation, this pressure may be direct, as with the lobbying from candy manufacturers headquartered in Sweden that contributed to the failure of a recent attempt to impose a tax on sugar in Finland (Hagenaars et al. 2017). Pressure from market interests is also, however, filtered through Europe. The EU's trade agreements with other entities, including World Trade Organization (WTO) agreements on labeling and standard setting, have an important impact on member states' ability to regulate both their internal health care market and product markets (Koivusalo et al. 2009; Koivusalo 2014). One interviewee pointed out that the large multinational corporations peddling alcohol, tobacco, and processed foods have lobbyists at both the EU and the WTO (interview FI3). And a review of the implementation of the 2001 National Public Health Programme in Finland found that joining the EU "increased commercial interests and the strength of the lobby system, leading to the prioritization of economic objectives over public health objectives" (Kokkinen et al. 2017).

Under these circumstances, Finnish politicians and policy-makers seeking to promote population health and health equity have come to view many forms of product market regulation as an uphill battle. Regulation of product markets has not achieved the status of a taboo in Finland; in fact, the introduction of legislation taxing sugary foods and tobacco has, as is the case in many other European countries, been initiated by conservative governments and with the primary expressed aim of increasing revenue (Hagenaars et al. 2017). However, European regulations have softened or overturned such legislation. While product market regulation that complies with EU trade policy is possible in Finland, the type of comprehensive intervention that characterized the twenty-five years of the North Karelia project is no longer on the table.

The Finnish Taboo in Comparative Perspective

The proscriptions against taxing capital incomes, devaluation, and deficit spending in Finland that I have described earlier in this chapter bring to mind the British and French experiences discussed in Chapters 4 and 5. As in Britain, center-left Finnish politicians feared financial markets' response to raising taxes on capital income, albeit for slightly different reasons. Both governments feared capital flight and hoped to retain middle-class support, but Finnish politicians appeared less worried about the domestic consequences of taxing capital than about the need to maintain standing in international markets.

The motivations for a ban on new public spending in Finland were similar to those in France, especially in the wake of the recession, when public spending as a share of GDP rose dramatically in Finland and threatened Finland's market standing and credit rating. Unprompted, one respondent made the comparison to the French situation explicit: "I'm sure the Finnish Social Democrats followed very closely what happened to Mitterrand" (interview FI8). At the same time, as in France, political leaders also used Europe as a way to justify beneficial changes. For example, in 1997, the SDP argued that membership in the EMU would allow Finland to "detach itself from the vicious cycle of inflation and devaluations" that until then had constrained its economic development (Timonen 2003, 44). And, as in France, new political taboos in Finland responded to fears of how international markets would respond, but were driven as well by an ideational shift that had already begun in Finland well before the onset of the strong *markka* policy in the mid-1980s.

But the taboos that emerged in Finland in response to international market liberalization and Europeanization were also in some ways quite specific to Finland's social democratic welfare regime. The high degree of societal consensus on social equality and the necessity for openness to international trade made Finland's regulation of domestic markets for goods and services central to the postwar political economy. When confronted with liberalizing pressures in the 1990s, these features created distinctive political sticking points, to which Finnish politicians responded by introducing new political taboos. Pressured by EU law and international commercial actors to limit public provision of primary health services and to curtail interventions in markets for food, alcohol, and tobacco, Finnish politicians could have fought back or even exited from international agreements in order to demonstrate their commitment to maintaining an equitable society. Instead, they chose to reframe the problem of inequality – specifically health inequality – to accommodate the taboos.

THE REFRAMING

Finnish governments' health policy agendas in the postwar period prioritized population health, and sought to improve it by reducing inequalities in health and health care. But as the broader environment in which health policy-making occurred changed, so too did the way that Finnish policy-makers approached the problem of health inequalities. By the early 2000s, the Finnish health policy establishment had, for the most part, adopted the international framing of health inequalities as socioeconomic inequalities in health status caused by inequalities in the social determinants of health. This reframing of Finnish health policy resulted from the interaction of the Finnish social democratic welfare regime with neoliberal ideas and forces beginning in the 1980s, which reshaped the landscape for health policy.

From the conclusion of the Second World War to the mid-1980s, the Finnish government sought to implement its public health agenda using two main tools: public service provision and regulation of product markets. Finland invested heavily in preventive health care, building a comprehensive, integrated network of health and social services that were run by municipalities but strongly directed from the center, in a way that resulted in reducing inequalities between poorer and wealthier individuals and parts of the country. The government also followed the lead of the public health establishment in seeking to reduce exposure to risk factors that were related to early mortality and that dispro-portionately affected lower-SES individuals and regions. In practice this meant introducing both health education campaigns and structural interventions. The latter included state action to shape product markets in order to induce indi-viduals to change their diets and health-related behaviors such as exercise and tobacco and alcohol consumption.

These policy tools became more difficult to wield by the late 1990s. As we saw in the previous section, political taboos around public service provision and difficulties enacting product market interventions contributed to subtle but consequential changes in the way Finnish policy-makers approached the prob-lem of health equity. The new frame deemphasized unequal access to health services as a cause of health inequalities, and shifted attention to upstream causes of health and illness. And whereas the Finnish public health model through the 1980s was strongly focused on reducing exposure to proximate risk factors for disease, in the early 2000s health policy discourse began to include more references to upstream inequalities in income and education as the underlying causes of health inequalities. In Chapter 7, I will examine how this shift in the framing of health inequalities set the stage for subsequent policies. The remainder of the present chapter considers in greater detail how and why the problem of health inequalities was reframed in Finland beginning in the early 2000s to match the international health inequalities consensus frame.

The Old Finnish Health Inequality Frame: Medical Care and Proximate Risk Factors

Finnish policy-makers have concerned themselves with inequalities in health status between different population groups since early in the postwar period. Section 19 of the Finnish Constitution specifies that public authorities must provide to all citizens, regardless of their personal characteristics, "adequate social, health, and medical services," and one of the key mechanisms the government has used to promote health equity has been universal public services (*Suomen Perustuslaki, 2 Luku, 19§*). Immediately after the war, and in response to a shortage of doctors in many areas of the country, the government established public maternal and child health services in all municipalities. Because at that time much of the country was rural and poor, and because the preventive care provided by the clinics covered all women and children at a critical period in the life course, this innovation was "very important from an equity point of view" (interview FI7). Beginning in 1955, the Finnish government also embarked on an ambitious program to provide access to curative medical care to previously excluded regions and population groups. In 1955, Finland had only two major hospitals, in Helsinki and Turku; over the next twenty years, the government built twenty new public hospitals, beginning in the poorest parts of the country (interview FI7).

In 1964, Finland introduced a universal, public sickness insurance program to complement existing occupationally based provision for which only some categories of workers were eligible. The 1964 law covered the costs of medical treatments, medications, maternity care, and sickness cash benefits (beginning in 1967, doctor fees were reimbursed as well).[3] However, as one respondent who was a political activist at the time put it, by the 1970s, "the idea was very strong in Finland that sickness insurance wouldn't solve the equity problem in health" (interview FI8). In a process parallel to the UK experience, but characterized by more intentional data collection and policy evaluation, policy-makers in Finland learned from population health status surveys carried out in 1964 and 1967 that significant socioeconomic and regional inequalities in health status remained, even after the rollout of a national sickness insurance program. In response, the year 1972 saw the passage of the Primary Health Care Act, which established the system of public health centers run by the municipalities providing preventive, primary, and social care services free at the point of service. Once again, in pursuit of greater equity in health, the rollout of

---

[3] Parliament of Finland, Law 364/1963, "Health Insurance Act," July 4, 1963, www.Perfar.Eu/Policies/Health-Insurance-Act-3641963, n.d.

the program was intentionally started in the poorest, most rural areas of the country (interview FI5).

The Primary Health Care Act defined health policy as "health and medical care aimed at the individual and his or her environment and related activities aimed at maintaining and promoting the state of health of the population."[4] This emphasis on treating the environment as well as persons was the second critical element of Finnish health policy in the postwar period. Political and economic circumstances in Finland in the 1960s (including the rapid transition to an industrial economy, the presence of a large, viable Communist party, and the governing Social Democratic Party's leadership) created an opening for a radical, community-based approach to preventive health services and to health equity among public health policy-makers that prevailed through the 1970s (interviews FI5; FI8; FI13). As we saw in the previous section, the Finnish government supported significant interventions in product markets as a way to change the public health environment. Regulating, taxing, and subsidizing markets for alcohol, tobacco, and foodstuffs was a way to reduce exposure to risk factors in the population at large; and since these risk factors were concentrated in poorer regions and among lower-income people, this was also an important route to creating greater health equity.

In the early 1970s, Finnish policy-makers began more explicitly to address the problem of inequalities in health, making Finland "among the first European countries to adopt the task of reducing socioeconomic health inequalities as an explicit health policy objective," as a later policy document would proudly announce (Finnish Ministry of Social Affairs and Health 2009, 196). A 1972 report of the Economic Council established the aim of health policy as improved population health as well as a more equal distribution of health, "using these two phrases together long before these terms were used by the WHO in their Health For All statement" (interview FI5). Finland became a pilot country for the Health For All program in 1986, and reducing health inequalities has been included as an objective in all Finnish health policy programs since that year (Finnish Ministry of Social Affairs and Health 2009, 4). In 1993, the government of Finland revised their national Health For All strategy, putting an even greater emphasis on health equity. With the expiration of the 1993 HFA strategy in 2001, the government adopted a new public health plan, Health 2015. Throughout this period, Finnish policy-makers attempted to coordinate actions to improve population health and reduce health inequalities by working in a coordinated way across sectors, making Finland an early adopter of the Health in All Policies approach as well (Kokkinen et al. 2017, 2).

[4] Parliament of Finland, Law 66/1972, "The Public Health Act," Chapter 1, Section 1, January 28, 1972, www.finlex.fi/fi/laki/alkup/1972/19720066.

Despite the attention to socioeconomic inequalities in health and the adoption of cross-sectoral approaches in Finland, however, it would be a mistake to conclude that Finnish policy-makers were framing health inequalities in a way that was precociously consistent with the international consensus frame already in the 1980s. To be sure, Finnish outlooks and experiences shaped the subsequent development of the international consensus through the international attention garnered by the North Karelia project, Finnish participation in the HFA program, and, perhaps most of all, through Finnish physician Leo Kaprio's role as director of the European regional office of the WHO from 1967 to 1982. But the consistent attention to health care services and healthy lifestyles as the main sources of health inequity was decidedly different from the international consensus about health inequalities that would emerge in the 1990s and 2000s at the European level: the latter was much more focused on non-behavioral and upstream determinants of health inequalities.

One reason for the differences between the Finnish and international health inequality frames was the importance in Finland of occupationally based health care coverage. Unlike Britain or Sweden, the other key influencers of the international consensus developing during this period, Finland did not have a National Health Service. Finland's health care system instead consisted of three parts: the primary health centers, which as we have already seen were designed to reduce health inequalities; the public sickness insurance program, which in the 1970s was still not fully developed, and covered private health care provision only at a low level; and an occupational health system, codified in 1978, which offered employees access to basic health services complementary to the public system. Initially intended to cover only preventive services and occupational hygiene, the occupational health system was expanded at the last minute to cover the cost of medical treatments "to compensate for the slow development of [public] primary health care in urban industrial centers" (interview FI8). As a result, members of the active labor force got preferential health care, which made the health care system less equitable even as it was expanded. This development had another, longer-term consequence: as in France, pursuit of health equity became linked in the public mind to the issue of health care coverage.

Another factor that helped to distinguish between the Finnish approach to health inequalities in the 1980s and 1990s and the British/Swedish approach that was more dominant with European international circles at that time was the strong influence of American epidemiology. One interviewee attributed this influence to the fact that after World War II, Finland was the only country that repaid its war debts to the United States. In return, the interviewee said, the US government sponsored a large number of Finnish scholars to undertake advanced training in the United States (interview FI3). Finnish researchers' and policy-makers' close connections with American health researchers in the 1950s and 1960s led to a strong emphasis in the Finnish public health field on chronic disease epidemiology, and to a particular focus on lung cancer and cardiovascular disease and their associated behavioral and biomedical risk factors. Kaprio, like many Finnish public health experts at that time, did his doctoral training in the United States. Finland was one of the countries represented in the US-based Seven Countries Study, which was launched in 1958 under the leadership of Ancel Keys, and explored the relationship between dietary patterns and coronary heart disease. Martti Karvonen, one of the lead Finnish researchers in the Seven Countries Study, went on to become a key player in developing the North Karelia project, and eventually General Director of the Finnish Institute of Occupational Health. These connections between the United States and Finland led Finland to be more integrated into the American, biomedical tradition of public health than into the European social medicine tradition – in fact, "[o]nly in the last fifteen years has there been more contact with EU countries than with the US, partly for political reasons" (interview FI3). It also led Finland to develop "a strong medical epidemiological tradition," especially in cardiovascular disease and cancer (interview FI11).

Beginning in the 1970s, Finnish public health policy was "pretty purely risk-factor oriented and about disease control," partly as a result of the focus on diseases that were preventable by modifying health-related behaviors (interview F17). Reports one interviewee, "We had such an epidemiological approach, we tended to forget the causes of the causes" (interview FI11). A focus on modifiable risk factors, more than structural causes of health inequalities, was also encouraged by Finland's relative socioeconomic equality: "In the 1980s and early 1990s, Finland was one of the most equal countries. So, people said that health inequalities were not related to social inequality" (interview FI10).

In line with the health inequalities frame dominant in Finland for much of the postwar period, the 2001 national public health program, Health 2015, while not mainly focused on health inequalities, laid out a strategy for promoting health equity through two prongs: improved access to services and better control of modifiable risk factors. There are thirty-six action items in the program, of which two explicitly mention the goal of enhancing health equity. Action 16 states that "health care must be developed in a way that will guarantee everyone equal, sufficient, and high-quality services, so that regional and socioeconomic status does not limit access to the necessary services," while Action 17 specifies that social welfare and health care services must be developed "so as to ensure that everyone, regardless of socioeconomic status or origin, is able to get understandable information about ... health and its promotion, together with the chance to influence decision-making concerning their own health." However, as a subsequent policy document notes, "the goals of health promotion and disease prevention" were "overshadowed" by proposals for the development of hospital services (Finnish Ministry of Social Affairs and Health 2009, 197).

Despite these limitations, however, Health 2015 marked a transition from the old Finnish health inequalities frame, which blamed a lack of health equity on insufficient access to care and on modifiable lifestyle factors, to a new frame that was more strongly aligned with the international health inequalities consensus. Health 2015 set targets for reducing by one-fifth mortality differences between men and women, between groups with different educational attainment, and between different occupational groups, with a focus on improving the health status in deprived groups, policy ideas that were common in European health equity documents of the period.

The Early 2000s and the New Frame

The new health inequalities frame adopted in Finland beginning in the early 2000s was not a radical departure from the approach adopted in Health 2015. It did, however, shift the emphasis from access to health and social services as a cause of health inequalities to a more multisectoral approach. In the realm of public health interventions, it similarly shifted the emphasis from creating the conditions for changing health behaviors at the individual and community level to focusing on the upstream causes of health and illness. While the risk-factor orientation of Finnish public health did not disappear, beginning in the early 2000s, government strategies and public discourse paid more attention to inequalities in education, employment, and income as sources of health inequalities.

The Vanhanen government that held office from 2003 to 2007 was a Centre Party–led coalition with the Social Democratic and Swedish People's parties. The Ministry of Social Affairs and Health (MSAH), which was led by a Social Democratic minister, acknowledged in its 2003 health program that health inequalities could not be reduced through actions in the health service sector alone. The government committed itself to cross-sectoral action to reduce health inequalities, stating that "a concerted effort will be made to narrow any health-related inequalities among the different population groups through resolute health and social policy action and by foregrounding health and social welfare concerns in public decision-making and practical measures" (quoted in Finnish Ministry of Social Affairs and Health 2009, 198). In 2004, the government established TEROKA, whose acronym stands for "Reducing Socioeconomic Health Inequalities in Finland." TEROKA was a pilot project created with the goal of reducing health inequalities. It brought together researchers from KTL (the National Institute of Public Health), STAKES (the National Research and Development Centre for Welfare and Health), and TTL (the Finnish Institute of Occupational Health). The steering committee also included representatives from the MSAH, the Finnish Center for Health Promotion, and the Association of Local and Regional Authorities.

TEROKA served as "a catalyst and activator in drawing attention to health inequalities" (Sihto and Palosuo 2008). In 2005, the TEROKA partners initiated a discussion with MSAH "on the need to start preparing an explicit multisectoral action plan" for reducing health inequalities (Sihto 2008, 15).

The MSAH's 2006 Social and Health Report to the Parliament identified reducing health inequalities as a major priority and recommended that the government prepare a broad plan of action to this end (Risikko 2009, 5). The MSAH requested that TEROKA generate a background paper to inform this plan, which TEROKA provided in 2007. The government released the English-language translation of the memo, *Socioeconomic Health Inequalities: An Essential Societal Challenge in Finland. A Memorandum for Socio-Political Ministerial Group*, in 2009. This background paper linked reducing health inequalities to other desiderata of the government: raising the retirement age, securing the ability to provide sufficient services to meet demand, and reducing public spending (Sihto 2008, 16–18). As such, it "may also have been an important input to convince the policy-makers that there [was] a need for such an action plan" (Sihto and Palosuo 2008, 1).

The bulk of the 240-page TEROKA memo documents the widening of socioeconomic health inequalities, mainly operationalized as inequalities across groups defined by educational attainment and occupational status, since 1980. The memo summarizes existing research and new analysis conducted for the report showing that inequalities in mortality, in physical and mental health and functional capacity, in health-related behaviors, and in the use of health care services have either remained steady or increased since 1980. It also discusses health and social policy measures that could be undertaken to reduce health inequalities in Finland.

In most respects, the TEROKA memo corresponds precisely to the international consensus framing of health inequalities. The relevant health inequalities are explicitly defined as inequalities in health status by socioeconomic group. The document cites earlier successful efforts to reduce regional and gender inequalities in mortality and life expectancy as a rationale for focusing on SES inequalities, noting, "It is important to consider why we have been successful in reducing health inequalities between regions and genders, but socioeconomic differences have remained unchanged or even increased" (Finnish Ministry of Social Affairs and Health 2009, 16).[5] And the authors note that SES inequalities in health are morally problematic: "All health inequalities that are in principle preventable can be considered unfair and unjust" (24).

The TEROKA memo was received by the second Vanhanen government (2007–10), of which the Social Democrats were no longer a part. Health Minister Paula Risikko, who represented the center-right National Coalition party, wrote a preface to the memo that presented a causal analysis that is largely in line with the older Finnish frame: she linked inequalities in health

---

[5] The report's authors contrast abundant data on gender and place of residence with the relatively sparse data in Finland on health by educational, occupational, and income groups, suggesting that "[p]erhaps the scarcity of data on health inequalities in earlier national health reports is also explained by a lack of interest in what is an inherently difficult topic" (Finnish Ministry of Social Affairs and Health 2009, 16).

outcomes to "structural aspects of health services and the way those services are targeted and allocated," and while she acknowledged that "the reasons for health inequalities lie partly in broader social factors and in the general conditions for well-being," she also added that "health inequalities are increased by socio-demographic differences in the risk factors for major public health diseases" (Finnish Ministry of Social Affairs and Health 2009, 5). The memo itself, though, explains the genesis of health inequalities in a way that is much closer to the causal stories in the international consensus frame.

The introduction describes changes in Finnish society over the past twenty-five years that have had an impact on health inequalities, including the recession, rising unemployment, increasing income inequality, a growing proportion of people (especially those with children) living on low incomes, social policy decisions that reduced social security benefits and reduced the relative condition of the poorest, and cuts to alcohol taxes, alongside broader economic changes such as the collapse of the Soviet Union, EU enlargement, and broader changes affecting living and working conditions – some of which "may also have contributed to increasing socioeconomic inequalities in health" (Finnish Ministry of Social Affairs and Health 2009, 14).

Chapter 2 of the memo, which is dedicated to laying out a theoretical model for the genesis of health inequalities, draws heavily on ideas that are central to the development of the international consensus. The report follows the UK Black Report in considering explanations based on artifact, selection, culture and behavior, and materialist/structuralist explanations. It refers also to psychosocial mechanisms, citing Wilkinson and Marmot's *Social Determinants of Health: The Solid Facts* (WHO Regional Office for Europe 2003), and presents a reproduction of a diagram from Mackenbach (1994) showing "factors influencing socioeconomic health inequalities" and potential intervention points (Finnish Ministry of Social Affairs and Health 2009, 32). The conclusion of the TEROKA team, like that of the Black Report authors, is that "[s]ocio-economic health inequalities are deeply entrenched in the structures of modern society. The structures and processes that inherently engender social and other inequalities are reflected in the totality of people's social position. These inequality-engendering processes are manifested in the unequal distribution of power, esteem, wealth, and other resources in society. Health inequalities thus reflect the hierarchic construction and order of society as a whole" (22).

The report does not use the language of "social determinants," and it is still further from claiming that upstream income or educational inequalities are "fundamental causes" of health inequalities (Link and Phelan 1995). Furthermore, the authors argue that the explanatory models they review pay insufficient attention to health care services, given that health services utilization varies by social position (Finnish Ministry of Social Affairs and Health 2009, 32). Nevertheless, they explain that "[m]any aspects of the physical environment and material living conditions such as poverty, low income, economic hardship, working conditions, housing standards, and the living environment are linked with health, and contribute to socioeconomic health inequalities" (p. 31), and acknowledge that, while "health behaviours account for a significant proportion of socioeconomic differences in morbidity and mortality in Finland" (pp. 30–31), "individual factors are not independent of the wider context" (p. 29). In sum, the causal explanations for health inequalities presented in the TEROKA memorandum are largely consistent with the international consensus framing of the time.

The treatment recommendations and mechanisms put forward in the report are also consistent with the international consensus. The report recommends working to enhance equity in access to health services and to incorporate health equity goals into all health promotion activities carried out in the health sector. At the same time, it urges the government to "strengthen intersectoral cooperation in the search for ways to intervene in the causes of health differences and in implementing those interventions" (p. 205). Specific policy recommendations are for the most part limited to the old Finnish stand-by of product market regulation: "pricing and agricultural policy tools to keep the prices of vegetables at an affordable level" (p. 156), "a substantial rise in alcohol tax," "restrictions on [alcohol] advertising, licensing regulations and ... retaining the retail monopoly system" (p. 206), "regulation of tobacco prices and availability, advertising bans and the promotion of non-smoking environments" (p. 206), and "general business and industry policy measures, agricultural policy measures as well as pricing policy and taxation measures" (p. 205). However, the report also urges the government to "find ways to curb the rapid growth of income differentials and particularly to reduce poverty in families with children" (p. 205), arguing that "[a]t the most fundamental level, the narrowing of health inequalities requires a social policy that addresses social inequality in general" (p. 195). The TEROKA memorandum recommends action at all levels of government, but points out that, despite the reduced role for policy steering by the central government after the 1994 reform of the system of state funding for services provided at the local level, there are certain types of interventions that only the central government can perform: "Income distribution policy, alcohol and tobacco policy, and poverty reduction, for example, all call for national action" (p. 229).

A National Action Plan on Health Inequalities

The TEROKA group's memorandum informed the second Vanhanen government's preparations for a National Action Plan (NAP) on health inequalities, which was meant to complement the government's multisectoral Health Promotion Program (2008–11) (Sihto and Palosuo 2008, 1). A separate NAP on health inequalities was deemed necessary because "inequalities persist despite the efforts undertaken through health and social policy," which were the subject of the Health Promotion Program (Finnish Ministry of Social Affairs and Health 2008, 3). Seven working groups – on Health in All Policies, municipalities, alcohol and tobacco, health and social services, children and youth, working-age people, and monitoring – were convened to inform the planning. In 2008, the government launched the NAP, which proposed actions in three main areas: social welfare policies (e.g., poverty, education, employment, working conditions, housing); promoting healthy behaviors, particularly in disadvantaged groups; and promoting equity in the use of health and social services.

The stated objective of the NAP was "to reduce social inequalities in work ability and functional capacity, self-rated health, morbidity and mortality by leveling up" (Finnish Ministry of Social Affairs and Health 2008, 3–4). If the borrowing of the term "leveling up" in the objective statement from Dahlgren and Whitehead's working paper for WHO Europe (WHO Regional Office for Europe 1991) offers a first signal that the NAP would conform to the international consensus framing of health inequality, the definition of health inequalities, which also draws heavily on Dahlgren and Whitehead, confirms it: "Health inequality refers to unjust variations in health. That means health differences [that are] clearly affected by social factors, the occurrence of which cannot be interpreted solely as the result of a person's exercise of free choice or unavoidable biological factors. When we speak of health inequalities, we usually specifically mean socioeconomic differences" (Finnish Ministry of Social Affairs and Health 2008, 22). In laying out the causes of health inequalities, the NAP also relies on iconography strongly linked to the international consensus, reproducing a diagram from Diderichsen et al. that also appears frequently in WHO publications (Diderichsen et al. 2001; Finnish Ministry of Social Affairs and Health 2008, 28). The causal language of the NAP, which locates the sources of health inequalities primarily in social forces that result in an unequal distribution of the social determinants of health, is similarly resonant with the international consensus: "Behind the differences between population groups there lies an unequal distribution of material, social, informational and cultural resources in society. The reasons for health inequalities are thus bound up with social structures (e.g. income distribution and the education system) and with working and living conditions. Working and living conditions detrimental to health are links in a chain that leads from poor socioeconomic status to poor health.... Health inequalities between social groups are not the result of some natural law, but the result of human activities and social decisions" (pp. 26–27).

The general policy approach laid out in the NAP is also consistent with the international consensus frame's emphasis on cross-sectoral coordination and action to reduce inequalities in the social determinants of health through targeted universalism (which is labeled in the NAP as a "dual" strategy "aimed at both the most disadvantaged groups and the largest groups that find themselves in the middle of the health care spectrum" [p. 30]). It argues that "[s]ocial determinants of health and the processes behind the inequalities must be addressed" through "[p]ersistent, multisectoral work" (p. 4). The NAP devotes almost a full page to laying out the principles of Health in All Policies (HiAP), to demonstrating HiAP's Finnish roots, and to heralding its compliance with the international consensus (p. 29).

The NAP was designed to complement Health 2015, which was still in force, and to coordinate with a number of other concurrent plans of the government in sectors such as health promotion and health services; employment, entrepreneurship, and work life; children, youth, and families; KASTE (the National Development Plan of Social Welfare and Health Care); nutrition and physical activity; alcohol policy; and a project restructuring municipalities and services (pp. 19–22). The fifteen action items proposed in the NAP were related to those other programs, but targeted "areas where progress in reducing health inequalities is considered to have been inadequate." Most importantly, all were actions that could at least begin, and in some cases could be completed, "during the term of the present Government" (p. 18).

As a result, the specific policy proposals taken as a group fell considerably short of a comprehensive attack on inequalities in the social determinants of health, despite the NAP's claim to "target the reasons behind health inequalities and to cut the chains of cause-and-effect at various policy levels" (p. 27), "first and foremost" by influencing "the socioeconomic resources of well-being, such as education, incomes and employment" (p. 27). For example, in the area of social policy, possible intervention points mentioned in the NAP included reducing poverty through reform of social security benefits and income transfers to families; education sector interventions to improve health prevention and promotion in schools, reduce dropouts, improve vocational training, and increase opportunities for recreational activities; development of a social guarantee for youth; job-creation and services for the long-term unemployed and those on disability or rehabilitation pensions; and work on the problem of homelessness. However, the NAP proposed only two actual interventions in this area: introducing health services for students in vocational education and strengthening health promotion efforts carried out by the Institute for Occupational Health in occupations and sectors "where factors detrimental to health are present and harmful lifestyles are common" (p. 41).

The range of concrete interventions designed to reduce health inequalities by influencing lifestyles and promoting access to services is, predictably, broader. Tobacco and alcohol taxes were to be raised, municipalities were required to introduce substance abuse prevention and services, and unspecified government actions in the area of nutrition and exercise were to be taken. Municipalities were directed to improve rehabilitation services and those directed at the unemployed and immigrants, and plans were announced to include data on health and other needs as a basis for allocating funding for social and health services. At the same time, the NAP, like the TEROKA memo that preceded it, warns that "political and economic decisions that affect health are increasingly made at the EU level and globally" (p. 28). While central government ministries, local governments, NGOs, churches, and social partners are all exhorted to participate in reducing inequalities, there are notable gaps in what these entities are asked to do. At the national level, multiple ministries and their activities that bear on health inequalities are identified, but reducing socio-economic inequality through tax policy is not on the list. At the municipal level, the overriding obligation seems to be to cut costs, despite calls to increase service provision in some areas: "The fact that a large proportion of the population fails to achieve the attainable level of health means extra costs and loss of revenue for municipalities.... An emphasis on corrective and acute care means more expenses for local government. The promotion of health is considered the most effective way of cutting growth in health care costs over the long run" (p. 67). And the social partners are held responsible for "disseminating information through their own information channels about how to promote health and reduce health inequalities and by actively supporting development of occupational health promotion and health equity" (pp. 71–72), but not for producing a more equitable wage distribution.

Increasing Salience of Health Inequalities

But if the full force of the international consensus's policy recommendations for reducing underlying social inequalities was muted in Finland, as it was also in England and France, the 2000s nevertheless marked a significant change in the role of health inequalities in politics and in public discourse in Finland. "Five years ago [i.e., in 2009] nobody except researchers knew about [health inequalities]. But then it got onto the agenda. Now many people use the words, and while only some understand, it's used in public discourse" (interview FI2). Content analysis of *Helsingin Sanomat*, the main Finnish newspaper, starting in 1990 confirms this assertion.[6] From 1990 until 2005, fewer than five articles that were mainly about the problem of health inequality were published each year. After 2005, the number increased dramatically, peaking in 2012 when *Helsingin Sanomat* published fourteen articles focused on the problem of inequalities in health status.

Among politicians and policy actors, attention to health inequalities has also increased in recent years, in part because of the actions of researchers to publicize them: TEROKA's action plan "got the issue in the media, and we also did a lot of outreach with municipal-level people and at the ministry to get the word out" (interview FI2). Among senior MSAH officials, "[n]ot all of them have realized until recently how unequal the health system is. But nowadays, since the last five years, they would understand that" (interview FI6). Politicians who are not health policy specialists are also aware of the issue of health

---

[6] Searches were conducted in the newspaper's archive for terms related to health inequalities and hand-coded for relevance by a Finnish-speaking research assistant. Variants on the following terms were entered in the catalog search: *terveyserot* (health inequalities), *hyvinvointierot* (differences in well-being), and *terveydenhuolto erot* (health care differences).

inequalities. In fact, "[t]hat's the main issue in politics [in health policy]. If you listen to politicians and their speeches, I think they are already in the stage of listing problems: number one is health inequalities, number two is primary health care. They are well trained" (interview FI11). Other respondents concur that health inequality is recognized as a problem across the political spectrum: "Everybody in national politics ... knows about the problem. Of course, the interpretation for this development is different, depending on who you are" (interview FI12); "The differences are mainly in what the parties want to do about it" (interview FI10).

A failed reform to the health care system in 2015 was framed in terms of health inequality, which generated further attention to the issue: "The health inequality issue was on the rhetoric of this reform rather strongly. I was surprised how strong it was in the rhetoric. There was no mechanism to do anything about health inequalities [in the proposed reform], but in the rhetoric it came through.... [E]ven the prime minister argued for the reform in order to reduce health inequalities" (interview FI8). The Conservative government's program also contained a promise to reduce health inequalities, although according to one respondent, it "didn't really mean anything" (interview FI2).

Domestic Politics and the International Consensus

The long-standing association between Finnish researchers and the WHO helps explain why health equity was on the agenda of both the WHO and the Finnish government in the 1970s–1990s. But the connection between Finland and European-level health policy bodies is not sufficient to explain the reframing of Finnish health equity discourse to match the international consensus. More important is the response of Finnish politicians on both the center-left and center-right, who found in the reframed issue of health inequalities a valuable way to express their support for greater equity despite growing economic inequality and the exhaustion of traditional Finnish health policy tools.

Even in the heyday of Finnish cooperation with the WHO's Health For All strategy, Finland did not always toe the WHO line. As one respondent noted, "We had a Health For All strategy, but the emphasis on equity was not as strong as in the WHO. It was there, but only as one aim. From the WHO's perspective, the Finnish HFA strategy was too health-services oriented" (interview FI8). Nevertheless, a rather negative review of the first round of the Finnish HFA strategy on the part of WHO officials (WHO Regional Office For Europe 2002) did cause the Finnish government to introduce a stronger equity component in 1993, and in more recent policy documents, Finnish policy-makers express concern with Finland's reputation in the WHO and at the European level: "The WHO assessment of the Finnish policy of health promotion [in the 1990s] pointed out that a policy aimed at increasing health equality should be made a key area of development and implementation in intersectoral cooperation and at the national level. Other international assessments [i.e., UK Presidency of the EU 2006] have also drawn attention to the fact that Finland still has not had a strategy for reducing health disparities" (Finnish Ministry of Social Affairs and Health 2009, 208).

There is some evidence for a reverse flow of ideas during the 1990s, from Finland to the WHO, particularly in the concept of Health in All Policies. One respondent averred that "Health in All Policies moved from Finland into the EU health policy space" (interview FI10). At the same time, international bodies have had limited power to coerce or even encourage Finnish policy-makers to change their positions. According to interviewees, even the work of the landmark WHO Commission on the Social Determinants of Health had a rather limited impact in Finland. While the NAP bore many similarities to the proposals put forward by the CSDH, one respondent pointed out: "These kinds of things often happen in parallel.... Probably the fact that the Marmot Commission had been set up made it easier to set up the work here. You can get some power from the international referents. But I wouldn't say [the NAP] was inspired by them" (interview FI6). This respondent went on to assert that the staff of the EU commission "are not supposed to interfere with national business, and if they did they would do much more harm than good" because they are largely "ignorant" of the issues around health inequalities (interview FI6).

Pressure from European-level health policy bodies cannot, then, explain the reframing of Finnish health policy debates to match the international consensus in the early 2000s. To understand that shift, we need to take a closer look at Finnish politics in the wake of the economic crisis in the early 2000s. One respondent explained that "from about 1990 onward," there was a "growing consciousness that we don't have an equitable ... system in health and social care" and that "the institutional system we had built in 1970s was one of the reasons the health care system ... was unable to compensate for health inequal-ities" (interview FI8). But full realization of the problem was delayed until after 1994, when significant cuts to social benefits were introduced, and income inequality began to climb. These facts on the ground had an impact on how health inequalities were interpreted. As one respondent explained, during the 1980s and early 1990s health inequalities were generally not linked to social inequalities, which were quite small. "But after the crisis, social policy changed, and inequalities in life expectancy also got bigger," and so the causes of health inequalities were reinterpreted (interview FI10). The timing of the reframing of health equity as a problem of upstream inequalities thus coincided, perhaps not surprisingly, with the growth of these inequalities.

Given the large shift in Finnish social and economic policy after 1994 (and under a center-left–led government) toward permitting greater socioeconomic inequality, the rhetorical invocation of the international consensus health inequalities frame might initially seem surprising. However, just as in Britain and in France, politicians in Finland seem to have found this frame useful as a way of signaling their interest in equity just when they had deprived themselves most completely of the policy tools to deal with it. Changes in the political and economic environment after the crisis had rendered many of the traditional tools held by Finnish policy-makers for dealing with health inequalities obsolete. Hence at the same time as "the economists are loudly saying that it's important to have [inequality as an] incentive in income structures, wage setting, and salary setting structures," there is "a very strong emphasis on reorganizing health and social services to promote equity" (interview FI4).

According to several respondents (interviews FI4; FI5; FI12), parties of the left (the SDP, the farther-left Left Alliance, and the green party) have shown a particular interest in health inequalities and "understand quite well that it's about more general welfare policies and [socioeconomic] inequality" (interview FI5). However, an important difference between the Finnish case and what occurred in England and France is that in Finland, the center-right was nearly as committed to the idea of equity as was the center-left, and hence had just as much interest in using the issue of health inequalities to communicate that commitment. In one interview, I described how British Labour politicians in the 1990s had used the issue of health inequalities as a way of drawing attention to the Conservatives' poor record on inequality, and asked if a similar dynamic had existed in Finland. "Actually," the interviewee responded, "I think it's a bit the reverse here. The issue of equality is such an important value in the Nordic public debate, and for the right it's easier to emphasize their pro-equality position by talking about health inequalities, because it doesn't concern distributing income, which is more difficult for them" (interview FI12). Another respondent described the center-right's embrace of health equity as "tactical," with the issue used as a way to push for privatization of public services: "The center-right brought up equity as a critique of the [2015 health services] reform proposal. [They said,] 'We note that there are inequities. We have a social insurance-supported private sector, and strongly privatized occupational health which shows how it should be done.' So, they link inequity with their ideas about privatizing, or introducing public–private competition" (interview FI8).

When I expressed surprise that the center-right raised the issue of socioeconomic inequities in health, a topic that in Britain was more strongly associated with the left, another interviewee conceded that "[i]t's dangerous [for the right] to talk about health inequalities, because somebody else will bring up the social determinants of health. If the right wing brings [the issue of health inequalities] up, and offers privatization as a solution, the left can offer a different solution. But our right [in Finland] tried consciously to take the arguments of the left" (interview FI8). Nevertheless, according to this respondent, health inequality was an easier issue than economic inequality for the Finnish right, because "[n]obody benefits from bad health of poor people; but there are people who benefit from low salaries" (interview FI8). Another respondent reported, "The [right-wing National Coalition Party] Minister of Labour last spring said it's more important to reduce health inequalities than to reduce income inequalities ... they obviously don't understand the causal mechanisms [linking income inequality and health inequality]. But the income inequality issue is very important to the conservative parties in general. They don't want to hinder growing income inequalities. They think it's essential for growth." As a result of this desire to avoid reducing income inequalities, "it's the Conservative governments that have been doing more on health inequalities" (interview FI5).

In sum, then, health inequalities are "recognized as a problem by all parties" (interview FI10), because "[i]t's something that allows politicians to talk in very concrete terms about inequality" (interview FI12). The issue is particularly valuable because while all parties are expected to uphold the Finnish value of equality, there are also pressures not to take too strong a stand against income inequality. "On the right there is unwillingness to talk about income inequality. In fact, in this country there have been strong voices from some of the richest people that one should stop interfering so strongly in the economy, that democracy is a threat against the economy" (interview FI7). On the left, too, though, it is "politically problematic" (interview FI1) to raise this issue of income inequality. "Solidarity is not a very fashionable term any more" (interview FI7); "It's somehow easier to talk about health inequalities than about income inequality, because those people who are poor can be blamed for being lazy, but those people who die younger can't always be blamed for that" (interview FI12). This makes SES inequalities in health a particularly useful issue in the current Finnish political milieu, and helps to explain why the reframing of health inequalities in Finland beginning in the 2000s was accompanied by a surge in political interest in the topic.

CONCLUSION

For much of the postwar period, Finnish society was simultaneously exposed to external markets and protected from this exposure by extensive intervention in domestic service and product markets. These characteristics are common to the social democratic welfare regime in the *trente glorieuses*, in which robust, tax-financed public social services compensated for the wage moderation necessary to an export-oriented economy, socialized the costs of human capital formation, and contributed to equalizing life chances. Internal product market regulation further promoted equity by shaping the environment in which people made choices about their consumption and leisure habits. Pressure to liberalize markets, which came about with the shift to a neoliberal policy paradigm and the development of the European single market in the 1990s, therefore implicates the very core of the Social Democratic regime. The economic orthodoxy that shuns taxes on capital and high incomes further undermines the egalitarian ethos both by directly promoting income and wealth inequality and by narrowing the financing base for public services and transfer programs.

In Finland, the old cross-party consensus on the need for strong state action to create equity even if within normal budgetary constraints gave way over a period of about ten years starting in the mid-1980s to a new cross-party consensus on a neoliberal version of the doctrine of "economic necessity" (Kettunen 2006). Steep recession in the early 1990s imposed constraints on social spending across the board, and entry into the European Union further deprived the Finnish government of the ability to subsidize and regulate product markets, which had hitherto been a key tool for creating health equity in Finland. Intervention in domestic product and service markets and taxation of high incomes have become political sticking points in Finland since the 1980s, leading politicians and policy-makers to do them quietly and unobtrusively or to avoid them entirely.

One way that Finnish politicians have attempted to avoided the sticking points associated with the collision between the social democratic socioeconomic model and the neoliberal environment of the 1980s and beyond is by talking about inequality in ways that shift attention away from the policy tools that the collision has rendered taboo. Beginning in the early 2000s, Finnish health policy, which had always emphasized the need for greater equity, underwent a subtle but important change that allowed politicians to do just that. Discussions about health policy in Finland during the postwar period and through the 1990s emphasized a strong role for equitable, publicly provided services and for intervention in product markets to shape individual health behaviors. The issue of health inequalities was reframed, beginning early in the 2000s, as a problem of inequalities in upstream social determinants of health, which were less amenable to either health services or product market interventions. This turned championing the issue of health inequalities into a "safe" way for politicians to support the core social democratic value of equality in a neoliberal era.

The reframing of health inequalities to match the international consensus "social determinants of health" model coincided with a renewed attention to the issue of health equity among politicians. As we shall see in Chapter 7, though, it did not result in policies that were likely to reduce either health inequalities or the underlying social inequalities said to cause them.

7

In and Out of the Overton Window

*How Talking about Health Inequality Made
the Problem Harder to Solve*

INTRODUCTION

In the preceding three chapters, we saw how politicians and policy-makers in England, France, and Finland reframed the issue of inequality in the 1990s and 2000s. In each country, public discourse about the problem of inequality – how the problem was defined, what caused it, who was responsible for solving it, and how best to do that – underwent important changes during this period. Reframing inequality in this way was facilitated by the availability of an international consensus on health inequality at the European level, whose development was described in Chapter 3. The reframing of inequality resulted in large part from the efforts of politicians who wanted to maintain their credibility as defenders of societal equity, but who were increasingly unwilling to advocate classical welfare policies like redistributive taxation, substantial public spending on services, or intervention in product markets.

But reframing inequality was not only a rhetorical change; it also had important consequences for both policy and politics. This chapter is devoted to examining one such consequence: a shift in the Overton window around inequality. When politicians adopted the international consensus frame that defined health inequality as a problem arising over a long period of time from inequalities in multiple, often quite distal, social determinants of health (SDOH), the Overton window – the range of policy approaches that appeared to be reasonable and feasible responses to the problem of inequality – shifted. And this movement of the Overton window helps to explain why inequality is so resilient even when many politicians and policy-makers would prefer that inequality be reduced, and make good-faith efforts to do so.

The concept of the Overton window is named for Joseph Overton, who was a political strategist at the Mackinac Center for Public Policy, a libertarian think tank at the University of Michigan. Overton's work involved teaching policy entrepreneurs how to move libertarian ideas into the mainstream of conservative thought and ultimately onto the Republican Party platform. Joseph Lehman, a colleague at the Mackinac Center, disseminated Overton's notion of the "window of political possibility" after the latter's untimely death in a plane crash. What Lehman termed the "Overton window" is the range of policy solutions to a public problem that are, at any given moment, "politically acceptable, meaning officeholders believe they can support the policies and survive the next election" (Lehman n.d.). Inside the Overton window are ideas that voters are likely to view as politically acceptable, "sensible," "sane," or that are in fact already-existing policy. On either side of the Overton window, outside the frame, lie proposed policies that are "radical" or "unthinkable" and currently not politically acceptable (see Figure 7.1).

The Overton window can shift to include previously radical or unthinkable ideas when public opinions about policy move, and Overton and Lehman themselves viewed moving the window as a long-term, even generational project (Lehman n.d.). Examples of such projects include the sustained campaigns by the "outriders" of neoliberalism in Britain (Jones 2014) – think tanks such as the Institute of Economic Affairs, Center for Policy Studies, and Adam Smith Institute – to cultivate neoliberal policy ideas that were later adopted by Thatcher. In the United States, efforts by the Koch brothers and other billionaires to normalize in conservative political circles the ideas that taxes are a form of tyranny and that government regulation of business is an assault on freedom were in the same vein (MacLean 2017; Mayer 2017). The concept of the Overton window has also been used recently in journalistic and even academic contexts to explain the sudden political viability of previously unthinkable policy choices such as Brexit or banning Muslims from entering the United States (Marsh 2016; Morgan and Patomäki 2017; Simonovits 2017). Hence, there is some confusion in current usage about whether the Overton window can be moved quickly and easily by politicians who simply assert that their preferred policies are now credible, or whether the window's placement instead depends on slower-moving societal changes that are not fully under the control of political actors.

I use the concept of the Overton window shift here to describe a change that was at least partly a result of politicians' agency – in particular their conscious decisions to avoid discussing taboo policies that would invoke political conflict. When New Labour chose to eliminate redistribution as a policy option, when Mitterrand took a U-turn to embrace fiscal discipline, or when Finnish politicians chose to lower taxes on alcohol, they contributed to shifting the Overton window in a way that marginalized certain policy levers for reducing inequality. In other words, the shift in the Overton window occurred because politicians' beliefs about which policies were politically reasonable and viable changed, and they acted accordingly. But politicians' beliefs about what was politically reasonable and viable, and the taboos they sought to avoid, were rooted in longer-term changes over which they, as individuals, had less control: the

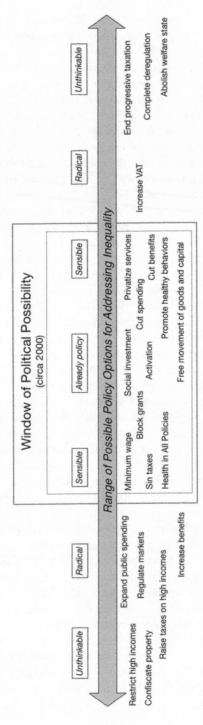

FIGURE 7.1 The Overton window around inequality

broader underlying shift from a Keynesian or Nordic to a neoliberal policy paradigm (P. Hall 1986; Fellman 2008), and changes in the environment that altered center-left parties' electorates and empowered international financial and regulatory actors with neoliberal agendas.

If the political taboos arising from the interaction between postwar welfare regimes and neoliberal policy ideas and power configurations help explain which policies for dealing with inequality currently lie outside the Overton window, the availability of an alternative framing of inequality in the form of the international health inequality consensus frame helps to explain what lies inside the window. Both what seems politically impossible – the traditional mechanisms embedded in liberal, conservative-corporatist, and social democratic regimes for managing inequality – and what seems possible – the complex tools of multisectoral, multilevel governance associated with the international health inequality consensus frame – constrained governments' efforts to reduce inequality. Shifting the Overton window resulted in *excluding* from use the policies that would reduce inequalities in the farthest upstream determinants of health and are thus likely to have the largest effect on health inequalities (WHO Regional Office for Europe 1991) and in *including* policy tools that were unlikely to be effective because they are bureaucratically complex, prone to drifting downstream, require new streams of funding, and are likely to be politically demobilizing.

A lack of evidence about what works, an absence of political will to solve the problem, opposition from corporate interests, and the EU's market-making activities all placed obstacles in the way of reducing health inequalities. But the discursive construction of inequality that results from reframing it in order to avoid taboos is another important reason why this form of inequality is so persistent.

This chapter describes the shift in the Overton window and its effects on policy outputs in each of the three country cases in turn. Each country section shows how the Overton window around inequality moved once inequality was reframed as a problem related to inequalities in the social determinants of health. In all three cases, the new placement of the Overton window excluded policies that had been central to the welfare regime's efforts to reduce inequality before the onset of neoliberalism but that in more recent years have become politically taboo, and included policies linked to the international consensus on health inequality. Each country section then establishes, to the extent possible given available data, how socioeconomic inequalities in health status were affected by the policy strategies that national governments adopted. Finally, the country sections describe the main mechanisms through which the shift in the Overton window inhibited national and subnational governments' efforts to reduce inequality. A concluding section of the chapter synthesizes the empirical findings from across the three country studies to develop a more general explanation for why the shift in the Overton window, induced by a desire to avoid taboo policy mechanisms, made it harder to reduce health inequalities.

ENGLAND: REDISTRIBUTION IS "OUT," COMPLEX
CROSS-SECTORAL INITIATIVES ARE "IN"

Chapter 4 showed that when New Labour decided to take up health inequalities as a campaign issue in the mid-1990s, they excluded from their repertoire of policy responses some of the tools of economic management that had been used by previous Labour governments to limit inequality. Taxation of top incomes and corporate profits and incomes policies designed to limit wage dispersion were taboo topics for Labour, whose leadership judged that they would be punished by the electorate, the media, and the City of London if they threatened to regulate wages or tax high incomes more heavily. To the extent that the government tried to reduce health inequalities that resulted from unequal distribution of resources, it was through poverty reduction measures, which aligned with Labour's new emphasis on equality of opportunity. Creating more equal opportunity lay inside, and redistribution outside, the Overton window around health inequality in New Labour's England.

Also inside the window lay Labour's preferred tool for reducing health inequalities, particularly in the first phase of its health inequality program (1997–2003): cross-sectoral policy coordination to reduce inequalities in mid-stream (including poverty) and downstream social determinants of health. There were known problems with this approach, which had been tried unsuccessfully in Britain the 1970s, but it aligned with Labour's government-wide emphasis on "Joined-Up Government." The result of these efforts was reduction in poverty, but little success in combating inequalities in either income or health. After 2003, when it became clear that the attempt to reduce health inequality through coordinated action on multiple midstream social determinants was not producing the desired results, more behavioral interventions appeared on the policy agenda, and the English NHS was made more explicitly responsible for reducing health inequalities.

Taken as a whole, Labour's strategy was not a success. Evaluations of individual cross-sectoral programs were generally negative; the government failed to deliver on its numerical targets for reducing health inequalities; and socioeconomic inequalities in health increased during the period of Labour's government and beyond. Early reviews of the government's health equity agenda were already quite negative. The Health Action Zones, Sure Start, and smoking cessation programs designed to reduce inequalities were found to have little to no impact on inequalities in health outcomes in the short run (Judge and Bauld 2006; Bauld et al. 2007; Belsky et al. 2007; UK Department of Health 2007; 2009c; Melhuish et al. 2008; Stafford et al. 2008). Moreover, government mortality monitoring in 2008 found that relative inequalities in life expectancy at birth between deprived "spearhead" areas[1]

---

[1] The spearhead areas were a group of seventy local authorities scoring in the bottom quintile of the English Index of Multiple Deprivation, which includes measures of income, employment, education and training, housing, crime, and health outcomes. Intensive interventions would be undertaken by

and the average for England and Wales in fact grew larger from the 1995 baseline to 2008 (UK Department of Health 2009b). Similarly, the gap in infant mortality between "routine and manual" occupational group versus all occupations in England and Wales increased by 23 percent between 1998 and 2008 (UK Department of Health 2009a).

By 2009, when the government conducted a review of its health inequality policy (UK Department of Health 2009c), there had been no reduction in mortality gaps between socioeconomic groups or areas characterized by different levels of deprivation, despite the target of a 10 percent reduction. Inequalities in some social determinants (child poverty, housing quality, educational attainment, flu vaccination) had been reduced, but relative inequalities in other health behaviors and outcomes (child road accidents, teen pregnancy, smoking, cardiovascular disease [CVD] and cancer mortality) were either stable or growing (UK Department of Health 2009c; Mackenbach 2011). The next year, the Marmot Review (UK Secretary of State for Health 2010) found that there had been no reduction in inequalities in self-assessed health, either.

Sobering findings like these led Johan Mackenbach, a leading scholar and policy advocate in the European health inequalities field, to conclude in 2011 that "in terms of its own targets, the English strategy has failed" (Mackenbach 2011, 574). To those who argued that the strategy simply needed more time to work, given that "the timeline linking determinants to life expectancy may stretch over decades," Mackenbach responded that in fact government policies can make inroads rather quickly. He noted that "life expectancy in 'spearhead areas' increased by 2.3 years in the 10 years since the baseline for the targets was set. The 'problem' is that life expectancy in non-spearhead areas (or in higher socioeconomic groups) has increased even more rapidly" (Mackenbach 2011, 572).

The few studies that have examined time trends in health inequalities more recently also find that health inequalities in England have remained steady or increased. Bennett et al. (2015) found a growing gap in life expectancy between the most and least deprived areas in England between 1981 and 2012, and Newton et al. (2015), who consider a shorter time span that better approximates the period in which we might expect to find an impact of the Labour strategy, conclude that "there has been little if any improvement in inequality in life expectancy across regions of England: by 2013, people living in the most deprived areas have not yet reached the levels of life expectancy that less deprived groups had in 1990" (Newton et al. 2015, 2264). (Newton et al. also note that in more deprived areas, declines in mortality from CVD have been largely offset by larger increases in death rates from cirrhosis of the liver, mental and substance use disorders, and neurological diseases, mainly Alzheimers, compared to less deprived areas [p. 2265].) Buchan et al. (2017) found

primary care trusts in these areas to achieve the target set in 2004 of reducing the gap in life expectancy between spearhead areas and the general population by 10 percent by 2010.

that gaps in premature mortality widened from 1995 to 2012 between the north and south of England, which are large, heterogeneous areas that nevertheless also reflect a social gradient (in the five northern regions, 11.7 percent of neighborhoods are in the most deprived decile, while in the four southern regions, only 3.6 percent are). And Gelder et al. (2017) found that relative occupational inequalities in mortality from all causes, CVD, external causes, and other causes aside from cancers increased quite markedly from the early 1990s to the late 2012.

The broad scope of policies undertaken, uncertainty about latency periods and appropriate lag structures, and the dearth of controlled intervention studies mean that it is difficult to make strong causal inferences connecting the lack of improvement in inequalities to the policy strategy pursued by the Labour government. There is some favorable evidence, too. A recent review (Hu et al. 2016) summarized a series of intervention studies that found small reductions in inequalities in smoking prevalence between spearhead areas and others, beneficial effects of Sure Start initiatives on children and their families living in deprived communities, and minor improvements in inequalities in infant and maternal health outcomes. Barr et al. (2014) also found an association between year-on-year increases in NHS allocations (part of which were due to a new funding formula introduced in 2002 to better target resources to deprived areas in order to reduce inequalities) and reductions in mortality amenable to health care in the area.

However, it is safe to conclude based on the most recent available data that the large investments that the Labour government made in reducing inequalities in health status through coordinated action on multiple social determinants of health did not bear fruit in the form of significantly narrowed inequalities in mortality or life expectancy. Moreover, even if Labour's strategy might have prevented health inequalities from becoming even worse than they would have otherwise been, trends in health inequalities in England after the introduction of Labour's most ambitious policies to reduce health inequalities did not differ significantly from those in other European countries that did not have similar-scale interventions (Hu et al. 2016).

Labour's policies did not succeed in reducing income inequality, either. Labour's spending policies, which increased benefits especially for single-parent families and pensioners, were distinctly more redistributive toward the poor than the policies carried out under conservative governments in the 1980s and 1990s. But while Labour slowed the growth of income inequality in the United Kingdom, inequality was not in fact reduced. This is because the redistributive effects of Labour's policies were in most years outstripped by increases in the inequality of earnings, particularly at the very top end of the income distribution (Gregg 2010; McKnight and Tsang 2013).

It is impossible to say for certain what effect reducing income inequality would have had on health inequalities in England if it had occurred: "There were no policies addressing income inequality as such" (Mackenbach 2011,

570). Nevertheless, Mackenbach attributes the Labour government's failure to reduce health inequalities in accordance with its targets to "lack of a democratic mandate to take more radical action. Labour had been elected on the basis of a party programme that simply did not include a radical redistribution of income or wealth" (p. 573). Other scholars concur that the failure to address income and class inequalities in England made it impossible for the Labour government to address the root causes driving health inequalities (G. D. Smith et al. 2001; Mackenbach 2011). However, the lack of government actions to reduce economic inequality was not the only reason that Labour's program to reduce health inequalities floundered. In fact, what was inside the Overton window around inequality once Labour had reframed the problem as an issue of health caused just as much trouble as what was shifted outside the window by the reframing.

Many of the early reviews of the English strategy argued that a central problem was the government's hurried adoption of policies without any real evidence about what was likely to work (e.g., Macintyre et al. 2001; Judge and Bauld 2006). However, even if it had been available, scientific evidence would not necessarily have been taken up in a way that led to effective policy. In fact, evidence about health inequalities was filtered and transformed by policy-making institutions under Labour in ways that made it much more difficult to reduce inequalities (Smith 2013a). One of the main stumbling blocks was the decision to focus on multisectoral actions requiring extensive bureaucratic coordination that was very difficult to sustain. Efforts at coordinated cross-sectoral policy-making had been tried under Labour governments in the 1970s (see Blackstone and Plowden 1988; Challis et al. 1988), and the 1996 IPPR health policy paper raised the failure of the 1970s-era Joint Action for Social Policy as a cautionary tale (Coote and Hunter 1996, 16). In light of this history, New Labour's enthusiasm for "Joined-Up Government" is perhaps surprising – but as we saw in Chapters 3 and 4, the health inequalities problem frame that was dominant in Britain at the time relied heavily on cross-sectoral action as the main policy solution.

Cross-sectoral policy-making in the arena of health inequalities seems to have encountered many of the same difficulties as those that impeded joined-up social policy in the 1970s (Exworthy and Hunter 2011). Even when considering only the two most powerful departments, health and treasury, coordination problems were rife: "With a newly appointed minister for public health, the Department of Health was a focal point for policies to tackle health inequalities throughout the first term. The second term was marked by the increasing involvement of the Treasury. Despite an appearance of coordination and complementarity, a dual leadership would inevitably become a source of duplication, conflict, ambiguity and blurred accountabilities in the delivery of the health inequalities agenda" (Sassi 2005, 89).

Similarly, attempts to promote the national-level policy agenda of reducing health inequalities using local-level policy levers proved disappointing.

The twenty-six Health Action Zones established in 1998 and 1999 aimed to bring together social service, voluntary, and business organizations, user groups, and local NHS bodies in order to develop programs to improve population health and tackle health inequalities in these areas. However, a major evaluation study concluded that despite accomplishments in getting health inequalities on the agenda and developing potentially helpful new initiatives, Health Action Zones did not contribute to reducing health inequalities (Bauld et al. 2005).

Beyond the difficulties inherent in cross-sectoral action (which in any event would arguably be lessened at the local level, where policy actors may have preexisting relationships and benefit from geographic proximity), there are several factors that likely contributed to the less-than-inspiring results of the Health Action Zone and Sure Start programs. One was insufficient financing. Despite being "by far the best resourced of all the Western European strategies to reduce health inequalities which started during the decade" (Mackenbach 2011, 570), devolution of responsibility for reducing health inequalities to local governments and NHS primary care trusts occurred without a concomitant transfer of funds adequate to do the job (Benzeval and Meth 2002; Sassi 2005; House of Commons Health Committee 2009). Another was the difficulty of generalizing from strategies that emerged at the local level to a broader national strategy, especially when limited national-level steering resulted in widely varying local experiences (Hunter et al. 2010, 85). Third was the tendency for area-based initiatives to shift attention away from policy levers capable of effecting systemic change across multiple locales. As an interviewee who was a policy advisor to the Blair government reported, "At the beginning, the Labour government's approach was quite area-based," because policy-makers feared that "if you focus on individual households, it's really hard to get the job done, because you have to be everywhere at once" (interview UK3). A downside of this strategy, however, was that with area-based approaches, "a lot of people got left out.... For example, workless adult households can be found everywhere, not just in deprived areas" (interview UK3).

As a result of the decision to attack inequality through the social determinants of health broadly, Labour's attempts to reduce health inequalities required attention to health inequalities on the part of multiple ministries and departments. It also necessitated collaboration between local government, national government, and the health service, and the ability to track both process and output goals and sustain policy focus over the long time period necessary to observe any effects on health inequalities. Moreover, all of this had to be done in a context in which there was a great deal of uncertainty about the effects that any given policy change, let alone multiple policy changes occurring at the same time, would ultimately have on health inequalities.

As the difficulties inherent in a multisectoral, multilevel policy approach to health inequalities mounted, policy drifted toward interventions on more downstream health determinants such as health care access and health behaviors. The Department of Health was a natural leader in cross-sectoral efforts, but its involvement led to a partial medicalization of the problem of health inequalities. An important vector for medicalization was institutional filtering, a mechanism of path dependence that constrains policy innovation to occur within the framework of existing institutions (Weir 1992; K. E. Smith 2013a; 2013b). In this case, the medical model of health embodied in institutions with a dominant role in inequalities policy – the Department of Health and the NHS – affected the outputs of policy-making even when many of the policy actors involved both understood and were committed to the non-medical, social determinants paradigm (Asthana et al. 2013; Smith 2013b).

Katherine Smith (2013a) argues that in England the power of medical actors in the health field led departments of health to initially be made responsible for health inequalities. These departments have control over health policy levers but not other policy fields, and their policy-makers sought out policy ideas related to those tools they had at their disposal. In addition, disease- and issue-based "silos" between and within departments prevented the diffusion of cross-cutting ideas about health inequalities. Policy-makers were more likely to encounter ideas that mapped onto their own specialized areas of responsibility, and ideas that did not fit with a department's niche tended to get blocked or reshaped. Finally, Smith argues, historical decisions to prioritize certain areas for attention shaped future priorities. For example, health inequalities targets were chosen not because they were the best targets, but because they mapped onto existing priorities. Mackenbach (2011) echoes this observation, arguing that the English health inequalities strategy failed in part because from the long "shopping list" of potential targets presented by scholars, policy-makers chose those that were most convenient given their preexisting objectives and commitments.

Medicalization of health inequalities policy, like the focus on poverty and the difficulties of cross-sectoral policy-making, contributed to shifting the Overton window around inequality away from structural solutions enacted through economic management and toward a more individualistic, neoliberal set of policy responses. Some aspects of the medicalization of health inequalities occurred largely by accident. For example, to compensate for a new NHS funding formula introduced in 2002 that threatened to produce sudden declines in resources directed to deprived areas, additional payments were directed to these areas with the stated goal of reducing health inequalities. Once these allocations were in place, however, a "meta-narrative that links addressing HI to levels of NHS funding" (Asthana et al. 2013, 179) developed that "effectively sideline[d] the macroprocesses of social inequality, legitimizing the kind of society that neoliberal government has produced in the United Kingdom" (pp. 175, 167).

As New Labour's time in office wore on, it shifted its emphasis on midstream social determinants even further downstream. This was particularly evident in the government's increasing reliance on efforts to change individual behaviors beginning with the 2004–7 English public health strategy *Choosing Health: Making Healthy Choices Easier* (UK Secretary of State for Health 2004). One reason for the shift in emphasis may have been a desire to generate "quick wins" in order to meet the government's health inequality targets (K. E. Smith and Bambra 2012, 101). Indeed, one of the appeals of reverting to the problem of health behaviors is that behavior-based policies do not require cross-sectoral cooperation and can hence be enacted and implemented more quickly (F. Baum and Fisher 2014).

The latter years of Blair's tenure as prime minister were dominated by conflict over his decision to involve the United Kingdom in the US-led invasions of Iraq and Afghanistan, and those of Gordon Brown's premiership were dominated by the global financial crisis. Nevertheless, Labour made a consistent and concerted effort to reduce health inequalities in England throughout their thirteen years in government, a period long enough to assess the implementation and the short- and medium-term results of their policies. The results have been disappointing when considered from the standpoint of either health equity or societal equity more generally. Policy tools designed to reduce inequalities simultaneously in a wide array of social determinants of health proved overwhelmingly unwieldy, resulting in scattershot efforts and improvements in health equity, but little that could be interpreted as a successful national approach to the problem. Further- more, the government's reluctance to engage in substantial leveling of the income distribution was at the core of the failure to substantially shift the course of health inequalities. The shift in the Overton window away from the politically taboo but technically familiar policy solutions of economic regulation and redistribution, and toward a more politically palatable set of highly technocratic tools, made it more difficult to reduce either health inequalities or the funda- mental economic and social inequalities that underlay them.

FRANCE: SPENDING ON REDUCING UPSTREAM INEQUALITIES IS "OUT," REGIONAL CROSS-SECTORAL INITIATIVES ARE "IN"

The tools that French policy-makers used to combat health inequalities in the 2000s were, as we saw in Chapter 5, a result of the political taboo against public spending that center-left politicians adopted in an attempt to maintain credibility with international financial actors and the EU. Mitterrand's eco- nomic policy U-turn in 1982 inaugurated an era in which economic liberaliza- tion, deregulation of first the peripheral and then the core labor market, and fiscal restraint – all of which were seen by politicians as requirements for France to maintain its position at the core of EU – came to be accepted necessities for the center-left. France's conservative-corporatist welfare regime meant that in the 1980s and 1990s, governments relied on public spending to contain the inequalities generated by France's rapidly dualizing labor market. But by the 1990s and accelerating throughout the 2000s, even compensatory "social anesthesia" (Levy 2005) spending – including spending on France's already expensive medical care system – became taboo. From the 1980s to the 2000s, the way that French politicians and policy-makers discussed the problem of health inequalities shifted in response.

Health equity in France had traditionally been seen as a problem of an unequal supply of health services throughout mainland France, the solution to which was rationalizing public spending on health care to meet medical needs in different territories. This frame was useful to politicians in an era when budgets for medical care were under some pressure, but not yet subject to serious austerity measures. By the late 2000s, though, and especially after the global financial crisis, the international consensus framing of health inequality as a problem of socioeconomic inequalities in health outcomes caused by underlying social inequalities became a more useful frame for politicians. It drew attention away from medical care services, which would require more spending, and directed it toward relatively inexpensive primary prevention and multisectoral initiatives to reduce inequalities in the social determinants of health. Many such initiatives were already in place in France, and they dovetailed nicely with the gradual regionalization of the health care system undertaken in the 1990s in an attempt to gain tighter central control over health care costs. However, as in England, the Overton window around the new health inequalities frame in France contained complex policy instruments requiring extensive coordination across government sectors and levels of government, while excluding the kinds of economic and social policy interventions that would be more likely to significantly reduce inequalities in the upstream determinants of health inequalities.

Under the traditional, territorial framing of health inequalities in France in which the main emphasis was on reducing variations in health care service provision across geographic areas, subnational solutions to the problem were at the center of the Overton window. Most of these concerned the management and financing of medical care, but there were several territorially based, multisectoral initiatives to remediate social exclusion, particularly in urban areas, that went beyond the health care sector and provided a scaffolding for efforts in the late 1990s. Indeed, a key recommendation of the 2009 High Council for Public Health (HCSP)'s report (HCSP 2009) was that these initiatives be better coordinated by a national-level body with real expertise in health inequalities.

There were also several other preexisting cross-sectoral initiatives that aimed directly at the issue of health inequalities, all at the subnational level. A 1998 law had mandated the formation of *Programmes régional d'accès à la prévention et aux soins* (Regional Programs for Preventive and Health Care Services Access [PRAPS]), which were regional-level plans designed to combat health problems related to social exclusion. While focused solely on marginal populations, rather than the full social gradient, and emphasizing service delivery rather than the underlying social causes of disease, the PRAPS were intended to help coordinate the activities of the health and social service sectors in order to improve the health of low-income and otherwise marginalized populations.

In 1999, *atelier santé ville* (ASV), or "city health workshops," were established by the inter-ministerial Committee on Cities (*Comité Interministériel des Villes* [CIV]) to complement the PRAPS and to ensure that reducing socioeconomic and territorial health inequalities was a top priority for cities.

The ASVs were to bring together primary care professionals and experts to work with representatives from the housing, education, social services, social insurance, and environmental sectors. The first ASV programs were experimentally launched in 2000–2001 in two pilot departments, and progressively rolled out in other areas and integrated into subsequent urban and health legislation. In 2006 the French government effectively nationalized the program, integrating the ASV into all target neighborhoods of the *Contrat urbain de cohésion sociale* (Urban Contract for Social Cohesion, an intergovernmental contract between the central government and localities).

Beginning in 2009, as the issue of *inégalités sociales en santé* (socioeconomic inequalities in health, or ISS) gained greater prominence in French political and health policy discourse, policy levers that were more compliant with the international health inequality consensus frame were layered on top of the new, regionalized arrangements for managing health care. From 2009 onward, the strategy for addressing health inequalities in France placed primary responsibility for reducing socioeconomic inequalities in health on the Regional Health Agencies (ARS) that had been created by the Law on Hospitals, Patients, Health and Territory (*Loi HPST*).[2]

Under the *Loi HPST*, the ARS, while technically regional bodies, act as arms of the central administration. The French health ministry has historically been rather weak (Rochaix and Wilsford 2005; Briatte 2010), but the creation of the ARS is the culmination of a process, beginning with the Juppé reforms of the mid-1990s, by which the French central state has progressively asserted its role in the health care system (Minvielle 2006; Axelsson et al. 2007; Hassenteufel et al. 2010; Tabuteau 2010).[3] The reorganization of multiple local, departmental, and regional bodies into the ARS consolidated central state control while effectively removing authority from local-level bodies and bringing the social insurance funds closer to heel. The ARS were large new agencies with substantial powers. One respondent likened the ARS for the region of Île-de-France to the health ministry of a small country such as Switzerland or Denmark, and described the ARS as powerful "states within the state" (interview FR37). ARS directors were to preside over *Commissions de coordination des politiques publiques de santé* (Coordinating Commissions for Public Health), which coordinated the activities and financing of all of the actors in the health field in a region. They thus had the

---

[2] The *Loi HPST* aimed to address the issue of health inequalities in other ways, too. For example, it exhorted physicians to accept their Hippocratic responsibility to provide care to all comers, in an attempt to stop the practice of refusing to treat patients without private supplementary insurance; and the law for the first time integrated public health into the same administrative apparatus as health care policy, a development hailed by many public health professionals as signaling a growing appreciation of the role of prevention and health promotion in producing health and reducing health disparities. However, under the *Loi HPST* the ARS were endowed with primary responsibility for reducing social inequalities in health.

[3] Traditionally, the most powerful actors in the French health care system have been the doctors, insurance funds, and local authorities.

potential to reshape old pathways of health policy-making in ways that could induce policy-makers to pay more attention to health inequalities.

Even after the adoption of the international consensus health inequality frame by the 2000s, then, the French approach to solving the problem of health inequalities was built on the foundations of the territorial, medical care-centric frame that had dominated French policy in the 1980s and 1990s. Cross-sectoral efforts to reduce inequalities in the social determinants of health were for the most part subnational initiatives, even if by the early 2000s they were being integrated into an overall health system architecture under the *Loi HPST* that had some levers for central steering. The 2016 Health Law created an interministerial committee under the office of the prime minister charged with ensuring that public policies across the board in France were attentive to their impact on health, and developing coordinated strategies for acting on the social determinants of health to reduce health inequalities. However, responsibility for reducing health inequalities remains with the ARS, and the focus of the Macron government has been on health education, prevention, and access to medical care, rather than on reducing inequalities in upstream social determinants of health. Macron's health minister announced in November 2017 that the administration would be shifting the priorities of the *Stratégie national de santé* (SNS) to ensuring access to medical care and prevention. The December 2017 Prevention Plan announced new education, labeling and price initiatives for tobacco and alcohol, a web portal to launch by the end of 2018 with nutrition information, and vitamin supplements for women trying to conceive, but it proposed no upstream interventions. In sum, regional-level cross-sectoral initiatives to address social inequalities in health, along with refinements to the medical care insurance system to reduce cost-related barriers to accessing health care, are still the main policy tools that lay inside the Overton window around health inequality in France.

Neither social policy levers at the national level, nor macro-economic policies, nor labor market regulation have so far been harnessed to address social inequalities in health outcomes, and health inequalities reports in France do not tend to recommend such solutions (see the Appendix). Inequalities in longevity and healthy life expectancy by occupation have been discussed in the context of pension reform, but any actions taken within the pension system to account for these inequalities would be remedial and would not address the causes of health inequalities.

One reason that broader social policy interventions have remained outside the Overton window around health inequalities in France may be that both the minimum wage and social transfers in France are set at levels high enough to contain poverty, and the growth of income inequality has been moderate. A cross-party consensus in place since the 1980s has gradually shifted the burden of taxation down the income scale, resulting in a slightly regressive tax and transfer system; but it has maintained revenues at a level high enough to finance generous social spending (Théret 1991; Cazenave et al. 2011; Sterdyniak 2015). In other words, with existing redistributive and social policies already doing a reasonably good job of controlling income inequality, what would be gained from asking for further reductions in socioeconomic inequality as a way to reduce health inequalities?

There is surely something to this argument. But while cash transfers are relatively generous and redistributive in France, other upstream social determinants of health such as education are much less equally distributed – yet acting on them remains outside the Overton window given the constraints on substantial new state spending. France was the European country with the largest social inequalities in educational performance measured in the OECD's 2015 PISA educational assessment (OECD 2016), a result that a recent high-level report by the French department of education pinned squarely on faulty educational policy (CNESCO 2016). Meanwhile, per pupil spending on education fell by 10 percent in the ten years between 2007 and 2017, and three times more public resources are spent on the highly selective *grandes ecoles* than on "those university courses in which young people from socially underprivileged backgrounds are concentrated" (Piketty 2017). Educational inequalities and a relatively weak system of vocational training have resulted in a surplus of low-skilled workers and a shortage of employment, an unhealthy equilibrium from which successive French governments have long struggled to find an exit (Piketty 2017). Even so, French health inequality policy documents have not highlighted addressing these kinds of educational inequalities as a way to reduce health inequalities, despite the potentially large impact this could have.

Fully assessing the impact of the placement of the Overton window on efforts to reduce health inequalities in France is still not possible. We do know that from the late 1990s to the 2000s—that is, before the *Loi HPST* was enacted—relative inequalities in mortality by education and occupation were already declining slightly (Gelder et al. 2017). No longitudinal studies have yet reported on the period since 2009, let alone linked any observed changes to implementation of policies to reduce health inequalities by the hundreds of regional health agencies and ASVs throughout France. The 2004 Public Health law did charge the health ministry with tracking health inequalities by socioeconomic status, however, which it has done since 2007. Data from studies conducted by the Directorate of Research (DREES) from 2007 to 2017 and published in the periodical *L'état de santé de la population en France* (The Health Status of the Population in France) show that inequalities in self-reported health (overall health, chronic illnesses, and long-standing limiting conditions) between managers and professionals, on the one hand, and blue-collar and agricultural workers, on the other, have held steady or increased slightly (see Figure 7.2).

If there has not been a decisive, immediate reduction in health inequalities in France, this is hardly cause for alarm, given the extended causal chains and latency periods involved in an approach focused on reducing health inequalities by acting on inequalities in the social determinants of health. As the ARS began their work, there were indications that the international health inequalities consensus had made inroads with regional as well as national health policy-makers,

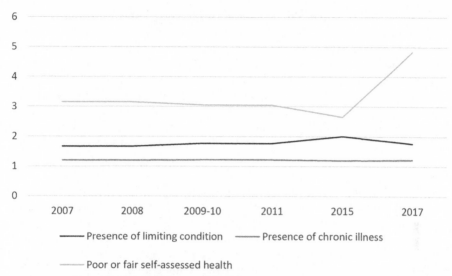

FIGURE 7.2 Inequalities in self-reported health in France since 2007. Rate ratios for blue-collar workers compared to managers/professionals.
Source: DREES 2007; 2008; 2010; 2011; 2015

and that efforts to reduce health inequalities would not be limited to reducing inequalities in health care access. For example, one study of four regional health projects implemented by 2012 found references to key international touchstones such as the Ottawa Charter of the WHO, the Dahlgren and Whitehead rainbow model, and the social gradient (Stachenko et al. 2017, 99). Moreover, given the history of cross-sectoral efforts to improve health at the local level, and given the integration in 2009 of these efforts into regional bodies invested with considerable power, there are reasons for optimism that the strategy of addressing socioeconomic inequalities in health through cross-sectoral action coordinated at the regional level could be effective.

However, the lack of data on health status aggregated to the appropriate geographic level for addressing health inequalities has handicapped efforts to evaluate policy interventions (Stachenko et al. 2017, 100). Before the 2004 health law there was no legal mandate for policy evaluation, and as a result, data were not collected on health outcomes or on the effects of policies on health (interview FR21). Health insurance claims data, which are maintained by the social insurance funds, could provide a reasonable substitute source of information about health status, but the head of the social insurance agency has not given the ARS permission to use their data at the regional level (interview FR31).[4] As a result of

---

[4] An official at the main health insurance fund avers that lack of resources to prepare the data for extraction and public use constitute the main barrier to sharing access (interview FR15).

the lack of good data on health outcomes, "It's not just that we don't have a clear idea [of what is working to reduce health inequalities]; we do not have *any* clue about the impact" of policies, reported the head of a major health policy research agency funded by the state (interview FR22). Moreover, national health ministry officials lack information about what policies the ARS are pursuing in individual regions to try to reduce health inequalities. Ministry officials meet regularly with representatives of each ARS and read their annual reports, but as of 2013, when I concluded my interviews, the ministry had not compiled an inventory of specific actions on health inequalities undertaken by the ARS, and had conducted no evaluations of such initiatives to determine whether they were effective (interview FR23).

Indeed, despite the considerable powers of the new ARS, implementation of policies to reduce health inequalities under the *Loi HPST* got off to a slow start. It took until February 2011 for ARS directors to sign the "multi-year contracts of objectives and means" (*Contrats pluriannuels d'objectifs et de moyens*, or CPOM) with the French government setting out their goals and proposed methods for achieving them. (The national steering committee mandated a list of thirty required themes to be included by each ARS in their CPOM, one of which was reducing health inequalities within their region. Subsequent funding levels would be set depending on progress toward meeting the targets agreed to in the CPOM [interviews FR5; FR6].) Similarly, the creation of the ARS initiated a new framework for developing local health contracts (*contrats locaux de santé* [CLS]) into which the ASV should have fit, but in fact they did so somewhat awkwardly, slowing the rollout of the ASV nationally.[5]

Quite apart from the slow start, the French strategy for addressing social inequalities in health seems to have been undermined by many of the same issues that plagued efforts to act on health inequalities in England. The first was that despite the integration of medical care, insurance, and public health into a single body, and despite that body's ability to convene multiple stakeholders in the *Commissions de Coordination de Santé Publique*, the ARS lacked many of

---

[5] Importing the ASV directly into the *Loi HPST* would have formalized an arrangement under which the national government effectively targeted certain areas for the purposes of reducing territorial inequalities in health, while national policies are not allowed to differentiate in their treatment of different localities. French urban policy has long honored this legal principle in the breach, but merging the ASV into the ARS would have done so explicitly. There was also a question of how to integrate local programs into the wider regional health policies being established by the ARS. The eventual solution was that ARS and local collectivities in charge of the ASV programs were to arrive at CLS contracts collaboratively, which would benefit the ASVs by giving them articulation into the broader regional health policy, and benefit the ARS by giving them access to the expertise and policy learning about how to reduce health inequalities that had been developed by the ASVs. As a result of clarifying the relationship with the ARS, the ASV programs again began to multiply, and by 2013 there were 286 ASVs in France covering almost all of the urban areas designated by the French government as "sensitive" (the equivalent of British "deprived areas").

the tools and policy levers that they would have needed to make substantive progress in reducing health inequalities. This meant that the main policy lever for addressing health inequalities that was inside the Overton window was very unlikely to lead to success.

A lack of funding to carry out interventions that could reduce health inequalities also hindered the ARS. The bulk of the ARS budgets is dedicated to health care services, but as of 2014, there was no adjustment in hospital payments for the average health status of patients in a hospital's catchment area, and no possibility of allocating health care resources for non-clinical activities such as smoking cessation programs (interview FR32). Respondents saw the ARS as being underfunded generally, but especially with respect to allocations for their public health competencies, which was only 6 percent of their total budget (interviews FR8; FR10). One interviewee contrasted the 30 million Canadian dollars invested in nutrition programming in Quebec, about which he had just learned, with his own agency's current activity: providing data for a local nutrition initiative that was producing a cookbook on how to prepare cabbage. In his view, ARS staff routinely asked his organization for appropriate data regarding health inequalities and asked for help designing appropriate interventions, but "they lack the resources to do anything to address the underlying problems" responsible for creating health inequalities within the regions (interview FR10). Adequately funding the ARS was not a policy option within the Overton window, given the government's taboo on increasing public spending.

The ARS also lacked the authority to consistently implement their initiatives. One interviewee was enthusiastic about the general principle behind the regionalized approach, but reported, "The big problem, of course, is that they have no tools to intervene. They can try to identify medical deserts, incentivize doctors to move there, group services into medical care 'homes' (*maisons*), but at the end of the day, these do not get at the underlying social determinants of health" (interview FR10). And while the ARS incorporated medico-social services such as home health visits and elder care, they did not have control over most levers of social policy at the regional or local level: competence for social welfare, infant and child policy, education, and occupational health all resided elsewhere. As a result, the ARS, whose creation was closely tied to long-standing efforts to reorganize the hospital system culminating in the *Loi HPST*, have remained mainly focused on health care service delivery (Stachenko et al. 2017, 101; interviews FR5; FR10).

Stachenko et al.'s study of four ARS' efforts on health inequalities revealed difficulties incorporating a "notion of transversality" (i.e., cross-sectoral coordination) into the work of the ARS. At the time of their study, the intersectoral commissions for public health had not yet succeeded in "sensitiz[ing] actors outside the health field to the impact of their actions on health, and even less to harmoniz[ing] the many financing mechanisms within the various sectors of society" (Stachenko et al. 2017, 101). Stachenko et al. found a few instances of ARS successfully collaborating on initiatives to improve housing conditions and literacy, but described an overall "lack of clarity in division of

responsibility between the CCPS and the Committees of Regional Administration (*Comités de l'Administration Régionale*)" (the latter are chaired by the
prefect of the Region and are supposed to ensure the coherence of state-led
activities at the regional level across sectors.) To their respondents in the ARS,
the complexity of these administrative mechanisms for inter-sectoral coordination made the situation difficult to read, and it was not always clear how the
two bodies were supposed to work together (Stachenko et al. 2017, 101).

Local-level cross-sectoral work at the municipal, departmental, and regional
levels has in some instances been more successful, and national-level steering of
the regionalized health system has increased. Even so, the central government
has yet to develop effective means for identifying and disseminating best
practices developed at the local and regional level. Stachenko et al.'s study
found evidence that best practices were rarely disseminated, and promising
programs were in fact often threatened with defunding or discontinuation
(p. 100). Ministry officials I interviewed also described marked differences in
the approaches of different ARS directors to the issue of health inequalities,
making it difficult to arrive at a shared policy vision based on the sum of
activities in the various regions (interviews FR23; FR24; FR25).

Among national-level policy makers too, a shared vision for how to
approach health inequalities has been elusive, despite some convergence in
recent years on a set of ideas that is basically compliant with the international
health inequalities consensus frame. Respondents describe lingering differences
of opinion between health researchers and policy professionals, between elected
officials and Health Ministry staff, within the Health Ministry, and between the
Ministry and the HCSP, over the priority to accord to certain types of actions
(interviews FR20; FR27; FR30; FR33; FR35). Recommendations for increased
cross-sectoral work at the national level have run into the expected problems of
coordination, turf battles, and health care system dominance.

Some researchers and civil servants expressed skepticism that politicians possess
the political will to tackle health inequalities from their root causes. A longtime
health equity advocate worried that "maybe it's too utopian – but to really reverse
the social gradient we need, I think, a kind of general strategy" to reverse the trend
of health resources going to those who need it the least. Such a strategy is
hampered, though, by political realities. Said one senior health ministry official,
politicians "have to think in terms of the issues they will be held accountable for
next week or tomorrow," but "any action on SDOH, or any kind of prevention,
has a limited impact in the short term" (interview FR30). Strategy discussions with
the Health Minister's top aides surrounding the announcement of the SNS focused
on whether it was too "dangerous to put forward something [like reducing health
inequalities] that you're not going to be able to solve that easily, and that people
don't necessarily see how you're going to address" (interview FR30). The budgetary climate posed a particular obstacle: politicians are simply "not willing" to take
on big, expensive problems like unemployment or improving life chances in
deprived areas, and "any solutions have to be very low cost" (interview FR10).

Many French health policy specialists see the new inter-ministerial committee for health introduced in 2016 as a long-awaited step in the right direction that could help to generate political will for tackling health inequalities at the national level (Stachenko et al. 2017; interviews FR30, FR37, FR40). But it is hardly a magic bullet: inter-ministerial committees carry their own political risks – "other ministers [fear] that health issues will interfere with their own agenda" (interview FR30). Furthermore, there are questions about whether the inter-ministerial committee will have the funding or the support from other agencies needed to work effectively. One senior health ministry official laughed out loud when I asked if there would be any new staff hired for the inter-ministerial committee. "New staff?" he asked incredulously. "Do you have any idea how things are around here these days?!" He went on to explain, "The idea is not to create new resources"; existing resources within the health system would need to be reallocated. The larger problem, though, "will likely be to find some support from the other ministers. To have a functioning working group you need the other ministers to be really involved" (interview FR27).

Budgetary constraints may provide an opening for more work on prevention and promotion. Said one interviewee, "I think they do understand that prevention and health promotion are important, that these are a possible ways of saving money. And that's not bad.... They're figuring out how many health promotion workers they could pay for instead of building a hospital" (interview FR37). Moreover, this respondent opined that "I can't imagine that it [prevention and promotion] can be done without any social perspective [i.e., an eye to social inequalities in health] – even if they [health ministry officials] don't know a lot about that" (interview FR37). But while the health sector itself may reorient, social inequalities in health are tied in France to a cost-cutting agenda, and so the Overton window shift has precluded actions on inequalities in the upstream social determinants of health. Ultimately, declared one interviewee, "[t]he most important thing that French policy makers could do to reduce inequalities in health status would be to reduce social inequalities. Really the answer is how you tackle the economic crisis. How you reduce unemployment, have a good standard of living for the population" (interview FR19). But these are precisely the policies that have moved out of the Overton window.

The issue of health inequality was reframed in France in line with the international health inequality consensus because the latter offered politicians a way to appear simultaneously to address problems in the French health system and reduce public expenditure. Moving from a territorial framing of health equity to what is, in reality, a hybrid of territorial and socioeconomic approaches should have led to a greater emphasis on reducing upstream inequalities in the social determinants of health. But the taboo on social spending that provided the impetus for the reframing also limited the range of policy responses that could actually be engaged in order to deal with upstream inequalities. The rhetorical framing of health inequality in France after the crisis has thus generated an apparent convergence between the French and international approaches to the problem, but without the policy interventions that would be expected under the international consensus framing.

FINLAND: UPSTREAM INTERVENTIONS ARE "OUT," MIDSTREAM INTERVENTIONS ARE "IN"

In 1990, Finland was one of the most egalitarian countries in the world. By the end of the 1990s, though, after a severe economic crisis and a major reorientation of public policy that reduced downward redistribution and lightened the tax burden on capital income, income inequality had risen dramatically. This reorientation of social and economic policy coincided with Finland's entry into the European Union in 1995, which restricted the Finnish government's ability to intervene in product and service markets. By the 2000s, the framing of the problem of health inequality in Finland had shifted fully to accommodate new taboos on redistribution and market regulation. As in France, it was the reframing of health inequality in particular, and not inequality in general, that moved the Overton window around inequality in Finland, but even this was enough to make ameliorating social inequality more broadly a more difficult task.

As we saw in Chapter 6, Finnish policy-makers have been attuned to the problem of health inequalities since the early postwar period, and by the 1970s reducing health inequalities was a central goal of Finnish health policy. The Finnish approach to improving population health and reducing inequalities from the 1970s through the 1990s stood on two legs: integrated public service provision focused on primary care, and regulation of product markets to affect the availability and price of products that were perceived as either health-harming (alcohol, tobacco, saturated fats, salt) or health-enhancing (fruits and vegetables, unsaturated fats). The international consensus framing of health inequality, which Finnish politicians and policy-makers adopted beginning in the early 2000s in its Health 2015 program and National Action Plan, was different. By shifting attention to upstream determinants of health such as income and education, the international consensus frame helpfully directed attention away from the investment in public services and intervention in product markets that had marked earlier Finnish health equity discourse, but that had become politically taboo.

But this apparently innocuous reframing of inequality also had political risks: as one Finnish respondent who had been closely involved in producing the 2005 National Action Plan (NAP) for reducing health inequalities put it, "Health is such an easy issue for politics because everyone agrees ... and can be used by all political parties ... but when you come to the determinants of health, then the controversies and differences of interest come out immediately.... [I]f you understand that this may require redistribution of resources, then we are in a hot political area" (interview FI5). To avoid getting burned, Finnish politicians adopted the international consensus framing of health inequalities as resulting from inequalities in upstream social determinants of health, but eschewed the redistributive and other policy recommendations that went along with that causal story. "In principle the NAP includes 'social determinants of health' thinking," an interviewee told me, "but the difficult questions – about redistribution – are not touched at all" (interview FI5).

This meant that redistributive social policy shifted out of the Overton window, and the parts of the international consensus that were less threatening remained within it. In Finland, Health in All Policies (HiAP) took center stage. HiAP requires collaboration across multiple sectors to reduce inequalities in the social determinants of health. The NAP, for example, included proposals for reducing homelessness, alleviating poverty by raising benefits, and helping the unemployed to return to work; some additional services for new immigrants and improved coordination of existing social services with primary health care; and interventions to promote healthier behaviors through higher taxes on tobacco and alcohol and by improving access to healthy foods in workplaces. These policies were to be carried out through collaboration across national government ministries, coordination with municipalities (to whom several of the policies were delegated), and a plan to monitor outcomes.

A final report on the NAP by the Finnish National Institute for Health and Welfare (THL) (2012) lauded the fact that "the reduction of health inequalities was prominently included in public and political debate during the past electoral period" (p. 10). It concluded, "The current Government Programme demonstrates that reducing health inequalities is a generally accepted social goal" and noted approvingly an increase in "public awareness of the co-operation needed to tackle these problems" (p. 10). However, the THL report also found that health inequalities had not improved at all since the NAP was put into place, and worried that "[t]he measures selected are not necessarily comprehensive enough for addressing health inequalities, or appropriately aimed, or sufficiently addressing the root causes of health inequalities" (p. 10).

Scholarly evaluations of health inequalities trends in Finland confirmed the THL's assessment. One study found that life expectancy inequalities across income groups had in fact grown larger between 1998 and 2007, due mainly to stagnating life expectancy in the lowest income group (Tarkiainen et al. 2012). Another declared "a major failure in reaching the equity goals in Finnish health care" after examining trends in mortality amenable to medical care in 1992–2008 (Lumme et al. 2012, 906). Socioeconomic inequalities in hospital-ization for psychiatric disorders and alcohol abuse among teens were also found to have increased despite the efforts of the NAP (Kokkinen et al. 2015; Liu et al. 2016). The most recent comprehensive reviews of health inequality trends in Finland have also found that the Finnish government's policies that were aimed at reducing inequalities had limited impact. Gelder et al. (2017) noted an increase in inequalities in all-cause mortality by education and occu-pation between the early and late 2000s. While the rate of increase of health inequalities among women slowed during this period, the long-term trend of linearly increasing inequality in mortality among Finnish men since the mid-1980s remained steady, and does not appear to have been abated by policy changes associated with the reframing of health inequality in the mid-2000s.

These results are perhaps surprising in light of the political buy-in that the Finnish strategy has enjoyed. The National Action Plan "has been accepted by different political parties in two consecutive governments and is 'consensual' in this sense" (Sihto and Palosuo 2008, 1). Ministry of Social Affairs and Health (MSAH) staff reported in 2014 that "our Minister is quite committed to Health in All Policies" (interview FI9), and a cross-ministerial network for promoting health and reducing inequalities continued the successes of the cross-sectoral Advisory Board for Public Health in eliciting cooperation from ministries for the environment, education, agriculture and forestry, trade and employment (interviews FI6; FI9). Cross-sectoral efforts, if anything, have been even "better at the local level" (interview FI9), where municipalities are required to report every four years on outcomes and measures taken to improve health and reduce health inequalities across all sectors of local government. One respondent further reports that "the whole-of-government approach [to health inequalities] allows for more centralized steering" (interview FI10), which, at least in theory, could result in more successful efforts to reduce inequalities.

The MSAH has also shown an interest in continuing to reduce exposure to behavioral risk factors through work on physical activity, nutrition, alcohol, and tobacco, and has achieved some important results. The Finnish government is "the first in the world to aim for a smoke-free country. We have the lowest tobacco consumption rates in Europe. It's very exciting. And smoking is now declining faster in lower SES groups. Smoke-free workplace programs have worked" (interview FI3). But health promotion activity has also moved upstream. According to one high-ranking career ministry official, "[W]hat we think is the bigger picture here is larger inequalities in society, like socioeconomic inequality, that influence these other determinants. Socioeconomic position and education determine how people can choose how they live. In our ministry, there's quite a strong view that all of this is influenced by SES" (interview FI9).

Beyond the rhetorical commitment, there are also funds available to pursue reducing health inequalities. This official reported that earmarking tobacco taxes for health promotion to address the health impacts of upstream factors "has created a positive cycle, helping the politics to survive. Much of the work on health inequalities has been supported by that. It's not huge money, but sometimes any money is important in terms of supporting the things that the ministries themselves can't say or promote. Quite often there are things that Ministries should do, but they can't step out of their own sector. You need to get the NGOs and public pressure activated to give political space for people to act. And this money supports that. It gives health promotion a political voice, makes it so that it's not just silent work within the administration" (interview FI9).

Why did the policies adopted by the Finnish government beginning in the 2000s under the new health inequalities frame produce such disappointing results despite the normative commitment of ministry officials, the tradition of cross-sectoral cooperation, the cooperation of local governments, and the earmarked financing to legitimate the goal of acting on the social determinants of health? One important reason is that while the reframing of health inequality in the 2000s focused attention on upstream determinants of health, it did not create the conditions for acting on these upstream determinants. In other words, the reports that were prepared to advise the government's policy-making in the area of health inequalities could recommend policies that were by now taboo in Finnish politics – for example, reducing socioeconomic inequality or regulating product markets – but governments could not necessarily enact them. These policies had shifted out of the Overton window.

Many respondents argue that the political environment in Finland since the 1990s, which has favored policies that resulted in increased social inequality, is at the root of the problem (interviews FI5; FI6; FI7; FI10; FI12). Even where actions on health inequalities have been successful – one respondent identified work on the prison population and other especially vulnerable groups – "there have been bigger wheels turning around at the same time, so you can never catch up" (interview FI10). Those "bigger wheels" were the broader economic policy constraints under which politicians were operating, and the policies that resulted from these constraints: reduction of tax rates on corporations and capital earnings, decreasing progressivity of income taxes, reduction in social benefits, and increases in user fees for services.

One report commissioned by the government had warned that many of the policy levers that had been used to combat health inequalities in Finland in the past were no longer available as a result of the fact that "political and economic decisions with health implications are no longer taken only at the national, regional and municipal level, but increasingly at the EU and global level as well" (Finnish Ministry of Social Affairs and Health 2009, 196). For example, the authors point out, in alcohol policy, "decision-making has largely been ceded to the level of the European Union. In this situation, the national and local health policy tools available are largely confined to traditional health education focused on living habits, which is still to prove its effectiveness in reducing health inequalities" (p. 201). As a result, "It is no longer possible, to the same extent as before, to rely on the old alcohol policy tools of high prices and restrictions on availability to prevent and contain alcohol-related harms" (p. 146).

Independent analyses of the NAP and Health 2015 programs largely concur that the strategies that were available to promote health equity in an earlier period in Finland were now politically impossible, and that this resulted in policies that were unable to combat rising health inequalities. A recent assessment of implementation of Health 2015 found that economic objectives were prioritized over public health outcomes as a result of "increased commercial interests and the strength of the lobby system" associated with Finland's joining the EU (Kokkinen et al. 2017). The same study noted that "the changing relationship between the state and the market, manifested in market deregulation and increasing influence of pro-growth arguments," hindered the implementation of Health 2015. A separate study identified "inequality-increasing mechanisms ... activated by welfare state retrenchment, which included the liberalization of financial markets and labour markets, severe austerity measures, and narrowing down of public sector employment commitment," as key drivers of increases in mental health inequalities in Finland in recent years (Kokkinen et al. 2015).

Meanwhile, the policies that remained inside the Overton window – cross-sectoral collaboration and multiple actions on midstream and downstream social determinants of health such as poverty, unemployment, housing, or health education – proved more difficult than expected to implement successfully. Despite efforts at cross-sectoral collaboration, health equity was easily pushed to the side by more pressing concerns. One respondent described a view that "[e]conomics is the big boy, you have to get Finland going again, you can't talk about the small, soft things like health" (interview FI6). According to this respondent, the MSAH was not consulted when the Ministry of Finance made important decisions that affected health such as changes to the progressivity of the tax code (interview FI6). Another respondent went further, averring that "the hard sectors" like finance and trade are "never involved in *any* Health in All Policies activities" (interview FI0). A recent study of mandatory Health Impact Assessment in Finland from 2007 to 2014 confirmed that fewer than one-third of tax bills that should have been evaluated for their effects on health impacts were scored. Bills addressing the "structural determinants of health (e.g. income and wealth distribution)" were not scored, because "[t]here is less experience in Finland of detecting and evaluating their contribution to population health, and evidence of these upstream health determinants is often in conflict with someone's vested interests or political ideology" (Aaltonen et al. 2018, 697).

Interviewees also described difficulties with cross-sectoral collaboration that are familiar from the English and French cases: a lack of leadership from the highest levels to "commit the different sectors to doing what needs to be done" (interview FI7); a lack of understanding of and commitment to the issue of health inequality even on the part of senior MSAH officials; political conflict between ministries (e.g., the industry and trade ministry seeks to increase labor supply, while in MSAH "there are people who are much more left-wing" [interview FI9]); lack of financial and human resources, including expert staff (e.g., in developing the NAP, "the most complicated health policy problem one could take on," one ministry official reports, "[w]e had few people and most of them were researchers, and most of them had no policy or implementation expertise" [interview FI11]); and conflicting imperatives from concurrent policies (e.g., the more behaviorally focused Health Promotion Programme that was released concurrently with the NAP [interviews FI2; FI10]).

The devolution of responsibility for solving the problem of health inequalities to lower-level actors created still more problems of implementation and accountability. Local-level implementers did not always have access to the best tools for reducing health inequalities. As one respondent pointed out, "if you consider the social determinants of health, you see that many of the risk factors are decided at the national level or even international level" (interview FI7). Several respondents also reported a lack of clarity in national-level instructions to municipalities about the goals and processes that would lead to a reduction in health inequalities. For example, the NAP required that local governments consider the health impacts of policy decisions, including examining the impact of policies on the health of different groups. But "[w]hen legislators worked on this they meant SES groups, but they didn't write that into the law, and so municipalities have mainly interpreted that as meaning by age and gender" (interview FI2).

Just as the French government has still to discover what the regional health agencies have actually done to try to reduce health inequalities, in Finland national oversight is spotty. One respondent at the national level explained, "We do have a health promotion questionnaire that we send to municipalities regularly.... But we are not using the welfare reports as a follow-up measure, and they are not required even to be in electronic form, or to use the same format, or the same indicators. So we have a general sense that they are doing good work and it's going well, but we really don't know for sure" (interview FI9).

Insufficient financing of municipal efforts, linked to broader policies of fiscal restraint, also hindered efforts to meet the health equity goals in Finnish government programs. Finnish municipalities are responsible for financing a share of the cost of the public services they deliver, supplementing funds received as block grants from the central government with tax revenues raised locally. Beginning with the 1993 reform of state financing, the central government's share of health and social service spending has declined, and by 2001 municipalities were responsible for roughly two-thirds of these costs. As Kokkinen et al. (2017) describe, the shift to block grants after 1993 deprived the central government of the ability to steer local-level policy, including mandating implementation of policies to promote the goals of health programs like Health 2015. Some municipalities acted on their own to try to meet Health 2015 goals, but most municipalities cut funding for health promotion efforts after its passage, in part in order to cover the costs of health services that were, unlike health promotion activities, mandated. Other municipalities outsourced health promotion and prevention activities to private providers in order to generate budgetary savings, and only 5 percent of municipalities enacted the Health Impact Assessment mandated in 2005 and 2010 legislation because it did not come with any new funding streams for technical support or monitoring (Kokkinen et al. 2017).

Ontological issues related to the nature of the social determinants of health framework – causal complexity, long lag times between cause and effects, and difficulty in identifying concrete entry points for intervention – constituted further hindrances to effective inter-sectoral and inter-governmental action on health inequalities, according to interviewees (interviews FI11; FI12). The authors of the TEROKA memo (Finnish Ministry of Social Affairs and Health 2009) note that health inequality is a much more difficult policy problem to resolve than some others: "The very complexity and diversity of the causal chains makes it much harder to find well-targeted structural measures to reduce health inequalities than to identify measures to reduce, say, poverty. Health cannot be 'redistributed' in the same way as income, where distributions can be adjusted by means of various social income transfers" (p. 199).

Taken together, these difficulties with multilevel and cross-sectoral governance of health inequalities not only created a weaker-than-ideal response to health inequalities, but also served to direct attention away from the policy mechanisms that could have been used to remediate inequalities in the underlying social determinants of health. As we have seen, some of these mechanisms had already been explicitly ruled out under the neoliberal economic and managerial consensus that took hold in Finland starting in the mid-1980s, and intensified after the recession and EU accession. The motivation for politicians to take up the issue of health inequalities was at least in part to be able to claim to be paying attention to inequality without activating these taboos and calling into question the reigning economic policy orthodoxy. It is a striking irony that even as Finnish policy-makers shifted their understanding of health inequalities upstream, the policy remedies for addressing upstream determinants remained stubbornly out of reach.

CROSS-COUNTRY ANALYSIS: WHY ARE HEALTH INEQUALITIES SO HARD TO REDUCE?

The international consensus on health inequalities described in Chapter 3 proposes a clear and consistent set of policy recommendations for reducing health inequalities. The key elements include working in a coordinated fashion across policy sectors (and not only in the health sector) to reduce inequalities in multiple upstream determinants of health; addressing the social, economic, and environmental factors that shape individual choices rather than simply exhorting individuals to change their health behaviors; exercising political leadership at the national level to coordinate efforts that may be best under-taken or even formulated at the subnational level and with community involve-ment; adopting policies aimed at flattening the entire social gradient in health rather than just improving health among the most deprived; and redistributing power and resources in order to eliminate the social inequality that is ultimately responsible for producing health inequalities.

Some researchers and policy-makers remain skeptical that these policies would reduce health inequalities, even if implemented. Many of the same arguments about alternative causes of health inequalities that the authors of the Black Report considered and overturned – that people with worse health select into lower-SES groups; that the measurement of socioeconomic inequality tends to exaggerate health differences; that behaviors like smoking, exercise, and diet are personal choices; that absolute deprivation harms health but inequality does not – continue to resurface in contemporary scholarly and political debates.[6] And because the

---

[6] Some agree in principle that socioeconomic inequality causes health inequalities, but do not advocate increasing economic equality as a way to increase equality in health because of concerns about the non-Pareto optimality of redistribution (e.g., Deaton 2002).

level of socioeconomic inequality in a polity cannot be experimentally manipulated, we will never be able to prove in an econometric sense that reducing socioeconomic inequality will cause a reduction in the size of health inequalities. However, research in the field of health inequalities has demonstrated conclusively that inequalities in upstream social determinants are associated with inequalities in a variety of health outcomes, and there is now isolated but compelling scientific evidence that there is a causal link (see Chapter 3). So, there is reason to believe that if governments intervened forcefully to correct inequalities in the fundamental causes of health inequalities, they could succeed in narrowing the absolute and relative gaps in health status between socioeconomic groups.

Yet as we have seen, even when national politicians and policy-makers have acknowledged health inequality as a public problem and eventually adopted a framing of the issue that conformed to the international consensus frame, they did not adopt the full range of policies recommended by the international consensus. Policies aimed at correcting inequalities in downstream and mid-stream social determinants of health, including poverty, were inside the Overton window around health inequalities, but English, French, and Finnish programs aimed at reducing health inequalities in the 1990s and 2000s excluded policies that would flatten the social gradient in health by redistributing income, narrowing wage inequalities, or investing substantially in public education and training. Those strategies, which were politically taboo, remained outside the Overton window. The reframing of inequality in line with the international health inequality consensus has thus, paradoxically, shifted the Overton window away from possible solutions to the problem of inequality that address inequalities in upstream social determinants of health.

An expansive agenda for cross-sectoral actions on midstream and downstream social determinants of health, carried out across multiple levels of government, remained within the Overton window. But relying on these policy levers may have done as much to hamper effective action against health inequalities as ignoring what was outside the window did. There are two main reasons why. First, the level of coordination required by cross-sectoral and multilevel governance frequently surpasses the capacity of even the most committed governments. Second, when coordinated efforts to reduce simultaneously inequalities in multiple upstream social determinants of health fail, the result is that health policy-making tends to drift downstream, to more familiar medical and behavioral interventions that have already proven ineffective.

The country case studies presented here have shown just how difficult and elusive truly coordinated cross-sectoral policy-making can be, even when efforts are sustained over long periods of time and backed by strongly committed leadership at the central level. This is not surprising. Indeed, Wismar et al. (2013) found that in the arena of health inequalities policy, inter-sectoral committees often do not work as planned. There are many requisites for successful cross-sectoral policy-making (Kickbusch 2010), including clarity about individual and shared goals; capacities (resources, skills, and knowledge) for joint action; relationships on which to base cooperative action; clear, well-conceived policies that can be implemented and evaluated; clear roles and responsibilities; and plans to monitor and sustain outcomes. Equally, there are many barriers to making policy when multiple sectors, ministries, and/or levels of government are involved. These include coordination problems, contests over allocation of financing, clashing objectives, principal-agent problems when those who want an initiative to succeed are not those who implement its various strategies, and intellectual and communication differences. Even when initially supported at a high level, cross-sectoral policy-making often also confronts issues of sustainability: when dedicated budgets run out, specialist staff move on and are not replaced, management reforms redirect attention to narrower goals, supporters in key positions change jobs, new priorities and ideas attract attention, ministers and governments change, or bureaucracies drift away from some activities and assume politicians will not notice (Greer and Lillvis 2014, 8–9).

The difficulties of cross-sectoral policy-making are compounded in the area of health by the need to negotiate the roles and resources of (public) health versus medical actors; and health versus other sectors. Kickbusch (2010, 14) points out that "the health sector itself must be willing to cooperate with other sectors. But the health sector is a particularly vertical configuration, driven by a strong 'functional imperative,' with a concentration of specialist medical knowledge and very well organised professional special interests." Furthermore, it is often unclear why it would benefit other sectors to join the health sector in attacking such a difficult problem and why other agencies should spend their funds on health when health care is already such a large expenditure area (Kickbusch and Buckett 2010, 5). Bringing the medical sector into play has other consequences, too, for the effectiveness of efforts to reduce both health inequalities and inequalities in upstream social determinants. The cordoning-off within departments and subdepartments of policies addressing different diseases and health conditions, as well as historical decisions to prioritize certain health problems over others, means that some ideas within the dominant health inequalities frame are translated more or less intact into policy, while others – including the need to act on the upstream determinants of health – are often transformed or ignored when the health sector is a central actor (Smith 2013a). Moreover, a belief in individualism links neoliberalism and the medical model of health, and makes the two meta-frames especially compatible (see, e.g., Navarro 2009; Rushton and Williams 2012; F. Baum and Fisher 2014). This resonance may allow neoliberal ideas to influence policy styles in institutional settings like health ministries that are dominated by actors who have a medicalized understanding of health (see, e.g., Asthana et al. 2013).

Medicalization of inequality policy tends to push interventions toward downstream social determinants like access to medical care, but it is merely one aspect of the broader tendency toward downstream "drift" that seems inherent to efforts at cross-sectoral and multilevel coordination. The complexity and difficulty of sustaining cross-sectoral coordination and a common pattern of devolving responsibility to subnational actors without commensurate resources mean that these well-intentioned policies often fail. When this occurs, the default is older, more medicalized, individualized, and behaviorally based public health interventions. This dynamic creates "lifestyle drift": a tendency for public health initiatives informed by a broad social determinants approach to be replaced over time by interventions designed to shift individual lifestyle factors (Popay et al. 2010, 148). Of course, this does not occur only for practical reasons; governments make policies that "privilege behavioral health promotion despite the considerable information available about [social determinants of health]" because these policies have ideological appeal. They are "likely to be more acceptable to political actors sympathetic to a neoliberal worldview because they define health in terms of individual biology and risky health behavior as primarily a product of individual choice" (F. Baum and Fisher 2014, 216). But the high bar for successful cross-sectoral and multilevel governance of inequality means that such downstream drift would likely occur even without the ideological push. In a survey of health inequalities researchers in the United Kingdom, Katherine Smith (2013b) found that even though they share "a widely-held consensus that upstream, macro-level policy interventions are likely to be more effective in reducing health inequalities," the specific policy proposals that these researchers support "usually involve relatively downstream interventions relating to lifestyle behaviors and health services" (p. 53). This occurs because complex, upstream policy interventions lack the kind of iron-clad evidence base that would make researchers comfortable endorsing these policies to policy-makers (p. 53).

In fact, complexity and ideological resistance to evidence are characteristics of social problems that Rittel and Webber (1973) identify as "wicked" (as opposed to "tame"). Wicked problems are those which, in a pluralist society with no objective definition of the public good, "cannot be meaningfully correct or false; and it makes no sense to talk about 'optimal solutions' to these problems.... Even worse, there are no solutions in the sense of definitive answers" (p. 155). Analysts of policy-making have come to understand health inequality as a paradigmatic wicked problem (Blackman et al. 2006; Harrington et al. 2009; Petticrew et al. 2009; Kickbusch 2010; Exworthy and Hunter 2011). As one commentator has noted, "policy making about health inequalities takes place in a fog of disagreement about goals, controversy about causes and uncertainty compounded by ignorance about means" (Klein 2003, 55). Horn and Weber's (2007) notion of "social messes" is also *a propos*: social messes have the additional characteristics that most problems are connected to other problems; data and evidence about how to solve the problem are often missing or uncertain; and there are numerous possible intervention points, the consequences of which are hard to foresee. Together, these characteristics create problems that are surrounded by uncertainty and ambiguity, and are highly resistant to change.

The international consensus health inequality problem frame and the policy response privileged by this frame shine a spotlight on many of these characteristics. The social determinants of health causal interpretation and the cross-sectoral treatment recommendation highlight the complexity of causation and the multiple systems that are involved and must be recruited into the solution. Many of the processes said to produce health inequalities operate over the life-course, and so the outcomes of interventions are bound to be distal. Furthermore, the moral evaluation inherent to the health inequalities frame – exonerating individuals and blaming market inequalities and govern-ment policies for health inequalities – brings into sharp focus how value-laden are both the definition of and the solutions to the problem of health inequality. When problems are causally complex and full of value conflicts, it is tempting for politicians and policy-makers to try to cut through the wickedness by aiming policy interventions at the more proximate rather than the more distal causes. Health inequalities research may contribute to this tendency: "mapping out the processes through which differences in social status give rise to health inequalities may seem to politicians to offer possibilities of intervention without addressing the fundamental causes" (Wilkinson 2006, 1230). But wicked prob-lems by definition cannot be solved (Pacanowsky 1995; Raisio 2009).

Reframing social inequality as a problem of health inequality makes inequal-ity into a wicked problem, resistant to solution, when in fact relatively straight-forward solutions to the underlying problem of socioeconomic inequality are still available. Socioeconomic inequality is a less wicked problem. It is still ideologically contested terrain, of course; but the causal processes are better understood, the causal chains are shorter, and the policy tools – redistributive taxation, labor market regulation, and the like – are easier for a single, often powerful, ministry to implement.

As the central tools for containing inequality in postwar welfare regimes came to be taboo, the way policy-makers framed the issue of inequality, particularly health inequality, has also shifted in England, France, and Finland. Framing health inequalities as a result of inequalities in the social determinants of health has allowed politicians to show their commitment to the idea of equality, while replacing fraught debates over economic policy with the more universally palatable exhortation of better health for all. With this shift in framing of the problem of inequality came a shift in the policies that seemed like reasonable responses to the problem of inequality. In theory, the inter-national consensus framing of health inequalities could have moved the Overton window away from downstream determinants of health inequality like health care, diet, and smoking and shifted policy attention further upstream, to determinants like education and income. But in practice the policies needed to reduce upstream inequalities remained taboo, and attempts to address inequalities in midstream social determinants of health fell on the sword of their own technocratic complexity. As a result, reframing inequality was a successful rhetorical device, but it produced neither politically daring policies aimed at tackling fundamental socioeconomic inequalities nor success-ful reduction of health inequalities in the shorter term.

8

Regimes of Inequality

INTRODUCTION

In this book, I have set out to explain why rising inequality has become a more or less permanent feature of life in most of the rich, industrialized democracies of Europe in the last thirty years. This has occurred despite public opinion in European societies that is staunchly opposed to inequality and supportive of state efforts to create more equitable societies (Osberg and Smeeding 2006; Kenworthy and McCall 2008; Kohut 2013; Sorapop and Norton 2014), and despite a growing consensus among experts that current levels of inequality are undesirable and even dangerous. My approach has been to study the politics and policy-making surrounding health inequalities, which most public health experts believe are closely linked to socioeconomic inequalities, but which policy-makers have tended to try to solve using different kinds of tools from those designed to impact directly the distribution of income and wealth.

As with income inequality, health inequalities have resisted most efforts on the part of governments to reduce them, and are continuing to grow. We saw in Chapter 3 that, by the early 2000s, researchers and European-level health policy elites had come to a widely shared consensus that inequalities in health status exist, despite quasi-universal access to health care, are morally unjust and hence constitute a public problem, are caused primarily by inequalities in socioeconomic resources, and can be reduced only by concerted efforts to curtail inequalities in the "upstream" social determinants of health (SDOH) such as income and educational and political inequalities. Politicians in most European countries, too, have accepted this view of health inequalities as a public problem, yet have been remarkably slow to enact the policies that the international consensus view stipulates as necessary to solve the problem. Chapters 4–7 examined attempts to reduce health inequalities in England, France, and Finland in order to explain why.

Despite a decade or more of sustained attention to the problem of socio-economic inequalities in health in each of the three countries profiled in the earlier chapters, health inequalities have not been appreciably reduced. Moreover, the overall picture in most countries for which there are good data is of steady or increasing gaps in health status and mortality – particularly (but not only) between the lowest and highest income and educational groups (Gelder et al. 2017). Much of this increase in relative inequality is driven by faster improvements for higher-socioeconomic status (SES) groups than for lower groups. However, there are notable exceptions that point to troubling underlying trends. In the United States, for example, declining life expectancy among middle-aged whites has been the subject of considerable public attention (Achenbach and Keating 2016; McKay 2017). A recent study also found large declines in average life expectancy in 2014–16 in two-thirds of rich, democratic countries (Ho and Hendi 2018). Even where inequalities are "merely" driven by slower improvement for the worse-off, though, they remain troubling. How can we explain the persistence of health inequalities despite good-faith efforts by governments to lessen them?

One reason that SES inequalities in health persist is that inequalities in the upstream determinants of health have also grown since 1980. While the timing of the increase has varied across countries, income and wealth have become substantially more unequally distributed in all of the rich industrialized countries (OECD 2011). Educational inequalities appear to have increased in some countries as well (Oppedisano and Turati 2015). One could argue that we can't know for sure that policies enacted to try to reduce health inequalities have failed, precisely because the underlying inequalities continue to grow. However, even if it were true that some interventions have helped prevent greater health inequalities from emerging as a consequence of increasing income and educational inequalities, the underlying problem remains to be addressed: Why is it that neither health inequalities nor inequalities in the underlying causes have been successfully reduced, despite sustained public and policy attention?

The dominant explanations for the phenomenon of resilient inequality in the economics and policy literatures do not provide ready answers. Economic forces can engender significant capital accumulation on the part of the rich if left uninterrupted over long periods of time (Piketty 2014). But the key lesson that we ought to take away from Piketty's explanation for rising inequality is not that these forces are inexorable, but rather that they can be contained through political action. Similarly, in politics it is simply not the case that the interests of capital holders always prevail to set the level of acceptable income inequality or social mobility. In the rich industrialized democracies, cross-class coalitions that include both capital-holders and unpropertied laborers have negotiated a variety of ways to contain inequality. And while it is true that in general a stronger, more organized, and better-represented center-left has led to more equitable societies, increasing inequality in the late twentieth and early twenty-first centuries cannot be attributed solely to center-right rule. Center-left leaders and parties have frequently embraced policies and practices that have led to increasing inequality.

Finally, it is not the case that increasing inequalities in either SES or health have occurred simply because policy-makers lacked information about the problems or how to solve them. Some public health specialists continue to argue that governments are unable to reduce health inequalities because researchers have not provided them with a solid evidence base about the causal pathways linking socioeconomic inequalities and health or the policy interventions that would interrupt those pathways (Petticrew et al. 2009). Yet many others maintain that despite some lacunae (e.g., a lack of randomized controlled trials demonstrating the efficacy of specific policy interventions), there is more than enough evidence from other sources on which policy-makers can and should act (see, e.g., Pickett and Wilkinson 2015).

This evidence and a blueprint for policy action have been summarized in widely publicized reports such as those authored for the WHO and the European Union by Michael Marmot (WHO 2008; WHO Regional Office for Europe 2013) and the Lancet-University of Oslo Commission report (Ottersen et al. 2014). By the turn of the twenty-first century, a strong consensus among public health researchers and policy elites working at the international level in Europe framed health inequalities as a result of underlying inequalities in the social determinants of health, and prescribed a policy response that involved collaboration across multiple sectors of government, coordinated at the national level, to reduce inequalities in the determinants of health. These included both social determinants proximate ("downstream") to health outcomes, such as health care, nutrition, or housing, and those more distal ("upstream"), including inequalities in income and political power. Many governments have accepted these blueprints as a model for action. Yet in each of the three country case studies in this book, even when the issue of health inequalities entered mainstream political debate in a way that was compatible with the international health inequality consensus frame, policy-makers have failed to enact policies that are consistent with that frame and that could help to reduce inequalities both in health and in the underlying social inequalities. Understanding why this is so helps us understand why containing the growth of inequality has become so difficult starting in the 1990s.

Comparative Taboos

The international consensus framing of health inequalities as a problem linked to underlying social inequities, and as a problem best solved by cross-sectoral policy actions aimed at altering the distribution of the upstream social determinants of health, began to take hold in Europe in the early 1980s (this process is described in Chapter 3). It emerged earliest in Britain, diffused through international and scholarly networks into the WHO, and from there into the European Union. By 2014, and in some cases substantially earlier, the issue of socioeconomic inequality in health status had appeared on the political agenda in much of western Europe, and indeed in the rich democracies more generally. The international health inequalities frame came with little in the way of either carrots or sticks to encourage adoption; politicians, most often on the center-left, took it up of their own accord. Why?

The case study chapters show that in all three countries, politicians adopted the international framing of health inequalities as a solution to a political problem: the problem that arose when the strategies for managing social inequality that were embedded in postwar welfare regimes came into conflict with neoliberal ideas, policies, and practices starting in the 1980s. Center-left politicians, for the most part, believe in the goal of creating more equitable societies; as one senior official in France put it, "For socialists there is a value in being able to talk about inequalities" (interview FR30). But in England, France, and Finland, politicians also feared financial markets' response to raising taxes on capital income, albeit for slightly different reasons in each country. All governments feared the domestic consequences of taxing capital and hoped to retain middle-class support by keeping taxes low. French and Finnish politicians also worried about restraining public spending (which threatened their countries' sovereign bond ratings and standing with international markets) and about running afoul of the European Union's liberal market order. Reframing inequality as a matter of health allowed politicians to claim to take action to reduce inequality while avoiding the politically sensitive topics of redistribution, public spending, and market intervention.

But reframing inequality as a matter of health, however politically appealing, does not appear to have made it any easier to solve. On the contrary, the medicalization of inequality may actually have made it more resilient. Despite important, systemic differences between the three countries whose experiences are detailed in Chapters 4–7, in each of the country cases we can observe a consistent sequence of events that links core aspects of postwar welfare regimes to the eventual approach taken to dealing with the interlinked problems of socioeconomic and health inequalities. This sequence involves three steps, as illustrated in Figure 8.1.

The first step in the sequence is the emergence of political taboos against using the central tools of economic and social policy that policy-makers had used to contain inequality from the 1950s through the 1970s. These taboos come about when postwar settlements, which had set political limits on the extent of inequality that markets could be allowed to generate, came into conflict beginning in the 1980s with a new set of ideas about the proper relationship between governments and markets. It is important to note that these taboos were not hard constraints on what politicians and policy-makers could do to reduce inequality. They were given force by the perceptions of these politicians and policy-makers about what would happen should they fail to heed the prescriptions of the new neoliberal policy paradigm, in particular in light of the growing influence of mass media and international financial market actors.

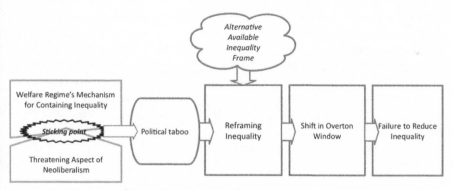

FIGURE 8.1 Regimes of inequality: mapping the argument

Taboos were most likely to develop around the policy levers that were central to containing inequality in the postwar period, which were different in the various European welfare regimes, but which in every case contradicted key tenets of the neoliberal policy paradigm.

In the liberal welfare regimes, which did not have strong corporatist institutions or social insurance systems through which to channel large sums of money to working-class citizens, containing inequality relied on having a left party that could periodically enter government and enact a redistributive tax and spending agenda. But taxing middle incomes was anathema in the Thatcherite version of neoliberalism, and taxing high incomes even more problematic in the finance-centric version of the neoliberal paradigm that moved to center stage beginning in the mid-1990s. As the center-left in the United Kingdom came to accept key tenets of neoliberalism, part of that ideological convergence between parties involved center-left politicians agreeing to an astonishingly explicit taboo against redistribution.

In the conservative-corporatist welfare regimes, the core mechanism for containing inequality, particularly in times of economic adjustment, was public spending. But after Mitterrand's U-turn in 1983 committed France to a course of fiscal restraint in order to secure France's place in the European Union, openly advocating public spending as a means of promoting greater social equality became taboo. Other topics were also off-limits in French politics, too – for example, open discussion of the fact that racial and ethnic minority groups were systematically socioeconomically disadvantaged. But especially on the center-left, advocating an overall increase in public spending to reduce social inequalities became a central taboo not only because it would make fiscal restraint more difficult but also because it would have laid bare the conflict between the old French social model and the left's embrace of the European project's neoliberal underpinnings.

The social democratic welfare regimes of the Nordic countries developed in small, open economies necessarily exposed to external markets, and so the key mechanisms for containing inequality in the postwar period were those that buffered citizens from exposure to markets while also protecting their ability to participate in them. These included public provision of high-quality social services like education and preventive health care that could prepare all citizens to participate effectively in the market, broad-based taxation in order to finance these services, and direct controls over product markets to ensure individual health and well-being. All three of these policy tools became politically sensitive in Finland starting in the late 1980s, when first Finland's currency and then internal markets for products and services became more closely linked to the neoliberal framework of the European monetary system and the single market.

Variable Reframing

The emergence of taboos triggers the second step in the sequence linking the politics of health inequalities to the broader politics of inequality. Politicians on the center-left were affected most strongly by the new taboos, because they adopted the premises of neoliberal governance that were most challenging for their postwar settlements, but at the same time still sought to appeal to an electoral base that expected social protection. (Only in Finland, where a society-wide preference for equality affected politics across much of the political spectrum, did center-right politicians face some similar challenges.) As political actors cast about for new ways to discuss inequality that allowed them to be "for" equity without proposing redistribution, greater public spending, or extensive public intervention in markets for services and goods, the topic of health inequalities offered an enticing alternative.

By the 1990s, scholars and policy entrepreneurs at the international level had put forward a new way of understanding inequalities in health, which provided a ready alternative to politicians and policy-makers who were looking for new ways of talking about the problem of inequality. The new international consensus on health inequality explicitly linked health inequalities to social inequality more broadly. As outlined in core policy documents of the World Health Organization and the European Commission's directorate for Health and Consumer Protection, the international consensus stipulated that inequalities in health were best understood as products of underlying socioeconomic inequalities, rather than insufficient access to health care or a lack of knowledge on the part of individuals about the health consequences of their personal lifestyle choices. The international consensus on health inequalities also proposed a new set of policy tools for dealing with health inequalities (chief among them was cross-sectoral action on the upstream causes of health inequalities) that were not yet subject to any taboos.

Just as the taboos differed in each country, however, so too did the precise way in which inequality was reframed. The most obvious and wholesale reframing of inequality took place in the United Kingdom. New Labour's rhetoric all but replaced discussion of remediating income and wealth inequalities through redistribution with talk of reducing inequalities via social investment in human capital – including health. In France, a long-standing commitment to securing equity through a territorially uniform distribution of state services (including health care) delayed reframing of the issue of inequality in terms of socioeconomic differences of health status. It was only when the EU Fiscal Compact made any further spending in the health sector impossible that the issue of health inequality was decisively reframed in public and policy discourse: the international consensus's focus on cross-sectoral action provided a way to be in favor of further development of the health system without incurring additional public spending. In Finland, the entire postwar period had been marked by attention to socioeconomic inequalities in health, but the priority had been on ensuring access to services and modifying lifestyle factors. Entry into European markets constrained Finnish policy-makers from intervening in public services and product markets, which prompted a gradual shift in health policy discourse to focus on further upstream social determinants of health. This shift began during the period of Social Democratic–led government following EU accession in 1995.

Reframing the issue of inequality in general, or health inequalities in particular, as a problem related to inequalities in the upstream socioeconomic determinants of health should have produced policies designed to combat those upstream inequalities in health. However, a remarkable similarity across all three of our country cases is that reframing inequality has generally not resulted in such policies. National plans put into place with the explicit intention of reducing socioeconomic health inequalities have resulted in some isolated successes, but also in a devolution of responsibility for reducing health inequalities to local-level actors without sufficient oversight or resources, continuing dominance of the health sector instead of true cross-sectoral cooperation, health promotion interventions that focus on altering individual lifestyle choices rather than broader structural reforms, and a focus on alleviating poverty rather than reducing income inequality.

The Overton Window

This consistent package of policy outputs – which is consistently inconsistent with the recommendation of the international health inequalities consensus for coordinated, multisectoral action, led by national governments, that reaches beyond the health sector to reduce or eliminate the inequalities in the upstream social determinants of health – leads us to the third step in the process linking health inequalities to the broader issue of inequality. Reframing inequality has paradoxically made it harder for governments to reduce either health inequalities or broader social inequalities because the reframing shifts the Overton window around inequality.

Recall that the Overton window is the range of policy options that appear as acceptable or reasonable responses to a particular public problem. We have already seen that the rise of neoliberal discourses, policies, and power configurations in Europe prompted center-left politicians to avoid discussing certain policies, many of which had been central to postwar welfare regimes' control of inequality. These taboo policies lay, conveniently, outside the Overton window for health inequalities. The Overton window that is framed by the international consensus view of health inequalities implied a different policy tool for dealing with inequality: coordinated policy action across multiple sectors and levels of government in order to reduce inequalities in both downstream (e.g., health care, nutrition, housing) and further upstream (e.g., income, education) determinants of health.

Not surprisingly, given its complexity, cross-sectoral work to reduce health inequalities turned out to be much harder to pull off than the public health experts shaping the international consensus had anticipated. The medical care sector often continued to dominate policy-making, while critical decisions affecting the distribution of upstream social determinants of health were made by finance and economy ministries who were not subject to the discipline of Health in All Policies mandates. Coordination across levels of government also proved difficult, due to a lack of effective steering from the national level and/or to devolution of responsibility without adequate financing. Finally, while all of the governments in question set to work on reducing poverty as a critical cause of poor health, nowhere did they enact policies to reduce income inequality, which many public health experts argue is as important as material deprivation in causing health inequalities.

The failure of governments to follow their own policy advice when it came to health inequalities occurred because the location of the Overton window around health inequalities made the problem much more difficult to solve. On the one hand, the fact that the international health inequalities frame redirects attention away from policy tools that had become taboo under the neoliberal consensus was likely a motivation for politicians to take up the new frame. On the other hand, politicians and policy-makers who truly wish to reduce health inequalities need to be able to address the underlying causes – and the new frame introduces several obstacles to doing so that reinforce politicians' self-censorship when it comes to using straightforward redistributive, compensatory, or market-conditioning policy mechanisms.

One such obstacle is that reframing social inequality as a problem of health medicalizes the problem of inequality, making it seem less amenable to systemic or structural solutions that act directly on the income distribution. Even when actors understand the social determinants paradigm and are committed to reducing health inequalities, the power of medical actors in the health field, the disease- and issue-based silos between and within departments, and historical decisions to prioritize certain health problems mean that some ideas within the dominant health inequalities frame are translated more or less intact into policy, while others – like the need to act on the upstream determinants of health – are transformed or ignored (K. Smith 2013b; Schrecker 2015).

Beyond medicalization, framing the issue of social inequality as a problem of health inequalities, and the issue of health inequalities as one of socioeconomic inequalities in health resulting from inequalities in multiple social determinants of health, makes the problem appear more difficult to solve. During the postwar period there has been a consensus among policy-makers that more egalitarian wage structures, high levels of tax on high earners, and higher social transfers for those with low incomes result in lower inequality – even if parties may disagree about whether these policy choices could also negatively affect economic growth and aggregate welfare. In other words, policy-makers and the public generally understand economic inequality as a relatively straightforward and immediate result of how the labor market and the tax and transfer systems distribute and redistribute the gains of economic activity in society. As framed in the international consensus, however, health inequalities are the result of multiple, interacting, distal causes that operate over the full life course. The social determinants causal interpretation and the cross-sectoral treatment recommendation highlight the complexity of causation and the multiple systems that must be recruited into any solution of the problem of health inequalities.

Furthermore, the fact that the international health inequalities problem frame exonerates individuals and instead blames market inequalities and government policies for health inequalities brings into focus the normative underpinnings of both the definition of and proposed solutions to the problem of health inequalities. This is an attribute of "wicked problems" (Rittel and Webber 1973), and indeed many health policy analysts have described health inequalities as just this type of problem (see, e.g., Blackman et al. 2006; Harrington et al. 2009; Petticrew et al. 2009; Kickbusch and Buckett 2010; Exworthy and Hunter 2011). Wicked problems involve disputes over the definition of the public good and thus have no definitive solutions. Further, evidence about how to solve wicked problems is often missing or uncertain, and there are numerous possible intervention points, the consequences of which are hard to foresee. Together, these characteristics create problems that are surrounded by uncertainty, and are likely to seem insoluble using policy approaches within the current repertoire of policy-makers. The international consensus on health inequalities framed inequality as a wicked problem that requires governments to engage with complex, unfamiliar policy tools requiring a great deal of coordination and patience, while the relatively simple and familiar policy tools that could be used to act directly on socioeconomic inequality fall outside the Overton window. As a result, focusing public attention on SES inequalities in health outcomes has contributed to making the problem of inequality harder to solve.

HOW AND WHY NEOLIBERALISM MATTERS FOR HEALTH INEQUALITIES

The analysis in this book has focused on what happened when the combination of policy tools used to moderate stratification in postwar welfare regimes confronted the complex of ideas, practices, and power that we have referred to using the umbrella concept of neoliberalism. Many have challenged the idea that neoliberalism is an entity in the world that can have any causal force. They claim, instead, that neoliberalism is merely a rhetorical trope, a pejorative that lumps together a wide variety of disparate things that proponents of managed capitalism happen to find objectionable (see, e.g., Boas and Gans-Morse 2009). I take a different approach.

Beginning in the 1980s, a relatively coherent bundle of things that we can collectively label as neoliberalism entered European politics. This bundle contained newly prominent ideas (e.g., a belief in markets' superior capacity to aggregate preferences in a way that produces societally optimal outcomes, or a preference for monetarist macroeconomic policies), new policy practices (e.g., deregulation, privatization, New Public Management, market liberalization), and a set of actors imbued by these ideas and practices with new power in politics (e.g., international financial actors, ministries of finance and trade, European regulators, multinational corporations).

By the 1990s, neoliberalism had become embedded as a new reality in European politics, and it changed the way that political elites talked about and sought to manage the problem of social inequality. But the component elements of the bundle did not affect every country equally. Neoliberalism changed the politics of inequality in Europe starting in the 1980s because the central policies that each of the postwar welfare regimes used to contain inequality was challenged, and often rendered less effective, by one or more specific aspects of neoliberalism. The collision between the welfare regimes of the *trente glorieuses* and neoliberalism thus looked different in each regime, but this does not mean that neoliberalism was irrelevant, any more than it means that the old welfare regimes were irrelevant, in shaping the new regimes of inequality that emerged beginning in the 1990s.

Public health scholarship has recognized the link between health outcomes (including health inequalities) and neoliberalism (see, e.g., Koivusalo et al. 2009; De Vogli 2011; Mooney 2012; Glasgow and Schrecker 2015; Schrecker and Bambra 2015; Schrecker 2016a; Farrants and Bambra 2018). Indeed, the report of a recent major commission on health inequalities concluded that "implementation of the primary tenets of neoliberalism" has been "disastrous for public health" (Ottersen et al. 2014). However, taken as a whole, the public health literature has struggled to come to a comprehensive understanding of how and why the transformation of politics in Europe starting in the 1980s has been so detrimental to health equity. One recent critical review argues that to understand "how, specifically, public health is imbricated in the various manifestations of neoliberalism" researchers need to come to grips with "how, where and in what forms do the various processes of neoliberalism impact public health" and "when, where, and in what ways the economic, political and cultural intersect with health" (K. Bell and Green 2016, 242). It is hard to disagree either with the ambition of this project or with the sentiment that we need to disaggregate beyond the headlines that "neoliberalism kills" (Mooney 2012) or "politics makes us sick" (Schrecker and Bambra 2015). The challenge is how to combine a general understanding of what neoliberalism *as a whole* does to health equity with a recognition of the specific processes and mechanisms at work in any given setting.

My research shows that there is something about the politics of inequality in a neoliberal era that does affect health inequalities in a way that is more generalizable than the specific effects of individual policies or practices. The neoliberal environment wears different guises – for example, the removal of constraints on European markets for goods, limits on public spending that affect social services, or barriers to taxing high incomes in order to redistribute – that are more or less salient to the economy and politics in different national contexts. These different facets of neoliberalism affect public health and health inequalities through different mechanisms and to different extents in different countries – but they are nevertheless three faces of the same neoliberal environment. The public health community could limit itself to working on the commercial determinants of health (e.g., trade deals involving alcohol, tobacco, and big food), and leave aside the quest to understand the effects of neoliberal politics on health equity more broadly. But if it did, it would be missing the bigger picture: not only how a broader range of practices like financial system deregulation, new public management reforms, or austerity policies are related to health inequality, but also why political champions of health equity have failed to deliver on their promises.

Neoliberal politics harms health equity in ways that are predicted by the logic of fundamental causation. Fundamental cause theory stipulates that inequalities in health status across socioeconomic groups are a consistent feature of social life across place and time, despite occasional good-faith efforts to reduce them, because the resources associated with high SES – knowledge, money, power, prestige, and beneficial social connections – can be deployed flexibly to meet emerging risks to health even as access to protection against older health risks diffuses to lower-SES groups (Link and Phelan 1995). Because health risks and protective factors are always changing as new causes of illness (e.g., sedentary lifestyles) and new health technologies (e.g., screenings that can detect cancers at an early stage) emerge, those with an abundance of flexible resources will be best positioned to avoid risks and to be early adopters of health-promoting technologies. In this sense, inequalities in the flexible resources associated with higher SES are the "causes of the causes" of socioeconomic inequalities in health.

The logic of fundamental causation tells us that in order to reduce SES inequalities in health, it is necessary to do at least one of two things: to reduce socioeconomic inequality and the inequalities in flexible resources that go with it or to weaken the connection between the possession of flexible resources and the ability to improve one's health. The international health inequality frame's consistent recommendation to take action to reduce social inequality as a way to address the problem of health inequity indicates that the frame is premised on the theory of fundamental causation. Yet even when they have adopted this frame, governments have failed either to enable fundamental redistribution or to break the link between SES and health. The findings of this book help to explain the underlying political mechanisms that produced this result, which is linked to the politics of neoliberalism.

WELFARE REGIMES, NEOLIBERALISM, AND
REGIMES OF INEQUALITY

We have seen that politicians tend to reframe inequality as a problem of SES inequalities in health when the old mechanisms for managing social inequality in a pre-neoliberal era come to seem politically untenable. This reframing has the potential to helpfully focus politicians' attention on the upstream, fundamental causes of health and health inequalities, but for reasons discussed in Chapter 7, it does not tend, in fact, to produce policy action that can address those fundamental causes. At the same time, the reframing also reinforces politicians' choice to disengage from the rhetoric and policy tools associated with directly reducing socioeconomic inequality because it offers a new repertoire of policies designed to affect health. The shift to the international health inequalities frame thus accompanies an acceptance on the part of center-left politicians of limits on government actions that could actually help to break the link between SES and health.

The broader context within which social inequality exists is important for understanding the politics of inequality. Regimes of inequality – both the postwar welfare regimes and the neoliberal-inflected regimes that have developed since the 1980s – provide this context. Regimes are a particular kind of context, though. Because regimes are made up of interconnected parts – power configurations, ideas, institutions, and practices – they tend to be relatively stable (Kratochwil and Ruggie 1986; Harris and Milkis 1989; Taylor-Gooby 1996; Wilson 2000; P. Hall 2015). This means that they also tend to shape inequality in ways that are resilient over time. This, in turn, is why shifting to a new political language of health inequalities does not end up changing the difficult politics of social inequality under neoliberalism all that much.

The engine of both continuity and change in regimes is the interaction over time between different attributes of societal organization that make up the regime: in the case of regimes of inequality, the structure of the economy, the nature of political competition, the capacities of the state and other actors, the internal workings of parties, the vernaculars for dealing with social problems, and the points of friction between the domestic and supranational orders. Arguments about regime trajectories rest on insights about institutions that are both historical and configurational. By contrast, "treating inequality as a 'variable' in statistical analysis (as opposed to an explanatory category in social analysis) renders it decontextualized and depoliticized," argued Poland et al. in the influential journal *Social Science and Medicine* (1998, 791). Poland et al. contend that it is "misplaced emphasis" to put "so much effort into finding plausible biological and psychological mechanisms to explain the relationship between class and health" if we at the same time "fail to consider how and why social and economic inequities are produced and sustained in the first place" (p. 791). Much the same could be said of contemporary political science approaches to understanding the politics of inequality, which remove processes of distribution and redistribution from their political, institutional, and normative contexts.

The trends now are to model societal inequality as cause or consequence of the interactions between abstract, impersonal entities such as "elites" or "democracy" (Acemoglu and Robinson 2000; Boix 2003; Ansell and Samuels 2014) or to engage in micro-level dissections of individual preferences and behaviors (see, e.g., Barnes 2013; Schmidt-Catran 2016; Trump 2018). Many such works – including those I have cited here – are outstanding examples of political science scholarship that have launched productive debates in the field. Yet attempting to understand inequality by abstracting it away from the institutions that shape it in a polity and from the political choices behind those institutions seems to me, to borrow Poland et al.'s (1998) words, misplaced emphasis. Similarly, understanding how the politics of inequality affects the preferences and behaviors of individual voters tells us something vitally important about how and why inequality matters, but the notion that inequality can be understood purely as a result of demand from the electorate seems to obscure a large part of the potentially relevant political landscape.

My argument draws on insights of an older, institutionalist literature that is more deeply historical and configurational. This view prioritizes understanding how different attributes of societal organization occur together over time in specific places to create political outcomes. In this book I have approached the politics of inequality as something that constitutes, and is constituted by, policy institutions and political strategies. The central players are the actors whom the public entrusts with the task of trying to solve society's most pressing problems, including containing the inequality that capitalism generates within bounds sufficient to maintain political order. Regimes of inequality are the institutional expression of the answers to this problem that political actors devise, and that electorates ratify.

In this work, I have harnessed Gøsta Esping-Andersen's central insight that welfare regimes are interlocking and self-reinforcing systems of public policy, political-electoral institutions, and economic regulation that are oriented around creating and maintaining a certain level of social (in)equality. And while I did not set out to write a book that would update Esping-Andersen's regime theory for a neoliberal age, it became clear during the course of researching how policy-makers tried to address the related problems of health inequalities and underlying socioeconomic inequalities since 1980 that the welfare regimes constructed during the postwar period cast very long shadows indeed.

The postwar welfare regimes described by Esping-Andersen were not static constructions, and by the late twentieth century had developed far beyond the initial outlines suggested by the coalitions in place at the time of their formation. But a key insight of regime theory is that welfare states have a characteristic structure that pushes them to change in particular directions when confronted with new environmental conditions. For example, the growth of the middle class in the 1960s and 1970s presented a challenge to the logic of both social democratic and liberal regimes: how to retain political support for the welfare state among increasingly prosperous citizens when benefits were flat-rate or means-tested, and relatively low. However, the regimes evolved differently in response to this challenge. Social democratic welfare states upgraded the level of universal benefits and expanded public social services and female labor force participation in tandem in order to generate the necessary tax revenues to pay for such upgrading. In the liberal regime, however, further public intervention would not have been ideologically permissible as it was under social democracy, and increasing inequality was permissible, as it would not have been under social democracy. Hence the liberal solution was to allow middle classes to opt out of the public welfare regime in favor of private provision. (In the conservative-corporatist regime, meanwhile, a stratified system of benefits already allowed for the consumption tastes of middle-class recipients, and required little change at that stage.)

Beginning in the 1980s, the internationalization and deregulation of finance markets; the construction of a single, liberal European market; and the rise of a neoliberal economic policy paradigm among policy-makers and politicians have posed new challenges to old welfare regimes. These developments have affected each welfare regime, and indeed each individual state, differently. While the central challenge for each regime remains the same as it has ever been – how to contain the inequalities generated by markets in ways that are acceptable in a democratic polity – starting points for neoliberalization also differ widely across countries within the EU, with consequences for the politics of inequality.

Different pathways to resilient inequality occur because the characteristic systems put into place to tame and contain market-generated inequalities in the immediate postwar period continued to affect social policy and social outcomes even as they were substantially transformed by the forces of neoliberalism. None of the welfare regimes underlying the original *Three Worlds of Welfare Capitalism* (Esping-Andersen 1990) was able to contain the growth of inequality, but this growth was channeled in different directions, and at different times, due to the specific ways in which central institutions of each welfare regime interacted with different aspects of neoliberalism.

In one sense, then, neoliberalism caused welfare regimes to converge on a higher level of inequality. However, the specific path was different in each of our cases, resulting in equifinality rather than true convergence. In all three cases, the interaction between the transnational/international and domestic orders during a period in which the fundamental economic policy paradigm was shifting created institutionally specific yet functionally equivalent sticking points for politics, and in so doing put each of these states on distinct trajectories to the same higher-inequality endpoint. It is easier to see why equifinality occurs when we understand neoliberalism not as an autonomous force in the world but as a mixed bag of ideas, actors, practices, power relationships, and policies that prioritizes market outcomes over political regulation, any one of which may be more or less relevant for the politics of inequality depending on the shape of the welfare regime with which it interacts; and when we understand the politics of inequality as being shaped by regimes: bundles of institutions and norms that embody, with some lag, societal bargains about the level of allowable inequality in a society.

CONSTRUCTING INEQUALITY

This brings us to a final theoretical contribution of this work, which is to make clear that what we take as the problem of inequality is itself politically constructed. How politicians and policy-makers talk about inequality is constrained by available data, but only partially: most governments and experts in western Europe have enough information about a wide range of social indicators to at least identify basic patterns of stratification, and decide whether or not to frame them as problematic or worth talking about in politics. What, then, determines which inequalities politicians choose to emphasize? And what are the consequences – for politics and for inequality – when politicians try to redefine what inequality is? In taking up these questions, this book has highlighted that the politics of inequality involves contestation not only over how much inequality is desirable in society but also over what counts as inequality, and ultimately what kinds of policy instruments can be used to deal with it.

This is an important lesson for political science, which as a discipline knows but sometimes forgets that many of the things we take for granted as "natural kinds" – for example, racial categories, nation-states, or markets – are in fact outcomes of earlier, hard-fought battles over meaning-making.[1] Public health advocates, too, may be less aware than they should be of the range of choices that have already been made when health inequality emerges as a public problem. Researchers in epidemiology tend to be acutely attuned to the consequences of their methodological choices about which health indicators to use, or how to characterize mathematically the distribution of health in society, but they may not be equally sensitive to the consequences of their decisions about

---

[1] In fact, not only is inequality in the category of things that seem natural but are politically constructed; we would be hard-pressed to measure inequality at all without making recourse to some of these other contested, constructed categories.

how to conceptualize the groups affected by inequality, much less to why it might matter that they examine inequalities in health rather than in the under-lying determinants.

I suspect that many, if not most, researchers and policy advocates who have made it their life's work to shine a spotlight on health inequalities have done so at least in part because they are broadly concerned with the lives and life-chances of those at the bottom end of the social ladder. In this sense, it may not seem to matter very much whether politicians choose to speak out about health inequality versus socioeconomic inequality. This research has shown, though, that it *does* matter how politicians talk about inequality. Whether we consider economic inequality as a problem of wage dispersion versus an issue of concen-tration of wealth in the hands of the top 1 percent ought to affect who mobilizes politically, and around what potential policy solutions. Similarly, framing the issue of social inequality as a problem of "social investment" rather than as a maldistribution of societal resources, or framing health inequalities as a prob-lem of the geography of health care provision versus inequalities in the social determinants of health, will affect the political and policy response to inequality.

Inequality is a category that has multiple possible meanings that are subject to political contestation and construction. But while these different meanings have consequences for politics and policy, the case studies in this book have shown that the way inequality is framed does not necessarily cause a policy response that is consistent with that frame. Bergeron et al. (2014) have argued that the characteristics of the actors involved (e.g., the power and identities of problem framers versus policy enactors), characteristics of the frames them-selves (e.g., whether they challenge the status quo, their degree of complexity and specificity), and the broader ecology of social problems that actors are attempting to deal with can all affect the extent to which policy outputs match policy frames. In the case of health inequalities, the relative centrality of medical as compared to public health actors, the resonance of medicalized understand-ings of health inequality with the neoliberal meta-narrative, and the complexity of the policy remedy all made it less likely that shifting the framing of inequality to focus on health would substantively change policy outputs. In other words, the health inequalities frame did not have the characteristics that would have allowed policy actors to alter established patterns of policy and rhetoric that precluded redistributing, public spending, and regulating markets as tools for reducing inequality.

IMPLICATIONS FOR POLICY AND POLITICS

Researchers and advocates in the field of public health have worked hard to get the issue of health inequalities on the political agenda – and as the case studies in this book show, they have succeeded to a very great extent, even when circumstances have been least propitious. But raising political and public awareness of health inequalities has come at a cost. Taking up the issue of socioeconomic inequalities in health has led to a shifting of the Overton window away from policies that could be expected to reduce underlying inequalities in socioeconomic resources, which ultimately will hamper efforts to reduce health inequalities. The implications of this finding for public health advocacy are disconcerting: promoting health equity may actually require advocates to step away from the issue whose salience they have worked so hard to raise.

One reason is that reframing inequality in general as an issue of health inequalities invites medicalization of the issue of inequality, and this may in turn lead – for a variety of institutional and ideational reasons spelled out ably by Asthana et al. (2013), Smith (2013a), and others – to the dominance of individualist over structuralist thinking and health sector–focused interventions over actions in further upstream policy domains. Both of these are likely to hinder efforts to reduce inequalities in either health or the underlying social causes.

Another reason that reframing the issue of social inequality in terms of health is likely to make the job of promoting equity more difficult is that, despite some philosophers' and bioethicists' attachment to the idea of health as a "special" good deserving of heightened moral value, health equity may simply not generate much excitement among voters. Survey research in a variety of national contexts suggests that the mass public views health inequities in ways that are very similar to how they view underlying inequalities in income or education (Blaxter 1997; Rigby et al. 2009; Julia Lynch and Gollust 2010; Gollust and Lynch 2011; Knesebeck et al. 2016). Moreover, there is evidence that detaching the issue of inequality from the traditional policy instruments with which it is associated depresses public support for reducing inequality (Evans and Tilley 2012a; 2012b; 2017; Touzet 2018). So, reframing inequality as a matter of health to take advantage of the public's allegedly greater attachment to equity in the health sphere is unlikely to generate the public pressure required to keep policy-makers focused on the task of reducing inequality.

When inequality in health, rather than social inequality writ large, is reframed to meet the international consensus definition (as occurred in Finland and France), the domain of inequality does not shift, and the consequences for politics and policy may seem less stark. However, a focus on the internationally approved social determinants of health framing can divert attention away from inequities in health care provision and/or in exposure to modifiable risk factors, which could at least in principle be reduced using regular health policy tools. The new framing emphasizes instead work on multiple upstream inequalities, requiring unwieldy forms of coordination and implying policy actions that may not be politically possible, such as reducing income inequality. As a result, growing emphasis on the problem of health inequalities in these countries, too, may ultimately be self-defeating.

What should public health advocates who care about health equity do under these circumstances? One solution may be to revise the policy package that has been recommended to go along with the international consensus definition of health inequalities. It is probably not the heightened salience of the issue of health inequalities per se, but rather the policy remedies that have been emphasized in the international consensus, that pose the most immediate obstacle to reducing health inequalities. Two elements of the consensus policy package – the focus on cross-sectoral work and related efforts to decentralize day-to-day responsibility for reducing health inequalities – appear, based on my case studies, to be particularly damaging. While reducing inequalities in the upstream social determinants of health is critical for reducing health inequalities, cross-sectoral policy coordination is unlikely to be the best way to achieve that goal. As we have seen, repeated efforts to enact forms of "joined up government," including but not limited to the Health in All Policies framework, have proved disappointing, even in countries with generally high-quality public administration and significant steering capacity. Insisting on cross-sectoral work as a key part of the policy response to health inequalities is likely to lead to pyrrhic victories in which social ministries give over more of their power to health actors, and the ministries holding most of the power to shape the socio-economic distribution – finance and the economy – are at the table only in their roles as enforcers of austerity.

Decentralizing responsibility for solving the problem of health inequalities is also likely to be a dead end. Effective collaboration to reduce the impact of inequities in some of the social determinants most proximate to health is already occurring in most countries at the local level, simply because these smaller policy-making settings allow experts in housing, social services, health services, vocational training, and the like to meet face-to-face, and often over a shared local services budget. However, as we saw in the case studies, mandating that subnational actors take responsibility for securing gains in health equity without ensuring that they have the resources to do so has led to predictably disappointing results. In the United Kingdom, devolution of responsibility for reducing health inequalities to local governments and National Health Service primary care trusts occurred without the transfer of funds that would have been needed to address the scope of the problem; in France, responsibility for reducing health inequalities was delegated to the regional health agencies, which had been created with the express intent of reducing health sector spending; and in Finland, block-granting national government funding for municipal services has resulted in under-investment in health promotion at the expense of curative care. Despite the optimistic theorizing of some economists and public administration scholars about the capacity of decentralization to reduce inequality (Tibout 1956; Bankauskaite and Saltman 2007; Rodríguez-Pose and Ezcurra 2010; Kroneman et al. 2012), decentralization is not itself a panacea for inequity. If the policy package associated with health inequalities continues to emphasize to too great extent the importance of local control without concomitant attention to the need for local resources, reducing health inequalities will remain an elusive goal.

Where does this leave political actors on the center-left, who remain committed to the cause of creating a more equitable society? They must appeal to an electorate desirous of equality, but are also constrained by their own beliefs about what is politically possible in a neoliberal era. Can they use the issue of health inequalities as a way to reintroduce effective redistributive policy after three decades of neoliberal hegemony? Possibly, but the conclusion I draw from the case studies in this book is that policy-makers interested in reducing *either* social inequalities *or* health inequalities would do better to eschew the health inequalities problem frame and instead stick to tested, effective remedies for social inequality consisting of taxation, redistribution, and labor market regulation. These policies may seem too politically risky to consider, and near impossible to enact in a neoliberal era, but they have the benefit of being relatively straightforward to manage and to implement by a single ministry.

Creating more equitable societies in a neoliberal era requires a difficult task of political navigation. The passengers who boarded the metro in Byker in the opening paragraph of this book still need to cross over a wide chasm if they are to have the same healthy life expectancy, or the same chance of growing up in a household that isn't poor, as the folks in Gosforth – but nothing about bridging this chasm is easy. To avoid discussing redistributive and regulatory policies that would invite the wrath of powerful market actors, politicians may well be tempted to adopt a health inequality frame, which increases the difficulty of policy-making but seems more politically attractive. But this apparently easier path may ultimately be a more dangerous one. Taking on powerful market actors requires political ingenuity, but it is made easier by public opinion that is generally supportive of greater equality and by the availability of policy tools such as taxation, redistribution, and labor market regulation that are relatively straightforward and within the range of technical feasibility for economic policy-makers.

CONCLUSION

From the end of the Second World War until the late 1980s, democratic competition in much of western Europe was a highly institutionalized process involving parties with loyal constituencies, tied to ideological traditions and auxiliary organizations, and with relatively clear-cut policy alternatives. In the 1950s and 1960s, the major parties in northwestern Europe were distinctive in their approach to cultural issues such as the importance of the church or avoiding Communism, but often shared a considerable degree of consensus about the direction of economic policy. By the late 1960s, though, the mainstream parties in many European countries presented sharply contrasting economic policy agendas: on the left, social democratic, socialist, and Euro-communist parties offered an agenda of expansionary welfare state and macroeconomic policies that appealed to industrial and public-sector workers. On the right, conservative, liberal, and some Christian democratic parties appealed to capitalists, professionals, and the self-employed by promising to lower taxes and protect the sanctity of private property. Under these circumstances, a vote for the center-left or center-right offered clear policy alternatives, and alternation in government often resulted in significant policy change.

With the convergence in the 1990s of mainstream parties on quite similar neoliberal economic and social policies, however, alternation of the major parties in government no longer produces distinct strategies of economic management. Center-left and center-right parties have staked out only minor differences on key policy issues ranging from the priority to be placed on employment versus inflation to the proper degree of regulation of international financial flows. From the point of view of both major political tendencies, then, there is no longer any alternative to neoliberalism, to borrow Margaret Thatcher's famous phrase. The policy agenda that supports the relatively free movement of goods, capital, and people, particularly within the European region, may have economic and political benefits in the aggregate, but it has also resulted in both rising economic inequality and rising health inequalities.

The turn to neoliberalism is by definition a turn away from using the power and resources of the state to protect working- and (many) middle-class voters. It is also, however, a rhetorical turn. And when center-left parties cease to try to mobilize voters on class lines, this makes their voters available for recruitment by other parties on the basis of other identities and preferences (e.g., nationalism, regional identity, ethnic identity) (Evans and Tilley 2012a; 2012b). If the center-left wishes to regain the support of voters now being drawn away by populist and nationalist parties, it will need to rethink how it talks about inequality. Center-left politicians have tied their own hands when it comes to reducing social inequality, insisting that it is either too dangerous or fundamentally undesirable to do anything that would upset the neoliberal market order. As a result, they have begun to frame the problem of social inequality in new ways. Inequality is a problem to be solved no longer by redistribution or political regulation of the market, but instead by taking on more distal, technocratic issues like social investment and health inequalities. This new framing of inequality allows politicians to signal that they are still in favor of greater equity, but, as I have shown, it also makes the problem of inequality much harder to solve.

If politicians, including but not limited to those on the center-left, want to be "for" equity, they must insist on using the policy levers that they already know can work to reduce inequality: redistributive taxation, public spending, and market regulation. It will require some boldness to break with twenty-five years of taboo, but politicians should take heart in the knowledge that the public, the pontiff, and the IMF all agree that inequality needs to be brought to heel. And if Brexit, the resurgence of reactionary right-wing nationalist parties, and the election of Donald Trump have taught us anything, it is that taboos can be broken.

Appendix

Content Analysis of Government and Commissioned Health Inequality Reports

INTRODUCTION

Chapters 3–7 draw on quantitative and qualitative content analysis of the problem frames put forth in reports on the issue of health inequality that have been either produced or commissioned by national governments in England, France, and Finland; by the World Health Organization's Regional Office for Europe (WHO Europe); and by the European Union. There were two main goals of the analysis: to determine whether there is an international consensus health inequality frame reflected in European-level documents post-2003 and to examine the similarities and differences between the frames used by different national governments and the international consensus. This appendix sets forth the criteria I used to assemble the body of reports, lists the reports for each country and international organization, and describes the coding scheme and procedures that I used to generate systematic, comparable information about the contents of the reports.

SELECTION CRITERIA FOR REPORTS

Content analysis was undertaken in order to produce a summary of how the issue of health inequality is framed as a public problem in the major health inequality reports produced in each country or at the European level. The period from which reports for the systematic content analysis are sampled varies according to the analytic focus of each chapter. For the analysis of WHO Europe and EU documents, which examines the international consensus frame in its fully fledged form, the time period is limited to 2003–14 (2014 is the last year for which I can be sure that I have comprehensive coverage of the universe of documents produced). For the country chapters, I was interested in exploring the evolution of discourse over time, and so the sampling of reports begins earlier, in 1980. This choice of starting point reflects the tremendous importance of the Black Report, which was released in 1980, in setting the agenda for government attention to health inequalities in the contemporary period. For England, apart from the Black Report, I analyze the health inequality frame in the documents produced by or for the Labour governments of 1997–2010. This is because I am particularly interested in Labour's framing of the issue, which is quite different from the conservative frame. For France, where there is more bureaucratic continuity and the issue of health inequality is less politically polarized, I include all relevant reports produced between 1980 and 2014, regardless of the government composition at the time of their release. The same is true for Finland, with the notable distinction that only Finnish reports with an official English-language translation were coded.

To identify the universe of relevant health inequalities reports produced by each government or international organization in the appropriate time period, I began by surveying the secondary literature on public health and health policy in each country to construct a timeline, including all mentioned government or government-sponsored publications. Next I searched the web sites of (1) the national health ministries, (2) any subsidiary organizations that these ministries' websites linked to, and (3) government publications offices, in order to identify any additional policy documents related to health inequalities. Finally, I conducted Google searches for documents whose titles included the words "health" and variants on inequality, disparity, difference, divide, and gap, in order to identify any documents that might have been omitted based on the literature and government website searches. When reports were commissioned rather than produced by a government or organization's own staff, I included only reports that were issued without disclaimers, and hence could be read as reflecting the official views of the issuing organization.

From the lists of documents generated using these strategies, I then selected major reports primarily concerned with health inequalities. "Major" reports are those produced by the top level of the organization in question (e.g., a ministry of health, a directorate general), rather than by a subsidiary department. Reports that are "primarily" concerned with health inequalities (1) contain the term "health" and "inequality," "equity," "disparity," "gap," or similar in the report title or (2) dedicate at least three-quarters of the report to the problem of health inequalities. Publications that met the above criteria for inclusion but that were constituted by individual chapters on diverse topics relating to health inequalities and attributed to separate authors were excluded. General reports on the health system that were commissioned directly by the health minister or the national executive or legislature and that contained information on health inequalities were also not included in the content analysis, although some are described in the country chapters. Reports that focused only on techniques for tracking and measuring health inequalities or on one small part of the overall problem: – for example, health inequalities in a particular geographic area or affecting specific subpopulations, particular diseases or outcomes rather than overall health, or particular policy tools or mechanisms to combat inequalities – were excluded. Both WHO Europe and the EU produce all of their documents in multiple languages. To ensure maximal comparability, I searched for WHO and EU documents using English-language search terms and analyzed the English-language versions of their documents. All reports included in the content analysis are listed in Table A.1.

TABLE A.1 *Health inequality reports included in the content analysis*

English Reports

Fair Society, Health Lives. The Marmot Review. Commissioned by the Secretary of State for Health. Ed. Michael Marmot, 2010, 231 pp.

Health Inequalities: Progress and Next Steps. Department of Health, 2008, 82 pp.

Health Inequalities. Third Report of Session 2008–2009 (vol. 1). House of Commons Health Committee, 2009, 130 pp. (document includes Report and Formal Minutes; only the Report was coded)

Independent Inquiry into Inequalities in Health. Ed. Donald Acheson, 1998, 140 pp.

Inequalities in Health. Report of a Research Working Group. Ed. Douglas Black, 1980, 369 pp. (appendixes were not coded)

Reducing Health Inequalities: An Action Report. Department of Health, 1999, 41 pp.

Tackling Health Inequalities: A Programme for Action. Department of Health, 2003, 73 pp.

Tackling Health Inequalities: 10 Years On. Department of Health, 2009, 140 pp.

Tackling Health Inequalities. 2002 Cross-Cutting Review. Department of Health and Treasury. Ed. Yvette Cooper, 2002, 63 pp.

European Union Reports

Action on Health Inequalities in the European Union: The EU Health Programme's Contribution to Fostering Solidarity in Health and Reducing Health Inequalities in the European Union, 2003–13. European Commission – DG SANCO, 2014, 187 pp. (only front matter and pp. 1–25 were coded; remainder is details of individual actions to reduce HI)

Health Inequalities: A Challenge for Europe. An independent, expert report commissioned by the UK Presidency of the EU. Ed. Ken Judge, Stephen Platt, Caroline Costongs, and Kasia Jurczak, 2006, 50 pp.

Health Inequalities in the EU: Final Report of a Consortium. European Commission – DG SANCO. Ed. Michael Marmot, 2013, 175 pp.

Health Inequalities: Europe in Profile. An independent, expert report commissioned by the UK Presidency of the EU. Ed. Johan Mackenbach, 2006, 46 pp.

The Health Status of the European Union: Narrowing the Health Gap. European Commission – DG SANCO, 2003, 58 pp.

Reducing Health Inequalities. European Parliament resolution of 8 March 2011 on reducing health inequalities in the EU, 2011, 13 pp.

(continued)

Reducing Health Inequalities in the European Union. European Commission – DG
Employment and DG SANCO, 2010, 23 pp.
Report on Health Inequalities in the European Union. Commission staff working
document. 2013, 45 pp.
Solidarity in Health: Reducing Health Inequalities in the EU. Communication from the
Commission to the European Parliament, the Council, the European Economic
Committee, and the Committee of the Regions, 2009, 11 pp.

Finnish Reports
*Health Inequalities in Finland. Trends in Socioeconomic Health Differences,
1980–2005.* Ministry of Social Affairs and Health. Ed. Hannele Palosuo, Seppo
Koskinen, Eero Lahelma, Elisa Kostiainen, Ritva Prättälä, Tuija Martelin, Aini
Ostamo, Ilmo Keskimäki, Marita Sihto, and Eila Linnanmäki, 2007, 240 pp.
National Action Plan to Reduce Health Inequalities 2008–2011. Ministry of Social
Affairs and Health, 2008, 79 pp.

French Reports
Allocation régionale des ressources et réduction des inégalités de santé. Ministère de
l'Emploi et de la Solidarité and Haut Comité de la santé Santé publique, 1999, 189 pp.
*Les inégalités devant la santé. Rapport au ministre des Affaires sociales et de la Solidarité
nationale*, by Sylvie LeRoux, 1984, 140 pp.
Les inégalités sociales de santé: déterminants sociaux et modèles d'action. Inspection
générale des affaires sociales [IGAS]. Ed. Marguerite Moleux, Françoise Schaetzel,
and Claire Scotton, 2011, 124 pp.
Les inégalités sociales de santé: sortir de la fatalité. Haut Conseil de la santé publique
[HCSP], 2009, 99 pp.
*Inégalités territoriales, environnementales et sociales de santé. Regards croisés en
régions: de l'observation à l'action.* Secrétariat général en charge des ministéres
sociaux and Commissariat général au développement durable, 2014, 68 pp.

WHO Europe Reports
Concepts and Principles for Tackling Social Inequities in Health: Levelling Up Part 1, by
Margaret Whitehead and Göran Dahlgren. WHO European Office for Investment for
Health and Development, 2006 (first edition 1991), 34 pp.
The Equity Action Spectrum: Taking a Comprehensive Approach, by Margaret
Whitehead, Sue Povall, and Belinda Loring, 2014, 29 pp.
European Strategies for Tackling Social Inequities in Health: Levelling Up Part 2, by
Göran Dahlgren and Margaret Whitehead. WHO European Office for Investment for
Health and Development, 2006 (first edition 1991), 137 pp.
Governance for Health Equity in the WHO European Region, by Chris Brown and
Dominic Harrison, 2013, 63 pp.
*Putting Our Own House in Order: Examples of Health-System Action on Socially
Determined Health Inequalities*, by Sarah Simpson, 2010, 73 pp.
*Review of Social Determinants and the Health Divide in the WHO European Region:
Final Report*, Michael Marmot, review chair, 2013 (updated reprint 2014), 188 pp.
Social Determinants of Health: The Solid Facts, 2nd edition, ed. Richard Wilkinson and
Michael Marmot, 2003 (first edition 1999), 31 pp.

CODING PROCEDURES

To draw measurements of the problem frame from these documents, I began by reading each document in its entirety. I used grounded coding to flag elements that recurred across the documents; for example, explanations of where health inequalities come from, statements about what kinds of policy changes might help reduce inequalities, and even recurrent single words such as "solidarity" or "outrage" that might indicate the type of moral framework that the authors of the documents were drawing on to justify their concern with the issue.

Once the grounded coding was complete, I grouped the codes into categories representing the five key elements of a policy frame: the definition of the problem, the moral evaluation, the explanation for the problem's genesis (causal stories), the proposed remedies (treatment recommendations), and the entity responsible for enacting those remedies (treatment responsibility). Based on the recurrent codes in each category, I constructed a codebook that would allow me to characterize the contents of any document according to its ideas relative to each element of the policy frame.

To make the discussion of my coding and analytical procedures easier to follow, it will help to first define some terms. Reports have been grouped into *corpora*: a group of documents from a particular country or, in the case of the "international" corpora, from both WHO Europe and the EU. *Elements* are the component parts of a frame: the problem definition, moral attribution, causal story, treatment attribution, and treatment recommendation. An *idea* is the "answer" to the question posed by each element (e.g., What is the problem definition? What is the treatment recommendation?) The coded elements and their respective associated ideas are shown in Table A.2. The full codebook and coding instructions are available from the author on request.

Reports were coded by human coders using Version 12 of MaxQDA. A team of five students (two French-English bilingual speakers, one Finnish-English bilingual speaker, and two native English-speakers) was trained to identify ideas in the documents and to tag each occurrence of an idea. The units of observation were sentences (including bullet points) and figures (graph, chart, table, map). Contiguous sentences containing the same idea code were counted as a single occurrence of the idea. Once each pair of coders could consistently code samples of reports from each country in the same fashion at least 90 percent of the time, training was complete. Multiple coders were assigned to code documents in each corpus in order to ensure that measured differences between the corpora reflected differences in the text and not individual coding "styles." Inter-rater reliability was reassessed periodically throughout the coding process to ensure a continuing high level of agreement.

MaxQDA's tools for analyzing the similarity of documents do not standardize for the length of the document or allow for grouping of codes hierarchically into multiple elements. For that reason, I report here the number of coded occurrences of every idea for each element, and calculate the prevalence of ideas

TABLE A.2 *Codes*

Outcome

HEALTH STATUS (e.g., mortality, morbidity, life expectancy, self-rated health, presence of chronic conditions, mental health, suicide, obesity, BMI, addiction, diet, exercise, tobacco, alcohol or drug use, sexual behavior)

HEALTH CARE (accessibility, quality, timeliness, appropriateness, utilization of health care; used only when health care is the outcome that is unequal; not used if health care is the cause of inequalities in health status)

Group

SES (socioeconomic status: income, wealth, employment status, occupation, prestige, educational attainment, geographic areas characterized by the SES of their residents or by SES-related characteristics of the area such as weak labor markets; e.g., deprived areas, poor neighborhoods)

AREA (Parts of the country not characterized solely by SES, e.g., urban/rural, by region or province, capital city vs. the rest; international comparisons not coded with this code)

GENDER (male, female, transgender, non-binary)

RACE/IMMIGRATION (groups characterized by race, ethnicity, religion, language, immigration status)

DISABILITY (the disability must be a characteristic of the group, not the health outcome that is the subject of the inequality, e.g., people with disabilities get worse health care)

Moral Attribution

JUSTICE (e.g., equity, justice, fairness, morality, solidarity, and other related terms)

INEQUALITY (e.g., inequality, disparity, gap, and other related terms)

RIGHTS (in the context of a right to health or to health equity)

Causal Stories

STRUCTURAL (structural discrimination, institutional racism; income or wealth inequality [as opposed to poverty, deprivation]; fundamental causation; capitalism, class structure)

SOCIAL DETERMINANTS (natural environment, built environment, social environment; education, deprivation, and poverty; health behaviors, individual choices, risk factors *with* mention of structures shaping these behaviors, choices or risk factors)

INDIVIDUAL (health behaviors, individual choices, "risk factors" without mention of structures shaping these behaviors, choices, or risk factors; biological, genetic makeup)

HEALTH SYSTEM (availability of, access to, quality of health care or public health interventions; adequate financing; culturally competent care; health education)

Treatment Recommendations and Polity Proposals

(coded as recommendation if it is describing a general approach; coded as proposal if specific policy tools, settings are described)

ECONOMIC SYSTEM (e.g., introduce or raise minimum wage; limit unemployment spells by incentivizing hiring, reforming labor market; redistribute income [not just by increasing minimum income benefits]; limit capitalism; limit free trade)

POWER/POLITICAL (e.g., redistribute power in society; remove structural discrimination; empowering local communities or stakeholder groups not included)

STRUCTURAL BEHAVIOR (act on structures affecting individual health choices, e.g., tax or restrict marketing and sales of food, alcohol, tobacco; food, alcohol, and tobacco nutrition labeling or warning labels; subsidizing or encouraging availability of healthy foods; building more facilities for exercise; healthy city planning; health education and outreach in schools, workplaces, communities; health literacy; smoking cessation programs; creating "supportive communities")

DETERMINANTS (act on environmental, social determinants of health, e.g., improve education (but not health education); raise minimum income benefits, reduce poverty; limit unemployment spells through training, activation; housing quality or cost; transport; pollution; dangerous working conditions; improve social capital)

EMPOWERMENT (e.g., empowering, giving ownership to individuals, groups, civil society actors, stakeholders, local communities)

MINDSET (e.g., develop political will, leadership, change the way people think about health, reduce individual discrimination)

DATA (e.g., collect more, better data, more analysis of existing data, better impact assessment, more research; disease surveillance is not included; it is under HEALTH SYSTEM (causal story))

HEALTH SYSTEM (e.g. facilitating access, upgrading quality, appropriateness, placing greater emphasis on primary care, prevention, or health promotion, changing provider behavior – e.g., end discrimination, more attention to determinants – expanding use of screening, improving medical social services – e.g., home care for elderly, disabled – improving quality of medical education, increasing supply of providers, increasing funding for health care, improving public health infrastructure including disease surveillance)

INDIVIDUAL BEHAVIOR (used only for behavioral changes to be undertaken by individuals – e.g., stop smoking, dietary changes, more exercise – without mention of the social structures or policies shaping individual behaviors)

OTHER

Treatment Responsibility

SUPRANATIONAL ORGANIZATION (e.g., WHO, EU, WTO; cooperation between countries not included)

NATIONAL GOVERNMENT (this is the default if it says "government" but does not specify a level of government)

SUB-NATIONAL GOVERNMENT

MULTIPLE LEVELS of government

HEALTH SYSTEM ACTORS (e.g., health ministry, public health system, health care providers)

PRIVATE SECTOR (employers, firms, including multinational firms)

COMMUNITY (organizations, civil society, stakeholders)

SCHOOLS

INDIVIDUALS (taking responsibility for their own health)

OTHER

as a percentage of all ideas coded for a given element. Frequencies and the prevalence of each idea in each document in the international (WHO Europe and EU), English, and French corpora are shown in Table A.3a–d. Table A.4, which shows the prevalence of each idea in an entire corpus, allows for easier comparison across corpora. Quantitative results for the Finnish corpus are not presented here because there were only two Finnish reports with official English-language translations, both of which are discussed in detail in Chapters 6 and 7.

THE INTERNATIONAL CONSENSUS FRAME

The results of the content analysis of the International corpus show that the WHO and EU documents contain ideas about health inequalities that are so consistent that they can indeed be labeled as a "consensus." While there are some differences in emphasis between the EU and WHO documents and over time, most of the documents in the corpus supply substantially similar responses to the elemental questions of the health inequalities problem frame: What are health inequalities? What is their moral valence? Where do they come from? and How ought society respond to them?

How do the authors of the WHO and EU reports in our corpus explain health inequalities? In seven of the nine WHO documents, equity/inequity and other terms with a strong moral valence (e.g., injustice, unfairness, solidarity) are the dominant language in which health inequalities are discussed, comprising over 75 percent of moral attributions in the corpus. In the EU documents, the term "inequality" is preferred over "inequity": in all but one of the EU documents, a variant of the word "inequality" is the term of choice in at least 60 percent of moral attributions. However, it is worth noting that the official EU web portal for action on health inequalities uses language drawn from the final report of the WHO's Commission on the Social Determinants of Health (WHO 2008) to define health inequalities as "preventable and unjust differences in health status or in the distribution of health determinants between different population groups" (EuroHealthNet 2018). The reference to preventable and unjust differences reflects the Whitehead (1991) definition of health *inequities*, and signals that the term *inequalities* in EU documents should probably be taken as expressing a stance that health inequalities are more than simply morally neutral differences.

My team coded the documents for every mention of an inequality in health care or health and the social groups over which that inequality occurred (e.g., groups defined by socioeconomic status, geography, race/ethnicity, gender). In all documents save one (European Parliament 2011b), more than 70 percent of the inequalities mentioned were related to inequalities in health status rather than to health care. In all but two of the documents (European Commission 2009; European Parliament 2011b) more than half of these mentions were related to inequalities over socioeconomic groups. In fact, the definition of

TABLE A.3A *Frequencies and prevalence of ideas in documents in the WHO corpus*

Report	Group						Outcome		Moral Attribution			Causal Attribution			
	SES	Area	Gender	Race, Immigr.	Disabil.	Other	Status, Behav.	Health Care	Equity, Justice	Equality, Disparity	Rights	Pol, Econ System	Social Det.	Health Care	Individ.
SDOH The Solid Facts	13 93%	0 0%	0 0%	0 0%	0 0%	1 7%	12 100%	0 0%	2 15%	11 85%	0 0%	0 0%	12 92%	0 0%	1 8%
Levelling Up Part I	16 89%	2 11%	0 0%	0 0%	0 0%	0 0%	11 65%	6 35%	32 67%	9 19%	7 15%	0 0%	4 80%	1 20%	0 0%
Levelling Up Part II	31 89%	1 3%	3 9%	0 0%	0 0%	0 0%	34 100%	0 0%	20 69%	1 3%	8 28%	3 14%	18 82%	0 0%	1 5%
Putting Our Own House in Order	2 100%	0 0%	0 0%	0 0%	0 0%	0 0%	2 100%	0 0%	1 11%	1 11%	7 78%	7 10%	36 51%	24 34%	3 4%
Rev. of SD and the Health Divide	100 69%	6 4%	21 15%	13 9%	1 1%	3 2%	135 96%	6 4%	394 84%	48 10%	27 6%	77 23%	221 67%	17 5%	14 4%
Governance for Health Equity	10 83%	0 0%	1 8%	1 8%	0 0%	0 0%	12 100%	0 0%	11 24%	19 42%	15 33%	13 18%	44 61%	12 17%	3 4%
Equity Action Spectrum	7 100%	0 0%	0 0%	0 0%	0 0%	0 0%	7 88%	1 13%	205 84%	32 13%	8 3%	1 9%	10 91%	0 0%	0 0%
WHO Corpus TOTAL	179 77%	9 4%	25 11%	14 6%	1 0%	4 2%	213 94%	13 6%	665 78%	121 14%	72 8%	101 19%	345 66%	54 10%	22 4%

Report	Treatment Recommendations								Policy Proposals							
	Polit, econ sys	Social Det.	Health System	Comm Empwr.	Indiv. Behav.	Change Mndst.	Data Soln.	Other	Econ Sys +Pr.	Social Det.	Health Syst.	Comm Empwr.	Indiv. Behav.	Change Mndst.	Data Soln.	Other
SDOH																
The Solid Facts	8 / 35%	14 / 61%	1 / 4%	0 / 0%	0 / 0%	0 / 0%	0 / 0%	0 / 0%	0 / 0%	1 / 100%	0 / 0%	0 / 0%	0 / 0%	0 / 0%	0 / 0%	0 / 0%
Levelling Up Part I	2 / 29%	2 / 29%	2 / 29%	1 / 14%	0 / 0%	0 / 0%	0 / 0%	0 / 0%	0	0	0	0	0	0	0	0
Levelling Up Part II	9 / 23%	24 / 60%	0 / 0%	2 / 5%	4 / 10%	0 / 0%	1 / 3%	0 / 0%	0 / 0%	2 / 50%	0 / 0%	0 / 0%	0 / 0%	0 / 0%	2 / 50%	0 / 0%
Putting Our Own House in Order	6 / 5%	27 / 24%	35 / 31%	15 / 13%	2 / 2%	3 / 3%	25 / 22%	0 / 0%	0 / 0%	3 / 16%	4 / 21%	5 / 26%	0 / 0%	0 / 0%	7 / 37%	0 / 0%
Rev. of SD and the Health Divide	46 / 15%	136 / 44%	44 / 14%	36 / 12%	5 / 2%	4 / 1%	38 / 12%	1 / 0%	3 / 23%	5 / 38%	1 / 8%	4 / 31%	0 / 0%	0 / 0%	0 / 0%	0 / 0%
Governance for Health Equity	7 / 13%	11 / 20%	3 / 5%	19 / 35%	1 / 2%	2 / 4%	12 / 22%	0 / 0%	0 / 0%	0 / 0%	2 / 8%	5 / 20%	0 / 0%	1 / 4%	17 / 68%	0 / 0%
Equity Action Spectrum	6 / 20%	8 / 27%	3 / 10%	3 / 10%	0 / 0%	1 / 3%	9 / 30%	0 / 0%								
WHO Corpus TOTAL	84 / 15%	222 / 38%	88 / 15%	76 / 13%	12 / 2%	10 / 2%	85 / 15%	1 / 0%	3 / 5%	11 / 18%	7 / 11%	14 / 23%	0 / 0%	1 / 2%	26 / 42%	0 / 0%

Treatment Responsibility

Report	National Government	Cross-Ministerial Group	Subnational Government	Supranational Organization	Multiple Levels	Health System Actors	Private Sector, Comm. Individuals
SDOH The Solid Facts	1 100%	0 0%	0 0%	0 0%	0 0%	0 0%	0 0%
Levelling Up Part I	0	0	0	0	0	0	0
Levelling Up Part II	0	0	0	0	0	0	0
Putting Our Own House in Order	17 20%	1 1%	17 20%	2 2%	10 12%	31 37%	5 6%
Rev. of SD and the Health Divide	24 20%	0 0%	6 5%	33 27%	34 28%	8 7%	18 15%
Governance for Health Equity	27 30%	1 1%	8 9%	11 12%	17 19%	9 10%	16 18%
Equity Action Spectrum	2 20%	0 0%	0 0%	0 0%	4 40%	1 10%	3 30%
WHO Corpus TOTAL	71 23%	2 1%	31 10%	46 15%	65 21%	49 16%	42 14%

TABLE A.3B *Frequencies and prevalence of ideas in documents in the EU corpus*

Report	Group						Outcome		Moral Attribution			Causal Attribution			
	SES	Area	Gender	Race, Immigr.	Disabil.	Other	Status, Behav	Health Care	Equity, Justice	Equality, Disparity	Rights	Pol, Econ System	Social Det.	Health Care	Individ.
Health Status of the EU	14 64%	4 18%	3 14%	1 5%	0 0%	0 0%	19 83%	4 17%	6 46%	6 46%	1 8%	0 0%	11 35%	7 23%	13 42%
HI Europe in Profile	68 96%	1 1%	1 1%	0 0%	1 1%	0 0%	45 100%	0 0%	4 57%	3 43%	0 0%	0 0%	5 71%	0 0%	2 29%
HI A Challenge for Europe	0 0	0	0	0	0		0	0	54 92%	3 5%	2 3%	0 0%	3 100%	0 0%	0 0%
Solidarity in Health	4 50%	0 0%	1 13%	3 38%	0 0%	0 0%	6 86%	1 14%	14 16%	65 76%	7 8%	3 10%	20 67%	5 17%	2 7%
Reducing HI in the EU	14 74%	1 5%	0 0%	3 16%	1 5%	0 0%	14 70%	6 30%	7 70%	2 20%	1 10%	5 16%	23 72%	3 9%	1 3%
EP Resolution	8 36%	5 23%	5 23%	1 5%	2 9%	1 5%	9 45%	11 55%	18 50%	5 14%	13 36%	7 22%	12 38%	8 25%	5 16%
Commission Report on HI	40 89%	1 2%	3 7%	1 2%	0 0%	0 0%	34 85%	6 15%	25 76%	1 3%	7 21%	13 13%	65 63%	24 23%	2 2%
European Marmot Review	77 84%	2 2%	9 10%	4 4%	0 0%	0 0%	90 99%	1 1%	82 8%	934 91%	6 1%	1 1%	57 85%	3 4%	6 9%
Action on HU in the EU	1 20%	0 0%	1 20%	2 40%	1 20%	0 0%	2 100%	0 0%	5 100%	0 0%	0 0%	1 5%	14 64%	3 14%	4 18%
EU Corpus TOTAL	226 80%	14 5%	23 8%	15 5%	5 2%	1 0%	219 88%	29 12%	215 17%	1019 80%	37 3%	30 9%	210 64%	53 16%	35 11%

Report	Treatment Recommendations								Policy Proposals							
	Econ Sys+Pr.	Social Det.	Health System	Comm Empwr.	Indiv. Behav.	Change Mndst.	Data Soln.	Other	Econ Sys+Pr.	Social Det.	Health Syst.	Comm. Empwr.	Indiv. Behav.	Change Mndst.	Data Soln.	Other
Health Status of the EU	1 / 6%	5 / 29%	2 / 12%	0 / 0%	2 / 12%	1 / 6%	6 / 35%	0 / 0%	0 / 0%	0 / 0%	2 / 13%	0 / 0%	1 / 6%	0 / 0%	13 / 81%	0 / 0%
HI Europe in Profile	0 / 0%	1 / 100%	0 / 0%	0 / 0%	0 / 0%	0 / 0%	0 / 0%	0 / 0%	0	0	0	0	0	0	0	0
HI A Challenge for Europe	2 / 29%	4 / 57%	1 / 14%	0 / 0%	0 / 0%	0 / 0%	0 / 0%	0 / 0%	0	0	0	0	0	0	0	0
Solidarity in Health	3 / 11%	8 / 30%	6 / 22%	0 / 0%	1 / 4%	0 / 0%	9 / 33%	0 / 0%	0 / 0%	0 / 0%	1 / 20%	0	0 / 0%	0 / 0%	4 / 80%	0 / 0%
Reducing HI in the EU	3 / 14%	8 / 38%	2 / 10%	1 / 5%	4 / 19%	0 / 0%	3 / 14%	0	2 / 22%	4 / 44%	2 / 22%	0 / 0%	0 / 0%	0 / 0%	1 / 11%	0 / 0%
EP Resolution	7 / 17%	11 / 26%	13 / 31%	1 / 2%	3 / 7%	1 / 2%	6 / 14%	0 / 0%	1 / 3%	1 / 3%	17 / 57%	1 / 3%	1 / 3%	0 / 0%	9 / 30%	0 / 0%
Commission Report on HI	8 / 13%	21 / 34%	19 / 31%	3 / 5%	0 / 0%	0 / 0%	11 / 18%	0 / 0%	3 / 21%	8 / 57%	2 / 14%	0 / 0%	0 / 0%	0 / 0%	1 / 7%	0 / 0%
European Marmot Review	5 / 16%	9 / 28%	4 / 13%	4 / 13%	0 / 0%	0 / 0%	9 / 28%	1 / 3%	0 / 0%	0 / 0%	0 / 0%	1 / 100%	0 / 0%	0 / 0%	0 / 0%	0 / 0%
Action on HU in the EU	0 / 0%	10 / 20%	17 / 33%	2 / 4%	2 / 4%	2 / 4%	18 / 35%	1 / 0%	0 / 0%	1 / 13%	2 / 25%	0 / 0%	0 / 0%	0 / 0%	5 / 63%	0 / 0%
EU Corpus TOTAL	29 / 11%	77 / 30%	64 / 25%	11 / 4%	12 / 5%	4 / 2%	62 / 24%	1 / 0%	6 / 7%	14 / 17%	26 / 31%	2 / 2%	2 / 2%	0 / 0%	33 / 40%	0 / 0%

239

		Treatment Responsibility					
Report	National Government	Cross-Ministerial Group	Subnational Government	Supranational Organization	Multiple Levels	Health System Actors	Private Sector, Comm. Individuals
Health Status of the EU	6 / 21%	0 / 0%	1 / 4%	10 / 36%	3 / 11%	3 / 11%	5 / 18%
HI Europe in Profile	0 / 0%	0 / 0%	0	0	0	0	0
HI A Challenge for Europe	3 / 60%	0 / 0%	0 / 0%	0 / 0%	0 / 0%	2 / 40%	0 / 0%
Solidarity in Health	7 / 22%	0 / 0%	2 / 6%	16 / 50%	4 / 13%	2 / 6%	1 / 3%
Reducing HI in the EU	3 / 15%	0 / 0%	1 / 5%	6 / 30%	2 / 10%	3 / 15%	5 / 25%
EP Resolution	25 / 36%	0 / 0%	1 / 1%	24 / 35%	19 / 28%	0 / 0%	0 / 0%
Commission Report on HI	6 / 10%	0 / 0%	4 / 7%	23 / 38%	20 / 33%	7 / 11%	1 / 2%
European Marmot Review	0 / 0%	0 / 0%	0 / 0%	3 / 30%	5 / 50%	0 / 0%	2 / 20%
Action on HU in the EU	7 / 14%	0 / 0%	3 / 6%	15 / 29%	10 / 20%	5 / 10%	11 / 22%
EU Corpus TOTAL	57 / 21%	0 / 0%	12 / 4%	97 / 35%	63 / 23%	22 / 8%	25 / 9%

TABLE A.3C *Frequencies and prevalence of ideas in documents in the English corpus*

Report	Group						Outcome			Moral Attribution			Causal Attribution		
	SES	Area	Gender	Race, Immigr.	Disabil.	Other	Status, Behav	Health Care	Equity, Justice	Equality, Disparity	Rights	Pol, Econ System	Social Det.	Health Care	Individ.
Cross Cutting Review	105 68%	17 11%	13 8%	15 10%	3 2%	2 1%	131 87%	20 13%	4 100%	0 0%	0 0%	13 6%	158 76%	20 10%	17 8%
HI Programme for Action	2 50%	1 25%	0 0%	1 25%	0 0%	0 0%	3 60%	2 40%	17 94%	0 0%	1 6%	1 50%	1 50%	0 0%	0 0%
HI Progress and Next Steps	17 65%	2 8%	0 0%	2 8%	1 4%	4 15%	23 79%	6 21%	13 87%	0 0%	2 13%	1 20%	4 80%	0 0%	0 0%
Tackling HI 10 Years On	32 65%	3 6%	8 16%	6 12%	0 0%	0 0%	44 100%	0 0%	29 88%	1 3%	3 9%	1 100%	0 0%	0 0%	0 0%
Commons Health Committee	27 64%	2 5%	5 12%	3 7%	3 7%	2 5%	37 90%	4 10%	14 93%	0 0%	1 7%	2 11%	11 61%	2 11%	3 17%
Marmot Report	132 90%	5 3%	1 1%	3 2%	5 3%	1 1%	128 96%	6 4%	49 89%	4 7%	2 4%	82 14%	445 76%	35 6%	20 3%
UK Corpus TOTAL	315 74%	30 7%	27 6%	30 7%	12 3%	9 2%	366 91%	38 9%	126 90%	5 4%	9 6%	100 12%	619 76%	57 7%	40 5%

(continued)

Report	Treatment Recommendations								Policy Proposals							
	Econ Sys+Pr.	Social Det.	Health System	Comm Empwr.	Indiv. Behav.	Change Mndst.	Data Soln.	Other	Econ Sys+Pr.	Social Det.	Health Syst.	Comm. Empwr.	Indiv. Behav.	Change Mndst.	Data Soln.	Other
Cross Cutting Review	7 / 4%	100 / 54%	36 / 19%	13 / 7%	19 / 10%	0 / 0%	10 / 5%	0 / 0%	0 / 0%	8 / 67%	2 / 17%	0 / 0%	1 / 8%	0 / 0%	1 / 8%	0 / 0%
HI Programme for Action	3 / 6%	16 / 33%	13 / 27%	1 / 2%	15 / 31%	0 / 0%	0 / 0%	0 / 0%	0 / 0%	1 / 50%	0 / 0%	0 / 0%	1 / 50%	0 / 0%	0 / 0%	0 / 0%
HI Progress and Next Steps	2 / 3%	22 / 38%	15 / 26%	3 / 5%	9 / 16%	0 / 0%	6 / 10%	1 / 2%	0 / 0%	3 / 50%	1 / 17%	0 / 0%	2 / 33%	0 / 0%	0 / 0%	0
Tacking HI 10 Years On	2 / 11%	12 / 63%	4 / 21%	0 / 0%	0 / 0%	0 / 0%	1 / 5%	0 / 0%	0 / 0%	1 / 33%	2 / 67%	0 / 0%	0 / 0%	0 / 0%	0 / 0%	0
Commons Health Committee	0 / 0%	18 / 49%	17 / 46%	0 / 0%	1 / 3%	0 / 0%	1 / 3%	0 / 0%	0 / 0%	1 / 100%	0 / 0%	0 / 0%	0 / 0%	0 / 0%	0 / 0%	0
Marmot Report	101 / 13%	388 / 52%	102 / 14%	47 / 6%	28 / 4%	20 / 3%	65 / 9%	0 / 0%	14 / 6%	141 / 59%	44 / 18%	5 / 2%	11 / 5%	1 / 0%	22 / 9%	0
UK Corpus TOTAL	115 / 10%	556 / 51%	187 / 17%	64 / 6%	72 / 7%	20 / 2%	83 / 8%	1 / 0%	14 / 5%	155 / 59%	49 / 19%	5 / 2%	15 / 6%	1 / 0%	23 / 9%	0 / 0%

Treatment Responsibility

Report	National Government	Cross-Ministerial Group	Subnational Government	Supranational Organization	Multiple Levels	Health System Actors	Private Sector, Comm. Individuals
Cross Cutting Review	32 34%	0 0%	10 11%	0 0%	10 11%	15 16%	27 29%
HI Programme for Action	1 5%	3 14%	0 0%	0 0%	0 0%	13 62%	4 19%
HI Progress and Next Steps	21 72%	1 3%	0 0%	1 3%	0 0%	5 17%	1 3%
Tacking HI 10 Years On	0 0%	0 0%	0 0%	0 0%	0 0%	1 100%	0 0%
Commons Health Committee	12 75%	1 6%	0 0%	0 0%	0 0%	2 13%	1 6%
Marmot Report	77 15%	0 0%	98 19%	0 0%	42 8%	105 20%	205 39%
UK Corpus TOTAL	143 21%	5 1%	108 16%	1 0%	52 8%	141 20%	238 35%

TABLE A.3D *Frequencies and prevalence of ideas in documents in the French corpus*

Report	Group							Outcome		Moral Attribution			Causal Attribution			
	SES	Area	Gender	Race, Immigr.	Disabil.	Other	Status, Behav	Health Care	Equity, Justice	Equality, Disparity	Rights	Pol,Econ System	Social Det.	Health Care	Individ.
LeRoux Report	60 70%	16 19%	2 2%	2 2%	3 3%	3 3%	43 52%	39 48%	11 48%	4 17%	8 35%	29 17%	113 68%	20 12%	4 2%
Allocation Régionale	27 36%	44 59%	3 4%	0 0%	1 1%	0 0%	34 56%	27 44%	63 39%	90 56%	8 5%	24 16%	43 29%	62 42%	17 12%
ISS Sortir de la Fatalité	26 93%	0 0%	2 7%	0 0%	0 0%	0 0%	24 86%	4 14%	27 48%	14 25%	15 27%	15 6%	184 68%	56 21%	16 6%
ISS Déterminants Sociaux	11 92%	1 8%	0 0%	0 0%	0 0%	0 0%	11 92%	1 8%	18 78%	3 13%	2 9%	15 8%	150 76%	20 10%	13 7%
Inégalités Territoriales	5 63%	3 38%	0 0%	0 0%	0 0%	0 0%	4 80%	1 20%	39 71%	10 18%	6 11%	13 9%	117 84%	8 6%	2 1%
FR Corpus TOTAL	129 62%	64 31%	7 3%	2 1%	4 2%	3 1%	116 62%	72 38%	158 50%	121 38%	39 12%	96 10%	607 66%	166 18%	52 6%

Treatment Recommendations / Policy Proposals

Report	Treatment Recommendations								Policy Proposals							
	Econ Sys+Pr.	Social Det.	Health System	Comm Empwr.	Indiv. Behav.	Change Mndst.	Data Soln.	Other	Econ Sys+Pr.	Social Det.	Health Syst.	Comm. Empwr.	Indiv. Behav.	Change Mndst.	Data Soln.	Other
LeRoux Report	12 / 14%	14 / 16%	34 / 40%	7 / 8%	1 / 1%	3 / 4%	14 / 16%	0 / 0%	8 / 13%	19 / 30%	23 / 36%	2 / 3%	0 / 0%	2 / 3%	10 / 16%	0 / 0%
Allocation Régionale	50 / 18%	7 / 3%	135 / 48%	0 / 0%	1 / 0%	2 / 1%	85 / 30%	0 / 0%	0 / 0%	0 / 0%	7 / 39%	0 / 0%	0 / 0%	0 / 0%	11 / 61%	0 / 0%
ISS Sortir de la Fatalité	13 / 7%	49 / 25%	33 / 17%	7 / 4%	3 / 2%	5 / 3%	88 / 44%	0 / 0%	0 / 0%	1 / 6%	2 / 12%	1 / 6%	2 / 12%	0 / 0%	11 / 65%	0 / 0%
ISS Déterminants Sociaux	10 / 4%	66 / 28%	16 / 7%	18 / 8%	10 / 4%	24 / 10%	90 / 38%	0 / 0%	0 / 0%	20 / 49%	5 / 12%	0 / 0%	1 / 2%	0 / 0%	15 / 37%	0 / 0%
Inégalités Territoriales	8 / 9%	20 / 21%	0 / 0%	20 / 21%	1 / 1%	8 / 9%	37 / 39%	0 / 0%	0 / 0%	5 / 28%	1 / 6%	3 / 17%	0 / 0%	0 / 0%	9 / 50%	0 / 0%
FR Corpus TOTAL	93 / 10%	156 / 18%	218 / 24%	52 / 6%	16 / 2%	42 / 5%	314 / 35%	0 / 0%	8 / 5%	45 / 28%	38 / 24%	6 / 4%	3 / 2%	2 / 1%	56 / 35%	0 / 0%

(*continued*)

Treatment Responsibility

Report	National Government	Cross-Ministerial Group	Subnational Government	Supranational Organization	Multiple Levels	Health System Actors	Private Sector, Comm. Individuals
LeRoux Report	13 17%	0 0%	3 4%	0 0%	0 0%	32 41%	30 38%
Allocation Régionale	44 18%	0 0%	136 56%	0 0%	27 11%	31 13%	5 2%
ISS Sortir de la Fatalité	18 16%	3 3%	28 25%	8 7%	26 23%	15 13%	16 14%
ISS Déterminants Sociaux	53 17%	13 4%	98 31%	14 4%	46 15%	47 15%	44 14%
Inégalités Territoriales	23 16%	4 3%	68 47%	0 0%	17 12%	10 7%	23 16%
FR Corpus TOTAL	151 17%	20 2%	333 37%	22 2%	116 13%	135 15%	118 13%

TABLE A.4 *Frequencies and prevalence of ideas across corpora*

Report	Group						Outcome		Moral Attribution			Causal Attribution			
	SES	Area	Gender	Race, Immigr.	Disabil.	Other	Status, Behav.	Health Care	Equity, Justice	Equality, Disparity	Rights	Pol, Econ System	Social Det.	Health Care	Individ.
International Corpus	405 78%	23 4%	48 9%	29 6%	6 1%	5 1%	432 91%	42 9%	880 41%	1,140 54%	109 5%	131 15%	555 65%	107 13%	57 7%
English Corpus	315 74%	30 7%	27 6%	30 7%	12 3%	9 2%	366 91%	38 9%	126 90%	5 4%	9 6%	100 12%	619 76%	57 7%	40 5%
French Corpus	129 62%	64 31%	7 3%	2 1%	4 2%	3 1%	116 62%	72 38%	158 50%	121 38%	39 12%	96 10%	607 66%	166 18%	52 6%

Report	Treatment Recommendations								Policy Proposals							
	Econ Sys+Pr.	Social Det.	Health System	Comm Empwr.	Indiv. Behav.	Change Mndst.	Data Soln.	Other	Econ Sys+Pr.	Social Det.	Health Syst.	Comm. Empwr.	Indiv. Behav.	Change Mndst.	Data Soln.	Other
International Corpus	113 13%	299 36%	152 18%	87 10%	24 3%	14 2%	147 18%	2 0%	9 6%	25 17%	33 23%	16 11%	2 1%	1 1%	59 41%	0 0%
English Corpus	115 10%	556 51%	187 17%	64 6%	72 7%	20 2%	83 8%	1 0%	14 5%	155 59%	49 19%	5 2%	15 6%	1 0%	23 9%	0 0%
French Corpus	93 10%	156 18%	218 24%	52 6%	16 2%	42 5%	314 35%	0 0%	8 5%	45 28%	38 24%	6 4%	3 2%	2 1%	56 35%	0 0%

(continued)

				Treatment Responsibility			
Report	National Government	Cross-Ministerial Group	Subnational Government	Supranational Organization	Multiple Levels	Health System Actors	Private Sector, Comm. Individuals
International Corpus	128	2	43	143	128	71	67
	22%	0%	7%	25%	22%	12%	12%
English Corpus	143	5	108	1	52	141	238
	21%	1%	16%	0%	8%	20%	35%
French Corpus	151	20	333	22	116	135	118
	17%	2%	37%	2%	13%	15%	13%

"health inequalities" in general appears to have become nearly synonymous with SES inequalities in health status. By selecting for inclusion in the corpus only those documents that are about health inequalities in general, we risked focusing our attention only on documents that are about SES inequalities in health status. This does not appear to be entirely the case, however, as just two of the documents in our corpus (Simpson 2010; Whitehead et al. 2014) mentioned *only* SES inequalities. In the remaining fourteen documents, inequalities by gender and race/ethnicity together accounted for between 9 and 40 percent of group mentions.

When coding the reports, I asked my team to look for a wide variety of causal stories, ranging from individual behaviors (inequalities in health exist because some individuals choose to behave in unhealthy ways) to political economy accounts (e.g., the class structure in capitalist societies is responsible for inequalities in health). In between these two poles were a range of potential causal factors, some – like health care – more proximate to health outcomes (or further "downstream"), others, like the phrase "social determinants of health," further "upstream." The coders also distinguished between causal stories that located health-affecting behaviors such as smoking or exercise in individuals' choices, and explanations that related health behaviors to structural factors such as tobacco advertising targeted at low-income children or a lack of safe outdoor spaces. Finally, I asked them to note when socioeconomic inequality itself, rather than poverty or a lack of resources, was identified as the source of health inequalities.

Health care (access, quality, or affordability) and lack of health education were cited in one-fifth to one-quarter of causal explanations in the 2003, 2011, and 2013 EU documents, and in one-third of causal explanations in the 2010 WHO report (European Commission 2003; Simpson 2010; European Parliament 2011b; European Commission 2013; WHO Regional Office for Europe 2013). In the earlier EU documents, behavioral and biological risk factors at the individual level were prominent (42 percent of mentions in EU 2003, 29 percent in EU 2006), but receded over time (European Commission 2003; Judge et al. 2006; Mackenbach 2006). None of the WHO documents ever had more than 10 percent of causal explanations related to individual-level factors. Meanwhile, social determinants of health that were not labeled as such, but that are generally included in that framework – conditions related to the natural, built, or social environment that affect health; general (not health) education; poverty; or deprivation – accounted for the plurality of causal explanations in all but four of the documents. In the four remaining documents, the phrase "social determinants" itself was the most frequent causal explanation. Taken together, these two categories of explanation accounted for well over half of all causal stories in all of the documents in the corpus save the very earliest EU publication.[1] "Social determinants" as a phrase appeared at least

---

[1] This publication, *The Health Status of the European Union* (European Commission 2003), focused on behavioral and biological risk factors at the individual level as its dominant causal

once in every document in the corpus, and accounted for one-third or more of all mentioned causal explanations in nine of the sixteen documents.

While the dominant causal explanation for health inequalities in the WHO/EU corpus is social determinants, explanations focusing on further upstream political and economic determinants were also present. In the EU corpus, the 2009 European Parliament communication had the greatest share of structural causes (22 percent). Of the WHO documents, the Review of Social Determinants and the Health Divide was the most attentive to upstream structural causes of health inequalities (23 percent). That is to say, almost a quarter of the causal frames in this key report pinned health inequalities not on downstream factors like health care access or individual behaviors, and not even on mid-range factors like poverty or environmental factors, but rather on upstream political and economic realities (e.g., an "uncontrolled" market or privatization) (Whitehead and Dahlgren 2006; WHO Regional Office for Europe 2013).

The dominant causal story emphasizing multiple social determinants of health inequalities implies that the appropriate treatments would include cross-sectoral actions to reduce inequalities in multiple social determinants of health. Is this the case in these documents? Recall that WHO and EU publications dedicated to a single type of remedy for health inequalities (e.g., EU structural funds) or a single arena for action (e.g., within the health care system) were excluded from the corpus. The documents included in the corpus all have the potential, then, to identify a wide range of possible solutions to the problem of health inequalities. We coded the documents for both treatment recommendations and specific policy recommendations. The former are general approaches to solving the problem of health inequalities (e.g., by reducing poverty among the elderly), while the latter require specific actions (e.g., raising the minimum pension benefit). Coders looked for recommendations in the following categories: act on social determinants, act on the health system, act on individuals to change health behaviors, act on the political/economic system to redistribute power/resources, change the mindset of policy-makers, empower stakeholders, collect/analyze more data, and other. All of the documents in the corpus had more general treatment recommendations than specific policy proposals, only achieving near parity in *The Health Status of the European Union* (European Commission 2003). Of the specific policy recommendations, 59 percent were in the collect/analyze more data category, 33 percent in the health care system category, and 25 percent in the social determinants category. However, the more general treatment recommendations were more closely aligned with the social determinants causal frame. The plurality of attention (36 percent) was to social determinants, with only 18 percent of recommendations involving the health sector specifically. Remarkably, 14 percent of the

explanation (42 percent of mentions). Social determinants were the second most frequently cited causes of health inequalities (29 percent).

recommendations involved calls for changing political and economic systems to create better conditions for health equity. Such calls were slightly more frequent in the WHO corpus than in EU documents, which tended to emphasize health care system changes to a greater extent.

Thirteen documents in all (seven from the EU and five from the WHO) specified treatment responsibility. In five of the seven EU documents, the EU itself was allocated the plurality of responsibility, whereas WHO documents attributed responsibility more broadly to international, national, and subnational actors. It is worth noting that in only two of the reports was a plurality of attributions of responsibility directed at the health care system (Judge et al. 2006; Simpson 2010). Ten of the documents opined that coordination across multiple levels of government would be needed, and twelve asserted the importance of national-level leadership. Ten of the reports also attributed responsibility for solving the problem of health inequalities to non-governmental actors, but in all instances government received more attributions of responsibility.

In sum, analysis of the WHO Europe and EU documents confirms the hypothesis that the international corpus represents a consensus problem frame. First, the problem of health inequalities is defined primarily in terms of health status outcomes across socioeconomic groups; that is, health care access or other groups may also be mentioned, but the health outcomes and socioeconomic status (SES) predominate. Second, the words used in the corpus to discuss health inequalities convey a distinctly negative moral judgment: health inequalities are described as inequitable, unfair, or unjust, rather than as mere gaps, differences, or disparities. Third, the dominant causal story in the corpus is that health inequalities arise from inequalities in the social determinants of health, rather than primarily from health care services or from individual behaviors that are not shaped by other inequalities. Fourth, the remedies for health inequalities specified in the corpus are not limited to changing individual behaviors or the functioning of the health care system, but instead require actions across many sectors of government to reduce inequalities in the social determinants of health. Fifth and finally, in this corpus treatment responsibility is attributed to the national level of government, as well as to lower levels and to other societal actors. Meanwhile, the data presented in Tables A.3 and A.4 support the conclusion that the English corpus shows a greater level of agreement with the international consensus frame than does the French corpus. These results are discussed more fully in Chapters 4 and 5.

References

Published Works

Aaltonen, Natassa, Miisa Chydenius, and Lauri Kokkinen. 2018. "'First, Do No Harm': Have the Health Impacts of Government Bills on Tax Legislation Been Assessed in Finland?" *International Journal of Health Policy and Management* 7 (8): 696–98.

Abel-Smith, Brian, ed. 1995. *Choices in Health Policy: An Agenda for the European Union*. London: Dartmouth Publishing.

Abrahamson, Peter. 2010. "European Welfare States beyond Neoliberalism: Toward the Social Investment State." *Development and Society* 39 (1): 61–95.

Acemoglu, Daron, and David Autor. 2011. "Skills, Tasks and Technologies: Implications for Employment and Earnings." In *Handbook of Labor Economics*, edited by David Card and Orley Ashenfelter, 4B: 1043–71. Amsterdam: Elsevier.

Acemoglu, Daron, and James Robinson. 2000. "Why Did the West Extend the Franchise? Democracy, Inequality, and Growth in Historical Perspective." *Quarterly Journal of Economics* 115 (4): 1167–99.

Achenbach, Joel, and Daniel Keating. 2016. "A New Divide in American Death: Statistics Show Widening Urban-Rural Health Gap." *Washington Post*, April 10. www.washingtonpost.com/sf/national/2016/04/10/a-new-divide-in-ameri can-death/.

Acheson, Donald. 1998. "Inequalities in Health: Report on Inequalities in Health Did Give Priority for Steps to Be Tackled." *British Medical Journal* 317 (7173): 1659.

Adler, Nancy, and Judith Stewart. 2010. "Health Disparities across the Lifespan: Meaning, Methods, and Mechanisms." *Annals of the New York Academy of Sciences* 1186 (February): 5–23.

Aiach, Pierre, and Roy Carr-Hill. 1989. "Inequalities in Health: The Country Debate." In *Health Inequalities in European Countries*, edited by John Fox, 19–49. Aldershot: Gower.

Aizer, Anna, and Janet Currie. 2014. "The Intergenerational Transmission of Inequality: Maternal Disadvantage and Health at Birth." *Science* 344 (6186): 856–61.

Alber, Jens. 1988. "Is There a Crisis of the Welfare State? Crossnational Evidence from Europe, North America, and Japan." *European Sociological Review* 4 (3): 181–205.

Ansell, Ben, and David Samuels. 2014. *Inequality and Democratization*. New York: Cambridge University Press.

Arts, Wil, and John Gelissen. 2002. "Three Worlds of Welfare Capitalism or More? A State-of-the-Art Report." *Journal of European Social Policy* 12 (2): 137–58.

Asthana, Sheena, Alex Gibson, and Joyce Halliday. 2013. "The Medicalisation of Health Inequalities and the English NHS: The Role of Resource Allocation." *Health Economics, Policy and Law* 8 (2): 167–83.

Atelier no. 1. 1993. "Perspectives financieres du systeme de santé." Commissariat général du plan.

Atkinson, Anthony. 2015. *Inequality: What Can Be Done?* Cambridge, MA: Harvard University Press.

Axelsson, Runo, Gregory P. Marchildon, and José R. Repullo Labrador. 2007. "Effects of Decentralization on Managerial Dimensions of Health Systems." In *Decentralization in Health Care*, edited by Richard Saltman, Vaida Bankauskaite, and Karsten Vrangbaek. New York: Open University Press.

Baggott, Rob. 2010. *Public Health: Policy and Politics*. London: Palgrave Macmillan.

Bambra, Clare. 2007. "Going beyond the Three Worlds of Welfare Capitalism: Regime Theory and Public Health Research." *Journal of Epidemiology and Community Health* 61 (12): 1098–102.

2012. "Reducing Health Inequalities: New Data Suggest That the English Strategy Was Partially Successful." *Journal of Epidemiology and Community Health* 66 (7): 661–62.

2013. "In Defence of (Social) Democracy: On Health Inequalities and the Welfare State." *Journal of Epidemiology and Community Health* 67 (9): 713–14.

2016. *Health Divides: Where You Live Can Kill You*. Bristol: Policy Press.

Ban, Cornel. 2016. *Ruling Ideas: How Global Neoliberalism Goes Local*. Oxford, New York: Oxford University Press.

Bankauskaite, Vaida, and Richard Saltman. 2007. "Central Issues in the Decentralization Debate." In *Decentralization in Health Care*, edited by Richard Saltman, Vaida Bankauskaite, and Karsten Vrangbaek, 9. New York: Open University Press.

Barnes, Lucy. 2013. "Does Median Voter Income Matter? The Effects of Inequality and Turnout on Government Spending." *Political Studies* 61 (1): 82–100.

Barr, Ben, Clare Bambra, and Margaret Whitehead. 2014. "The Impact of NHS Resource Allocation Policy on Health Inequalities in England 2001–11: Longitudinal Ecological Study." *British Medical Journal* 348 (May): g3231.

Bartels, Larry. 2016. *Unequal Democracy: The Political Economy of the New Gilded Age*, 2nd edition. Princeton, NJ: Princeton University Press.

Bartolini, Stefano. 2007. *The Political Mobilization of the European Left, 1860–1980: The Class Cleavage*. New York: Cambridge University Press.

Baudoui, Remy. 1999. "L'aménagement du territoire en France, antécédents et genese, 1911–1963." In *L'aménagement du territoire 1958–1974*, edited by François Caron and Maurice Vaïsse. Paris: Éditions L'Harmattan.

Bauld, Linda, Ken Judge, Marian Barnes, Michaela Benzeval, Mhairi Mackenzie, and Helen Sullivan. 2005. "Promoting Social Change: The Experience of Health Action Zones in England." *Journal of Social Policy* 34 (3): 427–45.

Bauld, Linda, Ken Judge, and Stephen Platt. 2007. "Assessing the Impact of Smoking Cessation Services on Reducing Health Inequalities in England: Observational Study on JSTOR." *British Medical Journal* 16 (6): 400–404.

Baum, Andrew, J. P. Garofalo, and Ann Marie Yali. 1999. "Socioeconomic Status and Chronic Stress: Does Stress Account for SES Effects on Health?" *Annals of the New York Academy of Sciences* 896 (1): 131–44.

Baum, Fran. 2007. "Health for All Now! Reviving the Spirit of Alma Ata in the Twenty-First Century: An Introduction to the Alma Ata Declaration." *Social Medicine* 2 (1): 34–41.

Baum, Fran, and Matthew Fisher. 2014. "Why Behavioural Health Promotion Endures Despite Its Failure to Reduce Health Inequities." *Sociology of Health and Illness* 36 (2): 213–25.

Bayley, Hugh, Kevin Barron, Anna Coote, Howard Glennerster, Melanie Henwood, Ron Singer, and Rod Smith. 1996. *Health Crisis – What Crisis?* Fabian Pamphlet 574. London: Fabian Society.

Beckfield, Jason. 2004. "Does Income Inequality Harm Health? New Cross-National Evidence." *Journal of Health and Social Behavior* 45 (3): 231–48.

Beckfield, Jason, Clare Bambra, Terje Eikemo, Tim Huijts, Courtney McNamara, and Claus Wendt. 2015. "An Institutional Theory of Welfare State Effects on the Distribution of Population Health." *Social Theory and Health* 13 (3–4): 227–44.

Beckfield, Jason, and Katherine Morris. 2016. "State of the Union: Health." *Pathways* 2016 (2): 58–64. https://inequality.stanford.edu/sites/default/files/Pathways-SOTU-2016-2.pdf.

Bell, Daniel. 2008. *The Coming of Post-Industrial Society*. New York: Basic Books.

Bell, Kirsten, and Judith Green. 2016. "On the Perils of Invoking Neoliberalism in Public Health Critique." *Critical Public Health* 26 (3): 239–43.

Beller, Emily, and Michael Hout. 2006. "Intergenerational Social Mobility: The United States in Comparative Perspective." *The Future of Children* 16 (2): 19–36.

Belsky, Jay, Jacqueline Barnes, and Edward C. Melhuish. 2007. *The National Evaluation of Sure Start: Does Area-Based Early Intervention Work?* Bristol: Policy Press.

Bennett, James E., Guangquan Li, Kyle Foreman, Nicky Best, Vasilis Kontis, Clare Pearson, Peter Hambly, and Majid Ezzati. 2015. "The Future of Life Expectancy and Life Expectancy Inequalities in England and Wales: Bayesian Spatiotemporal Forecasting." *The Lancet* 386 (9989): 163–70.

Benzeval, Michaela, and Fiona Meth. 2002. "Health Inequalities: A Priority at a Crossroads; the Final Report to the Department of Health." London: Queen Mary, University of London. www.sphsu.mrc.ac.uk.

Benzeval, Michaela, Ken Judge, Margaret Whitehead, and King's Fund Centre. 1995. *Tackling Inequalities in Health: An Agenda for Action*. London: King's Fund.

Bergeron, Henri, and Constance Nathanson. 2012. "Construction of a Policy Arena: The Case of Public Health in France." *Journal of Health Politics, Policy and Law* 37 (1): 5–36.

Bergeron, Henri, Patrick Castel, and Abigail Saguy. 2014. "When Frames (Don't) Matter: Querying the Relationship between Ideas and Policy." LIEPP Working Paper 18. Paris: LIEPP. http://spire.sciencespo.fr/hdl:/2441/f6h8764enu2lskk9 p2084epkn/resources/wp-18-1.pdf.

Bergh, Andreas, Therese Nilsson, and Daniel Waldenstrom. 2016. *Sick of Inequality: An Introduction to the Relationship between Inequality and Health.* Cheltenham: Edward Elgar.

Berkman, Lisa, and Ichiro Kawachi. 2000. *Social Epidemiology.* New York: Oxford University Press.

Bernier, Aurelien. 2014. *La Gauche radicale et ses tabous. Pourquoi le Front de gauche échoue face au Front national.* Paris: Le Seuil.

Berridge, Virginia, ed. 2002. "Witness Seminar: The Black Report and The Health Divide." *Contemporary British History* 16 (3): 131–72.

Berridge, Virginia, D. A. Christie, and E. M. Tansey. 2006. "Public Health in the 1980s and 1990s: Decline and Rise?" Wellcome Witnesses to Twentieth Century Medicine, 26. London: Wellcome Trust Centre for the History of Medicine at UCL. http://qmro.qmul.ac.uk/xmlui/handle/123456789/2761.

Besse, G., J. Caudeville, F. Michelot, N. Prisse, and A. Trugeon. 2014. *Inégalités territoriales, environnementales et sociales de santé. Regards croisés en régions: de l'observation à l'action.* SGMAS et CGDD.

Blackman, Tim, Alexandra Greene, David Hunter, Lorna McKee, Eva Elliott, Barbara Harrington, Linda Marks, and Gareth Williams. 2006. "Performance Assessment and Wicked Problems: The Case of Health Inequalities." *Public Policy and Administration* 21 (2): 66–80.

Blackstone, Tessa, and William Plowden. 1988. *Inside the Think Tank: Advising the Cabinet 1971–1983.* London: William Heinemann.

Blakely, Tony. 2008. "Iconography and Commission on the Social Determinants of Health (and Health Inequity)." *Journal of Epidemiology and Community Health* 62 (12): 1018–20.

Blanpain, Nathalie. 2018. "L'espérance de vie par niveau de vie: chez les hommes, 13 ans d'écart entre les plus aisés et les plus modestes." INSEE Première 1687. Paris: Institut national de la statistique et des études économiques. www.insee.fr/fr/statistiques/3319895.

Blaxter, Mildred. 1997. "Whose Fault Is It? People's Own Conceptions of the Reasons for Health Inequalities." *Social Science and Medicine,* Health Inequalities in Modern Societies and Beyond, 44 (6): 747–56.

Block, Fred. 1992. "Capitalism without Class Power." *Politics and Society* 20 (3): 277–303.

Blyth, Mark. 2002. *Great Transformations: Economic Ideas and Institutional Change in the Twentieth Century.* New York: Cambridge University Press.

———. 2013. *Austerity: The History of a Dangerous Idea.* New York: Oxford University Press.

Boas, Taylor, and Jordan Gans-Morse. 2009. "Neoliberalism: From New Liberal Philosophy to Anti-liberal Slogan." *Studies in Comparative International Development* 44 (2): 137–61.

Bogdanor, Vernon. 2015. "General Election: Do Party Manifestos Still Matter?" *Financial Times,* April 15, online edition. www.ft.com/content/7418b410-e2c2-11e4-bf4b-00144feab7de.

Boix, Carles. 2003. *Democracy and Redistribution.* New York: Cambridge University Press.

Bourdieu, Pierre. 1998. *Acts of Resistance: Against the New Myths of Our Time.* Cambridge, MA: Polity Press.

Braveman, Paula, Susan Egerter, and David Williams. 2011. "The Social Determinants of Health: Coming of Age." *Annual Review of Public Health* 32 (1): 381–98.

Breen, Richard, ed. 2005. *Social Mobility in Europe*. New York: Oxford University Press.

Briatte, François. 2010. "A Case of Weak Architecture: The French Ministry of Health." *Social Policy and Administration* 44 (2): 155–71.

"British Political Speech." n.d. www.britishpoliticalspeech.org/.

Brown, Brian, and Sally Baker. 2012. *Responsible Citizens Individuals, Health, and Policy under Neoliberalism*. London: Anthem Press.

Brunner, Eric, and Michael Marmot. 2005. "Social Organization, Stress, and Health." In *Social Determinants of Health*, edited by Michael Marmot and Richard Wilkinson. New York: Oxford University Press.

Buchan, Iain, Evangelos Kontopantelis, Matthew Sperrin, Tarani Chandola, and Tim Doran. 2017. "North-South Disparities in English Mortality 1965–2015: Longitudinal Population Study." *Journal of Epidemiology and Community Health* 2017 (71): 928–36.

Burci, Gian Luca. 2015. "The European Union and the World Health Organization: Interactions and Collaboration from a Governance and Policy Perspective." In *The European Union in International Organisations and Global Governance: Recent Developments*, edited by Christine Kaddous. London: Bloomsbury Publishing.

Cairney, Paul. 2007. "The Professionalisation of MPs: Refining the 'Politics-Facilitating' Explanation." *Parliamentary Affairs* 60 (2): 212–33.

Cameron, David R. 1978. "The Expansion of the Public Economy: A Comparative Analysis." *The American Political Science Review* 72 (4): 1243–61.

Cazenave, Marie-Cécile, Jonathan Duval, Alexis Eidelman, Frabrice Langumier, and Augustin Vicard. 2011. "La redistribution: état des lieux en 2010 et évolution depuis vingt ans." *INSEE Références*. Paris: INSEE. www.insee.fr/fr/statistiques/fichier/1373891/FPORSOC11h_VE33Redis.pdf.

Challis, Linda, Rudolph Klein, Susan Fuller, Melanie Henwood, William Plowden, Adrian Webb, Peter Whittingham, and Gerald Wistow. 1988. *Joint Approaches to Social Policy: Rationality and Practice*. New York: Cambridge University Press.

Clift, Ben. 2014. "The Hollande Presidency, the Eurozone Crisis and the Politics of Fiscal Rectitude." *Sheffield Political Economy Research Institute*, SPERI Papers, 1 (10): 1–19.

CNESCO. 2016. "Inégalités sociales et migratoires: comment l'école les amplifie?" Paris: CNESCO. www.cnesco.fr/fr/inegalites-sociales-et-migratoires-comment-lecole-les-amplifie/.

Coburn, David. 2004. "Beyond the Income Inequality Hypothesis: Class, Neo-Liberalism, and Health Inequalities." *Social Science and Medicine* 58 (1): 41–56.

Commissariat Général du Plan. 1993. "Santé 2010: équité et efficacité du système de santé: les enjeux." Paris: Documentation Française. www.worldcat.org/title/sante-2010-equite-et-efficacite-du-systeme-de-sante-les-enjeux/oclc/29924184.

Cook, Robin. 2004. "Call It Recycling If You Must." *The Guardian*, December 17. www.theguardian.com/politics/2004/dec/17/labour.uk.

Coote, Anna, and David J. Hunter. 1996. *New Agenda for Health*. London: Institute for Public Policy Research.

Cronin, James E. 2004. *New Labour's Pasts: The Labour Party and Its Discontents.* London: Routledge.

Dahl, Espen, Jon Ivar Elstad, Dag Hofoss, and Melissa Martin-Mollard. 2006. "For Whom Is Income Inequality Most Harmful? A Multi-Level Analysis of Income Inequality and Mortality in Norway." *Social Science and Medicine* 63 (10): 2562–74.

Dahlgren, Göran, and Margaret Whitehead. 1993. "Tackling Inequalities in Health: What Can We Learn from What Has Been Tried?" Working Paper Prepared for the King's Fund International Seminar on Tackling Inequalities in Health. Ditchley Park: King's Fund.

Daniels, Norman. 1983. "Health Care Needs and Distributive Justice." In *In Search of Equity*, 1–41. The Hastings Center Series in Ethics. Boston: Springer. https://link.springer.com/chapter/10.1007/978-1-4684-4424-7_1.

Daniels, Norman, Bruce Kennedy, and Ichiro Kawachi. 2000. *Is Inequality Bad for Our Health?* Boston: Beacon Press.

Dathan, Matt. 2015. "Why Manifestos Aren't Worth the Paper They're Written on." *The Independent*, April 13, online edition. www.independent.co.uk/news/uk/politics/generalelection/general-election-why-manifestos-aren-t-worth-the-paper-they-re-written-on-but-the-one-reason-why-10172317.html.

De Vogli, Roberto. 2011. "Neoliberal Globalisation and Health in a Time of Economic Crisis." *Social Theory and Health* 9 (S4): 311–25.

Deaton, Angus. 2002. "Policy Implications of the Gradient of Health and Wealth." *Health Affairs* 21 (2): 13–30.

Diderichsen, Finn, Timothy Evans, and Margaret Whitehead. 2001. "The Social Basis of Disparities in Health." In *Challenging Inequities in Health: From Ethics to Action*, edited by Timothy Evans, Margaret Whitehead, and Finn Diderichsen. New York: Oxford University Press.

Docteur, Elizabeth, and Robert Berenson. 2014. "In Pursuit of Health Equity: Comparing US and EU Approaches to Eliminating Disparities." Timely Analysis of Immediate Health Policy Issues June 2014. Princeton, NJ, and Washington, DC: Robert Wood Johnson Foundation and Urban Institute. http://papers.ssrn.com/sol3/papers.cfm?abstract_id=2462922.

Dorling, Danny. 2015. "The Mother of Underlying Causes – Economic Ranking and Health Inequality." *Social Science and Medicine* 128 (March): 327–30.

DREES. 2006. "L'état de santé de la population en France en 2006." Paris: La Documentation Française.

——— 2007. "L'état de santé de la population en France en 2007." Paris: La Documentation Française.

——— 2008. "L'état de santé de la population en France en 2008." Paris: La Documentation Française.

——— 2010. "L'état de santé de la population en France en 2009–2010." Paris: La Documentation Française.

——— 2011. "L'état de santé de la population en France en 2011." Paris: La Documentation Française.

——— 2015. "L'état de santé de la population en France en 2015." Paris: La Documentation Française.

Dreier, Peter. 2011. "Roots of Rebellion: Moving in the Labor Lane." *New Labor Forum* 20 (3): 88–92.

Driver, Stephen, and Luke Martell. 2002. "New Labour's Third Way." In *Blair's Britain*, 67–95. Cambridge: Polity Press.

Durkheim, Emile. 1976. *The Elementary Forms of the Religious Life*. London: Routledge.

Dutton, Paul. 2007. *Differential Diagnoses: A Comparative History of Health Care Problems and Solutions in the United States and France*. Ithaca, NY: Cornell University Press.

Elsässer, Lea, Svenja Hense, and Armin Schäfer. 2017. "'Dem Deutschen Volke'? Die ungleiche Responsivität des Bundestags." *Zeitschrift für Politikwissenschaft* 27 (2): 161–80.

En Marche! 2017. "Les propositions d'Emmanuel Macron." Available at https:// en-marche.fr/emmanuel-macron/le-programme.

Engels, Friedrich. 1987. *The Condition of the Working Class in England*. Edited by V. G. Kiernan. Harmondsworth: Penguin.

Entman, Robert. 1993. "Framing: Toward Clarification of a Fractured Paradigm." *Journal of Communication* 43 (4): 51–58.

Esping-Andersen, Gøsta. 1990. *The Three Worlds of Welfare Capitalism*. Princeton, NJ: Princeton University Press.

——— 1996. "Welfare States without Work: The Impasse of Labour Shedding and Familialism in Continental European Social Policy." In *Welfare States in Transition: National Adaptations in Global Economies*, 66–87. London: SAGE Publications.

ESRC [Economic and Social Research Council]. n.d. "The Dahlgren-Whitehead Rainbow." https://esrc.ukri.org/about-us/50-years-of-esrc/50-achievements/the-dahlgren-whitehead-rainbow/.

Eurofound. 2017. "Social Mobility in the EU." Eurofound. www.eurofound.europa.eu/ publications/report/2017/social-mobility-in-the-eu.

EuroHealthNet. n.d. "Glossary." Health Inequalities (blog). www.health-inequalities.eu/ resources/glossary/#H.

European Commission. 2003. *The Health Status of the European Union: Narrowing the Health Gap*. Luxembourg: Office for Official Publications of the European Communities. http://ec.europa.eu/health/archive/ph_information/documents/health_ status_en.pdf.

——— 2009. "Solidarity in Health: Reducing Health Inequalities in the EU." Commission of the European Communities. https://eur-lex.europa.eu/legal-content/EN/TXT/?uri= CELEX:52009DC0567.

——— 2013. "Health Inequalities in the EU: Final Report of a Consortium." Brussels: European Commission. http://dx.publications.europa.eu/10.2772/34426.

European Parliament. 2011a. "Debates – Monday, 7 March 2011: Reducing Health Inequalities (Short Presentation)." www.europarl.europa.eu/sides/getDoc.do?type= CRE&reference=20110307&secondRef=ITEM-024&language=EN&ring=A7-2011-0032.

——— 2011b. *European Parliament Resolution of 8 March 2011 on Reducing Health Inequalities in the EU*. www.europarl.europa.eu/sides/getDoc.do?pubRef=-//EP// TEXT+TA+P7-TA-2011-0081+0+DOC+XML+V0//EN&language=EN.

Evans, Geoffrey, and James Tilley. 2012a. "The Depoliticization of Inequality and Redistribution: Explaining the Decline of Class Voting." *The Journal of Politics* 74 (4): 963–76.

2012b. "How Parties Shape Class Politics: Explaining the Decline of the Class Basis of Party Support." *British Journal of Political Science* 42 (1): 137–61.

2017. *The New Politics of Class: The Political Exclusion of the British Working Class.* Oxford: Oxford University Press.

Exworthy, Mark. 2002. "The 'Second Black Report'? The Acheson Report as Another Opportunity to Tackle Health Inequalities." *Contemporary British History* 16 (3): 175–97.

Exworthy, Mark, and David Hunter. 2011. "The Challenge of Joined-Up Government in Tackling Health Inequalities." *International Journal of Public Administration* 34 (4): 201–12.

Exworthy, Mark, David Blane, and Michael Marmot. 2003. "Tackling Health Inequalities in the United Kingdom: The Progress and Pitfalls of Policy." *Health Services Research* 38 (6p2): 1905–22.

Farrants, Kristin, and Clare Bambra. 2018. "Neoliberalism and the Recommodification of Health Inequalities: A Case Study of the Swedish Welfare State 1980 to 2011." *Scandinavian Journal of Public Health* 46 (1): 18–26.

Fellman, Susana. 2008. "Growth and Investment: Finnish Capitalism, 1850–2005." In *Creating Nordic Capitalism: The Business History of a Competitive Periphery*, edited by Susana Fellman, Martin Iversen, Hans Sjögren, and Lars Thue, 139–217. London: Palgrave Macmillan.

Ferrera, Maurizio. 1996. "The 'Southern Model' of Welfare in Social Europe." *Journal of European Social Policy* 6 (1): 17–37.

Finnish Ministry of Social Affairs and Health. 2006. *Health in All Policies: Prospects and Potentials.* Edited by Timo Ståhl. Helsinki: Ministry of Social Affairs and Health.

2008. *National Action Plan to Reduce Health Inequalities 2008–2011.* Edited by Tuulia Rotko, Marita Sihto, and Hannele Palosuo. Publications of the Ministry of Social Affairs and Health, 2008, 25. Helsinki: Ministry of Social Affairs and Health.

2009. "Health Inequalities in Finland. Trends in Socioeconomic Health Differences 1980–2005." Sosiaali-ja terveysministeriö. www.julkari.fi/handle/10024/111864.

Finnish National Institute for Health and Welfare. 2012. "Kuilun Kaventajat – Kansallinen Terveyserojen Kaventamisen Toimintaohjelma 2008–2011 – Loppuraportti ["Narrowing the Gap. The National Action Plan to Reduce Health Inequalities 2008–2011 – Final Report]." National Institute for Health and Welfare (THL).

2009. *The North Karelia Project: From North Karelia to National Action.* Edited by Pekka Puska, Erkki Vartiainen, Tiina Laatikainen, Pekka Jousilahti, and Meri Paavola. Helsinki: National Institute for Health and Welfare.

Foucault, Michel. 2012. *Discipline and Punish: The Birth of the Prison.* New York: Vintage.

Fourcade-Gourinchas, Marion, and Sarah Babb. 2002. "The Rebirth of the Liberal Creed: Paths to Neoliberalism in Four Countries." *American Journal of Sociology* 108 (3): 533–79.

Fox, John, ed. 1989. *Health Inequalities in European Countries.* Aldershot: Gower.

Fox, John, and Roy Carr-Hill. 1989. "Introduction." In *Health Inequalities in European Countries*, edited by John Fox, 1–18. Aldershot: Gower.

Freeman, Richard. 2006. "The Work the Document Does: Research, Policy, and Equity in Health." *Journal of Health Politics, Policy and Law* 31 (1): 51–70.

Gamble, Andrew. 1996. "The Legacy of Thatcherism." In *The Blair Agenda*, edited by Mark Perryman. London: Lawrence & Wishart.

Ganghof, Steffen. 2006. *The Politics of Income Taxation: A Comparative Analysis.* Colchester: ECPR Press.

Garrett, Geoffrey. 1998. *Partisan Politics in the Global Economy.* New York: Cambridge University Press.

Gatrell, Anthony, Jennie Popay, and Carol Thomas. 2004. "Mapping the Determinants of Health Inequalities in Social Space: Can Bourdieu Help Us?" *Health and Place* 10 (3): 245–57.

Gelder, Rianne de, Gwenn Menvielle, Giuseppe Costa, Katalin Kovács, Pekka Martikainen, Bjørn Heine Strand, and Johan Mackenbach. 2017. "Long-Term Trends of Inequalities in Mortality in 6 European Countries." *International Journal of Public Health* 62 (1): 127–41.

Gentile, Lisa. 2010. "The Battle for Health in France: The Role of Ideas and Discourse in Constructing the Political Economy of Health Policy Reform (1990–2010)." PhD dissertation, New York University. http://search.proquest.com/docview/815746550/abstract/F62F8806F1764DFDPQ/1.

Gilens, Martin. 2009. *Why Americans Hate Welfare: Race, Media, and the Politics of Antipoverty Policy.* Chicago: University of Chicago Press.

Gill, Stephen, and David Law. 1989. "Global Hegemony and the Structural Power of Capital." *International Studies Quarterly* 33 (4): 475–99.

Glasgow, Sara, and Ted Schrecker. 2015. "The Double Burden of Neoliberalism? Noncommunicable Disease Policies and the Global Political Economy of Risk." *Health and Place* 34 (July): 279–86.

Goldin, Claudia, and Lawrence Katz. 2008. "The Race between Education and Technology." In *Inequality in the 21st Century*, edited by David Grusky, 49–54. London: Routledge.

Gollust, Sarah, and Julia Lynch. 2011. "Who Deserves Health Care? The Effects of Causal Attributions and Group Cues on Public Attitudes about Responsibility for Health Care Costs." *Journal of Health Politics, Policy and Law* 36 (6): 1061–95.

Gorp, Baldwin van. 2007. "The Constructionist Approach to Framing: Bringing Culture Back In." *Journal of Communication* 57 (1): 60–78.

Gourevitch, Alex. 2015. "Look Not to the Peripheries." *The Current Moment* (blog). August 5. https://thecurrentmoment.wordpress.com/2015/08/05/look-not-to-the-peripheries/.

Graham, Hilary. 2004a. "Social Determinants and Their Unequal Distribution: Clarifying Policy Understandings." *Milbank Quarterly* 82 (1): 101–24.

——— 2004b. "Tackling Inequalities in Health in England: Remedying Health Disadvantages, Narrowing Health Gaps or Reducing Health Gradients?" *Journal of Social Policy* 33 (1): 115–31.

Gray, Alastair McIntosh. 1982. "Inequalities in Health. The Black Report: A Summary and Comment." *International Journal of Health Services* 12 (3): 349–80.

Great Britain Department of Health. 1996. "Variations in Health: What Can the Department of Health and the NHS Do?" www.scie-socialcareonline.org.uk/

variations-in-health-what-can-the-department-of-health-and-the-nhs-do-a-report-produced-by-the-variations-sub-group-of-the-chief-medical-officers-health-of-the-nation-working-group/r/a11G0000001813MIAQ.

Greenhouse, Steven. 1992. "U.S. and World: New Economic Order." *New York Times*, April 29. www.nytimes.com/1992/04/29/world/us-and-world-new-economic-order.html.

Greer, Scott. 2004. *Territorial Politics and Health Policy: UK Health Policy in Comparative Perspective*. Manchester: Manchester University Press.

——— 2014. "The Three Faces of European Union Health Policy: Policy, Markets, and Austerity." *Policy and Society* 33 (1): 13–24.

Greer, Scott, and Denise Lillvis. 2014. "Beyond Leadership: Political Strategies for Coordination in Health Policies." *Health Policy* 116 (1): 12–17.

Greer, Scott, and Paulette Kurzer. 2013. *European Union Public Health Policy: Regional and Global Trends*. London: Routledge.

Greer, Scott, Tamara Hervey, Johan Mackenbach, and Martin McKee. 2013. "Health Law and Policy in the European Union." *The Lancet* 381 (9872): 1135–44.

Gregg, Paul. 2010. "New Labour and Inequality." *The Political Quarterly* 81 (September): S16–S30.

Grossman, Emiliano. 2007. "Introduction: France and the EU: From Opportunity to Constraint." *Journal of European Public Policy* 14 (7): 983–91.

The Guardian. 2002. "Blair Calls for Wealth Redistribution," September 18. www.theguardian.com/politics/2002/sep/18/immigrationpolicy.socialexclusion.

Guignier, Sébastien. 2006. "The EU's Role(s) in European Public Health: The Interdependence of Roles within a Saturated Space of International Organizations." In *The European Union's Roles in International Politics: Concepts and Analysis*, edited by Ole Elgström and Michael Smith. London: Routledge.

Gusfield, Joseph. 1984. *The Culture of Public Problems: Drinking-Driving and the Symbolic Order*. Chicago: University of Chicago Press.

Hacker, Jacob, and Paul Pierson. 2010. *Winner-Take-All Politics: How Washington Made the Rich Richer – And Turned Its Back on the Middle Class*. New York: Simon and Schuster.

Hagenaars, Luc, Patrick Jeurissen, and Niek Klazinga. 2017. "The Taxation of Unhealthy Energy-Dense Foods (EDFs) and Sugar-Sweetened Beverages (SSBs): An Overview of Patterns Observed in the Policy Content and Policy Context of 13 Case Studies." *Health Policy* 121 (8): 887–94.

Hall, Peter. 1986. *Governing the Economy: The Politics of State Intervention in Britain and France*. New York: Oxford University Press.

——— 1989. *The Political Power of Economic Ideas*. Princeton, NJ: Princeton University Press.

——— 1993. "Policy Paradigms, Social Learning, and the State: The Case of Economic Policymaking in Britain." *Comparative Politics* 25 (3): 275–96.

——— 2015. "How Growth Regimes Evolve in the Developed Democracies." Working paper prepared for the 22nd International Conference of Europeanists. Paris, Harvard University. https://scholar.harvard.edu/files/hall/files/palierces_o.pdf.

Hall, Peter, and David Soskice. 2001. *Varieties of Capitalism: The Institutional Foundations of Comparative Advantage*. New York: Oxford University Press.

Hall, Peter, and Michèle Lamont. 2009. *Successful Societies: How Institutions and Culture Affect Health*. New York: Cambridge University Press.

Hall, Stuart. 2003. "New Labour's Double-Shuffle." *Soundings*, no. 24 (January): 10–24.

Hancher, Leigh, and Wolf Sauter. 2012. *EU Competition and Internal Market Law in the Health Care Sector*. New York: Oxford University Press.

"Hansard Online." n.d. UK Parliament. https://hansard.parliament.uk/.

Harrington, Barbara, Katherine Smith, David Hunter, Linda Marks, Timothy Blackman, Lorna McKee, Alexandra Greene, Eva Elliott, and Gareth Williams. 2009. "Health Inequalities in England, Scotland and Wales: Stakeholders' Accounts and Policy Compared." *Public Health* 123 (1): e24–e28.

Harris, Richard, and Sidney Milkis. 1989. *The Politics of Regulatory Change: A Tale of Two Agencies*. New York: Oxford University Press.

Hassenteufel, Patrick, Marc Smyrl, William Genieys, and Francisco Javier Moreno-Fuentes. 2010. "Programmatic Actors and the Transformation of European Health Care States." *Journal of Health Politics, Policy and Law* 35 (4): 517–38.

Hatzopoulos, Vassilis. 2010. "Public Procurement and State Aid in National Health Care Systems." In *Health Systems Governance in Europe: The Role of EU Law and Policy*, edited by Elias Mossialos, Govin Permanand, Rita Baeten, and Tamara Hervey, 379–418. Cambridge: Cambridge University Press.

Hay, Colin. 1999. *The Political Economy of New Labour: Labouring under False Pretences?* Manchester: Manchester University Press.

HCSP. 1994. *La santé en France*. Paris: Documentation Française. www.ladocumentationfrancaise.fr/catalogue/9782110099815/index.shtml.

——— 1998. *La santé en France 1994–1998*. Paris: Documentation Française.

——— 2009. "Les inégalités sociales de santé: sortir de la fatalité." Paris: Haut Conseil de la Santé Publique. www.hcsp.fr/explore.cgi/avisrapportsdomaine?clefr=113.

HCSP and Ministère de l'emploi et de la solidarité. 1999. "Allocation régionale des ressources et réduction des inégalités de santé." Rennes: Éd. ENSP. www.ladocumentationfrancaise.fr/var/storage/rapports-publics/014000733.pdf.

Heath, Anthony, Roger Jowell, and John Curtice. 2001. *The Rise of New Labour: Party Policies and Voter Choices*. Oxford: Oxford University Press.

Hernandez, Aguado I., Esteban P. Campos, Matamoros D. Catalan, K. Fernandez de la Hoz, T. Koller, and B. Merino. 2010. "Moving Forward Equity in Health: Monitoring Social Determinants of Health and the Reduction of Health Inequalities." Madrid: Ministry of Health and Social Policy.

Hickson, Kevin. 2004. "Inequality." In *The Struggle for Labour's Soul*, edited by Raymond Plant, Matt Beech, and Kevin Hickson. London: Routledge.

"History of the Black Report." 1999. Socialist Health Association. March 6. www.sochealth.co.uk/national-health-service/public-health-and-wellbeing/poverty-and-inequality/the-black-report-1980/the-origin-of-the-black-report/interpreting-the-black-report/.

Ho, Jessica, and Arun Hendi. 2018. "Recent trends in life expectancy across high income countries: retrospective observational study." *British Medical Journal* 362: k2562.

Hopkin, Jonathan, and Julia Lynch. 2016. "Winner-Take-All Politics in Europe? European Inequality in Comparative Perspective." *Politics and Society* 44 (3): 335–43.

Hopkin, Jonathan, and Kate Alexander Shaw. 2016. "Organized Combat or Structural Advantage? The Politics of Inequality and the Winner-Take-All Economy in the United Kingdom." *Politics and Society* 44 (3): 345–71.

Horn, Robert, and Robert Weber. 2007. "New Tools for Resolving Wicked Problems: Mess Mapping and Resolution Mapping Processes." Strategy Kinetics LLC. http://robertweber.typepad.com/strategykinetics/New_Tools_For_Resolving_Wicked_Problems_Exec_Summary.pdf.

House, James. 2016. "Social Determinants and Disparities in Health: Their Crucifixion, Resurrection, and Ultimate Triumph (?) In Health Policy." *Journal of Health Politics, Policy and Law* 41 (4): 599–626.

House of Commons Health Committee. 2009. "Health Inequalities." https://publications.parliament.uk/pa/cm200809/cmselect/cmhealth/286/28602.htm.

Houweling, Tanja, Anton Kunst, Martijn Huisman, and Johan Mackenbach. 2007. "Using Relative and Absolute Measures for Monitoring Health Inequalities: Experiences from Cross-National Analyses on Maternal and Child Health." *International Journal for Equity in Health* 6 (15).

Hsia, Renee, and Yu-Chu Shen. 2011. "Possible Geographical Barriers to Trauma Center Access for Vulnerable Patients in the United States." *Archives of Surgery* 146 (1): 46–52.

Hu, Yannan, Frank van Lenthe, Ken Judge, Eero Lahelma, Giuseppe Costa, Rianne de Gelder, and Johan Mackenbach. 2016. "Did the English Strategy Reduce Inequalities in Health? A Difference-in-Difference Analysis Comparing England with Three Other European Countries." *BMC Public Health* 16 (1): 1–12.

Huber, Evelyne, and John Stephens. 2001. *Development and Crisis of the Welfare State: Parties and Policies in Global Markets.* Chicago: University of Chicago Press.

Huber, John. 2017. *Exclusion by Elections: Inequality, Ethnic Identity, and Democracy.* New York: Cambridge University Press.

Hühne, Philipp, and Dierk Herzer. 2017. "Is Inequality an Inevitable By-Product of Skill-Biased Technical Change?" *Applied Economics Letters* 24 (18): 1346–50.

Huijts, Tim, and Terje Andreas Eikemo. 2009. "Causality, Social Selectivity or Artefacts? Why Socioeconomic Inequalities in Health Are Not Smallest in the Nordic Countries." *European Journal of Public Health* 19 (5): 452–53.

Hunter, David. 2012. "Tackling the Health Divide in Europe: The Role of the World Health Organization." *Journal of Health Politics, Policy and Law* 37 (5): 867–78.

Hunter, David, Jenny Popay, Carol Tannahill, and Margaret Whitehead. 2010. "Getting to Grips with Health Inequalities at Last?" *British Medical Journal* 340 (February): c684–c684.

Hurrelmann, Klaus, Katharina Rathmann, and Matthias Richter. 2011. "Health Inequalities and Welfare State Regimes: A Research Note." *Journal of Public Health* 19 (1): 3–13.

IGAS. 2011. "Les inégalités sociales de santé: déterminants sociaux et modèles d'action." Paris: IGAS. www.dialogue-social.fr/files_upload/documentation/201110211634150.Rapport%20IGAS%20Les%20inegalites%20sociales%20de%20sante%20%20D%C3%A9terminants%20sociaux%20et%20modeles%20d'action.pdf.

Ingebritsen, Christine. 2000. *The Nordic States and European Unity.* Ithaca, NY: Cornell University Press.

Inglehart, Ronald. 1971. *The Silent Revolution in Europe: Intergenerational Change in Post-Industrial Societies*. Indianapolis, IN: Bobbs-Merrill Company.

INSERM [Institut National de la Santé et de la Recherche Médicale]. 2000. *Les inégalités sociales de santé*. Paris: La Decouverte.

Irvin, George. 2008. *A Robin Hood Lesson for New Labour*. London: Compass.

Irwin, Alec, Orielle Solar, and Jeanette Vega. 2008. "Social Determinants of Health, the United Nations Commission of." In *International Encyclopedia of Public Health*, edited by Harald Kristian (Kris) Heggenhougen, 64–69. Oxford: Academic Press.

ISSP. 2009. "ISSP 2009 'Social Inequality IV.'" www.gesis.org/issp/modules/issp-modules-by-topic/social-inequality/2009/.

———. 2011. "Health and Health Care – ISSP 2011." https://dbk.gesis.org/dbksearch/sdesc2.asp?ll=10&notabs=&af=&nf=&search=&search2=&db=d&no=5800.

Iversen, Torben, and Anne Wren. 1998. "Equality, Employment, and Budgetary Restraint: The Trilemma of the Service Economy." *World Politics* 50 (4): 507–46.

Iversen, Torben, and David Soskice. 2006. "Electoral Institutions and the Politics of Coalitions: Why Some Democracies Redistribute More than Others." *American Political Science Review* 100 (2): 165–81.

Jackson, Ben. 2007. *Equality and the British Left: A Study in Progressive Political Thought, 1900–64*. Manchester: Manchester University Press.

Jenson, Jane. 2010. "Diffusing Ideas for after Neoliberalism: The Social Investment Perspective in Europe and Latin America." *Global Social Policy* 10 (1): 59–84.

Jones, Owen. 2014. *The Establishment: And How They Got Away with It*. London: Allen Lane.

Jospin, Lionel. 1999. "Déclaration de M. Lionel Jospin, Premier ministre, sur les orientations de la politique gouvernementale de la rentrée sous le signe de 'la transformation sociale et de la modernité partagée,' La Rochelle le 29 août 1999." Text. Vie Publique. August 29. http://discours.vie-publique.fr/notices/993002135.html.

Judge, Ken, and Linda Bauld. 2006. "Learning from Policy Failure? Health Action Zones in England." *The European Journal of Public Health* 16 (4): 341–43.

Judge, Ken, Stephen Platt, Caroline Costongs, Kasia Jurczak, et al. 2006. *Health Inequalities: A Challenge for Europe*. EuroHealthNet. www.europa.nl/health/ph_determinants/socio_economics/documents/ev_060302_rdo5_en.pdf.

Julia, Chantal, and Alain-Jacques Valleron. 2011. "Louis-René Villermé (1782–1863), a Pioneer in Social Epidemiology: Re-analysis of His Data on Comparative Mortality in Paris in the Early 19th Century." *Journal of Epidemiology and Community Health* 65 (8): 666–70.

Jusko, Karen. 2015. "Electoral Geography and Redistributive Politics." *Journal of Theoretical Politics* 27 (2): 269–87.

Juster, Robert-Paul, Bruce McEwen, and Sonia Lupien. 2010. "Allostatic Load Biomarkers of Chronic Stress and Impact on Health and Cognition." *Neuroscience and Biobehavioral Reviews*, Psychophysiological Biomarkers of Health, 35 (1): 2–16.

Jutz, Regina. 2015. "The Role of Income Inequality and Social Policies on Income-Related Health Inequalities in Europe." *International Journal for Equity in Health* 14 (October): 117.

Katzenstein, Peter. 1985. *Small States in World Markets: Industrial Policy in Europe*. Ithaca, NY: Cornell University Press.

2003. "Small States and Small States Revisited." *New Political Economy* 8 (1): 9–30.

Kautto, Mikko, Johan Fritzell, Bjørn Hvinden, Jon Kvist, and Hannu Uusitalo. 2001. *Nordic Welfare States in the European Context.* London: Routledge.

Kawachi, Ichiro. 2000. "Income Inequality and Health." In *Social Epidemiology*, edited by Lisa Berkman, Ichiro Kawachi, and Maria Glymour, 76–94. New York: Oxford University Press.

Kawachi, Ichiro, Bruce Kennedy, Kimberly Lochner, and Deborah Prothrow-Stith. 1997. "Social Capital, Income Inequality, and Mortality." *American Journal of Public Health* 87 (9): 1491–98.

Kawachi, Ichiro, S. V. Subramanian, and Naomar Almeida-Filho. 2002. "A Glossary for Health Inequalities." *Journal of Epidemiology and Community Health* 56 (9): 647–52.

Keman, Hans, and Paul Pennings. 2006. "Competition and Coalescence in European Party Systems: Social Democracy and Christian Democracy Moving into the 21st Century." *Swiss Political Science Review* 12 (2): 95–126.

Kenworthy, Lane, and Leslie McCall. 2008. "Inequality, Public Opinion and Redistribution." *Socio-Economic Review* 6 (1): 35–68.

Kettunen, Pauli. 2004. "The Nordic Model and Consensual Competitiveness in Finland." In *Between Sociology and History*, edited by Anna-Maija Cantrén, Markku Lonkila, and Matti Peltonen. Helsinki: Finnish Literature Society (SKS).

2006. "Le modèle nordique et le consensus sur la compétitivité en Finlande." *Revue internationale de politique comparée* 13 (3): 447.

Kickbusch, Ilona. 2010. "Health in All Policies: The Evolution of the Concept of Horizontal Health Governance." In *Implementing Health in All Policies: Adelaide 2010*, edited by Ilona Kickbusch, Kevin Buckett, and Government of South Australia, Department of Health, 11–24. Rundle Mall: Government of South Australia, Department of Health.

Kickbusch, Ilona, and Kevin Buckett. 2010. "Introduction." In *Implementing Health in All Policies: Adelaide 2010*, edited by Ilona Kickbusch, Kevin Buckett, and Government of South Australia, Department of Health, 3–10. Rundle Mall: Government of South Australia, Department of Health.

Kim, Jong In, and Gukbin Kim. 2017. "Socio-ecological Perspective of Older Age Life Expectancy: Income, Gender Inequality, and Financial Crisis in Europe." *Globalization and Health* 13 (August): 58.

Kinnock, Neil. 1985. "Leader's Speech, Bournemouth 1985." British Political Speech. www.britishpoliticalspeech.org/speech-archive.htm?speech=191.

Kitschelt, Herbert. 1994. *The Transformation of European Social Democracy.* New York: Cambridge University Press.

Klein, Rudolph. 1988. "Acceptable Inequalities?" IEA Health Unit Paper 3. London: IEA Health Unit.

2003. "Commentary: Making Policy in a Fog." In *Health Inequalities: Evidence, Policy and Implementation: Proceedings from a Meeting of the Health Equity Network*, edited by Mark Exworthy and Adam Oliver, 55–57. London: Nuffield Trust.

Knesebeck, Olaf von dem, Nico Vonneilich, and Tae Jun Kim. 2016. "Are Health Care Inequalities Unfair? A Study on Public Attitudes in 23 Countries." *International Journal for Equity in Health* 15 (1): 61.

Knutsen, Oddbjørn. 1998. "Expert Judgements of the Left-Right Location of Political Parties: A Comparative Longitudinal Study." *West European Politics* 21 (2): 63–94.

Kohut, Andrew. 2013. "Economies of Emerging Markets Better Rated during Difficult Times." Pew Research Center. www.pewglobal.org/2013/05/23/economies-of-emerging-markets-better-rated-during-difficult-times/.

Koivusalo, Meri. 2014. "Policy Space for Health and Trade and Investment Agreements." *Health Promotion International* 29 (suppl. 1): i29–i47.

Koivusalo, Meri, Ted Schrecker, and Ronald Labonté. 2009. "Globalization and Policy Space for Health and Social Determinants of Health." In *Globalization and Health: Pathways, Evidence and Policy*, edited by Ronald Labonté, Ted Schrecker, Corinne Packer, and Viven Runnels, 105–30. New York: Routledge.

Kokkinen, Lauri, Carles Muntaner, Anne Kouvonen, Aki Koskinen, Pekka Varje, and Ari Väänänen. 2015. "Welfare State Retrenchment and Increasing Mental Health Inequality by Educational Credentials in Finland: A Multicohort Study." *BMJ Open* 5 (6): e007297.

Kokkinen, Lauri, Carles Muntaner, Patricia O'Campo, Alix Freiler, Golda Oneka, and Ketan Shankardass. 2017. "Implementation of Health 2015 Public Health Program in Finland: A Welfare State in Transition." *Health Promotion International*, November, 1–11.

Korpi, Walter. 1983. *The Democratic Class Struggle*. Boston: Routledge & Kegan Paul.
———. 1985. "Power Resources Approach vs. Action and Conflict: On Causal and Intentional Explanations in the Study of Power." *Sociological Theory* 3 (2): 31–45.

Kratochwil, Friedrich, and John Gerard Ruggie. 1986. "International Organization: A State of the Art on an Art of the State." *International Organization* 40 (4): 753–75.

Krieger, Nancy. 1992. "Overcoming the Absence of Socioeconomic Data in Medical Records: Validation and Application of a Census-Based Methodology." *American Journal of Public Health* 82 (5): 703–10.

Kroneman, Madelon, Mieke Cardol, and Roland Friele. 2012. "(De) Centralization of Social Support in Six Western European Countries." *Health Policy* 106 (1): 76–87.

Krueger, Patrick, and Virginia Chang. 2008. "Being Poor and Coping with Stress: Health Behaviors and the Risk of Death." *American Journal of Public Health* 98 (5): 889–96.

Kuisma, Mikko. 2017. "Oscillating Meanings of the Nordic Model: Ideas and the Welfare State in Finland and Sweden." *Critical Policy Studies* 11 (4): 433–54.

Kunst, Anton, David Leon, Feikje Groenhof, and Johan Mackenbach. 1998. "Occupational Class and Cause Specific Mortality in Middle Aged Men in 11 European Countries: Comparison of Population Based Studies. Commentary: Unequal Inequalities across Europe." *British Medical Journal* 316 (7145): 1636–42.

Kurzer, Paulette, and Alice Cooper. 2011. "Hold the Croissant! The European Union Declares War on Obesity." *Journal of European Social Policy* 21 (2): 107–19.

Kus, Basak. 2006. "Neoliberalism, Institutional Change and the Welfare State: The Case of Britain and France." *International Journal of Comparative Sociology* 47 (6): 488–525.

"Labour Party Manifesto 1983." n.d. Labour Party Manifestos. http://labourmanifesto.com/1983/1983-labour-manifesto.shtml.

"Labour Party Manifesto 1987." n.d. Labour Party Manifestos. http://labourmanifesto.com/ 1987/1987-labour-manifesto.shtml.

"Labour Party Manifesto 1992." n.d. Labour Party Manifestos. http://labourmanifesto.com/ 1992/1992-labour-manifesto.shtml.

"Labour Party Manifesto 1997." n.d. Labour Party Manifestos. http://labourmanifesto.com/ 1997/1997-labour-manifesto.shtml.

"Labour Party Manifesto 2001." n.d. Labour-Party.Org. www.labour-party.org.uk/ manifestos/2001/2001-labour-manifesto.shtml.

"Labour Party Manifesto 2005." n.d. Labour Party. www.politicsresources.net/area/uk/ geo5/man/lab/manifesto.pdf.

"Labour Party Manifesto 2010." n.d. Labour Party. www.cpa.org.uk/cpa_documents/ TheLabourPartyManifesto-2010.pdf.

Lagarde, Christine. 2014. "Economic Inclusion and Financial Integrity: An Address to the Conference on Inclusive Capitalism." International Monetary Fund. May 27. www.imf.org/en/News/Articles/2015/09/28/04/53/sp052714.

Lahelma, Eero, and Olle Lundberg. 2009. "Health Inequalities in European Welfare States." *The European Journal of Public Health* 19 (5): 445–46.

Lansley, Stewart. 2011. "Redefining Poverty? Poverty and Social Exclusion." *Poverty and Social Exclusion* (blog). 2011. www.poverty.ac.uk/analysis-poverty-measurement-life-chances-government-policy/redefining-poverty#_edn19.

Leão, Teresa, Inês Campos-Matos, Clare Bambra, Giuliano Russo, and Julian Perelman. 2018. "Welfare States, the Great Recession and Health: Trends in Educational Inequalities in Self-Reported Health in 26 European Countries." Edited by María Carmen Díaz Roldán. *PLOS ONE* 13 (2): e0193165.

Lee, Kelley. 2008. *The World Health Organization*, 1st edition. New York: Routledge.

Lehman, Joseph. n.d. "A Brief Explanation of the Overton Window." The Overton Window. www.mackinac.org/overtonwindow.

Levitas, Ruth. 2005. *The Inclusive Society? Social Exclusion and New Labour*. New York: Springer.

Levy, Jonah. 2000. "France Directing Adjustment?" In *Welfare and Work in the Open Economy, vol. II: Diverse Responses to Common Challenges in Twelve Countries*, edited by Fritz W. Scharpf and Vivien A. Schmidt, 308–50. Oxford: Oxford University Press.

2005. "Economic Policy and Policy-Making." In *Developments in French Politics*, edited by Alistair Cole, Patrick Le Galès, and Jonah Levy, 3: 170–95. Basingstoke: Palgrave Macmillan.

2010. "Welfare Retrenchment." In *The Oxford Handbook of the Welfare State*, edited by Francis Castles, Stephan Leibfried, Jane Lewis, Herbert Obinger, and Christopher Pierson, 552–68. New York: Oxford University Press.

Leyland, Alastair, Ruth Dundas, Philip McLoone, and F. Andrew Boddy. 2007. "Cause-Specific Inequalities in Mortality in Scotland: Two Decades of Change. A Population-Based Study." *BMC Public Health* 7 (1): 172.

Link, Bruce, and Jo Phelan. 1995. "Social Conditions as Fundamental Causes of Disease." *Journal of Health and Social Behavior* 35: 80–94.

Linos, Katerina, and Martin West. 2003. "Self-Interest, Social Beliefs, and Attitudes to Redistribution. Re-addressing the Issue of Cross-National Variation." *European Sociological Review* 19 (4): 393–409.

Liu, Yang, Tomi Lintonen, Jorma Tynjälä, Jari Villberg, Raili Välimaa, Kristiina Ojala, and Lasse Kannas. 2016. "Socioeconomic Differences in the Use of Alcohol and Drunkenness in Adolescents: Trends in the Health Behaviour in School-Aged Children Study in Finland 1990–2014." *Scandinavian Journal of Public Health* 46 (1): 102–11.

Locke, Richard, and Kathleen Thelen. 1995. "Apples and Oranges Revisited: Contextualized Comparisons and the Study of Comparative Labor Politics." *Politics and Society* 23 (3): 337–67.

Lopez-Casasnovas, Guillem, Joan Costa-Font, and Ivan Planas. 2005. "Diversity and Regional Inequalities in the Spanish 'System of Health Care Services.'" *Health Economics* 14 (S1): S221–S235.

Lumme, Sonja, Reijo Sund, Alastair Leyland, and Ilmo Keskimäki. 2012. "Socioeconomic Equity in Amenable Mortality in Finland 1992–2008." *Social Science and Medicine* 75 (5): 905–13.

Lupu, Noam, and Jonas Pontusson. 2011. "The Structure of Inequality and the Politics of Redistribution." *American Political Science Review* 105 (2): 316–36.

Lynch, John, George Davey Smith, George Kaplan, and James House. 2000. "Income Inequality and Mortality: Importance to Health of Individual Income, Psychosocial Environment, or Material Conditions." *British Medical Journal* 320 (7243): 1200.

Lynch, John, George Kaplan, and J. T. Salonen. 1997. "Why Do Poor People Behave Poorly? Variation in Adult Health Behaviours and Psychosocial Characteristics by Stages of the Socioeconomic Lifecourse." *Social Science and Medicine* 44 (6): 809–19.

Lynch, Julia. 2016. "Class, Territory, and Inequality: Explaining Differences in the Framing of Health Inequalities as a Policy Problem in Belgium and France." *French Politics* 14 (1): 55–82.

Lynch, Julia, and Isabel Perera. 2017. "Framing Health Equity: US Health Disparities in Comparative Perspective." *Journal of Health Politics, Policy and Law* 42 (5): 803–39.

Lynch, Julia, and Sarah Gollust. 2010. "Playing Fair: Fairness Beliefs and Health Policy Preferences in the United States." *Journal of Health Politics, Policy and Law* 35 (6): 849–87.

Macintyre, Sally. 2002. "Before and after the Black Report: Four Fallacies." *Contemporary British History* 16 (3): 198–220.

Macintyre, Sally, Iain Chalmers, Richard Horton, and Richard Smith. 2001. "Using Evidence to Inform Health Policy: Case Study." *British Medical Journal* 322 (7280): 222–25.

Mackenbach, Johan. 2006. *Health Inequalities: Europe in Profile*. London: Produced by COI for the Department of Health. www.who.int/entity/social_determinants/resources/european_inequalities.pdf.

———. 2009. "Politics Is Nothing but Medicine at a Larger Scale: Reflections on Public Health's Biggest Idea." *Journal of Epidemiology and Community Health* 63 (3): 181–84.

———. 2011. "Can We Reduce Health Inequalities? An Analysis of the English Strategy (1997–2010)." *Journal of Epidemiology and Community Health* 65 (7): 568–75.

Mackenbach, Johan, and Anton Kunst. 1997. "Measuring the Magnitude of Socio-Economic Inequalities in Health: An Overview of Available Measures Illustrated with Two Examples from Europe." *Social Science and Medicine* 44 (6): 757–71.

Mackenbach, Johan, Caspar Looman, Anton Kunst, J. D. Habbema, and Paul van der Maas. 1988. "Regional Differences in Decline of Mortality from Selected Conditions: The Netherlands, 1969–1984." *International Journal of Epidemiology* 17 (4): 821–29.

Mackenbach, Johan, Irina Stirbu, Albert-Jan Roskam, Maartje Schaap, Gwenn Menvielle, Mall Leinsalu, and Anton Kunst. 2008. "Socioeconomic Inequalities in Health in 22 European Countries." *New England Journal of Medicine* 358 (23): 2468–81.

Mackenbach, Johan, Ivana Kulhánová, Barbara Artnik, Matthias Bopp, Carme Borrell, Tom Clemens, Giuseppe Costa, et al. 2016. "Changes in Mortality Inequalities over Two Decades: Register Based Study of European Countries." *British Medical Journal*, April, i1732.

Mackenbach, Johan, and Martijntje Bakker, eds. 2003. *Reducing Inequalities in Health: A European Perspective.* London: Routledge.

Mackenbach, Johan, H. van de Mheen, and K. Stronks. 1994. "A Prospective Cohort Study Investigating the Explanation of Socio-Economic Inequalities in Health in the Netherlands." *Social Science and Medicine* 38 (2): 299–308.

Mackenbach, Johan, Yannan Hu, Barbara Artnik, Matthias Bopp, Giuseppe Costa, Ramune Kalediene, Pekka Martikainen, et al. 2017. "Trends in Inequalities in Mortality Amenable to Health Care in 17 European Countries." *Health Affairs* 36 (6): 1110–18.

MacLean, Nancy. 2017. *Democracy in Chains: The Deep History of the Radical Right's Stealth Plan for America.* New York: Viking.

Maier, Charles. 1981. "The Two Postwar Eras and the Conditions for Stability in Twentieth-Century Western Europe." *The American Historical Review* 86 (2): 327–52.

March, James, and Johan Olsen. 1998. "The Institutional Dynamics of International Political Orders." *International Organization* 52 (4): 943–69.

Marmot, Michael. 2001. "From Black to Acheson: Two Decades of Concern with Inequalities in Health: A Celebration of the 90th Birthday of Professor Jerry Morris." *International Journal of Epidemiology* 30 (5): 1165–71.

———. 2005. "Social Determinants of Health Inequalities." *The Lancet* 365 (9464): 1099–104.

Marmot, Michael, George Davey Smith, Stephen Stansfeld, C. Patel, F. North, Jenny Head, Ian White, Eric Brunner, and A. Feeney. 1991. "Health Inequalities among British Civil Servants: The Whitehall II Study." *The Lancet* 337 (8754): 1387–93.

Marmot, Michael, Jessica Allen, Peter Goldblatt, Tammy Boyce, Di McNeish, Mike Grady, Ilaria Geddes, et al. 2010. "Fair Society, Healthy Lives: Strategic Review of Health Inequalities in England Post-2010." http://discovery.ucl.ac.uk/111743/.

Marmot, Michael, and Richard Wilkinson. 2005. *Social Determinants of Health.* Oxford: Oxford University Press.

Marmot, Michael, M. J. Shipley, and Geoffrey Rose. 1984. "Inequalities in Death: Specific Explanations of a General Pattern?" *The Lancet* 323 (8384): 1003–6.

Marsh, Laura. 2016. "A Theory of Everything." *New Republic* 247 (12): 6–8.

Marx, Karl. 1951. "Manifesto of the Communist Party." In *Selected Works*, by Karl Marx and Friedrich Engels. Vol. 1. London: Lawrence and Wishart.

Maslow, Abraham. 1943. "A Theory of Human Motivation." *Psychological Review* 50 (4): 370–96.

Matthijs, Matthias. 2016. "The Euro's 'Winner-Take-All' Political Economy." *Politics and Society* 44 (3): 393–422.

Mayer, Jane. 2017. *Dark Money: The Hidden History of the Billionaires behind the Rise of the Radical Right.* New York: Anchor.

McGinnis, J. Michael, Pamela Williams-Russo, and James Knickman. 2002. "The Case for More Active Policy Attention to Health Promotion." *Health Affairs* 21 (2): 78–93.

McKay, Betsy. 2017. "Death Rates Rise for Wide Swath of White Adults, Study Finds." *Wall Street Journal*, March 23, online edition. www.wsj.com/articles/death-rates-rise-for-wide-swath-of-white-adults-1490240740.

McKee, Martin, Tamara Hervey, and Anna Gilmore. 2010. "Public Health Policies." In *Health Systems Governance in Europe*, edited by Elias Mossialos, Govin Permanand, Rita Baeten, and Tamara Hervey, 231–81. Cambridge: Cambridge University Press.

McKnight, Abigail, and Tiffany Tsang. 2013. "Growing Inequalities and Their Impacts in the United Kingdom." Country Report for the United Kingdom. GINI Project. www.gini-research.org/system/uploads/513/original/United-Kingdom.pdf?1380182986.

McNamara, Kathleen. 1998. *The Currency of Ideas: Monetary Politics in the European Union.* Ithaca, NY: Cornell University Press.

Melhuish, Edward, Jay Belsky, Alastair Leyland, and Jacqueline Barnes. 2008. "Effects of Fully-Established Sure Start Local Programmes on 3-Year-Old Children and Their Families Living in England: A Quasi-Experimental Observational Study." *The Lancet* 372 (9650): 1610–12.

Mellor, Jennifer, and Jeffrey Milyo. 2001. "Reexamining the Evidence of an Ecological Association between Income Inequality and Health." *Journal of Health Politics, Policy and Law* 26 (3): 487–522.

Meltzer, Allan, and Scott Richard. 1981. "A Rational Theory of the Size of Government." *Journal of Political Economy* 89 (5): 914–27.

Miller, Gregory, and Edith Chen. 2013. "The Biological Residue of Childhood Poverty." *Child Development Perspectives* 7 (2): 67–73.

Ministère des Affaires Sociales et de la Santé. 2013. "Stratégie National de Santé (SNS)." Paris: Ministère des Affaires Sociales et de la Santé.

Ministère des Affaires Sociales et de la Solidarité nationale. 1985. "Les inégalités devant la santé." Collection des Rapports Officiels. Paris: La Documentation Française.

Ministère del'Emploi et de la Solidarité, and Haut Comité de la Santé Publique. 2002. *La santé en France 2002.* Paris: Documentation Française.

Ministère du Travail et des Affaires Sociales, and Haut Comité de la Santé Publique, eds. 1996. *La santé en France 96.* Paris: Documentation Française.

Minvielle, Etienne. 2006. "New Public Management à la Française: The Case of Regional Hospital Agencies." *Public Administration Review* 66 (5): 753–63.

Mishra, Ramesh. 1984. *The Welfare State in Crisis: Social Thought and Social Change.* London: Wheatsheaf Books.

Moene, Karle Ove, and Michael Wallerstein. 2001. "Inequality, Social Insurance, and Redistribution." *American Political Science Review* 95 (4): 859–74.

Montgomery, Scott, Mel Bartley, Derek Cook, and Michael Wadsworth. 1996. "Health and Social Precursors of Unemployment in Young Men in Great Britain." *Journal of Epidemiology and Community Health* 50 (4): 415–22.

Mooney, Gavin. 2012. "Neoliberalism Is Bad for Our Health." *International Journal of Health Services* 42 (3): 383–401.

Morgan, Jamie, and Heikki Patomäki. 2017. "Special Forum on Brexit." *Globalizations* 14 (1): 99–103.

"Morning Feature: Crazy Like a Fox?" 2009. *Daily Kos.* November 5. www.dailykos.com/story/2009/11/5/800804/-.

Mosley, Layna. 2000. "Room to Move: International Financial Markets and National Welfare States." *International Organization* 54 (4): 737–73.

Muntaner, Carles, Owen Davis, Kathryn McIsaack, Lauri Kokkinen, Ketan Shankardass, and Patricia O'Campo. 2017. "Retrenched Welfare Regimes Still Lessen Social Class Inequalities in Health: A Longitudinal Analysis of the 2003–2010 EU-SILC in 23 European Countries." *International Journal of Health Services* 47 (3): 410–31.

Navarro, Vicente. 2009. "What We Mean by Social Determinants of Health." *International Journal of Health Services* 39 (3): 423–41.

Navarro, Vicente, Carles Muntaner, Carme Borrell, Joan Benach, Águeda Quiroga, Maica Rodríguez-Sanz, Núria Vergés, and M. Isabel Pasarín. 2006. "Politics and Health Outcomes." *The Lancet* 368 (9540): 1033–37.

Navarro, Vicente, Carme Borrell, Joan Benach, Carles Muntaner, Agueda Quiroga, Maica Rodríguez-Sanz, Nuria Vergés, Jordi Gumá, and M. Isabel Pasarin. 2003. "The Importance of the Political and the Social in Explaining Mortality Differentials among the Countries of the OECD, 1950–1998." *International Journal of Health Services* 33 (3): 419–94.

Neumayer, Eric, and Thomas Plümper. 2016. "Inequalities of Income and Inequalities of Longevity: A Cross-Country Study." *American Journal of Public Health* 106 (1): 160–65.

Newton, John, Adam Briggs, Christopher Murray, Daniel Dicker, Kyle Foreman, Haidong Wang, Mohsen Naghavi, et al. 2015. "Changes in Health in England, with Analysis by English Regions and Areas of Deprivation, 1990–2013: A Systematic Analysis for the Global Burden of Disease Study 2013." *The Lancet* 386 (10010): 2257–74.

Niedzwiedz, Claire. 2016. "The Relationship between Wealth and Loneliness among Older People across Europe: Is Social Participation Protective?" *Preventive Medicine* 91 (October): 24–31.

Norwegian Directorate of Health and Care Services. 2007. "Report No. 20 (2006–2007) to the Storting: Nasjonal Strategi for Utjevne Sosiale Helseforskjeller [National Strategy to Reduce Social Inequalities in Health]." www.regjeringen.no/contentassets/bc70b9942ea241cd90029989bff72d3c/no/pdfs/stm200620070020000dddpdfs.pdf.

Norwegian Directorate for Health and Social Affairs. 2005. "Norwegian Plan of Action to Reduce Social Inequalities in Health." Oslo: Norwegian Directorate for Health and Social Affairs. https://helsedirektoratet.no/Lists/Publikasjoner/Attachments/280/Gradientutfordringen-sosial-og-helsedirektoratets-handlingsplan-mot-sosiale-ulikheter-i-helse-IS-1229.pdf.

OECD. 2011. *Divided We Stand*. Paris: OECD.
— 2016. *PISA 2015 Results, vol. I: Excellence and Equity in Education*. Paris: OECD Publishing.
— 2018. *A Broken Social Elevator? How to Promote Social Mobility*. Paris: OECD.
Oortwijn, Wija, Tom Ling, Judith Mathijssen, Maureen Lankhuizen, Amanda Watt, Christian Van Stolk, and Jonathan Cave. 2007. "Interim Evaluation of the Public Health Programme 2003–2008." Rand Corporation. www.rand.org/pubs/tech nical_reports/TR460.html.
Oppedisano, Veruska, and Gilberto Turati. 2015. "What Are the Causes of Educational Inequality and of Its Evolution over Time in Europe? Evidence from PISA." *Education Economics* 23 (1): 3–24.
Orloff, Ann Shola. 1993a. "Gender and the Social Rights of Citizenship: The Comparative Analysis of Gender Relations and Welfare States." *American Sociological Review* 58 (3): 303–28.
— 1993b. *The Politics of Pensions: A Comparative Analysis of Britain, Canada, and the United States, 1880–1940*. Madison: University of Wisconsin Press.
Ornston, Darius. 2018. *Good Governance Gone Bad: How Nordic Adaptability Leads to Excess*. Cornell Studies in Political Economy. Ithaca, NY: Cornell University Press.
Osberg, Lars, and Timothy Smeeding. 2006. "'Fair' Inequality? Attitudes toward Pay Differentials: The United States in Comparative Perspective." *American Sociological Review* 71 (3): 450–73.
Ottersen, Ole Petter, Jashodhara Dasgupta, Chantal Blouin, Paulo Buss, Virasakdi Chongsuvivatwong, Julio Frenk, Sakiko Fukuda-Parr, et al. 2014. "The Political Origins of Health Inequity: Prospects for Change." *The Lancet* 383 (9917): 630–67.
Pacanowsky, Michael. 1995. "Team Tools for Wicked Problems." *Organizational Dynamics* 23 (3): 36–51.
Palier, Bruno, ed. 2010. *A Long Goodbye to Bismarck? The Politics of Welfare Reforms in Continental Europe*. Amsterdam: Amsterdam University Press.
Parsons, Craig. 2003. *A Certain Idea of Europe*. Ithaca, NY: Cornell University Press.
Parti Socialiste. 1988. "Propositions pour la France. Texte adopté à La Convention Nationale du Parti Socialiste, Paris, 17 Janvier 1988." www.archives-socialistes.fr/ app/photopro.sk/archives/detail?docid=122916&rsid=4413&pos=3&psort=date debut:D&pitemsperpage=20&ppage=1&pbase=PRESSE&target=doclist#session history-ready.
Patterson, Andrew. 2017. "Not All Built the Same? A Comparative Study of Electoral Systems and Population Health." *Health and Place* 47 (September): 90–99.
Pearce, Jamie, Danny Dorling, Ben Wheeler, Ross Barnett, and Jan Rigby. 2006. "Geographical Inequalities in Health in New Zealand, 1980–2001: The Gap Widens." *Australian and New Zealand Journal of Public Health* 30 (5): 461–66.
Pekkarinen, Jukka. 2005. "Political Economy of the Finnish Welfare State." In *Welfare States and the Future*, edited by B. Vivekenandan and Nimmi Kurian, 161–77. London: Palgrave Macmillan.
Petley, Julian. 2005. "Hit or Myth." In *Culture Wars: The Media and the British Left*, edited by James Curran, Ivor Gaber, and Julian Petley, 85–107. Edinburgh: Edinburgh University Press.

Petticrew, Mark, Peter Tugwell, Vivian Welch, Erin Ueffing, Elizabeth Kristjansson, Rebecca Armstrong, Jodie Doyle, and Elizabeth Waters. 2009. "Better Evidence about Wicked Issues in Tackling Health Inequities." *Journal of Public Health* 31 (3): 453–56.

Phelan, Jo, Bruce Link, and Parisa Tehranifar. 2010. "Social Conditions as Fundamental Causes of Health Inequalities: Theory, Evidence, and Policy Implications." *Journal of Health and Social Behavior* 51 (suppl. 1): S28–S40.

Phelan, Sean. 2007. "Messy Grand Narrative or Analytical Blind Spot? When Speaking of Neoliberalism." *Comparative European Politics* 5 (3): 328–38.

Phillips, Louise. 1998. "Hegemony and Political Discourse: The Lasting Impact of Thatcherism." *Sociology* 32 (4): 847–67.

Pickett, Kate, and Danny Dorling. 2010. "Against the Organization of Misery? The Marmot Review of Health Inequalities." *Social Science and Medicine* 71 (7): 1231–33.

Pickett, Kate, and Richard Wilkinson. 2015. "Income Inequality and Health: A Causal Review." *Social Science and Medicine* 128: 316–26.

Pierson, Paul. 2001. "Post-Industrial Pressures on the Mature Welfare States." In *The New Politics of the Welfare State*, edited by Paul Pierson, 80–105. New York: Oxford University Press.

Piketty, Thomas. 2014. *Capital in the Twenty-First Century*. Cambridge, MA: Harvard University Press.

——— 2017. "Inequality in France." *Le Monde Blogs, Le blog de Thomas Piketty*. April 18. http://piketty.blog.lemonde.fr/2017/04/18/inequality-in-france/.

Piketty, Thomas, and Emmanuel Saez. 2001. "Income Inequality in the United States, 1913–1998 (Series Updated to 2000 Available)." Working Paper 8467. National Bureau of Economic Research. https://doi.org/10.3386/w8467.

——— 2006. "The Evolution of Top Incomes: A Historical and International Perspective." *American Economic Review* 96 (2): 200–205.

Piven, Frances Fox, and Richard Cloward. 2012. *Regulating the Poor: The Functions of Public Welfare*. New York: Knopf Doubleday.

Poland, Blake, David Coburn, Ann Robertson, Joan Eakin, et al. 1998. "Wealth, Equity and Health Care: A Critique of a 'Population Health' Perspective on the Determinants of Health." *Social Science and Medicine* 46 (7): 785–98.

Pollitt, Christopher, and Geert Bouckaert. 2017. *Public Management Reform: A Comparative Analysis – Into the Age of Austerity*. New York: Oxford University Press.

Pongiglione, Benedetta, and Albert Sabater. 2014. "The Role of Education at Young and Older Ages in Explaining Health Inequalities in Europe." *Population, Space and Place* 22 (3): 255–75.

Pontusson, Jonas, and David Rueda. 2010. "The Politics of Inequality: Voter Mobilization and Left Parties in Advanced Industrial States." *Comparative Political Studies* 43 (6): 675–705.

Popay, Jenny, Margaret Whitehead, and David Hunter. 2010. "Injustice Is Killing People on a Large Scale – But What Is to Be Done about It?" *Journal of Public Health* 32 (2): 148–49.

Pope Francis. 2014. "Inequality Is the Root of Social Evil." Tweet. @pontifex (blog). April 28.

Popham, Frank, Chris Dibben, and Clare Bambra. 2013. "Are Health Inequalities Really Not the Smallest in the Nordic Welfare States? A Comparison of Mortality Inequality in 37 Countries." *Journal of Epidemiology and Community Health* 67 (5): 412–18.

Prasad, Monica. 2005. "Why Is France So French? Culture, Institutions, and Neoliberalism, 1974–1981." *American Journal of Sociology* 111 (2): 357–407.

2006. *The Politics of Free Markets: The Rise of Neoliberal Economic Policies in Britain, France, Germany, and the United States.* Chicago: University of Chicago Press.

Przeworski, Adam, and John Sprague. 1986. *Paper Stones.* Chicago: University of Chicago Press.

Puska, Pekka, Pirjo Pietonen, and Ulla Uusitalo. 2002. "Influencing Public Nutrition for Non-communicable Disease Prevention: From Community Intervention to National Programme – Experiences from Finland." *Public Health Nutrition* 5 (1A): 245–52.

Rablen, Matthew, and Andrew Oswald. 2008. "Mortality and Immortality: The Nobel Prize as an Experiment into the Effect of Status upon Longevity." *Journal of Health Economics* 27 (6): 1462–71.

Raisio, Harri. 2009. "Health Care Reform Planners and Wicked Problems: Is the Wickedness of the Problems Taken Seriously or Is It Even Noticed at All?" *Journal of Health Organization and Management* 23 (5): 477–93.

Randall, Ed. 2001. *The European Union and Health Policy.* New York: Springer.

Raphael, Dennis. 2011a. "A Discourse Analysis of the Social Determinants of Health." *Critical Public Health* 21 (2): 221–36.

2011b. "Mainstream Media and the Social Determinants of Health in Canada: Is It Time to Call It a Day?" *Health Promotion International* 26 (2): 220–29.

Rathmann, Katharina, Timo-Kolja Pförtner, Klaus Hurrelmann, Ana M. Osorio, Lucia Bosakova, Frank Elgar, and Matthias Richter. 2016. "The Great Recession, Youth Unemployment and Inequalities in Psychological Health Complaints in Adolescents: A Multilevel Study in 31 Countries." *International Journal of Public Health* 61 (7): 809–19.

Raunio, Tapio, and Teija Tiilikainen. 2003. "Finland Joins the European Union." In *Finland in the European Union,* 20–40. London: Frank Cass.

Redelmeier, Donald, and Sheldon Singh. 2001. "Survival in Academy Award-Winning Actors and Actresses." *Annals of Internal Medicine* 134 (10): 955–62.

Reed, Adolph, and Merlin Chowkwanyun. 2012. "Race, Class, Crisis: The Discourse of Racial Disparity and Its Analytical Discontents." *Socialist Register* 48: 149–75.

Reeves, Richard. 2017. *Dream Hoarders: How the American Upper Middle Class Is Leaving Everyone Else in the Dust, Why That Is a Problem, and What to Do about It.* Washington, DC: Brookings Institution Press.

Rigby, Elizabeth, Joe Soss, Bridget Booske, Angela Rohan, and Stephanie Robert. 2009. "Public Responses to Health Disparities: How Group Cues Influence Support for Government Intervention." *Social Science Quarterly* 90 (5): 1321–40.

Risikko, Paula. 2009. "Foreword." In *Health Inequalities in Finland. Trends in Socioeconomic Health Differences 1980–2005,* edited by Hannele Palosuo, Seppo Koskinen, Eero Lahelma, Ritva Prättälä, Tuija Martelin, Aini Ostamo, Ilmo Keskimäki, Marita Sihto, and Elisa Kostiainen, 5. Stockholm: Ministry of Social Affairs and Health. www.julkari.fi/handle/10024/111864.

Ritsatakis, Anna. 1994. "Equity in Health and the WHO HFA Policy." In *Health Inequalities: Discussion in Western European Countries,* edited by Andreas Mielck and Maria do Rosário Giraldes, 204–5. Münster: Waxmann.

2000. "Experience in Setting Targets for Health in Europe." *European Journal of Public Health* 10 (suppl. 4): 7–10.

Rittel, Horst, and Melvin Webber. 1973. "Dilemmas in a General Theory of Planning." *Policy Sciences* 4 (2): 155–69.

Robson, Matthew, Miqdad Asaria, Richard Cookson, Aki Tsuchiya, and Shehzad Ali. 2016. "Eliciting the Level of Health Inequality Aversion in England." *Health Economics* 26 (10): 1328–34.

Rochaix, Lise, and David Wilsford. 2005. "State Autonomy, Policy Paralysis: Paradoxes of Institutions and Culture in the French Health Care System." *Journal of Health Politics, Policy and Law* 30 (1–2): 97–120.

Rodríguez-Pose, Andrés, and Roberto Ezcurra. 2010. "Does Decentralization Matter for Regional Disparities? A Cross-Country Analysis." *Journal of Economic Geography* 10 (5): 619–44.

Rushton, Simon, and Owain David Williams. 2012. "Frames, Paradigms and Power: Global Health Policy-Making under Neoliberalism." *Global Society* 26 (2): 147–67.

Ryner, J. Magnus. 2007. "The Nordic Model: Does It Exist? Can It Survive?" *New Political Economy* 12 (1): 61–70.

Sachs, Jeffrey. 2001. *Macroeconomics and Health: Investing in Health for Economic Development*. Geneva: World Health Organization.

Sapolsky, Robert. 2005. "The Influence of Social Hierarchy on Primate Health." *Science* 308 (5722): 648–52.

Sartori, Giovanni. 1970. "Concept Misformation in Comparative Politics." *American Political Science Review* 64 (4): 1033–53.

Sassi, Franco. 2005. "Tackling Health Inequalities." In *A More Equal Society?: New Labour, Poverty, Inequality and Exclusion*, edited by John Hills and Kitty Stewart, 69–92. Bristol: Policy Press.

Scheidel, Walter. 2017. *The Great Leveler: Violence and the History of Inequality from the Stone Age to the Twenty-First Century*. Princeton, NJ: Princeton University Press.

Schmidt, Vivien 2002. "Does Discourse Matter in the Politics of Welfare State Adjustment?" *Comparative Political Studies* 35 (2): 168–93.

——— 2007. "Trapped by Their Ideas: French Élites' Discourses of European Integration and Globalization." *Journal of European Public Policy* 14 (7): 992–1009.

Schmidt-Catran, Alexander W. 2016. "Economic Inequality and Public Demand for Redistribution: Combining Cross-Sectional and Longitudinal Evidence." *Socio-Economic Review* 14 (1): 119–40.

Schrecker, Ted. 2015. "Bringing (Domestic) Politics Back in: Global and Local Influences on Health Equity." *Public Health* 129 (7): 843–48.

——— 2016a. "Neoliberalism and Health: The Linkages and the Dangers: Neoliberalism and Health." *Sociology Compass* 10 (10): 952–71.

——— 2016b. "'Neoliberal Epidemics' and Public Health: Sometimes the World Is Less Complicated than It Appears." *Critical Public Health* 26 (5): 477–80.

Schrecker, Ted, and Clare Bambra. 2015. *How Politics Makes Us Sick: Neoliberal Epidemics*. London: Springer.

Sen, Amartya. 2002. "Why Health Equity?" *Health Economics* 11 (8): 659–66.

Seychell, Martin, Bartosz Hackbart, et al. 2013. "The EU Health Strategy – Investing in Health." *Public Health Reviews* 35 (1): 1–26.

Shaw, Eric. 2007. *Losing Labour's Soul? New Labour and the Blair Government 1997–2007*. London: Routledge.

Shonfield, Andrew. 1965. *Modern Capitalism: The Changing Balance of Public and Private Power*. Oxford: Oxford University Press.

Sihto, Marita. 2008. "Reducing Health Inequalities in Finland – Experiences from TEROKA Project.Pdf." Presented at the Bertelsmann Stiftung, Berlin, July 10.

Sihto, Marita, and Hannele Palosuo. 2008. "Reducing Socioeconomic Inequalities in Health II." *Health Policy Monitor* (blog). www.hpm.org/survey/fi/a12/1.

Simonovits, Gabor. 2017. "Centrist by Comparison: Extremism and the Expansion of the Political Spectrum." *Political Behavior* 39 (1): 157–75.

Simpson, Sarah. 2010. *Putting Our Own House in Order: Examples of Health-System Action on Socially Determined Health Inequalities*. Copenhagen: WHO Regional Office for Europe.

Singh, Gopal, and Michael Kogan. 2007. "Persistent Socioeconomic Disparities in Infant, Neonatal, and Postneonatal Mortality Rates in the United States, 1969–2001." *Pediatrics* 119 (4): e928–e939.

Skocpol, Theda. 1995. *Protecting Soldiers and Mothers*. Cambridge, MA: Harvard University Press.

Smith, George Davey, and Daniel Dorling. 1996. "'I'm All Right, John': Voting Patterns and Mortality in England and Wales, 1981–92." *British Medical Journal* 313 (7072): 1573–77.

1997. "Association between Voting Patterns and Mortality Remains." *British Medical Journal* 315 (7105): 430–31.

Smith, George Davey, Shah Ebrahim, and Stephen Frankel. 2001. "How Policy Informs the Evidence: 'Evidence Based' Thinking Can Lead to Debased Policy Making." *British Medical Journal* 322 (7280): 184–85.

Smith, Katherine 2013a. *Beyond Evidence-Based Policy in Public Health*. London: Palgrave Macmillan.

2013b. "Institutional Filters: The Translation and Re-circulation of Ideas about Health Inequalities within Policy." *Policy and Politics* 41 (1): 81–100.

Smith, Katherine, and Clare Bambra. 2012. "British and Northern Irish Experiences." In *Tackling Health Inequalities: Lessons from International Experiences*, edited by Dennis Raphael, 93–122. Toronto: Canadian Scholars' Press.

Smith, Timothy, C. Tracy Orleans, and C. David Jenkins. 2004. "Prevention and Health Promotion: Decades of Progress, New Challenges, and an Emerging Agenda." *Health Psychology* 23 (2): 126–31.

Smyth, Paul, and Christopher Deeming. 2016. "The 'Social Investment Perspective' in Social Policy: A Longue Durée Perspective." *Social Policy and Administration* 50 (6): 673–90.

Solar, Orielle, and Alec Irwin. 2006. "Social Determinants, Political Contexts and Civil Society Action: A Historical Perspective on the Commission on Social Determinants of Health." *Health Promotion Journal of Australia* 17 (3): 180–5185.

Sopel, Jon. 1995. *Tony Blair: The Moderniser*. London: Michael Joseph.

Sorapop, Kiatpongsan, and Michael Norton. 2014. "How Much (More) Should CEOs Make? A Universal Desire for More Equal Pay." *Perspectives on Psychological Science* 9 (6): 587–93.

Stachenko, Sylvie, Jeanine Pommier, Cécile You, Marion Porcherie, Justine Halley, and Eric Breton. 2017. "Contribution des acteurs régionaux à la Réduction des inégalités sociales de santé: le cas de la France." *Global Health Promotion* 24 (3): 96–103.

Stafford, Mai, James Nazroo, Jennie Popay, and Margaret Whitehead. 2008. "Tackling Inequalities in Health: Evaluating the New Deal for Communities Initiative." *Journal of Epidemiology and Community Health* 62 (4): 298–304.

Stead, Martine, Crawford Moodie, Kathryn Angus, Linda Bauld, Ann McNeill, James Thomas, Gerard Hastings, et al. 2013. "Is Consumer Response to Plain/Standardised Tobacco Packaging Consistent with Framework Convention on Tobacco Control Guidelines? A Systematic Review of Quantitative Studies." Edited by Philippa Middleton. *PLoS ONE* 8 (10): e75919.

Sterdyniak, Henri. 2015. "The Great Tax Reform, a French Myth." *Revue de l'OFCE*, no. 5: 119–183.

Stone, Deborah. 1989. "Causal Stories and the Formation of Policy Agendas." *Political Science Quarterly* 104 (2): 281–300.

Strand, Mali, and Elisabeth Fosse. 2011. "Tackling Health Inequalities in Norway: Applying Linear and Non-linear Models in the Policy-Making Process." *Critical Public Health* 21 (3): 373–81.

Strauss-Kahn, Dominique, and Christian Sautter. 1998. "Une réform méthodique de l'impôt." *Le Monde*, July 23. www.lemonde.fr/archives/article/1998/07/23/une-reforme-methodique-de-l-impot_3668467_1819218.html?xtmc=&xtcr=7.

Suomen Perustuslaki [Finnish Constitution], 2 *Luku*, 19§. N.d.

Swank, Duane. 2005. "Globalisation, Domestic Politics, and Welfare State Retrenchment in Capitalist Democracies." *Social Policy and Society* 4 (2): 183–95.

Synnevåg, Ellen, Roar Amdam, and Elisabeth Fosse. 2018. "Public Health Terminology: Hindrance to a Health in All Policies Approach?" *Scandinavian Journal of Public Health* 46 (1): 68–73.

Tabuteau, Didier. 2010. "Loi 'Hôpital, Patients, Santé et Territoires' (HPST): des interrogations pour demain!" *Santé Publique* 22 (1): 78–90.

Tarkiainen, Lasse, Pekka Martikainen, Mikko Laaksonen, and Tapani Valkonen. 2012. "Trends in Life Expectancy by Income from 1988 to 2007: Decomposition by Age and Cause of Death." *Journal of Epidemiology and Community Health* 66 (7): 573–78.

Tarlov, Alvin. 1996. "Social Determinants of Health: The Sociobiological Translation." In *Health and Social Organization: Towards a Health Policy for the Twenty-First Century*, edited by David Blane, Eric Brunner, and Richard Wilkinson, 71–93. London: Routledge.

Taylor-Gooby, Peter. 1996. "The Response of Government: Fragile Convergence?" In *European Welfare Policy: Squaring the Welfare Circle*, edited by Vic George and Peter Taylor-Gooby, 199–218. London: Palgrave Macmillan.

Temmes, Markku. 1998. "Finland and New Public Management." *International Review of Administrative Sciences* 64 (3): 441–56.

Tervonen-Gonçalves, Leena, and Juhani Lehto. 2004. "Transfer of Health for All Policy – What, How and in Which Direction? A Two-Case Study." *Health Research Policy and Systems* 2 (8): 1–13.

Teune, Henry, and Adam Przeworski. 1970. *The Logic of Comparative Social Inquiry*. New York: Wiley-Interscience.

Théret, Bruno. 1991. "Néo-libéralisme, inégalités sociales et politiques fiscales de droite et de gauche dans la France des années 1980: identité et différences, pratiques et doctrines." *Revue Française de Science Politique* 41 (3): 342–81.

Thoits, Peggy. 2010. "Stress and Health: Major Findings and Policy Implications." *Journal of Health and Social Behavior* 51 (suppl. 1): S41–S53.

Thomas, Bethan, Danny Dorling, and George Davey Smith. 2010. "Inequalities in Premature Mortality in Britain: Observational Study from 1921 to 2007." *British Medical Journal* 341 (7767): 291.

Thomas, James. 2005. *Popular Newspapers, the Labour Party and British Politics.* London: Routledge.

Thomas, Richard, and Peter Turnbull. 2017. "Talking up a Storm? Using Language to Activate Adherents and Demobilize Detractors of European Commission Policy Frames." *Journal of European Public Policy* 24 (7): 931–50.

Tibout, Charles. 1956. "A Pure Theory of Local Expenditure." *Journal of Political Economy* 64: 416–24.

Timonen, Virpi. 2003. *Restructuring the Welfare State: Globalization and Social Policy Reform in Finland and Sweden.* Cheltenham: Edward Elgar Publishing.

Touraine, Marisol. 2014. "Health Inequalities and France's National Health Strategy." *The Lancet* 383 (9923): 1101–2.

Touzet, Chloé. 2017. "Winning the Votes, but Not the Minds. Why the French and British Left Turned to Fiscal Welfare to Support Low-Incomes." Prepared for presentation at the ESPANET Conference, Lisbon.

———. 2018. "Is Taking Less the Same as Giving More? Effects of the Switch to Tax Credits on Long-Term Support for Social Spending and Taxation in the UK." Prepared for presentation at the 25th Annual Conference of Europeanists, Chicago, IL.

Townsend, Peter, Margaret Whitehead, and Nick Davidson. 1992. *Inequalities in Health: The Black Report and the Health Divide,* new 3rd edition. London: Penguin Books.

Truesdale, Beth, and Christopher Jencks. 2016. "The Health Effects of Income Inequality: Averages and Disparities." *Annual Review of Public Health* 37 (1): 413–30.

Trump, Kris-Stella. 2018. "Income Inequality Influences Perceptions of Legitimate Income Differences." *British Journal of Political Science* 48 (4): 929–52.

UK Department of Health. 2007. *National Standards, Local Action Health and Social Care Standards and Planning Framework.* London: UK Department of Health.

———. 2009a. *Mortality Target Monitoring (Infant Mortality, Inequalities) Update to Include Data for 2008.* London: UK Department of Health. www.dh.gov.uk/en/Publicationsandstatistics/Publications/PublicationsStatistics/DH_109161.

———. 2009b. *Mortality Target Monitoring (Life Expectancy and All-Age All-Cause Mortality, Overall and Inequalities). Update to Include Data for 2008.* London: UK Department of Health. www.dh.gov.uk/en/Publicationsandstatistics/Publications/PublicationsStatistics/DH_107609.

———. 2009c. *Tackling Health Inequalities: 10 Years On: A Review of Developments in Tackling Health Inequalities in England over the Last 10 Years.* London: Department of Health.

UK Department of Health and Social Security. 1980. "Inequalities in Health: Report of a Research Working Group." www.sochealth.co.uk/national-health-service/public-health-and-wellbeing/poverty-and-inequality/the-black-report-1980/.

UK Presidency of the EU. 2006. "Health Inequalities: A Challenge for Europe." EuroHealthNet. www.europa.nl/health/ph_determinants/socio_economics/documents/ev_060302_rdo5_en.pdf.

UK Secretary of State for Health. 1992. "The Health of the Nation: A Strategy for Health in England." London.

1998. *Independent Inquiry into Inequalities in Health: Report.* Edited by Donald Acheson. London: Stationery Office.

2004. *Choosing Health: Making Healthy Choices Easier.* London: Department of Health London.

2010. "Fair Society, Healthy Lives: The Marmot Review. Final Report." Edited by Michael Marmot. www.instituteofhealthequity.org/resources-reports/fair-society-healthy-lives-the-marmot-review.

Vågerö, Denny, and Raymond Illsley. 1995. "Explaining Health Inequalities: Beyond Black and Barker: A Discussion of Some Issues Emerging in the Decade Following the Black Report." *European Sociological Review* 11 (3): 219–41.

Vail, Mark. 2009. *Recasting Welfare Capitalism: Economic Adjustment in Contemporary France and Germany.* Philadelphia: Temple University Press.

2018. *Liberalism in Illiberal States: Ideas and Economic Adjustment in Contemporary Europe.* New York: Oxford University Press.

Vallgårda, Signild. 2007. "Health Inequalities: Political Problematizations in Denmark and Sweden." *Critical Public Health* 17 (1): 45–56.

2008. "Social Inequality in Health: Dichotomy or Gradient?" *Health Policy* 85 (1): 71–82.

Villermé, Louis René. 1826. "Rapport fait par Villermé, et lu à l'Académie Royale de Médicine, au nom de la Commission de Statistique, sur une série de tableaux relatifs au mouvement de la population dans les Douze Arrondissemens Municipaux de la Ville de Paris, pendant les cinq années 1817, 1818, 1819, 1820 et 1821. 1826." *Archives Generales de Medecine* 10: 216–45.

Virchow, Rudolf. 2006. "Report on the Typhus Epidemic in Upper Silesia." *American Journal of Public Health* 96 (12): 2102–5.

Vliegenthart, Rens, and Liesbet van Zoonen. 2011. "Power to the Frame: Bringing Sociology Back to Frame Analysis." *European Journal of Communication* 26 (2): 101–15.

Weir, Margaret. 1992. "Ideas and the Politics of Bounded Innovation." In *Structuring Politics: Historical Institutionalism in Comparative Analysis*, edited by Sven Steinmo, Kathleen Thelen, and Frank Longstreth, 188–216. New York: Cambridge University Press.

Wel, Kjetil van der, Espen Dahl, and Heidi Bergsli. 2016. "The Norwegian Policy to Reduce Health Inequalities: Key Challenges." *Nordisk välfärdsforskning|Nordic Welfare Research* 1 (1): 19–29.

Whitehead, Margaret. 1991. "The Concepts and Principles of Equity and Health." *Health Promotion International* 6 (3): 217–28.

1998. "Diffusion of Ideas on Social Inequalities in Health: A European Perspective." *Milbank Quarterly* 76 (3): 469–92.

Whitehead, Margaret, and Göran Dahlgren. 2006. "Concepts and Principles for Tackling Social Inequities in Health: Levelling up Part 1." Studies on Social and Economic Determinants of Population Health. Copenhagen: WHO Regional Office for Europe. www.enothe.eu/cop/docs/concepts_and_principles.pdf.

Whitehead, Margaret, Sue Poval, and Belinda Loring. 2014. "The Equity Action Spectrum: Taking a Comprehensive Approach: Guidance for Addressing Inequities in

Health." Copenhagen: WHO Regional Office for Europe. www.euro.who.int/__ data/assets/pdf_file/0005/247631/equity-action-090514.pdf.

WHO. 1978. "Declaration of Alma-Ata International Conference on Primary Health Care, Alma-Ata, USSR, 6–12 September 1978." http://link.springer.com/10.1057/palgrave.development.1100047.

——— 1981. "Health for All by the Year 2000." Edited by Halfdan Mahler. *The Indian Journal of Pediatrics* 48 (6): 669–76.

——— 1999. *Health21: The Health for All Policy Framework for the WHO European Region.* Copenhagen: WHO Europe. Available at https://apps.who.int/iris/bit stream/handle/10665/272657/9289013494-eng.pdf.

——— 2008. *Closing the Gap in a Generation: Health Equity through Action on the Social Determinants of Health: Commission on Social Determinants of Health Final Report.* Edited by Michael Marmot. Geneva: World Health Organization, Commission on Social Determinants of Health.

WHO Europe. n.d. "Equity in Health Project: About the Project." World Health Organization Regional Office for Europe. www.euro.who.int/en/data-and-evi dence/equity-in-health-project/about-the-project.

WHO Regional Committee for Europe, ed. 2005. *The Health for All Policy Framework for the WHO European Region: 2005 Update.* European Health For All Series 7. Copenhagen: WHO Regional Office for Europe.

WHO Regional Office for Europe. 1991. *Policies and Strategies to Promote Social Equity in Health.* Copenhagen: WHO Regional Office for Europe.

——— 1998. *Social Determinants of Health: The Solid Facts,* 1st edition. Copenhagen: WHO Regional Office for Europe.

——— 1999. *The Solid Facts: Social Determinants of Health,* 1st edition. Oxford: Oxford University Press.

——— 2000. *Exploring Health Policy Development in Europe.* Edited by Anna Ritsatakis, Ruth Barnes, Evert Dekker, Patsy Harrington, Simo Kokko, and Peter Makara. Copenhagen: WHO Regional Office for Europe. www.cabdirect.org/abstracts/20002010387.html.

——— 2002. "Review of National Finnish Health Promotion Policies and Recommendations for the Future." Copenhagen: WHO Regional Office for Europe.

——— 2003. *Social Determinants of Health: The Solid Facts,* 2nd edition. Edited by Richard Wilkinson and Michael Marmot. Copenhagen: WHO Regional Office for Europe.

——— 2012. *Health 2020: A European Policy Framework and Strategy for the 21st Century.* Copenhagen: WHO Regional Office for Europe.

——— 2013. "Review of Social Determinants and the Health Divide in the WHO European Region: Final Report." Copenhagen: World Health Organization, Regional Office for Europe.

Wilkinson, Richard. 2006. "Politics and Health Inequalities." *The Lancet* 368 (9543): 1229–30.

Wilkinson, Richard, and Kate Pickett. 2009. *The Spirit Level: Why More Equal Societies Almost Always Do Better.* London: Allen Lane.

Wilson, Carter. 2000. "Policy Regimes and Policy Change." *Journal of Public Policy* 20 (3): 247–74.

Wismar, Matthias, David McQueen, Vivian Lin, Catherine Jones, and Maggie Davies. 2013. "Rethinking the Politics and Implementation of Health in All Policies." *Israel Journal of Health Policy Research* 2 (1): 1.

Woll, Cornelia. 2014. *The Power of Inaction: Bank Bailouts in Comparison.* Ithaca, NY: Cornell University Press.

Wood, Geof, and Ian Gough. 2006. "A Comparative Welfare Regime Approach to Global Social Policy." *World Development* 34 (10): 1696–712.

"World Income and Wealth Dataset." n.d. http://wid.world/.

Youde, Jeremy. 2012. *Global Health Governance.* Cambridge: Polity.

Ziglio, Erio. 2006. "Foreword." In *Concepts and Principles for Tackling Social Inequalities. Levelling Up (Part 2),* by Margaret Whitehead and Göran Dahlgren, viii. Copenhagen: WHO Regional Office for Europe.

Zysman, John. 1984. *Governments, Markets, and Growth: Financial Systems and the Politics of Industrial Change.* Ithaca, NY: Cornell University Press.

INTERVIEWS

Interview codes are as follows: FI, Finland; FR, France; INT, international (includes WHO and EU actors); UK, England.

Interview Code	Interviewee Role (primary)	Interview Date
FI1	Research	3/24/15
FI2	Civil service	3/18/15
FI3	Politics	3/18/15
FI4	Research	3/18/15
FI5	Research	3/20/15
FI6	Civil service	3/20/15
FI7	Civil service	3/23/15
FI8	Civil service	3/23/15
FI9	Civil service	3/18/15
FI10	Advocacy	3/19/15
FI11	Civil service	3/20/15
FI12	Research	3/17/15
FI13	Research	3/16/15
FR1	Research	6/10/11
FR2	Research	6/27/11
FR3	Politics	6/28/11
FR4	Research	6/7/11
FR5	Research	6/9/11
FR6	Research	6/9/11
FR7	Research	6/28/11
FR8	Research	6/28/11
FR9	Research	6/28/11
FR10	Research	6/23/11
FR11	Research	7/15/13
FR12	Research	7/11/13

Interview Code	Interviewee Role (primary)	Interview Date
FR13	Advocacy	7/17/13
FR14	Civil service	7/17/13
FR15	Civil service	7/16/13
FR16	Civil service	7/16/13
FR17	Civil service	7/16/13
FR18	Advocacy	7/11/13
FR19	Civil service	7/3/13
FR20	Civil service	7/3/13
FR21	Research	7/2/13
FR22	Civil service	7/2/13
FR23	Civil service	7/15/13
FR24	Civil service	7/15/13
FR25	Civil service	7/15/13
FR26	Research	7/15/13
FR27	Civil service	6/11/14
FR28	Advocacy	6/9/14
FR29	Advocacy	6/12/14
FR30	Civil service	6/18/14
FR31	Civil service	6/17/14
FR32	Research	6/16/14
FR33	Research	6/10/14
FR34	Research	6/17/14
FR35	Research	6/12/14
FR36	Politics	6/9/14
FR37	Advocacy	6/16/14
FR38	Research	6/18/14
FR39	Politics	6/13/14
FR40	Politics	6/20/14
FR41	Politics	7/15/14
INT1	Civil service	3/16/15
INT2	Research	3/16/15
INT3	Civil service	3/16/15
INT4	Research	6/1/18
INT5	Civil service	7/15/14
INT6	Civil service	5/30/13
INT7	Research	7/1/17
UK1	Politics	10/10/14
UK2	Advocacy	10/7/14
UK3	Politics	7/13/14
UK4	Politics	10/9/14
UK5	Research	9/22/14
UK6	Research	10/3/14

Index

Made in the USA
Coppell, TX
14 January 2022

71616640R00184